CULINARIA
Italy

CULINARIA
Italy
PASTA · PESTO · PASSION

CLAUDIA PIRAS · EUGENIO MEDAGLIANI

EDITORS-IN-CHIEF

RUPRECHT STEMPELL

PHOTOGRAPHY

Culinaria
KÖNEMANN

Abbreviations and Quantities

1 oz	= 1 ounce = 28 grams
1 lb	= 1 pound = 16 ounces
1 cup	= 8 ounces ★(see below)
1 cup	= 8 fluid ounces = 250 milliliters (liquids)
2 cups	= 1 pint (liquids)
8 pints	= 4 quarts
	= 1 gallon (liquids)
1 g	= 1 gram
	= 1/1000 kilogram
1 kg	= 1 kilogram
	= 1000 grams
	= 2¼ lb
1 l	= 1 liter
	= 1000 milliliters (ml)
	= approx. 34 fluid ounces
125 milliliters (ml)	= approx. 8 tablespoons
1 tbsp	= 1 level tablespoon
	= 15–20 g ★(see below)
	= 15 milliliters (liquids)
1 tsp	= 1 level teaspoon
	= 3–5 g ★(see below)
	= 5 ml (liquids)

Where measurements of dry ingredients are given in spoons, this always refers to the prepared ingredient as described in the wording following, e.g. 1 tbsp chopped onions BUT: 1 onion, peeled and chopped.

★The weight of dry ingredients varies significantly depending on the density factor, e.g. 1 cup flour weighs less than 1 cup butter.

Quantities in recipes have been rounded up or down for convenience, where appropriate. Metric conversions may therefore not correspond exactly. **It is important to use either American or metric measurements within a recipe.**

Quantities in recipes
Recipes serve 4 people, unless specified otherwise.
Exception: Recipes for drinks (quantities given per person).

PANINI – the different typeface indicates that this topic is relevant to an area wider than the region in question.

WARNING:
A number of recipes include raw eggs. It is advisable not to serve those dishes to very young children, pregnant women, elderly people or anyone weakened by serious illness. If in any doubt, consult your doctor. Of course, be sure that all the eggs you use are as fresh as possible.

© 2000 Könemann Verlagsgesellschaft mbH
   Bonner Strasse 126 · D–50968 Cologne

Art Director:	Peter Feierabend
Layout:	Michael Ditter
Project management:	Birgit Gropp
Assistance:	Freia Schleyerbach
Editor:	Daniela Kumor
Translation from Italian:	Giorgio Sinigalia, Peter Schelling, Stefanie Manderscheid
Travel organization (photography):	Bettina Dürr, Nina de Fazio
Photographic assistance:	Benjamin Holefleisch
Food stylist:	François Büns
Maps:	Studio für Landkartentechnik, Detlef Maiwald
Picture editor:	Mitra Nadjafi
Production:	Mark Voges
Reproductions:	Typografik, Cologne
Original title:	**Culinaria Italia**

© 2000 for this English edition:
Könemann Verlagsgesellschaft mbH

Translation from German:	Susan Ghanouni, Harriet Horsfield, Judith Phillips, Elaine Richards, Rae Walter, in association with First Edition Translations, Cambridge, UK
Typesetting:	The Write Idea, in association with First Edition Translations
Project management:	Béatrice Hunt, for First Edition Translations
Project coordination:	Nadja Bremse-Koob
Printing and binding:	Imprimerie Jean Lamour, Maxéville

Printed in France
ISBN 3–8290–2901–2

10 9 8 7 6 5 4 3 2 1

From an idea and original concept by Ludwig Könemann

CONTENTS

L'ARTE DELLA CUCINA ITALIANA

Whether a gastronomic tour of Italy, an elegant meal at the home of an Italian acquaintance, or "cooking Italian" back in one's own kitchen, the prospect is mouth-watering. It evokes memories, perhaps of holidays past, and the remembered flavors of culinary delights enjoyed in that land fringed with mountains, the land where the lemon tree blooms. Fine antipasti, and pasta of every shape and form, delicious sauces, fresh fish and seafood, crisp salads, fruit, and vegetables, straight from the garden; and pork, beef, wild boar, lamb, and even kid, all of the highest quality straight from the butcher. Last but not least are Italy's baked goods and desserts, from the savory focaccia to sugar-sweet confections such as cassata.

The popularity of *la cucina italiana* has never been greater. This is true not only of cooking in Italy itself, where traditional recipes are enjoying something of a renaissance, but also in other countries where there has been a revolution in what is called "Italian cuisine." The days when this meant simply pizza, spaghetti, and cheap Chianti in wicker-clad bottles, are long gone. Now, ambitious food retailers, excellent chefs, gastronomic experts, and whole armies of talented home cooks have ensured that authentic Italian specialties are known and available far beyond their country of origin. The customer asking for arborio or carnaroli rice by name has surely been exploring the art of making a good risotto; the one requesting a particular prosecco has perhaps spent the previous evening discussing that very winemaker. Today, almost everyone knows that freshly grated parmesan tastes better than the ready-grated packet variety, convenient though this is.

What is the key characteristic that makes Italian cuisine what it is? What particular charm has aroused such lively interest? Italian cuisine is not a single entity. There is great variety in a country of Italy's size; it is about 750 miles (1200 kilometers) from the Alpine peaks of the north to the toe of the "boot." The country also has two large islands, Sicily and Sardinia. Its changing geography from north to south results in a fascinating profusion of different foods; the distinct microclimates produce a great range of different sausages, hams, and cheeses – as well as the rich palette of Italian wines. The changing historical fortunes of the various regions have also left their mark on the cuisine. Sicilian cooking, for example, still reflects a degree of Arab influence to this day, and the Austro-Hungarian dish of goulash can still be tasted in Trieste.

Italian cuisine, then, cannot be seen as a unified tradition; on the contrary, each region has its own colors. Certain features are common to every city and province, such as the insistence on highest quality produce, and the love, care, and enthusiasm employed in preparing it.

People frequently travel long distances and pay slightly higher prices to buy from a favorite retailer or producer. All over Italy there are specialist producers dedicated to traditional methods. In Tuscany, for example, there are pork farmers devoting their efforts to preserving the *cinta senese* breed of pigs. These pigs lead a semi-wild existence, so keeping them is very cost-intensive, but their meat is of high quality and incomparable flavor. Although the producers realize that theirs is a niche product, they find that more and more consumers are looking for quality rather than quantity. Another example of this trend is the fact that cheese merchants are choosing to stock raw milk cheeses from small-scale cheese-makers – despite the distinct lack of enthusiasm shown by the food control legislators of the European Union for such resolutely noncompliant products.

The Italian table presents us with a veritable feast. The regional variation, the high quality of the produce, and a sense of tradition are its mainstays. Yet these alone are not enough: perhaps the true foundation on which this richly laden table rests is the Italian attitude to food and drink. Food in Italy means pure enjoyment, daily celebrated as a feast for the senses, in the company of family or friends, at home or in a good restaurant.

But now it is time to set out together on a journey of discovery. It will take us through 19 regions of this enchanting country that never loses its magic. Take a look inside the cooking pots, taste the wines, and meet interesting people. Listen to tales about our daily bread, tales from the earnest to the amazing. Did you know how to cheat the Devil with a cheese? Or how you can use a cake to save your life? *Culinaria Italy* will reveal this and more.

We hope you enjoy reading this book and sampling the many recipes it contains.

Good luck and *buon appetito!*

Claudia Piras

FRIULI
VENEZIA GIULIA

riuli lies away from the usual tourist track. The visitors who do reach this Alpine region bordering the former Yugoslavia choose it for its unspoiled natural beauties and relief from the hubbub of tourist hordes – and especially for its excellent cuisine and famous wines. For the gourmet, a place-name such as San Daniele del Friuli is synonymous with its famous hams, and Carnia in the far north with its delicious bacon and wonderful Montasio cheese, while Collio, Grave del Friuli, and Colli Orientali are music to the ears of those who love good wine. Winegrowers in the Friuli region made an early decision to aim for quality by consciously reducing the size of their yield. They are now among the best producers in Italy.

The region's cuisine keeps alive its Central European past. Trieste played a significant role in that history as a major trading port for the Danube area and Austrian monarchy. Faithful to the name the city had acquired as a "town of many peoples," its dishes mingle Austrian, Hungarian, Slovenian, and Croatian influences as well as local cooking traditions. In the beer halls, the clientele can enjoy Viennese sausages, goulash, and Bohemian hare, washed down with potent wine or beer, that "un-Italian" drink. Desserts of the flour-based type, including strudel, round off the meal.

The area known as Venezia Giulia has a cuisine that embraces and assimilates foreign influences; Friuli itself, the rest of the province, is more traditional. There, the simplest of ingredients are transformed into delicious dishes. The staple ingredient is polenta. Other regions may dismiss it as no more than the food of the poor, but between Udine and Tarvisio, Gorizia and Cortina d'Ampezzo it makes its appearance in innumerable variations: stirred, baked, served with sausage, with cheese, with fish, or with meat. The people of Friuli love their uncomplicated cuisine and regard it with pride. Spicy dishes often accompany pork, slowly roasted in traditional style over the *fogolar*, the open hearth in the kitchen. The appreciation of simple but flavorsome dishes, typical of this region, has produced true classics such as *jota*, a hearty bean soup with lashings of bacon, and *brovada*, turnips bottled in marc.

Previous double page: Caterina Castellani has been involved in the production and ripening of San Daniele hams for 50 years.

Left: The grapes that ripen on the fertile plains of Friuli not only produce impressive wines, but also various types of grappa, as here at Grave del Friuli.

PORK

Pork has always been popular in Friuli. It is still the custom for many families to rear their own pig, calling in the services of a peripatetic butcher and sausage manufacturer, called the *purcitar*, to process the meat. The slaughter of a pig remains to this day a ceremony with its own traditional rituals. The children are even granted a day off school, and everyone, young and old, impatiently awaits the arrival of the *purcitar*. A toast is drunk in wine or grappa, which is highly popular in Friuli, and events can begin.

Every part of the pig is used to prepare sausages and pork products, following traditional recipes. Use is even made of the blood and organ meat. They are mixed with raisins and pine nuts to create the typical Friuli delicacies *sanguinaccio* (other local names for blood sausage are *mule* or *mulze*) and *pan de frizze dolce* (a type of sweet bread with crackling).

Musetto is a boiled sausage popular in Friuli. The sausage meat is made of finely ground pork flavored with white wine or Marsala, together with rind and snout (hence the name, *muso* being the Italian for snout). It is richly seasoned with nutmeg, cinnamon, coriander, allspice, and pepper. The casings used are beef intestines, which accounts for the long, tapering appearance that is characteristic of *musetto*. It is not unlike *zampone*, a robust dish of stuffed trotter from Emilia Romagna. The difference is that, in Emilia Romagna, *zampone* is usually served with *bollito misto*, whereas in Friuli, *musetto* is mainly eaten with *brovada*. This is turnip marinaded in marc and then allowed to ferment. *Musetto* and *brovada* are combined in a hearty one-pot meal.

The better cuts of meat are used to make salami, including the specialty garlic salami. Pork products are still made in the traditional way, and a noted center for this is the small town of Sauris in Carnia, a northern region with an Alpine character. At some time in the past, people arrived here from Tyrol and Kärnten in Austria and from southern Germany, and one particular precious recipe that they brought with them was the method of making bacon, famous today across the whole of Friuli. The manufacture of bacon begins with the outer part of the ham joint, which is streaked with fat. This, the side of bacon, is salted and left to absorb the salt for seven or eight days. The next stage is the smoking: it is hung for a day in a smokehouse heated with juniper wood, and finally matured for about ten months. The method used to produce Sauris bacon is the same, except that the maturing period is 18 months. *Pancetta*, bacon made from belly of pork, is also produced here. *Pancetta* is smoked for 12 hours, and matures in "just" seven months.

The hams and sausages of Sauris are the pride of the town, and customers often travel long distances to buy Carnian specialties from one of the small firms producing them. The producers, aware of this, do their utmost to maintain their excellent standards of quality. The pork they use comes exclusively from Friuli; the animals are carefully tended and given the very best feed: corn, fruit, and grain, enriched with whey. The fact that Carnia is a cheese-producing area means that whey is abundantly available.

The specialties for which Sauris is known make a delicious wholesome but simple meal with bread. The combination tastes still better if the bread is a full-flavored one with caraway seeds.

SALSICCE AL VINO
Pork sausages in wine
(Illustration left)

4 SALSICCE
1 TBSP WHITE WINE VINEGAR
1 GLASS OF DRY WHITE WINE

Prick the *salsicce* a few times all over. Begin to fry them lightly, and sprinkle them with the white wine vinegar. When this has been absorbed or evaporated, pour on the wine and continue cooking. Serve the *salsicce* with slices of polenta, toasted under the broiler or in the oven.

Only a ham with the stamp of quality is a genuine San Daniele product. The riband is a further guarantee of controlled origin.

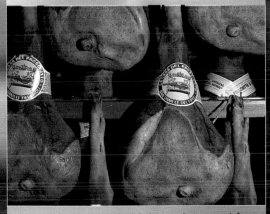

The regal hams of San Daniele have to be matured for at least ten months if their unmistakable flavor is to develop fully.

CORN

Corn is an undemanding crop that does not need special conditions, but it prefers warm, mild locations and humus-rich soils with good water retention.

Harvest time is in October. The cobs are removed from the plant and stored with their outer leaves intact, to prevent the kernels from drying out.

The 17th century was a time of hardship for the farmers of Friuli. The powerful city-state of Venice then ruled over the area, and not only did it show little interest in its hinterland; it drafted in the men of the region, the *friulani*, as soldiers to defend Venice from the Turks. The result was a lack of workers, with fields lying untended. Those few inhabitants who did not have to serve in Venice were hard put to find food. Famine was a common occurrence. Golden corn on the cob proved their salvation.

The great voyages of exploration of the 15th and 16th centuries did more than change men's geographical image of the world; they brought innovations in cooking too. Tomatoes, potatoes, beans, and of course corn appeared. These were at first regarded with scepticism by botanists and naturalists – some held them to be inedible if not actually poisonous – but they gradually came into use as food.

Corn (*Zea mays*) has a long history as a cultivated crop. It originates from the continent of America. Researchers have found evidence of its cultivation in the Tehuacán valley in Mexico as far back as the 5th century B.C. It was revered by the Aztec and Maya civilizations, and the corn god occupied an important place in the religious hierarchy.

Venetian merchants were already importing corn in the 16th century, but the real breakthrough did not come until a hundred years later, when it began to be cultivated in increasing quantity. It must have been around that time that corn arrived in Friuli. This foreign cereal plant brought an end to want and hunger in the region as farmers discovered it to be a useful source of nutrition, as well as an undemanding and easy crop to grow.

The region's cooks soon agreed on the best method of preparing it: following the long-established method used for lima beans, chickpeas, and buckwheat, it was ground into flour and turned into a thick porridge or pudding. The Venetians called this new corn *grano turco*, Turkish corn, since many foreign imports came via the East. In Friuli, it was called *blave*.

Polenta made from the corn soon became a highly popular dish in Friuli and the whole of northern Italy, eclipsing other types of cereal pudding, and even, in some areas, the traditional bread. A daily helping of polenta was often the only food eaten by poor mountain peasants.

Useful as it had been in preventing famine, corn had one big disadvantage, especially if it was the only foodstuff: it contains no niacin that can be used by the body. The medical significance of niacin is that it prevents pellagra. Large sections of the population were released from hunger only to suffer from this disease. It causes general weakness, impaired memory, and skin and nervous symptoms.

The modern balanced diet has thankfully put an end to this risk, and polenta features prominently on northern Italian menus. It is not for nothing that the Veneto is the largest corn-producing area in Italy, closely followed by Friuli, Lombardy, and Piedmont.

For some years, the farmers of these regions have been using traditional strains of corn with a more pronounced flavor, rather than hybrid varieties. This gives local traditional corn-based dishes a characteristic taste that is enjoying continued – or at least rediscovered – appreciation.

POLENTA PASTICCIATA AI GAMBERI
Polenta with shrimp
(Illustration below)

POLENTA (SEE BASIC RECIPE RIGHT)
BUTTER
GENEROUS 2 LB/1 KG SHRIMP
1 HANDFUL OF FRESH MUSHROOMS
1 CLOVE OF GARLIC, CHOPPED FINELY
1 TBSP CHOPPED PARSLEY
3/4 CUP/200 ML WHITE WINE
4 CUPS/1 LITER VEGETABLE STOCK
FRESHLY GROUND PEPPER
NUTMEG

Prepare the polenta to a soft consistency. Cool and cut into slices, and place them on a greased baking sheet so that the slices cover it completely, overlapping slightly. Preheat the oven to 350–375 °F (175–190 °C).
Clean the mushrooms and chop finely. Peel the shrimp and sauté them in a little butter in a saucepan. Add the mushrooms, garlic, and parsley. Pour on some of the white wine and vegetable stock, and bring to a boil. Add the rest only if needed. Season with freshly ground pepper and nutmeg, and arrange on top of the polenta slices. Bake for a few minutes in the preheated oven.

POLENTA AL BURRO
Polenta with butter

Prepare polenta to a firm consistency, and slice.
Grease a baking sheet with butter or lard, and arrange the polenta slices on it, side by side. Scatter with grated cheese and cinnamon, and sprinkle with melted butter. Bake in a preheated oven at 350–375 °F (175–190 °C).

FRIULIAN POLENTA

Following the arrival of corn in northeastern Italy in the 16th century, it quickly became an important staple food – especially in those areas of Carnia where people were poor and the task of feeding their families placed constant demands on the cooks. They now ate polenta at every meal: with milk for breakfast, with cheese at midday, and in the evening, as a porridge with vegetables, bacon, or butter.
Polenta accompanies almost all traditional dishes in Friuli to this day. There are three types: the traditional, yellow polenta, which can be served in a host of different ways; white polenta, made of light-colored corn flour, which is excellent served with broiled or baked fish, and can be broiled in its own right, and black polenta made from buckwheat. This last has a unique, slightly bitter flavor and is best simply served with butter and sardines.

BASIC RECIPE FOR POLENTA

SALT
1 CUP/250 G POLENTA FLOUR

Add a pinch of polenta flour to 3 cups/750 ml of salted water and bring to a boil. Slowly sprinkle in the rest of the polenta, stirring constantly. Stir more vigorously as the polenta thickens, to ensure an even consistency. Crush any lumps that form, by pressing them against the side of the saucepan. Once all the polenta has been added, reduce the heat and simmer for 45 minutes, stirring constantly. Take care during this time, as the polenta is very hot and can spurt out of the saucepan. The bottom of the saucepan becomes encrusted during the cooking. The polenta then begins to lift away from the encrusted base of the pan. This indicates that it is ready. Turn it out onto a board and smooth it flat with the back of a knife. Polenta can be cut with kitchen string when hot, and with a knife when cold.

GNOCCHI DI POLENTA
Polenta gnocchi

Dice leftover polenta and pour on boiling salted water. When heated through, drain and place on deep pasta plates. Top with grated smoked ricotta.

EVENING BY THE FOGOLAR

In Friuli there is a type of fireplace called a *fogolar*. This is more than just a fire for cooking food; it forms part of a traditional life style with a long history. It is the focus and meeting place where friends gather to eat, drink, talk, and argue, and it creates a cosiness that is all the more attractive on cold winter nights. It consists of a hearth where food is grilled over a wood fire, and often occupies the center of the kitchen, crowned by a massive flue. Here, people often cook a simple meal of pork, chicken, beans, root vegetables, or polenta – warming, nourishing food that is hardly *haute cuisine*, but is nonetheless delicious and makes for a delightful and often stimulating evening.

THE COAST

Friuli boasts an interesting coastline in addition to the beauties of its inland areas. There are two lagoons, Laguna di Grado and Laguna di Marano, both well worth a visit. The sleepy fishing port of Marano is one of the few places in Italy that cherishes unspoiled tradition, despite the proximity of Lignano Sabbiadoro and Bibione with their throbbing nightlife. Marano, in contrast, still has some old houses in the Venetian style, with gaily painted façades. There are even some traditional fishermen's straw-thatched dwellings – *casoni* – to be seen around the Laguna di Grado and the fishing village of Portogruaro.

The scenery of the lagoons is likewise more natural here than elsewhere. Between the distant shores lined with fishermen's houses, the broad expanse of the water is dotted with small, shrubby islands. As the tide ebbs, the sandbanks and mudflats are exposed, with their lush and varied growth of algae and other plant life.

In the historical past, the local center for this coastal region was the ancient Roman city of Aquileia. The settlement of the lagoons came about as the result of other events. Aquileia was a Roman Imperial trading city, whose citizens practiced a luxurious life style and a tolerance that enabled the early Christians to become established here; it became a stronghold of Christianity. It was destroyed and razed to the ground by the invading Huns. Most of the population fled to the islands of the lagoons, where they found abundant fish and marsh-land birds, though they lacked drinking water. Initially, they lived mainly on fish. As it is still done in the most northern part of Europe, they used the fish oil both for food and for practical purposes: to lubricate their tools, as fuel for their lamps, and to paint the hulls of their boats to make them watertight. It was a long time before Aquileia recovered from its destruction by the Huns. It began to regain some of its former glory in the Middle Ages, and became the seat of influential patriarchs with almost as much power as the pope in Rome.

The number and variety of fish around the coasts and lagoons of Friuli equal other parts of the Adriatic. Eel are a specialty of the calm waters of the lagoons. Fish varieties caught farther out to sea include mullet, sea bass, and gilt head bream. The fishermen's lives and methods have changed radically since the days of these first settlers; no longer do they set out to sea in traditional fishing smacks under sail, but in fast, powered boats. Traditional clothing has long since given way to T-shirts and blue jeans. In one respect, though, little has changed: fishing is a man's job, and the women's involvement starts with the fish soup. Locals claim that they can still identify distinct types among the fishermen: tall, muscular, ash blond men of Dalmatian ancestry; blond, blue-eyed fishermen from Caorle or Istria, who are seen as lively and always ready for a joke; dark-eyed and fiery men of Romagnan stock, nevertheless friendly and tolerant, and delighting in the sensual pleasures of life; and, lastly, the Venetians, reddish of face, typically with green or hazel eyes. They are seen as agreeable, cheerful, and a little garrulous, yet patient, peaceable, and full of common sense.

Anguilla ai ferri
Grilled eel
(Illustration far left, behind)

2 GUTTED FRESHWATER EELS, 1 1/4 LBS/600 G EACH

For the marinade:
OLIVE OIL
VINEGAR
SALT AND PEPPER

8 BAY LEAVES
CHOPPED PARSLEY
GRILLED SLICES OF POLENTA

Wash the eels, carefully cleaning off all the slime. Remove the heads, tails, and backbones, and cut into pieces about 3 inches/8 cm long. Open out and press as flat as possible. Mix the marinade ingredients and place the eels in it for several hours to absorb the flavors. Then remove and lay the pieces on a hot grill, skin side down. Scatter with bay leaves and cook for about 15 minutes. Turn and cook for another 10 minutes. Season with salt and pepper, and sprinkle with parsley. Serve with grilled polenta.

Anguilla fritta
Fried eel
(Illustration far left, in foreground)

4–5 GUTTED EELS, 1/2 LB/250 G EACH

For the marinade:
OLIVE OIL
LEMON JUICE
SALT AND PEPPER

ALL-PURPOSE FLOUR
OIL FOR FRYING
GRILLED OR ROASTED SLICES OF POLENTA

Choose small eels if possible. Wash them and clean thoroughly of slime. Remove the heads, tails, and fish bones and cut the eels into roughly 2 inch/5 cm pieces. Mix the marinade and leave the eel in it for at least 2 hours to absorb the flavors.
Drain the eels and coat in flour. Heat a generous quantity of oil, fry the eel, then remove and drain on paper towels before serving. Accompany with grilled or roasted polenta slices.

Risotto alla maranese
Seafood risotto
(Illustration left, center)

1/2 LB/200 G PREPARED SQUID
1/4 LB/100 G PREPARED SHRIMP
6–7 TBSP OLIVE OIL
1 CLOVE OF GARLIC, CHOPPED FINELY
3–4 TBSP CHOPPED PARSLEY
SALT AND PEPPER
1 LB/500 G MUSSELS
1 GLASS DRY WHITE WINE
1 3/4 CUPS/300 G RISOTTO RICE
VEGETABLE STOCK

Wash and slice the squid, not too finely. Wash the shrimp. Sauté both briefly in half the olive oil, with the garlic and parsley. Wash and clean the mussels, discarding any that are open. Cook them in the remaining oil until the shells have completely opened. Discard unopened mussels. Remove the flesh from the shells and add it to the shrimp and squid. Strain the cooking juices from the mussels through muslin, and add it to the seafood. Pour on the white wine. Add the rice, and simmer until tender. Add vegetable stock from time to time to prevent drying out. Allow the risotto to stand for a few moments before serving.

Scampi fritti
Fried shrimp

24 SHRIMP
2 EGGS
SALT AND PEPPER
OLIVE OIL FOR FRYING
2 TBSP ALL-PURPOSE FLOUR

Wash the shrimp and remove from their shells, discarding heads, tails, and innards. Beat the eggs and season with salt and pepper. Toss the shrimp in flour, then dip in egg and fry in the hot oil for a few minutes. Drain on paper towels and serve hot.

Coda di rospo al vino bianco
Monkfish in white wine

4 PORTIONS OF FILLETED MONKFISH
1 ONION, CHOPPED
2 CLOVES OF GARLIC, CHOPPED
1 STALK OF CELERY, CHOPPED
1 SPRIG OF ROSEMARY, CHOPPED
3 SPRIGS OF FLAT LEAF PARSLEY, CHOPPED
6 TBSP OLIVE OIL
SALT AND WHITE PEPPER
ALL-PURPOSE FLOUR
1 CUP/250 ML DRY WHITE WINE

Preheat the oven to 400 °F/200 °C. Wash the fish and pat dry. Briefly sauté the onion, garlic, celery, rosemary, and parsley in the olive oil in an ovenproof pan or casserole. Season the fish with salt and pepper, toss in flour, and sauté on both sides. Pour on the white wine, and bake for about 20 minutes. Then remove the fish and keep hot. Reduce the cooking liquid, strain it, and pour over the fish. Serve immediately.

Misto di pesce con salsa d'aglio
Fried fish in garlic sauce

4 SMALL, GUTTED PLAICE
4 SMALL, GUTTED RED MULLET
4 PORTIONS MONKFISH OR OTHER MARINE FISH, AS AVAILABLE
SALT
ALL-PURPOSE FLOUR
OLIVE OIL
LEMON WEDGES

For the sauce:
2 CLOVES OF GARLIC
1 BUNCH OF PARSLEY
6 TBSP OLIVE OIL
JUICE OF 1 LEMON
SALT

Wash the fish and pat dry. Rub the inside of the plaice and red mullet, and the outside of the monkfish, with salt, and coat them lightly in flour.
Crush the garlic and mix it with the parsley, the 6 tablespoons of olive oil for the sauce, and the lemon juice. Season with salt, and add more olive oil if necessary.
Heat olive oil in a skillet and sauté the fish for about three minutes on each side. Arrange on a plate to serve, garnished with lemon wedges and accompanied by the sauce.

WINEGROWING IN THE BORDERLANDS

There is always a fascination about wine grown in border regions that have seen the passage of many peoples. This region in the far northeast of Italy is no exception. From the earliest times, viticulture in this area has been influenced by Romans, Celts, Furlani, and Illyrians. This tract of country saw successive kingdoms come and go – Gothic, Lombard, Carolingian and Frankish rulers were followed by centuries of tension between the Habsburg Empire and Venice. Signs of Habsburg influence can mainly be found in the modern province of Gorizia; the social, political, and cultural sway of Venice has left its mark on Grave and Colli Orientali, areas where the production of red wines predominates. In modern times, vineyards in Collio, a region of hills, are owned and worked by winegrowers from Friuli and from Slovenia, with large estates on both sides of the border.

Single-variety white wines of the highest quality are produced in Collio from Chardonnay, Sauvignon, and Ribolla grapes.

WHAT DOES THE LABEL TELL US?

1 Producer country

2 DOC classification (or other classification: DOCG, IgT, or VdT = Vino da Tavola)

3 Producer or estate

4 Address of producer or bottling address (second applies if the wine is not made and bottled by the winegrower)

5 Grape variety (only applies to DOC wines, where the variety is specified)

6 Year

7 Classification

8 Alcohol content as alcohol by volume

9 Capacity of contents (℮ = EU standard bottle)

10 Producer bottled (wine made and bottled by the winegrower)

Colli Orientali

Although "Colli Orientali" means "Eastern Hills" this is not the easternmost wine-growing area of Friuli; Collio and Carso lie farther to the east. It surrounds the regional capital, Udine, in a crescent, and the area occupies the northwestern part of the range of hills to which Collio too belongs. The sweet wine Ramandolo comes from the northern tip of Colli Orientali. The gentle hills in the central part of the area offer the right climatic conditions for fine, elegant white wines. The southern part, facing the Adriatic, is suitable for creating great, powerful, red wines. Some of these are among the best products of Italian winemaking today.

Collio

Collio is the most famous winegrowing area in Friuli. The name means "hill." It does not lie entirely in Italy, since over half the area belongs to Slovenia. There, the area is called Brda; historically, it is a relic of the Austro-Hungarian Empire, which formerly ruled the entire region. Many Collio winegrowers also own vineyards on the Slovenian side,

but they are allowed to market their wines with an Italian label, thanks to a legal exception made under EU regulations. White wines are the great specialty of Collio: varietal wines made from Chardonnay, Sauvignon, and Ribolla grape varieties, and blended wines using several types. The hills of central Collio are among the few really excellent white wine producing areas in Italy. The southern slopes around Capriva and Cormóns also produce outstanding red wines, particularly those based on Merlot.

Isonzo, Carso, and the river plains of Friuli

The remaining areas of Friuli have to struggle to establish a reputation for themselves in competition with the top wine-growing areas of Collio and Colli Orientali. Nevertheless, they include the Grave region, which accounts for most of Friuli's wine production in terms of quantity. The Isonzo region in the south of Collio offers the delightful surprise of some outstanding Chardonnay and Sauvignon Blanc. And to the north of Trieste, in the limestone karst area of Carso, minute amounts of highly individual wines of marked character are being made from the local varieties Terrano and Vitovska.

Latisana, Aquileia, Annia, and Lison-Pramaggiore are generally known for clean-tasting, respectable mass-roduction wines.

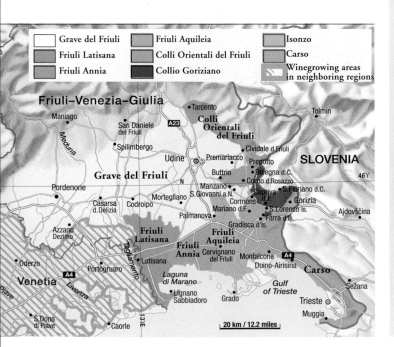

Grave del Friuli	Friuli Aquileia	Isonzo
Friuli Latisana	Colli Orientali del Friuli	Carso
Friuli Annia	Collio Goriziano	Winegrowing areas in neighboring regions

20 km / 12.2 miles

The winegrowing potential of this territory between the Alps and the Adriatic has only recently been developed, unlike other Italian regions. It offers travelers a beauty of landscape as yet unspoiled by mass tourism, and enjoys a climate with abundant sunshine, adequate rainfall, and a wide range of soil types, ideal for viticulture. It allows the cultivation of a number of grape varieties, both native and imported. The region initially established its reputation for its white varieties, especially Pinot Grigio, Chardonnay, and Sauvignon Blanc. Until a few decades ago, the vineyards here were mainly stocked with red varieties, but the market for the great, well-known red wines was dominated by Tuscany and Piedmont. The market for white wines, on the other hand, was growing exponentially, and the only internationally significant Italian wines in this category were from the Alto Adige.

Recent years have seen a return to red wines in all markets, and many winegrowers in Friuli have consequently begun to concentrate again on the red varieties. The region had a good foundation from which to begin. French varieties such as Cabernet Sauvignon and Merlot had been planted immediately after the great phylloxera disaster of the 19th century. Merlot has been the most widely grown variety in Friuli ever since the beginning of the 20th century, and excellent results have been achieved through the careful work done in both cultivation and winemaking. The finest growths of these two varieties correspond to what wine-drinkers have been looking for in the 1990s: they combine the structure and finesse of the great European wines with the juiciness and fruit of those from California and Australia.

Another great benefit of this region is the existence of many native varieties, still to be found here and there, having survived the years of mass wine production in some forgotten corner of an unworked vineyard. In the 1980s, a small group of winegrowers began to devote more attention to the Schioppettino, Refosco, Pignolo and Tazzelenghe vines they had. From these grapes, they made some powerful and highly individual red wines of great character.

There is also increasing use of native white varieties, especially Ribolla Gialla in the Collio region on the Slovenian border. This produces fine, fresh wines with good acidity, either as a single-variety wine or as part of a blend. Sweet wines produced from the Picolit and Verduzzo varieties are a specialty of the region. On the whole, the ones made from Verduzzo grapes, especially those from Ramandolo, are of much better quality.

Left: Collio produces excellent white wines, both varietal and blended types. In addition, the region has for some years been producing some respectable reds, some from French grape varieties such as Merlot, and others from local ones like Refosco.

SWEET DELIGHTS

The rule that a dessert wine is the right accompaniment to a sweet dessert dish applies in Friuli just as surely as elsewhere. A meal here might culminate in a slice of the traditional Friulian sweet yeast bread, *pinza*, or with *presniz* – made of pastry whorls generously filled with walnuts, hazelnuts, almonds, pine nuts, and raisins soaked in rum.

ITALIAN DESSERT WINES

Italy has a whole range of different types of dessert wine, though their reputation lags behind that of their French, German, and Austrian equivalents. Wine from selected, ripe grapes, and wine made from frosted ones, were known as long ago as Imperial Roman times. It was also common to sweeten dry ones, perhaps by adding honey. Even famous dry wines like Frascati, Orvieto, and Soave were produced in the sweet style, *abbocato*, for centuries.

Four main classes of sweet wine types are known in Italy today. Recioto, a type of *vin de paille* or "straw wine" is mainly produced in the Veneto. The grapes are left to dry out on wooden trestles for a few weeks after harvesting, before being pressed in the normal way. The wines have an intense sweetness, yet are light and fruity in flavor, ideal to accompany a light sweet course. Vin Santo is a very different wine. It comes mostly from Tuscany, though also from the Trentino region. For this, the grapes are air-dried, and the wines stored for a long period in small, hermetically sealed wooden casks in a warm loft. This gives the wines an oxidized character sometimes reminiscent of sherry. The most popular Italian sweet wine is certainly the sparkling Moscato d'Asti, along with Asti and Asti Spumante. The natural sweetness of the grapes is preserved by interrupting the fermentation process in the tank. This is done either by cooling the wine or by filtration. A good Moscato d'Asti is excellent with fruit salad or very light desserts, such as sorbets or fruit tarts. In Sicily, sweet wines are generally made from overripe grapes of the Moscato or Malvasia varieties. These have sufficient depth to drink with more substantial, creamy desserts, such as chocolate torte or cheese cakes. Wines from late-harvested grapes and selected ripe grapes (Spätlese and Auslese) in the tradition of the German-speaking countries are found in the Alto Adige region. The grape varieties used are also German.

The conditions of the Italian climate are not usually suited to noble rot, as for the grapes used in making French Sauternes and the Beerenauslese type of German and Austrian wine. A few winemakers are therefore using special chambers in which they recreate the climatic conditions, so that the harvested grapes can continue ripening under the appropriate high levels of humidity.

PINZA
Sweet yeast bread

GENEROUS 2 LB/1 KG ALL-PURPOSE FLOUR
2 1/2OZ/70 G FRESH YEAST (IF USING ACTIVE DRY YEAST, FOLLOW MAKER'S INSTRUCTIONS)
1 CUP/250 ML MILK
1 1/3 CUPS SUGAR (PREFERABLY SUPERFINE)
3 1/2 OZ/100 G BUTTER
6 EGGS
SALT
RUM
1 VANILLA BEAN

Mix together a generous ½ lb/250 g of the flour with the yeast and lukewarm milk to a batter. Leave to rise for 1 hour, then add another ½ lb flour, ½ cup/100 g sugar, 3 tablespoons/40 g melted butter, and 2 eggs. Mix carefully and leave for 2 hours. Preheat the oven to 400 °F/200 °C. Add and knead in the remaining flour, butter, sugar, 3 eggs plus 1 egg yolk, a pinch of salt, a dash of rum, and the pulp from the center of the vanilla bean. Leave to rise, then knead again and shape into a loaf. Place on a baking tray and bake for 30 minutes at 400 °F/200 °C. Reduce the oven temperature to 350 °F/180 °C and continue baking for about another 10 minutes until the crust has browned.

PRESNIZ
Pastry whorl dessert
(Illustration left)

For the pastry:
GENEROUS 2 CUPS/250 G ALL-PURPOSE FLOUR
1 CUP/250 G BUTTER
5–6 TBSP MILK
JUICE OF 1 LEMON
1 EGG
SALT

For the filling:
WALNUTS
HAZELNUTS
CHOPPED ALMONDS
PINE NUTS
RAISINS SOAKED IN RUM
CANDIED FRUITS

FLOUR FOR WORK SURFACE
BUTTER FOR GREASING PANS
1 EGG, BEATEN
CONFECTIONERS' SUGAR

Rub the butter into half the flour, and leave to stand overnight. Mix the remaining flour, milk, lemon juice, egg, and salt in a second bowl. Leave to stand for 1 hour. Then knead the two mixtures together, and roll out thinly into a rectangle on a floured cloth. Preheat the oven to 400 °F/200 °C.
Scatter the nuts and fruits for the filling over the pastry. Use the cloth to help roll up the pastry into a sausage shape. Then slice into rounds. Grease a baking dish with butter and lay the slices side by side to fill the dish. Brush the top with the beaten egg and bake for about 40 minutes. Sprinkle with confectioners' sugar before serving.

Tajut

The time-honored custom of *tajut* or *cajut* is one of the oldest drinking habits in Friuli. It dictates that, when two friends meet in the street, one stands the other a glass of wine. The recipient must respond by providing the second glass. In small villages in Friuli, several friends are likely to wander by and join the group, each receiving a drink and standing a round. Not surprisingly, *tajut* calls for a good deal of time – and for prior drinking practice. Fortunately for the drinkers, the wine is served in small glasses, thus averting the hangover that would otherwise have followed the sociable get-together.

Background: The custom of *tajut* is beginning to die out in Friuli. Here, Gianni is waiting for his friends outside a small *trattoria*.

GRAPPA

The origins of grappa, a clear spirit distilled from marc, lie shrouded in the past. It is made from the remains of the grapes after pressing, the Italian word *grappa* literally meaning "grape stalk". There is an early written record of this alcoholic product of the Alps and Alpine foothills, that dates from 1451. A native of Friuli by the name of Enrico made mention of a brew called *grape* in his last will and testament. The original use of grappa was to provide a sense of Mediterranean warmth in the chill climate of northern Italy.

Its career has led upward ever since, and grappa now enjoys a good reputation and a place in the European pantheon of fine food and drink. Huge differences in quality exist, as a result of rising demand, and a correspondingly wide spectrum of prices. These range from fairly cheap, industrially produced spirits made by a continual process to the more expensive products of traditional distilleries, which have greater sophistication. Here, individual batches are distilled, each of which is attended to with a craftsman's care. Single variety grappa has gained currency in recent years, though critics point out that this is only justifiable where the grape variety is a highly aromatic one such as Moscato, or muscat. Opinion also differs on whether grappa should be aged. The quality of the marc is certainly the main determinant of quality, along with the skill of the distiller. No amount of maturation in the cask can make up for poor quality grapes. Maturation does however harmonize and refine the flavors and aromas. A riserva or stravecchia is aged for at least twelve months, of which six are spent in the wooden cask. Oak casks give them their typical golden hue.

Young grappa is at its best when drunk slightly chilled, at 46–50 °F (8–10 °C) out of tall-stemmed glasses. Aged varieties are better drunk from a brandy glass at 61–64 °F (16–18 °C). Whatever its age (or even flavoring), however, grappa must always be crystal clear. Cloudiness or impurities are a sign of poor quality, as are a sooty, acrid or rotten odor.

In the Sibona grappa distillery in Piobesi d'Alba, Piedmont, the stills are used to make separate batches of spirit. The grape residue for each batch is heated by means of a waterbath.

Romano Levi's distillery in Neive, Piedmont, is of the traditional type, so the separate-batch method is used. Heating is done using the dried residue of the previous year's marc as fuel. The grappa is of the highest quality.

The furnace is burning fiercely, but excessively high temperatures will impair the marc. It is therefore heated inside a bath.

The marc is loaded into the heating vessel. Good quality marc comes from good, ripe, fresh grapes.

The distiller now seals down the lid. The furnace is stoked high, and heating of the still can begin.

The alcohol and aromatic substances rise as they vaporize, and enter the condensing coil, where the distillate liquesces.

THE MANUFACTURE OF GRAPPA

The process by which grappa is made begins with marc, the skins of the grapes that have been pressed. For the production of good grappa, the marc should still be as fresh and moist as possible. Mold and acidifying bacteria have not yet had a chance to multiply if the marc is fresh. The marc from red grapes will already have been fermented as part of the red wine production process, so it is ready for distillation. In white wine production, there is less skin contact, and the must is separated off before fermentation of the wine. The skins have still to be fermented before the marc can be distilled.

Care must be taken when heating the marc, or it will thicken and burn onto the bottom of the still. This has an adverse effect on flavor. There are two methods of preventing this: the first is to place the still inside a second container filled with water, so that the marc is heated in a *bagnomaria* or waterbath; the second is to heat it by means of steam. Both ensure that no direct heat reaches the marc, and that the temperature remains below 212 °F (100 °C).

Each of the various individual substances contained in the marc boils at its own particular temperature. Methyl alcohol, along with certain other alcohols (called polyhydric alcohols), is the first to evaporate from the bubbling mixture being distilled. Together these make up the *testa* or "head" of the distillate, which is an evil-smelling, poisonous mixture. Frustratingly for the distiller, the very next stage contains the alcohol that is wanted, as well as all the precious aromas that give the grappa its character. This demands considerable experience on the part of the distiller, who needs to have a good "nose" so as to separate off the *testa*, but capture the "heart" of the grappa, (*il cuore* as it is called in Italian). Only by acting at exactly the right moment can this be done, and the spirit collected free of impurities.

The distillation process is followed through observation portholes.

In the large grappa distillation plants, the process runs continuously, but the small, traditional distillers prepare each batch individually. The stills are emptied completely after each process, and refilled with fresh marc. The used marc is pressed and laid out to dry, to be used as fuel the following year. The ashes of the burnt marc are used in their turn, to fertilize the vines. It is hard to imagine a more efficient re-use of waste. A spirit that has been distilled with so much care needs to be truly appreciated and carefully handled. The connoisseur should store grappa in a cool, dry place. It is best to finish a bottle fairly quickly once opened; the delicate, volatile bouquet will not last beyond about three months.

Left: Grappa has made a remarkable transition from a spirit drunk by peasants to the height of fashion. The delightful bottles no doubt contributed to its success.

Grappa is traditionally drunk young and crystal clear. The variety chosen is a matter of taste.

Right: Romano Levi, regarded by many as the doyen of grappa, takes a sample from the cask.

Italian bars usually serve grappa in small, heavy-bottomed glasses, but a whole variety of specialized shapes can be found for the enjoyment of this drink.

TYPES OF GRAPPA

Interest in grappa was muted until recently. Especially in the more exalted gastronomic circles, it was thought of as merely a peasant drink. Its popularity has now risen to levels that would have been impossible without gifted distillers like Romano Levi, Luigi Orazio Nonino, Bruno Pilzer, Gioachino Nannoni, and certain others. Distillers of grappa used to travel from one vineyard to the next, distilling on the spot to provide the winegrowers with a potent drink to keep out the cold; now, modern distilleries are specializing. They are producing fine quality grappa, often from single grape varieties – Moscato or Traminer – capable of satisfying the highest expectations.

Distillation of grappa is not limited to Piedmont and Friuli: marc is widely available, since winemaking is carried on in most regions of the country. The most important areas of grappa production are Lombardy, Val d'Aosta, the Veneto, Trentino, and Alto Adige. Any grappa simply described as "Italian" is probably a blend of spirit from several regions. In Friuli, grappa made using marc from the sweet, low-yield grape variety Picolit is a specialty.

A TRADITIONAL DISTILLERY

Romano Levi is one of the best-known grappa distillers in Italy; certainly the one most pictured. His tiny distillery is located in Neive, Piedmont. It has the quaintness and reverence of age. He learned the craft from his father, eventually took over the distillery himself, and has altered nothing in the centuries-old production process. Watching him at work, it is clear to see that he would never dream of changing his methods – and their success proves him right. His output is only a couple of thousand bottles a year, but his products are known and appreciated far beyond Piedmont or even Italy. A number of customers travel far to buy from him. His grappa may not necessarily have the clarity of others, as is well known. Nor does he take that great an interest in flavor; this he happily admits himself. But there is great attraction in the personal attention he devotes to the bottles, lovingly created by him and adorned, once filled, with handwritten labels. They are a collector's item.

VENEZIA
VENETO

The city of Venice and the Veneto region, whatever the political links between them, are strikingly different in atmosphere and association. The city itself, truly the *grande dame* of the Adriatic, graces many a photograph album. Its romance never ceases to fascinate; the Veneto, in contrast, calmly boasts the finest of Palladian villas. These were mainly built as summer residences for the rich Venetian aristocracy eager to escape the heat and stench of the city's canals and alleyways. The healthy climate on the banks of the river Brenta provided an ideal retreat in the hottest months. The region is more than a backdrop for Venice, the former trading and seagoing power. In the territory from Padua to Verona – city of the once-powerful and dreaded Sforza family – and on to the eastern shores of Lake Garda, another Italy is revealed, with a character all its own. Venice, the *Serenissima*, seems part of a different world.

The cuisine of Venice likewise differs from that of the Veneto. Risotto is common to both, but the added ingredients on the coast are fish and seafood; away from the Adria, we find pumpkin, asparagus, radicchio, and frogs' legs being used. Beans and legumes feature in both areas; the traditional dish of *pasta e fagioli* combines pasta with beans. It is served lukewarm, usually with a dash of olive oil. *Risi e bisi*, a dish of rice with tender, young peas, has gained a place on menus both within and beyond the region.

Otherwise, the Veneto tends to favor heavier dishes, while some of the food served in Venice reflects the former glories of the *Serenissima*. Exquisite menus are created, with the use of exotic spices and fine sauces. Yet simple and traditional foods like stockfish or the dish of marinated anchovies or sardines called *sarde in saor* are not forgotten. In the Veneto, less fish is eaten. Meat and sausage are preferred, such as *sopressata*, a coarse-textured, pressed meat sausage, and garlic salami. The region is also one of the main producers of fine vegetables. Red radicchio from Treviso is one such specialty; asparagus from Bassano del Grappa is another.

Previous double page: Harry's Bar is one of the icons of Venetian gastronomy.

Left: The villas built by the architect Palladio (1508–1580) are world famous. Shown here is the Villa Foscari (built around 1560), also known as the Villa Malcontenta.

HARRY'S BAR

The history of the legendary Harry's Bar goes back to 1930, to the counter of another bar entirely: that of the eminent Hotel Europa-Britannia. There, Giuseppe Cipriani was mixing cocktails for a handful of guests able to defy the Great Depression. There were three Americans among them: a somewhat reserved young student, Harry Pickering, his aunt, and her lover. The trio made a few excursions now and again into St. Mark's Square, but otherwise saw little of the city, preferring to spend their time in the bar of the hotel. Their day began around 11 in the morning, when they ordered aperitifs before eating lunch on the terrace. They returned to the bar for drinks in the afternoon, and once more in the evening. Some two months later, an argument took place, and the aunt left, together with her young lover. Harry remained behind with a mountain of unpaid bar bills.

Harry's visits to the bar became fewer and fewer. On one of his rare appearances, Giuseppe Cipriani tried to discover the reason for this change in habits. Pickering had been one of his best customers; could he be ill, or in financial straits? The problem turned out to be financial. Giuseppe took pity on the young man, and lent him his hard-earned money – the not inconsiderable sum of 10,000 lire, which he had been saving to buy a bar of his own. The checks were all paid, and Pickering disappeared across the Atlantic, apparently for good. A few months later, however, he was back, to repay the debt – and gave Cipriani an extra 30,000 lire as an expression of thanks. The amount was enough to enable them jointly to open the bar that Giuseppe had dreamt of for so long.

As a mark of gratitude to Mr. Pickering, the name "Harry's Bar" was chosen. It was Giuseppe's wife Giulietta who found the premises: it was a former shop at no. 1323, Calle Vallaresso, near the landing stage where the boats stop for S. Marco. Just 485 square feet (45 square meters) in size, it was tucked away in a cul-de-sac, away from the bustle of St. Mark's Square itself.

Rossini
(Illustration above right)

Serves 1

Scant 1/4 cup/50 ml ice-cold strawberry purée
2/3 cup/150 ml well chilled Prosecco di Conegliano

Place the strawberry purée in a chilled glass. Top up with prosecco, stir quickly, and serve immediately.

Tiziano
(Illustration below right)

Serves 1

Scant 1/4 cup/50 ml cold red grape juice
2/3 cup/150 ml well chilled Prosecco di Conegliano

Put the grape juice into a chilled glass. Top up with prosecco, stir quickly, and serve immediately.

Bellini

Serves 1

Scant 1/4 cup/50 ml ice-cold purée of unpeeled white peaches
2/3 cup/150 ml well chilled Prosecco di Conegliano

Place the purée in a chilled glass. Top up with prosecco, stir quickly, and serve immediately.

Giuseppe Sereno, barman at Harry's Bar, mixes a Bellini, a drink made of white peach purée and well chilled Prosecco di Conegliano.

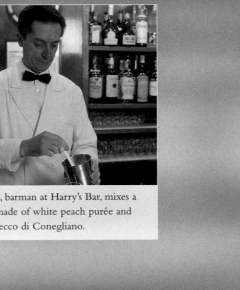

CARPACCIO DI CIPRIANI

Beef carpaccio, Cipriani style
(Illustration in background)

1/4 CUP/60 ML FRESHLY MADE MAYONNAISE
2–3 TBSP SINGLE CREAM
1 TSP MILD MUSTARD
1 TSP WORCESTER SAUCE
TABASCO; SALT
10 OZ/300 G FILLET STEAK
ROCKET SALAD (ARUGULA) TO GARNISH

Mix the freshly made mayonnaise, cream, mustard, and Worcester sauce until blended and creamy. Season with Tabasco and salt, and leave to rest for 15 minutes for the flavors to mingle.

Place the fillet steak in the freezer just long enough to become lightly frozen. Then cut the meat into wafer-thin slices and arrange on 4 individual plates or one large one. Pour over the mayonnaise sauce and garnish with rocket.

This made it ideal to attract a regular clientele, rather than passing custom. The choice proved a perfect one. Harry's Bar was an instant triumph as fashionable customers streamed in. It continued to be a favorite haunt of the contemporary jet set as time went on, for Harry's Bar has lost none of its appeal to the beautiful, rich, and famous. The list of such names is endless, including Ernest Hemingway, Somerset Maugham, the Rothschilds, Arturo Toscanini, Orson Welles, Aristotle Onassis, Maria Callas, Truman Capote, Peggy Guggenheim, Charlie Chaplin, Barbara Hutton, and even royalty, such as King Alfonso XIII of Spain, Queen Wilhelmina of the Netherlands, King Paul of Greece, Princess Diana and Prince Charles.

From the outset it was not only the drinks that exerted such attraction; delicious food accompanied them. Among the drinks dispensed by Giuseppe at the bar were simple but inspired creations such as Bellini and Tiziano. His most famous invention is probably a culinary one. One of the regular customers at Harry's Bar

during the 1950s was Amalia Nani Mocenigo, a lady from the highest ranks of the Venetian nobility. Her doctor had prescribed for her a diet rich in raw meat to counter slight anemia, and Giuseppe now created a unique dish of quite elegant simplicity. An exhibition of the works of the Renaissance Venetian artist Vittore Carpaccio, a painter famous for his brilliant reds, was taking place in the city at that time, and it was decided to name the dish after him. It consists of wafer-thin slices of raw fillet steak in a sauce of mayonnaise, lemon juice, Worcester sauce, cream, salt, and white pepper. Today this dish can be found on almost every Italian menu at home and abroad – albeit with variations. The original may still best be enjoyed at 1323 Calle Vallaresso.

Giuseppe Cipriani died in 1980, and the management of the bar passed to his son, Arrigo. The bar in fact bears his name, and always has done – Arrigo is the Italian equivalent of Harry. A lawyer, he had worked in the bar in his youth as often as he could, at the request

of his father. He took loving care of the small establishment, changing nothing. The one concession to modernity is a computerized cash desk. For maintaining its character he has earned the gratitude of his customers, and Harry's Bar seems proof against the tyranny of changing times and fashions.

THE OSTERIA DA FIORE

In the dark recesses of Calle del Scaleter, in the Sestiere San Polo area of the city, lies an outwardly unremarkable small establishment, a former wine shop that is now Maurizio Martin's restaurant, the Osteria da Fiore. This tiny, tucked-away gem is well worth the search. The restaurant seats just 40 people, and its decor, in the traditional style, is both pretty and unassuming. Above all, there is no better place to taste traditional Venetian fish dishes.

Mara Martin, who heads the kitchen, uses only freshly caught fish from the lagoon, such as gilt head bream, sea bass, and turbot, as well as seafood, including squid, octopus, and local varieties of mussel. Any lingering doubts over dried cod – the centuries-old staple of stockfish – are dispelled here by a delicious pureed dried cod dish that taunts the taste buds. Another of Mara Martin's specialties is *risotto nero*, in which the rice is colored by the ink from the octopus. The Osteria da Fiore is equally happy to entertain guests who simply want a glass of wine and a selection of tempting morsels.

RISOTTO NERO
Octopus risotto with ink
(Illustration below left)

Serves 4–6

GENEROUS 1 1/2 LBS/750 G OCTOPUS WITH INK SACS
2 CLOVES OF GARLIC
7 TBSP OLIVE OIL
JUICE OF 1 LEMON
1 ONION
1 CUP/250 ML DRY WHITE WINE
2 CUPS/750 ML FISH STOCK (HOMEMADE OR BOUGHT)
1 1/2 CUPS/250 G VIALONE RICE
SALT AND FRESHLY GROUND BLACK PEPPER
1 BUNCH OF FLAT LEAF PARSLEY, CHOPPED

Clean the octopus and place the intact ink sacs carefully in a bowl. Slice the octopus body and tentacles finely.
Chop the garlic finely and mix with the olive oil and lemon juice. Pour the mixture over the octopus and marinate for 20 minutes. Heat the fish stock and keep hot.
Chop the onion finely and sauté lightly in 4 tablespoons of olive oil in a saucepan. Drain the octopus, reserving the marinade. Add the octopus to the saucepan, stirring to seal on all sides. Then add the marinade and the white wine.
Open the ink sacs and carefully pour the ink into the saucepan. Simmer for 20 minutes, adding some of the hot fish stock from time to time. Add the rice and cook until it is tender and has absorbed the liquid. Stir it constantly, gradually adding the remaining fish stock. Season with salt and pepper, and garnish with chopped parsley.

ANDAR PER OMBRE – A VENETIAN CUSTOM

Venetians are said to love a glass of wine, and to enjoy a chat with friends and relations, at any time of day. How better to combine the two than in the custom of *andar per ombre*, which is a time-honored ritual in this city. There are several explanations as to how it came to be called this, but the words signify "let's seek out a cosy *osteria* for a drink and a bite to eat, and have a good talk." Some people think that the term comes from the travelling wine merchants, who used to follow the shadow of the Campanile on St. Mark's Square as the sun moved round, to keep their wine cool. Anyone who wanted a drink therefore had to go into the shade – *all'ombra*. Others say that the *ombra* is an old Venetian unit of measurement, equivalent to about half a cup (100 ml). The *ombretta* is smaller still. Almost every citizen of Venice has a favorite drinking haunt or *giro de ombre*. They head towards their chosen *osteria* around 11 in the morning and there meet other regulars. They chat, drink their *ombra*, and go their way. A number of *ombre* may be drunk in this way in the course of the day and ensuing evening, but the measures are too small to produce any severe aftereffects. The *giro de ombre* is perhaps best compared with its Spanish equivalent, the *tapeo*. There, people wander from one tapas bar to another in the early evening.

Risotto nero –
Octopus risotto with ink

Baccalà alla vicentina –
Dried cod Vicenza style

Baccalà mantecato
Puree of dried cod
(Illustration above)

1 DRIED COD, SOAKED
EXTRA VIRGIN OLIVE OIL (1/4 THE WEIGHT OF THE PIECE OF COD)
SALT AND PEPPER
NUTMEG
3 CLOVES OF GARLIC
1 SMALL BUNCH OF PARSLEY

Wash the cod and boil for 20 minutes. Drain it and remove any bones. Then cut into pieces. Using a blender, mix with the olive oil and a seasoning of salt, pepper, and grated nutmeg until creamy. Chop the garlic and parsley and stir into the fish puree. Serve either cold or lukewarm, with hot polenta.
Stockfish (dried cod) is dried in the sun. Unless bought ready-soaked, it must be prepared before use. It needs to be beaten with a meat mallet and soaked for 2–3 days in enough water to cover it, changing the water daily.

Baccalà alla vicentina
Dried cod Vicenza style
(Illustration left)

GENEROUS 2 LBS/1 KG SOAKED DRIED COD
6–7 TBSP EXTRA VIRGIN OLIVE OIL
3 CLOVES OF CHOPPED GARLIC
2 TBSP CHOPPED PARSLEY
SALT AND PEPPER
1 ONION, FINELY CHOPPED
4 CUPS/1 L MILK
NUTMEG
3 SARDINES
GRATED PARMESAN

Wash the dried cod and pat dry. Cut into pieces Place half the olive oil, the garlic, and 1 tablespoon of parsley in an oven-proof casserole. Then add the fish and seal on all sides. Season lightly with salt and pepper, and add the finely chopped onion. Remove from the heat and take out the garlic.
Warm the milk slightly and pour over the fish to cover completely. Grate in a little nutmeg, and simmer for about 2 hours until the milk is nearly all absorbed.
Meanwhile, preheat the oven to 430 °F (220°C). Heat the remaining olive oil in a small saucepan and soften the sardines in it, removing any bones. Pour over the cod. Sprinkle with the remaining parsley and grated Parmesan. Bake in the open casserole for about 10 minutes. Cut out crescent-shaped pieces of polenta and bake these to serve with the fish.

VENICE AND THE AUSTRIANS

Venice, the *Serenissima Dominante*, once ruled lands extending from Istria to Byzantium and from Dalmatia to the Levant. Many times in its history it has been "in peril" – yet it has always survived with a legendary tenacity. The decline of this proud, aristocratic republic may be traced to the invasion of Napoleon on 12 March 1797. Even then, it had an air of decay. The last Doge, Ludovico Manin, abdicated. Soon after, Venice was handed over by Napoleon to the Austrians. The French returned in 1806, and carried off everything they could carry. The Congress of Vienna once more assigned Venice to the Austrians, who continued to hold it for 50 years. During this time, they imported the pigeons, and transformed the former monarch of the seas into a sleepy, provincial town. In 1866, Venice fell to the newly created kingdom of Italy. The Venetians are not by nature rebellious – they are said to tread warily in political matters – but a citizens' revolution against the Austrians was attempted. On 22 March 1848, Daniele Manin (coincidentally a namesake of the last Doge) climbed onto a table in front of the Caffè Florian on St. Mark's Square and proclaimed the republic. His attempt ended in failure, but illustrates the fact that Venice's cafés and hotels do serve as places of assembly where resistance may grow. Venetians can spend days at a time sitting in cafés – some even used to have their post directed there. The city was bombarded by the Austrian General Radetzky to bring it into submission.

During that bombardment, the populace had to abandon its outer sectors, and seek refuge elsewhere. The more affluent of them chose the elegant Hotel Danieli. The opponents of Austria-Hungary made the Caffè Florian their meeting-place, duly coming under observation there by the Austrian Imperial and Royal secret police.

FEGATO DI VITELLO ALLA VENEZIANA
Calf liver Venetian style
(Illustration above)

1 LB/500 G ONIONS
5 TSP/25 G BUTTER
3–4 TBSP OF OLIVE OIL
1 TBSP CHOPPED PARSLEY
2 BAY LEAVES
1 LB/500 G CALF LIVERS
4 TBSP MEAT STOCK
SALT AND FRESHLY GROUND BLACK PEPPER

Peel and slice the onions into rings. Melt the butter in a skillet with the olive oil. Peel the onions and cut them into fine rings. Add the onions, bay leaves and parsley. Cover and cook gently for about 10 minutes. Cut the calf liver into 4 slices. Add to the onions, raise the heat, and add a little meat stock. Cook not too fiercely for 5 minutes. Remove from the heat, season with salt and freshly ground pepper, and serve with slices of polenta.

PANINI

Salmone
Small *tartine* usually in the form of an open, filled bread roll. Generously buttered, the salmon complemented by a squeeze of lemon juice.

Arrostino e zucchini
Roast meat with either sliced zucchini and thyme, or julienne strips of zucchini to add a crisp, fresh note.

Primavera
The Italian version of the sandwich, the *tramezzino* is made from sliced white bread, usually untoasted. Here, the filling is ham with lettuce salad.

Gorgonzola e tartufo
The wonderful flavor of truffles contrasts with the strong taste of Gorgonzola cheese. Another combination is Gorgonzola with chestnut honey.

Insalata di gamberetti
This *tramezzino* has a shrimp and lettuce filling, often with mayonnaise. It is served cold.

Salmone e insalata
Crisp lettuce, usually frisée, and smoked salmon are used together to create a light, elegant note.

Tonno e carciofini
A real classic among *tramezzini*, with a filling of tuna and hearts of artichoke. Succulent and flavorsome.

Carciofini e Würstel
Italian-style small sausages with a German name in a very Italian combination.

Spinaci e mozzarella
Fresh Mozzarella cheese with cooked spinach, seasoned with a little lemon juice and pepper, makes for a light, very digestible snack.

Piadina caprese
Piadina is a type of flat bread from Romagna. Here, it is filled with tomatoes and mozarella cheese.

Carciofini e salame
This small baguette has a piquant filling of strong salami and artichokes.

Prosciutto e formaggio
This type of *panino* is best eaten hot. The cheese then melts, so that its flavor mingles with that of the ham

Mozzarella e acciughe
This combination dates back to ancient Rome. The piquancy of the anchovies is tempered by the mellow cheese.

Parmigiana di melanzane
A southern Italian specialty fit for a king. Fried eggplant is baked with a melting cheese and tomatoes.

Croissant al prosciutto e formaggio
This combination with ham and cheese demands a hot, buttery tasting croissant. *Mignon croissants* are the type usually used.

Fiore di zucca
This recipe calls for zucchini flowers, stuffed with mozzarella cheese and an anchovy. They are then fried in light batter.

Speck e brie
Speck is the name given to a delicious smoked ham from the Trentino region.

Piadina mozzarella e funghi
Piadina, with toasted cheese and mushrooms, makes a delicious, quick snack.

Mozzarella e pomodori
This combination of buffalo-milk mozzarella and tomatoes is called *Caprese* in Italy. Capri is the place where it tastes best.

Bresaola, racletta e rucola
Wafer-thin *bresaola* air-dried beef is served with fresh cheese, rocket salad (arugula), and a dash of lemon juice.

Mozzarella e prosciutto
A cheese and ham combination. One refinement is to make the sandwich using *panbrioche*, which has a subtle sweetness.

Mozzarella e pomodoro
Completely fresh mozzarella is the key to this combination – cheese straight from the refrigerator is simply not as good. It tastes delicious with tomatoes.

Uovo e tonno
Sliced, hard cooked eggs add just the right consistency to tuna canned in oil, and enhance the flavor.

Prosciutto cotto, formaggio e pomodori
Many Italians who go out to work eat bread rolls or *tramezzini* at midday. The fillings usually include vegetables to make the meal complete – here, ham, cheese, and tomatoes.

Italian bars, motorway eating places, and snack bars serve sandwiches and *panini, tramezzini,* or *crostini* to go with the usual *espresso*. They are often magnificent artistic and culinary creations. The fillings reflect the regional choice of ingredients in the combinations offered: local sausage, cheese, tomatoes, ham, anchovies, tuna, and shrimp.

Venetian masks

The masks that featured in the original Venetian carnival are more than just imaginative items of costume: they represent a set tradition, and several have a long history. Some are a reminder of events in the city's history; the Plague Doctor is one such. It harks back to the devastating plagues of the 16th and 17th centuries. Others, like *Pantalone* and *Arlecchino* derive from characters of the *Commedia dell'arte*. They still have an essential place in the staging of carnival folly, long after Goldoni's theater reforms.

Bauta

Bauta was one of the most popular Venetian costumes. It featured a three-cornered hat and black veil with a white face mask, and could be worn by women as well as by men.

Arlecchino

Arlecchino is Harlequin, a typical *Commedia dell'arte* figure. The character is an impudent prankster, and wears a black face mask and soft hat above a costume made up of brightly colored patches.

Moretta

Moretta is the name for an oval, black face mask worn by a woman. It was kept in place by means of a knob at the back, which the wearer held between her teeth.

Pantalone

This is another typical *Commedia dell'arte* character, an ill-tempered old man whose face expresses his avarice. The figure symbolizes a self-made rich Venetian merchant.

The Plague Doctor

This costume is a reminder of the terrible plagues that affected the city during the Middle Ages and Renaissance. The doctor carries a wooden stick like the one used in those times to push back the bedclothes without having to touch the patient. Another feature is the mask, which is beaked. The beak used to be filled with sweet-smelling herbs to counter the stench of the plague.

Commedia dell'arte, The Pantaloon and Harlequin figures of old Italian comedy: Color lithograph, from a 17th century original illustration: from a history of grotesque comedy, "Floegels Geschichte des Grotesk-Komischen" ed. Friedrich W. Ebeling, 4th edition, Leipzig 1887, Plate 3.

Carlo Goldoni

Carlo Goldoni, the great reformer of Italian theater, was active in the middle of the 18th century. His reforms ensured that the ancient *Commedia dell'arte*, with its highly stylized characters such as *Capitano, Arlecchino,* and *Colombina,* went out of fashion. This opened the way for new characters. Goldoni himself was a true Venetian. As such, he loved good food and drink. He also loved his home city, though he left it in despair for Paris at the age of 55, following a quarrel with his theater colleagues Chiari and Gozzi. Goldoni's plays repeatedly show Venetian life. His 1756 comedy "Il campiello" (The Square), for example, contains the character of a *fritoler*, a woman who fries the delicious *fritole* sweetmeats. His "Le baruffe chiozzotte" (Quarrels at Chioggia), first performed in 1762, just before his departure for Paris, turns on a slice of fried melon. The melon proves to be a source of strife when a gondolier gives it to a young woman, one of a number of lovers. The couples are thrown into argumentative chaos by this innocent act.

Pietro Longhi (1702–1785), *Portrait of Carlo Goldoni*, 1760, Museo Correr, Venice

CARNEVALE

Despite the enormous interest excited by Venice's modern street carnival, some of the city's most devoted citizens insist on preferring the ancient customs, which are quite unlike the tourist event in St. Mark's Square. *Carnevale* in Venice used to be celebrated in great style. Vast sums were spent on costumes and on balls – with fierce competition between societies and associations as to whose would be the most glamorous, would have the most elaborate setting, or would be able to serve the most opulent meal.

For the inhabitants of this city, festivals offer a magnificent opportunity for indulgence in good food. In the past, though not today, their love of such creature comforts brought them considerable moral criticism. The ecclesiastical authorities reproached them from time to time for their eagerness to move on from the sermon or ceremony to the table on the feast days of the church. "Gluttony is the greatest sin of the Venetians," wrote the city chronicler Pietro Gasparo Morolin in 1841.

Special foods, whether unusual or traditional, were indeed the focus of the various occasions of the church year, as well as the carnival. According to the writer Tommaso Locatelli, Venice in 1830 resembled a festival ground – and this was at a time of serious economic and political difficulties in the city. "Spits were turned and fish grilled in preparation for that great communal dinner." Delicacies eaten during the carnival included *galani*, strips of sweet pastry, crisply fried and dusted in sugar, and *fritole* or *fritelle*, carnival doughnuts. Other sugary delights to sustain participants in the carnival through long nights of celebration were *zaleti* and circular *buranelli* from the island of Burano, still popular today. A specialty traditionally eaten on 21 November, the day of the *Madonna della Salute*, was – and occasionally still is – *castradina*, salted, lightly smoked and air dried lamb prepared as a stew. Fortunately, the eating of *baccalà*, an extremely popular dish, was not limited to any particular feast day. It was enjoyed all year round in various guises. Another year-round dish was the delicious *fegato alla veneziana*, liver with onions. The calendar is less strictly observed today than it was, and the tiny doughnuts for which Venice is famous, *fritole*, can now be purchased and eaten whatever the season of the year.

Left: Far from being a riotous event, the carnival in Venice has a seriousness and solemnity not found in those of other countries and cities.

Doughnuts

The cheerful hiss of doughnuts frying in deep pans of hot fat is a sound that evokes the pleasures and the magnificence of carnival in the time of the Doges. *Fritole* were made of yeast dough, of flour, yeast, sugar, and a dash of grappa or anise, with the occasional addition of raisins, golden raisins, or pine nuts. They were deep fried in fat and sold on the streets.

The makers and sellers of these delicacies, the *fritoler*, were constantly inventing new variations on their wares. Sometimes they added rice, sometimes melon flowers, sometimes salt or fish, or even the powerfully flavored *baccalà*.

Towards the end of the 18th century, the *fritoler* of Venice achieved such economic significance that they banded together in a guild, the *corporazione dei fritoler*.

The most famous Venetian doughnut maker was probably a man named Zamaria. He even appears in an early 19th century print, cooking his wares. The self-confident title of the print is, "Here is Zamaria at work."

Zaleti

Polenta flour buns
(Illustration left)

2 TBSP RAISINS
I SMALL GLASS OF GRAPPA
I CUP/250 ML MILK
6 I/2 TBSP/100 G BUTTER
2 CUPS/250 G POLENTA FLOUR
2 I/2 TSP BAKING POWDER
A PINCH OF SALT
2/3 CUP/120 G SUGAR
I TBSP/30 G SUPERFINE SUGAR, FLAVORED
WITH A VANILLA BEAN

Soak the raisins in grappa. Warm the milk and melt the butter in it. Mix the flour, baking powder, salt, and sugar in a bowl. Pour in the milk and butter, and mix to a smooth dough. Add more milk if needed. Stir in the soaked raisins. Preheat the oven to 355°F (180°C).

Line a baking tray with parchment. With floured hands, take out portions of dough and shape into elongated buns about 4 inches (10 cm) long by 1 inch (2 cm) wide. Bake in the preheated oven for about 15 minutes. Sprinkle immediately with vanilla flavored sugar and leave to cool.

Deep-fried buns have always been popular in Italy. In times gone by they were often sold by traders on the street.

Fritole

Doughnuts

I/2 CUP/50 G GOLDEN RAISINS
I 2/3 CUPS/200 G ALL-PURPOSE FLOUR (PLUS A
LITTLE EXTRA)
SALT
I/3 CUP/60 G SUGAR
I EGG
I/3 OZ/10 G FRESH YEAST (IF USING
ACTIVE DRIED YEAST, FOLLOW MAKER'S
INSTRUCTIONS)
3/4 CUP/200 ML MILK (NOT TOO COLD)
PEANUT OIL
GENEROUS I/4 CUP/50 G CONFECTIONERS'
SUGAR FLAVORED WITH A VANILLA BEAN

Soak the golden raisins in lukewarm water, then drain and toss in a little flour to coat. Sieve the flour into a mixing bowl and add a pinch of salt, sugar, the egg, and the golden raisins. Mix the yeast with half the milk. Pour into the bowl with the other ingredients and stir in. Then knead to a smooth dough, gradually adding the remaining milk . Leave in a warm place to rise for about 1 hour.

Heat the oil (about 1 inch/2 cm deep in a deep pan). Fry the dough a small spoonful at a time until browned on both sides. Lift out with a slotted spoon and drain on paper towels. Sprinkle the doughnuts with confectioners' sugar to serve.

PANDORO

Pandoro, a Venetian specialty (illustration in back
ground), is closely related to the *panettone* of Milan,
and is mainly eaten at Christmas time. Both have a
long history. *Pandoro* may go back to *nadalin*, a typical
home-baked Christmas cake, or to the *pan de oro*, a
type of golden bread served at the end of the meal by
well-to-do patrician families. At the height of the city's
splendor, the cake was finely dusted with real, powdered
gold. Today it is vanilla flavored confectioners' sugar that
covers the golden brown surface of the *pandoro*. A
portion of this sugar is sold packed inside every box,
and helps give a Christmas feel to this delicious and
light-textured cake.

Most *pandoro* today is commercially made, but the
factories do try to maintain the old recipes. The ingredients used are the traditional flour, sugar, eggs, butter,
and brewers' yeast, and nothing else, and the characteristic shape — a flattened cone with the ribbed sides
running to an eight-pointed star at the top — has been
preserved over the years.

MURANO GLASS

The island of Murano lies more than a mile (2 kilometers) north of Venice. Its fame rests on its glass, and can ultimately be traced to the fear of fire. Glassware was originally produced on the main island of Venice. It was a precious commodity that brought both riches and reputation to the *Serenissima*. The furnaces needed for glassblowing represented a considerable fire risk,

Murano, a small group of islets, has a population of around 5,000. Like most destinations in Venice, it is best reached by means of the *vaporetto*.

however, especially as open furnaces were used, and so, in the 13th century, the decision was made to transfer the Venetian glassblowers entirely and almost overnight to Murano. The islanders of Murano were given special privileges to ease the transition. For example, their daughters were permitted to marry into the Venetian nobility. With these privileges came restrictions; the glassblowers were forbidden on pain of death to leave, so that they would never divulge the secrets of their trade.

Today, we tend to think of Murano glass as brightly colored and ornate, but the fame of Venetian glass production was originally based on the particularly fine glass developed and made there in the 16th century. Murano became the supplier of incomparably light and elegant crystal glassware to the courts of

Gianni Seguso's glassworks are on Murano, on the Fondamenta Serenella. Here, he and his craftsmen create fine quality glassware by the traditional methods of the glassblower's art.

The glassblower's most valuable tool is the blowing iron (background). The end of this is used to gather the required mass of glowing, semi-molten glass.

A wooden mold or matrix is bathed in water and used to create the shape. The glassblower turns the molten glass on the mold.

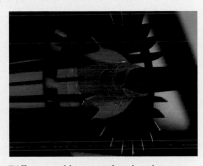
Different molds are employed to decorate and shape the glass. This one produces a ribbed effect.

The glassblower rolls the hot glass across the grid of the mold, in order to produce evenly spaced ridges.

The glassblower can further refine the shape using a wet wooden rod. Here, the circular base of a vase is being formed.

Europe. Despite the precautions taken, the secret of this precious clear glass filtered out to their competitors. Bohemian glassblowers in particular possessed the skill to produce glass of a quality to rival Venice. It was time for the men of Murano to invent something new. In the 17th century, the *soffiatori di vetro*, the glassblowers, developed a novel method of production, and launched onto the market their *reticello* glassware, soon highly sought after across Europe. This style features a network or lattice effect, of which Murano is still the leading producer. The creation of this latticework glass involves decorating the inside of a bulb of plain glass with opaque white or colored threads. The bulb of glass is blown and encased in a further layer, and the glassblower intertwines the threads into an amazing network with a few deft turns of the blowing iron.

The fine reputation of Murano glass has suffered somewhat since the 19th century, partly because of low-priced competing glassware from Hong Kong and Taiwan, and partly because of the manufacture of cheap, tasteless souvenirs in Murano itself. Individual items of high quality craftsmanship do not provide the income to remain competitive, and so most of the 50 glassworks in Murano make the sort of product that appeals to popular taste, the type seen on sale on every street corner.

A few outstanding representatives of the glassblower's art have ensured by their traditional craftsmanship that Murano has regained its name for glassmaking of the highest caliber. They measure their own achievements against the finest work of the past, in the conviction that their craft had reached its best at the time of the Renaissance. They are now trying to take up and continue these older traditions, though some of the shapes and designs they produce are extremely modern. Glass houses such as Taghapietra, Venini, Barovier & Toso, and Salviati have been in the vanguard of this development. Their workshops and sales rooms are well worth a visit, even for the most discriminating connoisseur.

Below: Murano is as synonymous with glass as Brussels is with lace. There are still glassworks on the island that seek to preserve the old, pre-industrial standards of quality, maintaining the high reputation of Murano glass.

BIGOLI – HOME-MADE PASTA

A demonstration of the *bigolaro* at the Volpato delicatessen in Mestre. The dough is forced through the holes that shape it into noodles.

The fresh pasta lands on a sieve and is then laid out and allowed to dry out before being cooked.

Before the invention of pasta machines and factory-produced noodles, long types of pasta were made at home using a traditional kitchen implement called a *bigolaro*. This is still sometimes done today. The pasta-making part of this machine is attached to one end of a three-foot (1 meter) long stool. A tube some 4 inches (10 centimeters) in diameter dispenses the pasta. The tube has interchangeable inserts, with holes of various sizes for the different shapes and thicknesses of the noodles. The pasta dough goes into the top of the tube and the cook turns a handle to force it through. By changing the insert, the cook can make thick or thin noodles (*bigoli*), *bigoli* with a hole down the middle, and so on, and cut them to the desired length.

The pasta was laid on a mesh of canes slung between two chairbacks to dry. Families used to lend their *bigolaro* to others who did not own one, or would make their pasta at the home of someone who had a machine. The customary way of thanking the owner of the *bigolaro* for their generosity was to give them some of the pasta. *Bigoli in salsa* is a typical Venetian dish. The combination of fresh pasta with a sauce of anchovies, olive oil, and onions is delicious.

BIGOLI IN SALSA
Pasta with anchovy sauce
(Illustration below)

4 SALTED ANCHOVIES
14 OZ/400 G BIGOLI (SPAGHETTI OR TRENETTE)
SALT
4 TBSP EXTRA VIRGIN OLIVE OIL
2 ONIONS
FRESHLY GROUND PEPPER
1 BUNCH OF FLAT LEAF PARSLEY TO GARNISH

Wash the anchovies, removing any bones. Cut small. Peel the onions and slice finely. Boil the pasta in plenty of salted water until *al dente* – just firm to the bite. Meanwhile, gently heat half the olive oil in a skillet and sauté the onions until soft, without browning. Add a little water if necessary. Add the anchovies and cook gently until they disintegrate. Remove from the heat. Stir in the remaining olive oil. Transfer the pasta to plates and pour over the sauce. Season with freshly ground pepper and garnish with whole parsley.

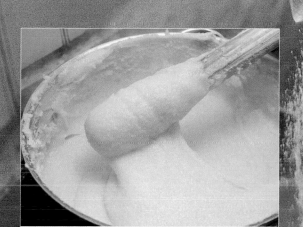

Exhausting as it is, the polenta must be stirred throughout the 40–45 minutes of cooking time. The task becomes harder as the polenta thickens

When cooked, the polenta is turned out onto a wooden board and smoothed over. It is cut with string when hot, but can be sliced with a knife once cold.

VENETIAN POLENTA

Polenta is a simple, even modest dish, yet it occupies an important place in the cuisine of Venice and the Veneto. The variations are almost endless. It can be eaten hot or cold, broiled, grilled, or cooked in the oven, served as a first course or baked main course, and accompanied by egg, fish, meat, or cheese.

Puddings made of ground millet, barley, or even beans were already well established in Venice, the Veneto, and Friuli, before corn swept onto the scene. Polenta from corn flour is still the most popular type, and the dish is felt to express family togetherness. The appetizing sight of a hot, golden, steaming meal of polenta creates a sense of warmth and comfort on cold winter days – a sense of home.

Polenta smells and tastes most appealing when cooked in the traditional way over a charcoal fire, when it absorbs the flavor of the smoke. It has to be prepared in a deep copper pot with a rounded cauldron base and no coating of zinc. This is because of the high cooking temperature, which would melt the zinc. The pot is either suspended over the fire by a chain, or can be placed directly on the hob. The metal rings of the hob can be removed as necessary to create a hollow where the cauldron can rest.

The pot is half filled with salted water. When this has boiled, the polenta flour is stirred in, adapting the amount to the consistency wanted. For a firm polenta, this is about 3 cups (350 g) of the flour, with about 2 teaspoons of salt. For a looser consistency, slightly less polenta flour or semolina is used. The fineness of the flour also affects the result: fine flour gives a smoother texture. The flour must be dry and free of lumps, and no more than a year old.

Cooking polenta is hard work. The mixture must be stirred constantly in slow, even, circular movements, occasionally switching direction to help the flour and water to blend thoroughly – and to ease the strain on the cook, especially towards the end of cooking, when the mixture is becoming stiff. A wooden stirring stick called a *mescola* is used for this task. One way of easing the effort is to call on many cooks to help; they will certainly not spoil the broth.

It takes about 40–45 minutes for the polenta to reach its optimum consistency. The cauldron is then lifted and swung toward a waiting wooden board for the contents to be tipped out. The polenta spreads across the board, helped along by smoothing it with a wetted knife. While it is still hot, polenta can be cut with a taut piece of string. When it has cooled down, it can be cut with a knife.

Special stirring machines are available today. These are fastened to the side of the pot, and achieve very respectable results, though they can never create the sense of affinity that develops when cooks stir the polenta themselves. When an artificial stirrer is used, many people also miss the togetherness of sitting around the kitchen with the aroma of cooking polenta wafting around them and their mouths watering in anticipation of a delicious meal.

LIFE ON THE LAGOON

The conduct and pace of life in Venice and on its neighboring islands are set by the surrounding water. In summer, as tourists delight in the vision of the canals sparkling in the midday sun, locals bemoan the stagnant reek in the side canal under their bedroom window. A change of season, and the worry is the threat of flooding, called *acqua alta*, arriving long after the tourists have returned to Tokyo, Toronto, Texas, or Telford, and bringing devastation to homes and business premises.

Yet it is equally to the lagoon that many Venetians owe their living. Some 30 miles (50 kilometers) long by 9 miles (14 kilometers) wide, dotted with innumerable islands, it supports a whole armada of fishermen, and Venice has the highest per capita consumption of fish and seafood of any Italian city. Everything has to be transported by boat in Venice and the surrounding area, making boatbuilding an important branch of local industry. Many of its inhabitants make their living as masters of vessels.

Malicious tongues claim that Venice is so beset by vanity that it banishes the less agreeable aspects of human existence from its shores. Death, for example, since the dead of the city are buried on a separate, burial island, the Isola di San Michele. It is easy for the city authorities to set aside a particular area; the number of reasonably inhabitable islands of all shapes and sizes is well nigh inexhaustible. A place was found in the 15th and 16th centuries to serve as a quarantine island, the Isola Lazzaretto Nuovo. This is where ships discharged passengers and crew showing symptoms that might indicate unwelcome illness. Burano is a fishermen's island and Murano belongs to the glass-blowers. Sant'Erasmo and Vignole are the city's kitchen garden, where its vegetables are grown. A visit to the island of Torcello can take in the restaurant Locanda Cipriani on the Piazza Santa Fosca.

Various means of transport are available to take the visitor around the lagoon and its islands. *Vaporetti* are motor-launches plying fixed routes to various destinations around the city like buses. Over longer distances, there are larger boats, two decks high, the *motonave*. The ferries are called *traghetti*, and there are also water-taxis, called *motoscafi*. Finally, Venice would not be Venice without its gondolas. With these, too, there is more than one type. The tourist gondolas can be booked for sightseeing trips, complete with musical accompaniment. Other gondolas, the *gondole traghetti*, are used by locals as ferries to cross the canals. They are inexpensive, but passengers need a good sense of balance if they are not to be seasick.

The Venetian lagoon extends between the rivers Brenta, Bacchaglione, and Sile, covering an area of about 225 square miles (58,660 hectares). Half of this area is tidal, the rest is the *Laguna Morta*, the dead lagoon. It is by no means empty of life, but is a fishing area. The catch can be plentiful, and is often to be found on the tables of the city's restaurants by the following lunchtime.

Above and background: Chioggia, situated on the lagoon some 28 miles (45 kilometers) south of Venice, is the unknown little sister of Venice itself. It is a place of greater simplicity – its palaces are less magnificent than those in the city of the Doges, and its campanile less impressive – yet the old town in particular has a charm of its own.

THE FISH MARKETS

The *mercato ittico all'ingrosso di Chioggia* is the country's largest fish market. It supplies fresh fish and seafood to the whole of northern Italy. The wholesalers' market is for the trade only, but consumers do have access to the retail market, the *mercato di pesce al minuto*. Fish is sold here twice a day, between five and six in the morning and around three in the afternoon. The fishermen bring in their catch and transfer it from the harbor to the floor of the market in large tubs. What follows is a selling process that seems entirely straightforward to the initiated, but may strike the observer as quite mysterious: instead of a noisy auction, there is a whispering process. One tradesman will whisper a price to a fisherman with a catch to sell. He may be surrounded by several other would-be buyers, but they cannot hear what is being said. If the offer is satisfactory, the fisherman nods his acceptance. If it is too low, he protests out loud. That is the sign to the others to whisper their offer for the catch – until the fish is finally sold.

Above and below: The fish market in Chioggia is famous for its great variety of fish and seafood.

How to tell if fish is really fresh

It is best to buy fish from a retailer you know and trust. If the fish is being sold whole, check that the eyes are clear and the gills bright red. Whether whole or filleted, the fish should have an appetizing smell of the sea. A "fishy" smell is to be avoided, as it is a sure sign that the fish is old. If you are able to, try the thumb test: quickly press the fish with your thumb. The flesh should spring back into shape almost at once. If the hollow left by the pressure remains, forget that fish and look for another retailer. Some types of fish are not sold freshly caught, so the above will not apply. Tuna and swordfish, for example, are "hung" for a while to tenderize them and develop their flavor.

The eyes should be bright and "lively," not dull.

The flesh should be firm and resilient, and not yield to pressure.

The gills should be red, and there should be no offensive smell.

Trade in fish takes place twice a day. The night's catch is sold in the morning, and the day's catch in the afternoon.

Orata, Marmora, Pagello (porgy)
The various types of porgy, gilt head bream *(orata)*, striped bream*(marmora)*, and sea bream *(pagello)* are all extremely suitable for baking.

Sardina, Sardella, Acciuga (sardine)
These tiny herring are popular all over the Mediterranean. Their flesh is oily, and tastes best freshly broiled and sprinkled with lemon juice. They are also good preserved in vinegar or oil.

Pesce San Pietro (John Dory)
Also called Peter-fish, this is quite expensive in practice, as the flesh accounts for only a third of its weight. It is best broiled, to preserve its excellent flavor.

Branzino, Spigola (sea bass)
Sea bass is probably the Italians' favorite fish. Its fine-textured but firm flesh can be prepared in many ways. A particularly delicious method is to bake it in a salt crust or wrapped in foil.

Triglia (striped mullet, goatfish)
Mullet, like salmon, is a good fish for making delicate pasta sauces. It is also good fried, broiled, boiled, or in fish soups.

Muggine (gray mullet)
The flesh of the mullet is good to eat, but it is most valued for its roe. *Bottarga di muggine* is regarded as a delicacy in Sicily and Sardinia, and is also expensive in the rest of Italy.

Anguilla, Bisato (eel)
Eels can live in salt or fresh water. The young elvers or glass eels are a traditional Christmas dish in many parts of Italy

Salmone (salmon)
For those who know salmon mainly as prepacked, smoked fish from a supermarket shelf, fresh salmon can be a revelation. The delicate, pink flesh is delicious broiled or when served with pasta.

Palombo (shark)
Adriatic sharks are not particularly good to eat, and have tended to disappear from most of the region's menus. It can still sometimes be found in Venice, under the name *vitello di mare* (sea veal).

Rombo (turbot)
In Italy, turbot *(rombo chiodato)* and brill *(rombo liscio)*, both flat fish, are eaten. They are filleted and steamed or poached in a sauce.

Rospo, Rana pescatrice (monkfish)
The monkfish or angler fish lives on the sea floor. As food, the tail flesh *(coda di rospo)* is much in demand, and has hardly any bones. Cooked, it tastes a little like lobster.

TEMPTING SARDINES

Sarde in saor is a fishermen's dish, but it is also a delicious one for mere landlubbers. Sardines and anchovies are the fish usually used. They are tossed in flour and fried in oil until golden. They are then lifted out, and layered in an earthenware dish. A finely chopped onion is fried without browning. White wine and vinegar are added, and the whole, with the cooking juices, is poured over the fish. An ancient Byzantine and Roman way of serving them was with raisins and pine nuts, especially in winter. They are a fairly high-calorie addition, but turn the dish into a feast. *Saor* can be refrigerated. It is served in Venetian restaurants, and is an excellent appetizer, accompanied by an aperitif. It is quite a match for the fish tapas of Spain.

SARDE IN SAOR
Marinated sardines

1 1/4 LBS/600 G FRESH SARDINES
ALL-PURPOSE FLOUR
1 1/4 LBS/600 G ONIONS
1/2 CUP/125 ML OLIVE OIL
1 GLASS OF RED OR WHITE WINE VINEGAR
SALT AND PEPPER
2 TBSP RAISINS
2 TBSP PINE NUTS

Clean and gut the sardines and cut off the heads. Wash the fish thoroughly. Pat dry and toss in flour. Heat half the olive oil in a skillet and fry the fish quickly until crisp, then drain on paper towels. Wipe the skillet clean.
Cut the onions into fine rings. Heat the remaining oil and sauté the onions until translucent. Pour on the vinegar and stir. Finally, season with salt and pepper, and add the raisins and pine nuts.
Place the sardines in a shallow dish, and pour on the marinade. Cover and transfer to the refrigerator to absorb flavors for 2 days.

SEAFOOD

Seafood – all the creatures of the deep apart from fish – is extremely popular in Italian coastal regions, and it is hardly surprising that there is such variety. A glance at the market stalls shows four main groups. First come the crustaceans, all the many types of shrimp and crayfish, as well as the crabs, then shellfish like mussels, clams, and scallops. Then there are the limpets and murex shells, and finally, squid, cuttlefish, and octopus. These delicious creatures are so different, but one thing is common to them all: the fact that they are all best eaten perfectly fresh. They then need almost no flavoring or elaborate preparation, so that the tangy freshness of the sea can be fully appreciated. Gentle cooking methods such as steaming, poaching, or light broiling are best.

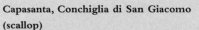

Calamaro (squid)
Squid are cephalopods like octopus and cuttlefish. They have round bodies with ten tentacles. Squid can be eaten in a seafood salad, or sliced and fried.

Seppia (cuttlefish)
Cuttlefish differ remarkably little from squid, though the body is smaller. They can be stuffed, baked, broiled, or stewed. The ink is often added to the cooking water to color pasta and rice dishes.

Cannolicchio, Cappalunga (razor shell)
The two halves of the shell look like a razor, and are nearly as sharp. The shellfish can be broiled, or eaten in a seafood salad.

Lumaca di mare (red abalone)
The meat is difficult to extract from the shells, but it is firm and full of flavor.

Vongola, Arsella (hard clam, Venus clam)
There are two varieties, *vongola verace* and *vongola gialla*. Both are good with pasta or as a main course.

Cozza, Mitilo (mussel)
Mussels are served cooked, though they used to be eaten raw like oysters. *Cozze* are good boiled and taste excellent with pasta dishes.

Capasanta, Conchiglia di San Giacomo (scallop)
Scallops are popular all over Italy, especially in seafood salads. They can also be stewed in white wine, and they make a delightful alternative stuffing for light, tender meats.

Dattero di mare (date shell)
A type of mussel that really does look like fresh dates. They are difficult to gather, because they secrete an acid to help embed themselves in the rock, making them very hard to dislodge. They can be eaten raw.

Scampo (tiger shrimp)
Shrimp, true lobsters and spiny lobsters are all closely related, so the terms tend to overlap. Freshly broiled, shrimp are a delight. Another excellent use is in fish soups.

Cannocchia (mantis shrimp)
These long shrimps can be boiled and eaten with parsley, garlic, and lemon juice. They make a fine ingredient for fish soups, and in seafood salads.

Granchio (crab)
Depending on size, crabs can be used in fish soups, stuffed, or served alone as a delicacy, seasoned with lemon juice and salt.

Grancevola (spider crab)
Spider crabs are cooked whole. The top shell is then removed and the flesh lifted out of the body cavity and claws.

CRABS

A huge variety of crabs and crustaceans lives around the Adriatic coast of Venice and the Veneto, yet all of them can be linked to one ancestor, the crab – *granchio* or *granzo* in Italian. Crustaceans are normally protected by their hard shell of chitin, and this does also make them difficult to eat and to handle in the kitchen. They do however need to shed their outgrown shells at certain seasons of the year, and the shell becomes softened at that time. The male casts its shell twice a year, in spring and autumn; the female, once, in the autumn. These soft-shelled crabs are seen as a specialty, and are prized by the canny fishermen of Venice and Chioggia, who diligently seek them out.

The female is called *manzaneta*. In the kitchen, it is boiled and prepared with oil, lemon juice, salt, pepper, parsley, and garlic. The male, *moleca* in the Venetian dialect, is a still more delectable morsel. It is dipped in beaten egg and fried in oil.

Right: The fishermen of Venice use creels, which are dragged across the floor of the lagoon, to catch crustaceans and crabs.

GRANZOLE OR MOLECHE RIPIENE
Stuffed crabs

2 EGGS
SALT
1 1/4 LBS/600 G LIVE CRABS
ALL-PURPOSE FLOUR
EXTRA VIRGIN OLIVE OIL OR PEANUT OIL FOR FRYING

Begin beating the eggs together, add a pinch of salt, and whisk. Wash the crabs in salted water, drain, and place in a bowl with the beaten eggs. Cover with a plate and weight it down. Leave in a cool place for at least 2 hours. The crabs will drink in the mixture.

At the end of the 2 hours, place the crabs one by one with the bread first in a big pot full of boiling water. Leave them in for 1–2 minutes, drain them, break off the legs, toss them in flour, and fry them in the hot oil. Drain on paper towels. Serve hot and crisp.

INSALATA DI MARE
Seafood salad
(Illustration left)

2 CLOVES OF GARLIC
JUICE OF 2 LEMONS
1 1/4 LBS/600 G SEAFOOD, WASHED AND CLEANED (E.G. SHRIMP, MUSSELS, BABY OCTOPUS, SMALL SQUID, CLAMS)
GENEROUS 1/4 CUP/90 ML OLIVE OIL
2 TBSP FINELY CHOPPED FLAT LEAF PARSLEY
SALT AND PEPPER

Pour the lemon juice over the garlic and leave to infuse for 1 hour. Then remove the garlic.

Meanwhile cook the seafood in a little water. Discard any mussels that are open when raw, or that do not open once they have been cooked.

Mix the lemon juice, olive oil, parsley, salt, and pepper. Turn the seafood in the sauce until coated, and leave in a cold place for the flavors to mingle and develop. Mix once more before serving.

ZUPPA DI COZZE E VONGOLE
Mussel and clam soup
(Illustration right)

2 CLOVES OF GARLIC
4 TBSP EXTRA VIRGIN OLIVE OIL
GENEROUS 1 LB/500 G MUSSELS
GENEROUS 1 LB/500 G HARD CLAMS
1 GLASS DRY WHITE WINE
3 TBSP CHOPPED PARSLEY
WATER OR FISH STOCK
4 SLICES LIGHTLY TOASTED WHITE BREAD
FRESHLY GROUND PEPPER

Chop the garlic a few hours in advance if possible, and stir it into the olive oil to flavor it. Wash and scrub the mussels and clams, discarding any open ones.

Heat the olive oil in a deep pan. Sauté the garlic, but do not let it discolor. Add the mussels and clams to the pan and begin cooking. Pour on the white wine, sprinkle in the parsley, and continue to cook all together until the mussels and clams have all opened. Discard any that remain closed when cooked. Pour in water or fish stock as needed. Transfer the mussels and clams to a bowl and pass the cooking liquid through muslin or a fine sieve to remove any vestiges of sand.

Return the mussels and clams to the cooking liquid. Place a piece of toasted bread in each soup plate, pour on the hot mussel soup, and season with pepper.

Zuppa di cozze e vongole – Mussel and clam soup

VEGETABLES FROM THE PO VALLEY

Radicchio from Treviso

It would be little short of a crime to describe radicchio from Treviso and Castelfranco as just "lettuce." Here in Italy, this delicious specialty is a vegetable in its own right, not a mere garnish. It is often eaten raw, sometimes broiled, roasted, or stuffed. An annual gathering even takes place in its honor near Treviso, at which the best gastronomic experts of the area assemble and rejoice in having available to them in the kitchens the finest radicchio in all Italy. A consortium dedicated to its supervision and protection has been created, to which eight precisely defined geographical communities belong.

A number of varieties of radicchio exist. *Radicchio variegato di Castelfranco* has a full, round head with loosely packed, creamy colored leaves splashed with red to violet variegation. Only small quantities are grown, so it is little known outside the area of production. The cultivation of this Castelfranco variety, like that of other types of radicchio, is labor and cost-intensive. The plants are biennials, related to chicory and endive. Sowing takes place in April, and the plants are thinned out about six weeks later. The leaves are removed in August to encourage new growth, and the Castelfranco transplanted into boxes before the arrival of the first frosts. These are placed in a darkened greenhouse, with the result that the plants cannot make enough chlorophyll to become green, and develop their characteristic pale color. Castelfranco is in season from December to April.

Radicchio di Treviso rosso tardivo has an elongated shape and purplish-red leaves with striking, thick, white ribs. It too is sown in April and thinned out six weeks later. The plants are bound up in September to blanch them by preventing light from reaching the inner leaves. They are dug up in the autumn and placed in water-tubs. This type of radicchio also goes to market from December onward. It is first stripped of its outer leaves, and then thoroughly cleaned, leaving just the tender heart. If it is to be eaten raw, as a salad vegetable, a dressing of robust wine vinegar and good olive oil is added to bring out its slightly bitter flavor. The dainty shape of the head would grace any plate, and it is never sliced or shredded, like lesser saladstuffs. *Radicchio di Treviso,* if it is the genuine article, should be served whole.

Radicchio di Treviso rosso precoce likewise has an elongated shape. The head is more compact and the veining of the leaves more delicate. It is also crisper than other varieties. The method of cultivation is the same as for the *tardivo* variety from Treviso.

Radicchio di Treviso rosso tardivo has purplish-red, loosely packed leaves with bold, white ribs. It is available from December to April.

Radicchio variegato di Castelfranco has a fairly compact heart and looser outer leaves. The pale color and splattered, red variegation are distinctive. It is available from December to April.

Radicchio di Treviso rosso precoce is a crisp variety with a compact head of closely-packed leaves characterized by their thick, white ribs and fine, white veins.

Radicchio di Chioggia is rounded and compact with dark purple leaves. It can be grown all year round. Its other name is *Rosa di Chioggia.*

BEANS FROM THE VENETO

Beans and pasta make a delicious combination, as connoisseurs will know. *Pasta e fasoj* – the Venetian name for this well-loved dish – is a true regional classic that owes its fine reputation to the many excellent varieties of tender beans grown between Lamon, Belluno, and Feltre. One such variety is the borlotto bean, perhaps the best variety in Italy, with its red freckled skin and good flavor. The beans are quite large and are usually sold dried.

Cannellino beans come originally from Tuscany, though they are now grown all over Italy. Delicate in shape and light in color, they are much used in gastronomy. They too are mostly sold dried. The beans produced in Lamon are similarly regarded as particularly fine and flavorsome.

The Italian name *fagiolini* refers to green beans. These are picked young and steamed to serve cold as a summer salad or hot to accompany a main dish. Varieties include Contender, the smallest, Bobis, slightly larger, and Stringa, like a pole bean or runner bean, which can grow to a length of 20 inches (50 centimeters). There are also white varieties of *fagiolini*, like Burro di Roquencourt – originally developed in France – and Meraviglia di Venezia, the "Venetian Wonder," a mangetout type. Beans are some of the oldest known foodstuffs, and have never been entirely forgotten by the great chefs. Now, the humble bean has made the transition from pauper's dish to the most exclusive menus, not only in Italy. There is even a delicious bean accompaniment for beluga caviar.

Borlotti beans are much esteemed. Spattered with red when raw, they turn green on cooking. This variety is ideal for salads, soups, and sauces.

Asparagus is grown around Bassano del Grappa, situated at the end of the Valsugana valley. Although the green type is grown, the area is best known for its white asparagus. Bassano asparagus enjoys DOC recognition.

ASPARAGUS FROM BASSANO

Asparagus enjoys great popularity in Italy. Three types are grown: green asparagus, produced mainly in Piedmont and Emilia-Romagna, a purple variety from Campania, often called *asparago napoletano* because it comes from that region, and white asparagus, which is grown almost exclusively around Bassano del Grappa on the River Brenta, in the Veneto. There is an annual asparagus festival in Bassano, for which the restaurants produce their latest culinary creations using asparagus, and their patrons vote to decide which is the best restaurant of the day.

White asparagus has to be blanched as part of the cultivation process. Earth is banked up around the plants, or dark plastic sheeting used, to prevent light reaching the emerging asparagus tips. This prevents them from synthesizing chlorophyll, and so keeps them white. Usually, only the first crop is blanched, with increasing amounts of the rest grown as green asparagus. This has the same, typical asparagus flavor, though it is generally less intense.

SQUASH AND PUMPKINS

The squash and pumpkin family is large and very varied, and much eaten in Italy. Even the well-known garden pumpkin with its orange flesh and green skin is widely enjoyed; in Venice and Chioggia, it is often served with pickled vegetables. In times past, traveling merchants plied their wares throughout Venice and the surrounding area, selling chestnuts, sweet potatoes, baked apples and pears, and slices of roasted pumpkin, *zucca barucca*. This variety has a spreading, squat shape like the turban of one of the Turkish ambassadors depicted in a painting by Vittore Carpaccio. It has a more pronounced flavor than other, more traditional members of this family of vegetables.

Asparagi in salsa
Asparagus with anchovy sauce
(Illustration below left)

GENEROUS 3 LBS/1.5 KG WHITE ASPARAGUS
SALT
4 HARD-BOILED EGGS
JUICE OF 1 LEMON
EXTRA VIRGIN OLIVE OIL
2 ANCHOVY FILLETS
1 TSP CAPERS
PEPPER

Peel the asparagus and tie in small bundles. Stand the
bundles upright in a tall saucepan of boiling salted water,
and cook for 10–20 minutes, according to thickness.
Remove and drain the asparagus, and untie the bundles to
let it cool.
Cut the boiled eggs in half and pass the yolks through a
sieve. Mix them with 2 tbsp lemon juice and enough olive
oil to create a liquid sauce. Chop the anchovies, capers, and
egg whites finely, and stir into the sauce. Season with salt
and pepper, and pour over the asparagus.

Zucca al latte
Pumpkin in milk

GENEROUS 2 LBS/1 KG YELLOW PUMPKIN
SALT
1/4 CUP/50 G SUGAR
GROUND CINNAMON
MILK

Preheat the oven to 350 °F (180 °C). Wash and peel the
pumpkin, and cut into pieces. Place in an ovenproof dish
(preferably terra cotta), season with salt, and bake.
Sprinkle the cooked pumpkin with sugar and cinnamon,
and serve on dessert plates. Pour over hot or cold milk
according to season.

Fasoj in salsa
Beans with anchovy sauce
(Illustration below right)

1 1/4 LBS/600 G FRESH BROAD BEANS OR 3/4 CUP/200 G DRIED
LIMA BEANS
1 CLOVE OF GARLIC
5 TBSP EXTRA VIRGIN OLIVE OIL
4 ANCHOVY FILLETS
1 TBSP CHOPPED PARSLEY
5–6 TBSP RED WINE VINEGAR
SALT
FRESHLY GROUND PEPPER

Shell the beans if using fresh. Cover with water, add a little
salt, and cover. Bring slowly to a boil. If using dried beans,
soak for at least 12 hours in lukewarm water before cooking. Remove from the heat when cooked, without draining.
Cut the garlic clove in half and sauté it lightly in a little
olive oil in a small saucepan. Add the anchovy fillets and
cook them until they melt. Add half the parsley, the vinegar,
salt, and a little pepper, and cook together for a few
minutes.
Drain the beans, transfer to a dish, and pour over the sauce.
Add a seasoning of pepper, cover, and leave to stand for
about 1 hour.
Sprinkle with the remaining parsley and serve lukewarm.

Risi e bisi
Rice with peas
(Illustration facing page below left)

2/3 CUP/50 G FINELY DICED BACON
2 ONIONS
8 TSP/40 G BUTTER
SCANT 1 LB/400 G FRESH, SHELLED PEAS
2 TBSP CHOPPED PARSLEY
4 CUPS/1 LITER CHICKEN STOCK
GENEROUS 1 CUP/200 G VIALONE RICE
SALT
1/2 CUP/50 G GRATED PARMESAN OR GRANA PADANO CHEESE

Dice the onions finely. Heat the stock. Melt half the butter
in another pan and sauté the diced bacon and onions without browning. Add the peas and 1 tablespoon of parsley. Add
one ladle of the stock, cover, and cook for 15 minutes. Add
the rice and a seasoning of salt. Cook gently over a low heat
for 20 minutes, little by little adding just sufficient hot stock
to keep the rice moist. Stir in the grated cheese and the
remaining butter and parsley. Leave to stand briefly before
serving.
Like risotto, this dish should be slightly moist, but not wet.
A further refinement is to boil a few pea pods in the
chicken stock and purée them, then pass them through a
sieve onto the rice.

Fasoj in salsa – Beans with anchovy sauce

Asparagi in salsa –
Asparagus with anchovy sauce

Radicchio rosso di Treviso al forno
Radicchio Treviso style
(Illustration below right, background)

1 1/4 LBS/600 G RADICCHIO ROSSO
EXTRA VIRGIN OLIVE OIL OR PEANUT OIL
SALT AND PEPPER

Wash the radicchio, and cut it in half or quarters, depending on size. Pat dry with paper towels. Place it in a flameproof baking dish or iron skillet, then drizzle with olive oil, season with salt and pepper, and broil for about 5 minutes with high heat, turning frequently. The radicchio is ready when cooked through and slightly crisp. Serve hot, immediately. Peanut oil is often used in place of olive oil in traditional Venetian cuisine, because of its more subtle flavor.

Pasta e fagioli alla veneta
Pasta with beans

1 1/2 CUPS/250 G DRIED BEANS (BORLOTTI OR LIMA BEANS)
1/3 CUP/30 G DICED BACON
1 ONION
1 CARROT
1 STALK OF CELERY
2 OZ/60 G BACON RIND
4 OZ/120 G TAGLIATELLE
SALT AND FRESHLY GROUND BLACK PEPPER

Soak the beans for at least 12 hours in advance in lukewarm water.
Chop the onion, carrot, and celery, and sauté them lightly with the diced bacon, over a low heat. Remove the pan from the heat and cool a little. Dip the bacon rind briefly in hot water to melt off some of the fat. Drain the beans and add them to the pan, together with the bacon rind. Cover with water and simmer. Froth will rise during the early stages of cooking. Skim this off with a slotted spoon. When the beans are cooked, pass about one third of them through a sieve, and return to the pan.
Now add the pasta and cook until al dente. Add a little more boiling water if the bean liquid is too thick. Season with salt and pepper. Remove the pan from the heat, take out the piece of bacon rind, and cut it into fine strips. When the fat begins to collect on the surface, transfer the pasta and beans to individual soup plates or a serving dish. Season generously with black pepper.
The traditional method of making this dish in the Veneto calls for pork fat only. In Liguria and Tuscany, a dash of olive oil is added just before serving, but this is not normally done in the Veneto.

Radicchio rosso di Treviso al forno –
Radicchio Treviso style

Risi e bisi –
Rice with peas

HUNTING AND FISHING IN THE VALLE SALSA

Valle Salsa is a name given to the delta of the River Po – it means "salt valley." As the river approaches the sea, the fresh and the salt water mingle, with a gradual increase in salinity. These waters are full of fish, and cover several square miles. The inflow and outflow of the water is controlled by a complex system of locks and dykes. Some of the pools are artificial, and there has been fishing here since time immemorial. The water at this point is more fresh than salt. Here, pike, carp, sturgeon, trout, tench, and pike-perch abound. The fish have no means of escape, so are fairly easy to catch. Large nets are let down into the water, suspended on crane-like structures and extending down to the river bed. Bait is attached, and then the only thing to do is to wait. By the next morning – if not before – a net full of fish can be hauled out.

In the southern section of the delta, where the water starts to become saltier, fishermen farm mussels and clams, or marine fish such as mullet, sea bass, gilt head bream, and sole. The area also offers crabs and shrimp. Eel, which is extremely popular all over Italy, is caught in great numbers across the whole delta region. The natural fauna of this broad, flat land includes frogs and the like.

The area around the river mouth was once sea marsh. The reclaimed fields and meadows won back from this boggy terrain were famed for their fertility, but life at the end of the 19th century was not always easy for the local populace. Sickness and a variety of risks to health were inevitably linked to a marshland existence, and infections were common, including malaria. The people of this tract of country remained there, however, because a good living could be made from agriculture and fishing. The Valle Salsa provided its inhabitants with a wide range of food in their immediate, natural environment, a distinct benefit in those times.

The *potentes*, the region's landowners, did no more than to order the peasants to tend the land: the meadows were to be grazed, woodland cleared, and acorns collected. In return, they granted the people the right to grow their crops on the land and to fish the waters. Fishing was of great economic importance in this region even then, as the peasants had to pay their fishing dues – *pisces amisseros* – in kind.

Hunting, too, has been carried on here since anyone can remember. Rights had to be formally agreed, on account of the sheer quantity of game involved, but a spoken agreement was enough, and order otherwise maintained by observing tradition. The number of game birds inhabiting the river flats was and is considerable: mallard, teal, wigeon, tufted duck, snipe, coot, curlew, and water rail, and many other wetland birds,

Right: Duck are hunted along the banks and in shallow waters. The hunting dog retrieves the birds without damaging them.

The mallard *(Anas platyrhynchos)* is a widely distributed species of duck. Italian huntsmen call the bird *anatra selvatica.*

The men lie in wait for the duck inside a cover of reeds. They kill them – using small shot – in the air, not on the water.

hotly disputed between the huntsmen on the one hand and ornithologists and nature protectionists on the other. The region's cuisine is known for the unusual game among the specialties it offers. These are often flavored with the wonderful white truffle, which grows in a few places between the Brenta, the Adige, and Po rivers.

The delta today attracts much tourism. Marked footpaths, bridle-paths, and cycle paths have been laid out, thanks to the relevant authorities, and excursions to historic sites put in place. But the visitor seeking no more than peace and quiet will be fascinated by the mysterious magic of the silence and expanse here in this flatland running down to the sea.

ANATRA ALLA VALLESANA
Wild duck with herb and anchovy sauce
(Illustration above)

Serves 6

FRESH SPRIGS OF THYME AND MARJORAM
3–4 PEPPERCORNS
1 GLASS OF WHITE WINE VINEGAR
2 WELL-HUNG, OVEN-READY WILD DUCK
CORN OIL OR PEANUT OIL
1 ONION
CHICKEN (OR OTHER POULTRY) STOCK
4 ANCHOVY FILLETS
1 GLASS OF WHITE WINE VINEGAR

Set aside some of the herbs for garnish, and chop the rest. Crush the peppercorns and mix with the vinegar, then marinate the duck in this mixture for at least 12 hours, turning frequently, to reduce the "gamey" flavor.
Drain off the marinade and joint the duck. Brown the pieces in oil.
Chop the onion and begin cooking it in a little oil and stock in a saucepan. Add the anchovies and melt them. Then add the pieces of duck, and pour on the white wine. Boil until the wine has evaporated, then cover and cook the

duck gently until done, adding hot stock little by little as required to prevent drying out.
Arrange the pieces of duck on a serving dish and pour over the cooking juices. Garnish with herbs, and serve with slices of toasted polenta.

BISATO SULL'ARA
Baked eel with bay

Serves 6–8

1 LARGE EEL (ABOUT 2 1/2 LBS/1.25 KG) OR 2 SMALLER EELS
(1 3/4 LBS/800 G EACH)
COARSE SALT
FRESHLY-PICKED, LARGE BAY LEAVES

Preheat the oven to 400 °F (200 °C). Skin and clean and gut the eel, then rub with a kitchen cloth to remove some of the shine. Cut into pieces about 3 inches/7.5 cm long, and layer with the salt and bay leaves in an ovenproof dish. Bake uncovered for about 30–40 minutes. Test occasionally with a skewer to see whether the eel is cooked.

WINES OF THE VENETO

The Veneto is one of the most important wine-producing areas of the Italian mainland. It lies only just behind the leaders, Sicily and Apulia, in vineyard area and production figures, but is far better known than its southern rivals. In terms of both quality and reputation, the region has a marked east-west divide. The province of Verona produces some of the most prolific and popular wines of Italy, Soave, Valpolicella, and Bardolino, as well as one of the country's great red wine types, Amarone. The wines of Breganze, Colli Berici, Lison-Pramaggiore, and even the Piave valley, on the other hand, are generally little known. Prosecco from this eastern part of the region is a solitary exception, though quality does not always live up to expectations. The region extends from Lake Garda in the west, along the foothills of the Alps, to the Adriatic lagoons

Background: The best Soave comes from the area around the Castello di Soave in the Verona region.

Valpolicella

The vineyards that produce this wine, one of Italy's most famous reds, lie on the slopes of the Alpine foothills north of Verona. The grape varieties used are Corvina or Corvinone,

Rondicella, and Molinara, with small quantities of other, native varieties. The bouquet is reminiscent of sour cherries, and the flavor dry, fruity, and not too heavy. The best are those from the Classico zone, around the small towns of Fumane, Negrar, and San Pietro. The wine is especially suitable as a partner for rich pasta dishes.

Amarone

Amarone wine is one of the most intense and powerful types that Italy produces, and accordingly high in alcohol. Valpolicella grapes are hung or spread out to dry in well-ventilated storage areas for two to three months. The drying

process concentrates the juice, giving the resulting wines an alcohol content of up to 16 percent. Well-made Amarone has a rich bouquet and full flavor. It can age for many years in the bottle. Recioto, the sweet version of Amarone in which the sugar has not all fermented to alcohol, is historically speaking older than Amarone, but has been rather forgotten in recent years.

Bardolino

This light, fruity red comes from the southeastern shores of Lake Garda. It is in principle made from the same grape varieties as Valpolicella, though

there are not many winemakers producing high quality wines. Bardolino is a quaffable wine, and well-made examples can be used to partner all sorts of fried fish, veal, and pasta dishes.

Soave

The best-known Italian white, Soave comes from a wine-producing region east of the city of Verona. It is made from the Garganega, Trebbiano di Soave, Chardonnay, and Pinot Blanc varieties, and is best drunk to accompany starters, fish, and

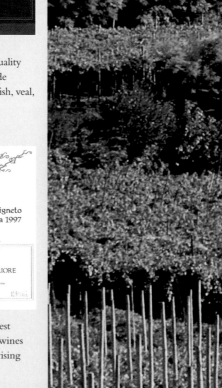

shellfish. The differences in quality between the best examples and the rest can be striking. The better wines come from the slopes of the Classico zone comprising Soave and Monteforte.

between Venice and Trieste. Vineyard slopes are mainly south-facing, and protected by the mountains. The region's really fine quality wines come only from these hills, whereas the bulk quantity wines come from the plain that lies between the foothills and the River Po or the River Adige. Soil types range from glacial gravels through weathered dolomite rocks to the fertile soils of the plain.

The grape varieties do not appear in the DOC names, which means that the most important varieties, other than Prosecco, are not generally familiar names. They include Garganega and Trebbiano, both white, the basis for Soave, Gambellara, and Bianco di Custoza, and the red varieties Corvina and its sport Corvinone, the main component of Valpolicella and Amarone, its dried grape variant.

FROM LAKE GARDA TO VERONA

The region's range of wines begins with the mainly white wines of the west. The DOC region of Lugana extends across the border from Lombardy, followed by Bianco di Custoza and the light, quaffable red, Bardolino, which all predominate in the vineyards of the southeastern corner of Lake Garda. To the north of

Verona, historic city of opera, lie the vineyards that produce Valpolicella. This, like Bardolino, is made from the Corvina grape among others, but the result has more power and body.

It is an ancient tradition to take some of the grapes from the Valpolicella harvest and spread or hang them on wooden trestles to dry. The wine from these is not made until December or January, when drying has increased the sugar content. Since usually not all the sugar is converted to alcohol, the resulting wine is sweet and full. It is called Recioto della Valpolicella. Sometimes, the natural yeasts do succeed in converting the sugar in these partially dried grapes to alcohol, producing powerful, markedly alcoholic, full-bodied wines. These began to be systematically made in the 1950s, under the name Amarone or Recioto Amarone. A third variant of this powerful Valpolicella wine type is *ripasso*, a method developed in the 1970s and 1980s. For this, fully fermented Valpolicella was added to the pressed grape skins from the fermented Amarone. These still contained sugar and yeasts, so that a further process of fermentation occurred. The wines produced by this method are often labelled Valpolicella Superiore or as Vino da Tavola.

VICENZA AND TREVISO

Moving eastward from Verona, the next wines are white: this is the home of Soave, and again, there is a sweet Recioto version. Soave, the best-known Italian wine along with Chianti, has long had to do battle against the image of being a cheap, mass-produced wine. A large number of winemakers have in fact striven to create genuinely good, dry and soft wines, some with a surprising capacity for aging. However, the negative image that this wine often has worldwide no doubt accounts for the fact that their achievements have so often not been recognized.

Gambellara is the twin of Soave, an otherwise little known wine from the neighboring province of Vicenza, not much associated with any great names. Mass production wines predominate from here on, from vast expanses of vineyard that stretch on toward the border with Friuli – and amid this anonymous profusion, a few islands of quality can be distinguished. Those worthy of note include the wines of Breganze, those of Colli Berici and Colli Euganei near Padua, and the Montello winegrowing region south of the small towns of Conegliano and Valdobbiadene, home of Prosecco.

PROSECCO

Prosecco is in fact the name of a grape variety, rather than that of a wine or wine-producing region. This delightfully sparkling white wine has risen greatly in popularity throughout Europe in the 1990s. The variety is not in itself remarkable; it is not over-endowed with the qualities of flavor and aroma that usually go with popularity. Its bouquet is somewhere between neutral and slightly fruity, certainly not rich and complex, and tasting the wine reveals few outstanding characteristics.

The origins of this grape are obscure. Some believe it to have come from a village of that name near Udine, and to resemble an old, native Friulian variety, while others think that it comes from Dalmatia. The reason for its cultivation in Treviso province lies in the series of very cold winters at the end of the 18th century, when the area's vineyards were almost completely destroyed by frosts, and this variety spread because it was hardy. The history of Prosecco begins in earnest in the 19th century, with the foundation of a *società enologica*, an enological society, by Antonio Carpené and his three partners. The society's aim was to bring champagne production to Italy.

The champagne idea did not materialize, but Prosecco di Conegliano-Valdobbiadene – to give it its full DOC name – did, and gradually became Italy's most popular sparkling wine. Winemakers, incidentally, do not always use the full name on their labels. It is produced by means of a second fermentation of the base wine in large pressure tanks. After aging for one month and attaining a bottle pressure of at least three atmospheres, the wine earns the right to the designation Spumante; it is otherwise termed Frizzante. Although Spumante commands the higher price, the difference in quality of the wine itself does not always correspond to this price difference.

Even the much-vaunted Cartizze from the steep slopes above Vidor, between Conegliano and Valdobbiadene, is not usually a better product than others from the same winegrower that do not happen to have this extra declaration of provenance on the label. DOC wines are not the sole type that emerge from the northeastern reaches of the Veneto; there are numerous imitations, which, being Vino da Tavola, can contain wine from other parts of the region and even beyond – even from distant Apulia.

Gregorio Bartolin produces an excellent Prosecco on his Ca' Salina estate at San Stefano di Valdobbiadene.

This refreshing, harmonious Prosecco is nowadays made in modern fermentation tanks. They are fitted with accurate pressure gauges.

Right: The range of Prosecco offered by the house of Ca' Salina includes a Brut, an Extra Brut, and a Rosé. The charm of Prosecco lies in its fine bubbles (far right).

The corks are inserted by machine (above) and secured with wire cages on account of the pressure (background).

TRENTINO
ALTO ADIGE

TRENTINO
ALTO ADIGE

CABBAGE AND POTATOES

BREAD, DUMPLINGS, AND
THICK SOUPS

BARLEY

FAREWELL TO WINTER

COUNTRY BACON

POLENTA

APPLES

FINE WINES OF THE ALTO
ADIGE

QUALITY WINE PRODUCTION
IN THE TRENTINO

Always overshadowed by the glories of the Alto Adige, the Trentino is no rich man's country; the peasant inhabitants of the land around Trento and Lake Garda have always had to struggle for their existence, tilling a harsh and infertile soil. Creature comforts counted for little, and regional specialties were therefore few. The main aim was to see the family fed, and the modest kitchen facilities that the houses afforded left no room for experimentation in cuisine. A historical event was to change all this. Around the year 1550, with the convening of the Council of Trient, the prelates of the Church arrived with their retinues of able cooks, and the art of cooking in the region was roused from its slumbers. Elaborate new recipes now found their way into the repertoire. Cooking methods for freshwater fish were learned from the ecclesiastical cooks. Only a few of these culinary secrets have been handed down. Two of them are *gnocchi con la ricotta* and *pollo ripieno alla trientina*, stuffed chicken Trento style. The Council of Trent was not the only influence on local cuisine. Later, dishes from the Republic of Venice were adopted, and further ideas from the Habsburg Empire.

The cuisine of the Alto Adige – sometimes called South Tirol – looks to a different tradition, one of Alpine specialties. It looks to the northeast corner of Europe, and bears elements of Slav, Austrian, and Hungarian cookery. One such dish is goulash, a regular Sunday treat. Others are the farinaceous dishes and strudels that betray Austrian influence. Potatoes, sauerkraut, and dumplings can be found on almost every menu. Many families make their own sauerkraut – which most Italian-speaking locals call *crauti*. In this region, lard is added. Dumplings are served as an accompaniment to a main dish (they are called *canederli* in the Trentino). The basic ingredient is leftover bread. Universal Italian ingredients like pasta, tomatoes, and olive oil have made their mark here, too, and it is this harmonious coexistence that makes the cuisine of the Alpine region so interesting.

Previous double page: The Franciscan bakery in Bolzano is the ideal place to try the local bread specialties, including "Schüttelbrot."

Left: Alto Adige and the Trentino are two very different regions, yet they have in common an impressively beautiful landscape, as here, at Castetel Beseno (Trentino).

CABBAGE AND POTATOES

Cabbage is grown all over the Alpine region and its foothills, as well as the Alto Adige and Trentino. White cabbage in particular plays an important part in the diet, and has the added advantage that it can be preserved for months as sauerkraut. This benefit was an important one in times past when preparing for a long winter. The traditional method is to slice the cabbage finely with a special knife, and layer the strips in a wooden barrel with coarse-grained salt, caraway seeds, and other flavorings like juniper and coriander. Once full, the barrel is closed with a lid of slightly smaller diameter. This is then weighted down with a large stone. Fermentation begins within a few days, forming lactic acid. The moisture is carefully spooned away. About four weeks later, the sauerkraut is ready to be used as required.

The popularity of sauerkraut has continued to this day, though not everyone now makes their own at home in a wooden barrel. Many of the Alpine dishes of the Alto Adige have sauerkraut as an accompaniment. Its popularity extended far beyond the Alps, however, for another of its benefits is to health. It has a high vitamin C content, so much so that it was taken to sea as provisions for long voyages, to protect the sailors against scurvy, the disease caused by vitamin C deficiency. It also contains vitamins B and K and the minerals iron, potassium, and calcium – and the bacteria responsible for the fermentation process are beneficial to the stomach and digestive tract, especially if the sauerkraut is eaten raw.

Potatoes have been long established in the Trentino and Alto Adige. It is even claimed that people in this region were the first to adopt it, and were soon thereafter making bread from it. Certainly it proved versatile, and was long a major item in local cuisine. It could be boiled and eaten with milk or cheese, and cold leftovers could be sliced and made into a salad with a salt and vinegar dressing. As a crop, potatoes are undemanding, and will grow even in the poorest soil. They are also a very healthy foodstuff, and contain plenty of protein, minerals, and vitamins.

The main use of potatoes in the Alto Adige and northern Trentino today is for potato dumplings – gnocchi – which are widely popular. On the other hand, polenta made with potatoes is a dish that is mainly confined to the area around Trento. It is served with local cheese or mixed pickled vegetables.

Fresh white cabbage is needed to prepare homemade sauerkraut.

The cabbage is grated or sliced finely.

Then the cabbage is layered into the sauerkraut pot with salt.

Caraway seeds and juniper berries may be added.

The cabbage is pressed down and weighted with a glass jar or a lid.

When the sauerkraut is ready, it can be used a portion at a time.

GNOCCHI CON LE PRUGNE
Potato gnocchi with plums
(Illustration in background)

GENEROUS 1 LB/500 G POTATOES
SALT
1 1/4 CUPS/150 G ALL-PURPOSE FLOUR
1 EGG
20 PITTED PLUMS
1 CUP/200 G BUTTER
1 CUP/100 G FRESHLY GRATED PARMESAN
OR GRANA PADANO

Boil the potatoes, remove the skins, and pass through a sieve. Add salt, and mix to a dough with the flour and egg. Shape into large gnocchi, and stuff each with a pitted plum. Boil the gnocchi in plenty of salted water. They rise to the surface when cooked. Lift them out immediately. Serve with butter and grated cheese.

ZUPPA DI CRAUTI
Sauerkraut soup

2/3 CUP/50 G DICED BACON
1 ONION, DICED
2 TBSP BUTTER
3 1/4 CUPS/800 ML STOCK
2 CUPS/260 G SAUERKRAUT
1 MEDIUM-SIZED POTATO
4 LARGE SLICES/150 G WHITE BREAD (3 CUPS WHEN DICED)
SCANT 1/2 CUP/100 ML SOURED CREAM
SALT AND PEPPER

Sauté the bacon and onion in 1 tablespoon of the butter. Add the stock and sauerkraut, and simmer for 30 minutes. Peel the potato and grate it (raw) into the soup. Bring to a boil. Dice the bread and fry it in the remaining butter. Remove the soup from the heat, and while it is still hot but not boiling, add the soured cream. Season with salt and pepper. Scatter with the croutons to serve.

GNOCCHI DI PATATE CRUDE
Raw potato gnocchi

GENEROUS 2 LBS/1 KG POTATOES
GENEROUS 2 CUPS/250 G ALL-PURPOSE FLOUR
SALT
6 1/2 TBSP/100 G BUTTER
5 OZ/105 G SMOKED RICOTTA CHEESE

Peel and grate the potatoes and mix with the flour. Shape into gnocchi as described in the recipe opposite, and cook in plenty of boiling, salted water. Serve with melted butter and ricotta.

Locally grown potatoes play an important role in the recipes of this Alpine region, although potatoes are also grown farther south.

Avezzana is one of the many potato varieties that grow around Avezzano in L'Aquila province, Abruzzi.

The very early variety **Agata** tends to remain firm when boiled. It is mainly grown in Emilia-Romagna.

In the potato-growing area around Viterbo in Lazio, a large range of varieties is cultivated. These are grouped together under the name **Viterbese**.

Pastagialla has yellowish flesh, and tends to remain firm when cooked. The whitish *pastabianca*, on the other hand, is floury.

Sieglinde is an early variety with yellowish flesh. It grows particularly well in Apulia and Sicily.

GNOCCHI CON LA RICOTTA
Gnocchi with ricotta

GENEROUS 2 LBS/1 KG POTATOES
GENEROUS 2 CUPS/250 G ALL-PURPOSE FLOUR
SALT
6 1/2 TBSP/100 G BUTTER
10 OZ/300 G SMOKED RICOTTA

Boil the potatoes and remove the skins while they are still hot. Pass them through a sieve or potato ricer. Gently work together the potatoes and flour to a smooth dough. Add a little salt. Shape pieces of the mixture into long rolls, about as thick as a finger, and cut into lengths about 1 inch/3 cm or so long. Place each on top of a fork, and press lightly with your thumb, rolling the edges slightly upward to create a rounded, dished shape.
Cook the gnocchi in plenty of boiling, salted water for a few minutes. Lift them out with a slotted spoon when they rise to the surface, and drain thoroughly. Serve with melted butter and ricotta cheese.

BREAD, DUMPLINGS, AND THICK SOUPS

Robust country bread is an essential element in the food of the Alto Adige. Even the names sound Austrian. Dunked into soups, or eaten to accompany the meal, there is always bread on the table. There is black whole wheat or rye bread, and a few bread varieties entirely special to the area – *Schüttelbrot*, *Vorschlag*, and *Paarl*. *Schüttelbrot* is a hard, unleavened bread that needs to be snapped in pieces like crispbread. *Vorschlag* is leavened, some 10 inches (25 centimeters) in diameter, and made of a mixture of rye and wheat flours. *Paarl* comes from the Val Venosta. The loaves come in pairs (the name means "pair") and consist of a sourdough rye bread. The pairs of loaves are an everyday reminder of the marriage partnership, and in the past, the loaves used to be baked singly if one of the spouses had sadly died.

The bread of the Alto Adige is often flavored with caraway, fennel, or aniseed. A still more typical addition is a native, white-flowered plant about 16 inches (40 centimeters) high, called "bread clover" *(Trigonella caerulia)*. The country women often grow this in their gardens, and townsfolk buy it from a herbalist, pharmacist, or health food outlet. A relative of fenugreek, it has a savory, almost spicy aroma.

In every country wine bar, a basket of various local breads is the first thing to be put on the table. These will always include Schüttelbrot and Paarl, which is traditionally flavored with "bread clover".

Bread is not only eaten at meals in its own right; it serves another purpose in the kitchens of Alto Adige: leftover bread and stale rolls are the basic ingredient in dumplings. Various other ingredients provide variety. The more substantial additions include bacon and cheese, and the lighter, but equally traditional ones are onions, spinach, mushrooms and the like. Beet dumplings are a great specialty. They are eaten with brown butter and grated parmesan.

Flour and the various grains are not only made into bread – or indeed dumplings – here. They are also used in delicious, thick soups. One tasty example of this is barley soup, which uses pearl barley, vegetables, and bacon. Flour-thickened soups include the simple, traditional one made just of flour with butter or lard, salt, and water. Other recipes recommend milk instead of water, or the addition of onions.

CANEDERLI
Bacon dumplings

6 SLICES/250 G STALE WHITE BREAD OR ROLLS (5 CUPS WHEN DICED)
3 EGGS
1 CUP/250 ML MILK
1/4 LB/100 G BACON, FINELY DICED
1 ONION
1 BUNCH OF FLAT LEAF PARSLEY
2 OZ/50 G SALAMI
6 TBSP ALL-PURPOSE FLOUR
SALT AND PEPPER
GRATED NUTMEG

Dice the bread or rolls, and place in a bowl. Mix the eggs and milk, pour over the bread, and leave to stand for 20 minutes, stirring occasionally.
Dice the onions finely. Chop the parsley. Sauté the diced bacon until the fat runs, then add the onion and half the parsley, and sauté for 2 minutes.
Dice the salami finely and add to the pan, along with the remaining parsley. Stir to mix, then add all to the soaked bread. Fold in the flour, and season to taste with salt, pepper, and nutmeg.
Bring about 3 pints/1.5 liters of water to a boil. With wet hands, form 10 evenly sized dumplings and cook until done.

ZUPPA DI FARINA TOSTATA
Flour soup
(Illustration below)

6 1/2 TBSP BUTTER
2 1/2 CUPS/300 G ALL-PURPOSE FLOUR
4 CUPS/1 LITER HOT MILK
SALT

Melt the butter in a saucepan and slowly blend in the flour until it begins to brown. Gradually add 4 cups/1 liter of water and the hot milk, stirring to blend and avoid lumps. Season with salt. Boil for about 20 minutes until the soup is creamy. Serve hot.

Crispy Schüttelbrot can be stacked upright in racks.

Canederli di pan grattato

Bread dumplings
(Illustration right)

3 CUPS/150 G DICED STALE WHITE BREAD
MILK
2 EGGS
BUTTER
1/2 ONION, CHOPPED
1 TBSP CHOPPED PARSLEY
1 CUP/50 G BREADCRUMBS
SALT AND PEPPER
GRATED NUTMEG
GRATED CHEESE

Soak the diced bread in milk. Beat together the eggs and
1/3 cup butter, and mix in the onion and parsley. Squeeze
out the bread and pass it through a sieve. Add the egg
mixture and the breadcrumbs. Season with salt, pepper, and
nutmeg, and leave to stand for a few minutes.
Shape the mixture into dumplings, and boil them in plenty
of salted water. Serve with melted butter and grated cheese.

Strangolapreti

Spinach dumplings

Serves 4–6

6 SLICES/250 G STALE WHITE BREAD (5 CUPS WHEN DICED)
2/3 CUP/150 ML MILK
GENEROUS 1 LB/500 G FRESH SPINACH
2 EGGS
4–5 TBSP ALL-PURPOSE FLOUR
SALT AND PEPPER
GRATED NUTMEG
3 1/2 TBSP/50 G BUTTER
A FEW SAGE LEAVES
1/2 CUP/50 G FRESHLY GRATED PARMESAN

Cut the bread into small dice, pour over the milk, and
stir well. Cover, and leave to soak for at least 2 hours.
Wash the spinach, and remove the stalks. Blanch for
2 minutes in plenty of boiling, salted water. Rinse in cold
water, drain, and cool. Then press to remove all moisture,
and chop very finely. Mix into the soaked bread, then
thoroughly knead in the eggs and flour. Season with salt,
pepper, and nutmeg.
Bring approximately 4 pints/2 liters of salted water to a boil
in a large saucepan. Shape a test dumpling between two
tablespoons, drop it into the water, and cook for about 5
minutes until done. If it is too dry, add more milk to the
dumpling mixture, and if too wet, more flour. Then shape
the remaining dumplings and lower them into the boiling
water to cook.
Lift them out with a slotted spoon, drain, and transfer to a
warmed dish. Melt the butter in a skillet and sauté the
sage leaves. Then add the dumplings to the pan and turn
until well coated with the butter. Serve, sprinkled with the
grated cheese.

Right: The frescos in Hocheppan castle chapel. The love of
dumplings in this region is nothing new! The frescos in the
castle chapel were painted in about A.D. 1200. Depicted
below the Virgin and Christ Child is a woman in a green
dress, eating dumplings out of a pan.

BEER

Alto Adige is Italy's beer country. The crystal-clear water that flows from the Eastern Alps above Merano made this an ideal area for the industry, as did the easy availability of natural mountain ice, which could be collected in winter to cool the cellars in summer. It is then no surprise that the art of brewing beer in this area dates back to the period between 985 and 993. Small brewers supplied private customers as well as coaching inns and the like. Sadly, almost none of the highly traditional small breweries has survived.

The one exception is the firm of Forst, founded by two entrepreneurs from Merano in 1857. It enjoys a very good annual turnover.

A man called Josef Fuchs took over the brewery in 1863, and founded a brewing dynasty that is now in its fourth generation. The family adheres resolutely to its motto of "quality respects nature – beer is nature." The beautiful building that houses the brewery is not called anything so prosaic; it is called the "Forst" after the firm itself. It produces an annual 18,492,600 gallons (700,000 hecto-

liters) of beer. The building also contains a restaurant, with rooms that can be booked for functions and weddings. The Forst beer then flows, as can be imagined. A range of beers is offered: a fresh, dry Pils, the exclusive V.I.P. Pils, the elegant, dry Forst Kronen, the Forst Premium, with its refreshing, fine effervescence, Forst Sixtus, a special Doppelbock beer that recalls the historic, monastic tradition of brewing, and Luxus Light, with a reduced calorie and alcohol content. The company is also the general representative in Italy for the British brewery names Allsopps, Arrol's, and John Bull. The Forst brewery has a second string to its bow. Having bought some springs on the Vigiljoch, it bottles the mineral water Merano Acqua minerale naturale San Vigilio.

The brewery's turnover is not the only sign that beer is gaining in popularity in Italy. The evidence is there to be seen, from Lake Como to Rome, that people are discovering the delights of a cold beer on a hot summer day, and finding that it tastes at least as delicious as a glass of red wine with pizza or a snack·

The Forst brewery at Tel (Töll) in Lagundo (Algund), Merano, is steeped in tradition. The brewing and bottling of the various beer types produced here, from Pils and Märzen to Bock, are done using ultra-modern equipment. The delightful rooms belonging to the brewery's own restaurant can be hired for private functions. Beer is then dispensed.

Minestra d'orzo
Barley soup

Generous 1 cup/200 g pearl barley
2 cups/500 ml stock
5 oz/150 g Belgian endive
1 carrot
1 stalk of celery
1/4 lb/50 g diced bacon (belly bacon is best)
3 1/3 tbsp butter

Soak the pearl barley in cold water for at least 1 hour.
Then pour off the water and place the barley in a
saucepan with the stock. Heat. Cut up the endive and
stir in. Simmer for about 1 hour.
Cut up the carrot and celery. Melt the butter in
another saucepan and brown the bacon and vegetables.
Add the barley and stock, and boil the soup for
another 30 minutes. Serve hot.

FAREWELL TO WINTER

Along the "Wine Road" of Alto Adige, the wine villages are strung out like pearls: Eppan, Tramin, Girlan, Kaltern, Kurtatsch, and Margreid. This area appears to have been inhabited since the earliest times, and the old rituals and traditions are preserved here. A multitude of wine festivals takes place here, and Shrove Tuesday is celebrated with carnivals like the large procession through the streets of Tramin. The terrifying masks parading among the gaily decorated floats recall the carnival costumes of the old Alemannic celebrations. The origins of this procession, which here in Alto Adige is called the Egetmann parade, are altogether darker. It goes back to a pre-Roman fertility cult, in which winter was driven out every year with various rites and a great deal of noise, and the nature spirits asked to send a good growing season and an abundant harvest in the vineyards.

Right: The Egetmann parade happens only every two years. Spectators are advised to wear old clothes – the proceedings involve smearing people with rust or shoe cream.

A LENTEN CARNIVAL DISH

Smacafam is a dish that was traditionally eaten in the closing days of the carnival. It is a baked mixture of buckwheat, corn, or wheat flour, bacon and sausages; the exact ingredients varied according to region. In some places, a sweet version of this traditional favorite is enjoyed.

SMACAFAM
Buckwheat bake

Serves 6

2 CUPS/500 ML MILK
GENEROUS 2 CUPS/250 G
BUCKWHEAT FLOUR
1 SMALL ONION
SALT AND PEPPER
4 TSP/20 G SHORTENING
1–2 WELL HUNG SALSICCE
SAUSAGES

Preheat the oven to 375 °F (190 °C). Gently heat the milk in a saucepan, and stir in the flour to create a smooth, soft batter, still fluid rather than stiff. Chop the onion finely and stir into the batter. Season with salt and pepper.
Grease a baking dish with lard and transfer the batter to the dish, to a depth of about 1 inch/2 cm. Break the sausage into pieces and distribute over the batter. Bake until brown (about 1 hour or less). Serve hot.

Bolzano/Bozen

Austrian as it seems to Italians, there is a Mediterranean feel to Bolzano (whose German name, Bozen, is also much used). Temperatures are mild during most of the year, though winter itself is cold. Its famous fruit market is held in the town square just as it was 700 years ago, when this town achieved importance as a trading place for goods from southern Germany and Lombardy, and with as much haggling and energetic debate. In the shadow of the parish church, all is color and bustle.

The modern face of the city is open and cosmopolitan, and no more than 80 years old; there has been much change. The original town of Bozen was German-speaking. It was a sleepy South Tirolean location half-forgotten by its Habsburg rulers in distant Vienna. The Peace of Paris in 1919 obliged Austria to hand over South Tirol (as this region was then called, and indeed sometimes still is) to Italy, then a relatively new country. Bozen then began to undergo a degree of Italianization. Mussolini's seizure of power led to an influx of Italian workers, merchants, and officials. Only the city center with its signs in both languages now retains any character of the former town. The outskirts, which sprawl as best they can between the rivers Talvera and Isarco, contain the same anonymous apartment blocks as the residential suburbs of most of Italy. Today's Bolzano is a location for industry, and a provider of jobs in the region – a role it has always had. It attracts people from the Alpine valleys looking for work.

Bolzano, the modern capital of Alto Adige, lies at the confluence of the Adige, Talvera, and Isarco rivers. Trade fairs and commerce have taken place here since the 12th century. The fruit market illustrates the town's talent for trade.

Three local languages

There are three languages spoken in the Trentino and Alto Adige: Italian, German, and Ladin. All three are officially recognized by the region's Statute of Autonomy. This official protection enables the Ladins in particular, some 40,000 in number, to preserve their language and culture from oblivion. The Ladins are descended from the original Rhaetian inhabitants of this area in pre-Roman times. They avoided Romanization by largely maintaining their own language. Certain elements were absorbed from Latin, so that Ladin became what linguists have defined as a "Romance idiom built on a Rhaetian substrate." It is related to the Romansh language spoken in Switzerland, and to the Friulian dialect encountered in northeastern Italy.

COUNTRY BACON

The cuisine of the Alto Adige is much influenced by that of the German-speaking countries that surround it, so the region's specialties are quite unlike those of the rest of Italy, and little to be found there. The bread called Schüttelbrot is an example. It is flavored with caraway, a spice hardly used in Italian cooking south of the Alps. Meat recipes, too, are different from Mediterranean ones. The people of the Trentino and Alto Adige enjoy pork, usually smoked, although it is also eaten unsmoked, as in the Lombard dish *bollito* or a pork roast.

Pork fat is turned into lard and used for frying. Two specialties made in this way are *Strauben* and *Kniekiachl*. The first are swirls of pancake batter, poured in a spiral into the hot fat; the second are made from yeast dough, by taking an apple-sized portion and pulling it into a cup shape, which is then fried and basted in lard, and filled with cranberry jam.

The country bacon of Alto Adige, *speck*, is a typical local product of excellent quality. The process involves first curing the legs of pork in salt and spices, using varying combinations of bay, juniper, pepper, nutmeg, cinnamon, and coriander. Each producer has a jealously guarded recipe. The next step in the process involves smoking and maturing.

The sides of bacon used to be hung in the chimney space above the domestic fire to be smoked, but today, smoking is done either by a cold smoking process, or at temperatures not exceeding 20 °C (68 °F), in well-ventilated smokehouses. This recreates the conditions of the chimney. Smoking takes about ten days, and during this time, the bacon absorbs the aromas of the wood. Juniper and pine wood are the types most used. Maturation takes about 20 weeks, and demands great skill. Good ventilation and a constant temperature are important, and the cool mountain climate of the region provides almost ideal conditions, whether the bacon is lean or fat. Each type of *speck* is able to develop the right consistency, which is neither too soft nor too hard.

A consortium of bacon producers for Alto Adige, the *Consorzio produttori speck dell' Alto Adige*, was formed in 1987. Its aim is to ensure today's consumers a bacon product that tastes as good as the traditional country bacon, despite the fact that industrial production methods have replaced the small-scale, handmade approach. All genuine bacon from Alto Adige bears a mark of quality, the emblem of the Consortium, stamped on the rind.

Local country bacon is an essential part of any snack or supper here. And in October and November, when the parties of revelers set out from inn to inn to taste the new wine after the harvest, they too welcome a tasty snack. There is bread, cheese, sausage, and, it goes without saying, *speck*.

Country bacon from the Val Pusteria valley in Alto Adige is a delicious and sustaining delicacy. Its worth is appreciated well beyond the local region.

POLENTA

One of the staples of people's diet in all the Alpine regions was always polenta. It is a simple dish, a pudding of buckwheat or barley flour, with the possible addition of potatoes or yellow pumpkin. Wheat flour only began to be used around 1650. Poorer people in the community would eat polenta instead of bread, serving it either on its own or with milk, cheese, or sausage.

Menus in Alto Adige still feature a number of polenta dishes. *Polenta nera* or "black polenta" is a delicious type, made of buckwheat flour, and served with anchovies "melted" in butter. Meat or game can be used, for a more elaborate meal. *Mosa* is a type of polenta made with milk, using one-third corn and two-thirds wheat flour. The flours are stirred into the boiling milk, and the resulting *polentina* is often served with melted butter.

Polenta nera
Buckwheat polenta with anchovies
(Illustration above)

2 1/2 cups/300 g buckwheat flour
6 1/2 tbsp butter
10 anchovy fillets in oil
Grated Parmesan or Grana Padano
Salt

Bring 4 cups/1 liter of salted water to a boil in a saucepan. Just before it boils, add the flour, stirring every addition. Boil for 40 minutes, stirring constantly. Transfer the cooked polenta to a buttered ovenproof dish. Preheat the oven to 465 °F (240 °C).
Cut the anchovies into pieces and sauté briefly in a little butter. Place on top of the polenta and sprinkle with grated cheese. Brown in the oven for 5 minutes.

Polenta con la zucca
Polenta with pumpkin

Peel a pumpkin weighing about 1¼ lb/600g and boil it in plenty of salted water until tender. Puree it. Boil the puree, together with corn polenta flour, in salted water for 50 minutes, stirring constantly (see recipe on page 19). Turn out onto a board and cool. Slice and serve with hot milk.

Polenta con la cipolla
Polenta with onions

Prepare a firm polenta (see recipe on page 19), and cool. Cut into slices of a finger's breadth. Chop onions finely and cook lightly in olive oil. Season with salt and pepper. Toast the polenta, top with onion, and serve hot.

South Tirolean Vesper

This meal (background) is an afternoon snack or early supper eaten in Alto Adige. It consists of smoked sausages, thin, crisp *Schüttelbrot*, boiled potatoes, wine, and *speck*. This may be the belly bacon or the smoked ham type, according to individual preference. If the meal is eaten out of doors, many people carve off wafer-thin slices or matchsticks of *speck* with their own pocket knives.

Asiago

The Asiago plateau has been used to pasture cows for around a thousand years. A cheese that bears its name is still made from the delicious milk produced by these cows in such a natural, organic context. *Asiago* received DOC status in 1978, and the consortium for its protection was founded a year later. It keeps strict watch over compliance with the production regulations, and now comprises about 100 dairies and warehouses. *Asiago* is by law required to come only from an area covering the provinces of Vicenza and Trento, and certain parts of Padua and Treviso.

This cheese specialty is available in a number of different types. It is rich in enzymes and protein, but has only a moderate fat content. *Asiago pressato* is a young cheese, made from whole milk and matured for 20 to 40 days. It has a mild flavor and pale color. *Asiago mezzano* uses a mixture of whole and skimmed milk, matures for at least three months, and has a more pronounced flavor than the younger version. *Asiago vecchio* has a maturation time of at least a year, and a characterful flavor. There is also an *Asiago stravecchio*, which matures for over a year, developing into a compact and extremely flavorful morsel.

Asiago can be used in many ways in cooking. The younger types can be eaten with bread as a snack or appetizer, the older varieties either grated over pasta or served with a cheese board and accompanied by a robust red wine – the perfect choice to round off an evening meal instead of a sweet course.

APPLES

Both the Trentino and Alto Adige are agricultural in character. Dairy farming, including on the mountain pastures, winegrowing, cereal crops, and fruitgrowing are all long established as important contributors to the local economy. Half of all Italian apples come from its small area of orchard in the Val di Non. The wide range of varieties and storage techniques ensures that the quantity and choice of apples in Italian markets is abundant from June to September. Much of the crop is exported to the rest of Europe. The fruit farmers of the Trentino and Alto Adige were incidentally the first to improve their methods so as to reduce the need for herbicides and pesticides.

The apple varieties grown here are so numerous that it is almost impossible to name them all. The category that includes Red Delicious and Golden Delicious is a significant one. The variety Stark Delicious, also called *delizia*, deserves special mention. It is a sub-variety of Red Delicious with a rich red skin. It keeps very well, although it does tend to become soft and sleepy in texture towards the end of its storage life. Golden Delicious has a golden green, slightly freckled skin, with a reddish tinge on its "sunny side." It has juicy, sweet, crisp flesh, and is one of the most popular apple varieties that the region exports. *Renetta del Canada* is also widely grown here. All three varieties ripen within a short time of each other, and are ready for picking from September 20 to early October.

Members of the umbrella organization Melinda, Val di Non, which comprises 16 local apple consortia, have to observe strict criteria. These not only relate to growing methods, but to the timing of the harvest. Agronomists and food chemists decide the correct moment for harvesting each variety and each orchard, based on an analysis of exactly when the starch in the apple has been converted into sugar. They set a final date for the completion of harvesting, to ensure that apples picked later do not become overripe and spoil too soon. The demanding time limits that this imposes on the apple growers of the consortium mean a period of hectic activity in the orchards. On average 275,000 tons (250,000 tonnes) of fruit has to be expertly picked and transferred to interim storage with as little time wasted as possible. From there they are taken to the centers in Italy or abroad. It is vital to transport them to cold storage as quickly as possible, within 12 hours. Every hour of warmth and daylight beyond that shortens storage time by three weeks.

Morgenduft (Mela imperatore) is a finely scented apple with a sweet, sharp aroma and fresh character. It is especially good for stewing and baking.

Golden Delicious is greenish-yellow, becoming golden yellow with a slight rosy blush as it ripens. It has a delicately juicy, sweet flesh.

Granny Smith has risen to fourth place among the apple varieties most grown in Alto Adige. It is crisp and juicy, with a sharp flavor and firm flesh.

Idared, a bright red variety, originates from the USA and Canada. It has a sweet but sharp flavor, keeps well, and is well suited for use in stewing or baking.

Gloster is a refreshing apple with a mild flavor and delicate, fruity acidity. It is easily recognized by its shape, tapering toward the base.

Jonathan has long been one of the most popular varieties. It has a sweetish, delicate acidity, and is related to Jonagold, another popular apple.

Alto Adige grows more apples than the Trentino; the ratio of production between the two is 70:30.

Renette du Canada is a dry, rough-skinned apple. It is greenish-yellow, ripening to rusty red.

Royal Gala is a crisp apple with low acidity and a sweet aroma. It is a cross between Kidds Orange and Golden Delicious.

Elstar is juicy, refreshingly sharp, and aromatic. Unfortunately, it cannot be stored for long periods.

DELICIOUS WAYS WITH APPLES

Apple fritters are popular everywhere. This simple, easy-to-prepare treat consists of apple slices – usually Golden Delicious – that are coated in batter before being deep fried in oil or shortening.

FRITELLE DI MELE
Apple fritters
(Illustration left)

Serves 6–8

1 TSP DRIED YEAST (IF USING ACTIVE DRIED YEAST, FOLLOW
MAKER'S INSTRUCTIONS)
3 1/2 TBSP BUTTER
1/2 CUP/125 ML MILK
SCANT 1/2 CUP/50 G ALL-PURPOSE FLOUR
3 EGGS, BEATEN
SCANT 1/2 CUP/50 G CONFECTIONERS' SUGAR
8 APPLES
VEGETABLE OIL FOR FRYING

Dissolve the yeast in a little warm water. Melt the butter and mix thoroughly to a smooth batter with the milk, flour, beaten eggs, yeast, and ¼ cup of the sugar.
Peel and core the apples using an apple corer. Slice into thin rings, and sprinkle with the remaining sugar. Dip the apple rings into the batter one by one and deep fry them until golden brown, in batches.
Drain on paper towels and serve hot.

SWEET TEMPTATION AT CHRISTMAS

Zelten is a specialty of both the Trentino and Alto Adige, yet each area has its own interpretation. In Alto Adige, it consists mainly of dried fruit – figs and raisins – and candied citrus fruit, as well as hazelnuts, almonds, and pine nuts. Only a small amount of flour is added. In the Trentino, the quantity of flour equals the quantity of fruit and nuts.
This specialty is eaten on Christmas Day itself in Alto Adige. Stored in the right conditions, it will keep until Easter.

ZELTEN
Christmas cake

For the cake mixture.
SCANT 1/2 CUP/50 G RAISINS
1 1/4 CUPS/200 G DRIED FIGS, CHOPPED
SCANT 1 CUP/100 G CHOPPED FILBERTS
GENEROUS 1/3 CUP/50 G CHOPPED
ALMONDS
GENEROUS 1/3 CUP/50 G PINE NUTS
3/4 CUP/100 G DICED CANDIED FRUITS
1/2 GLASS GRAPPA
1/3 CUP/80 G BUTTER
2/3 CUP/120 G SUGAR
2 EGGS

1 2/3 CUPS/200 G ALL-PURPOSE FLOUR
5 TSP/10 G BAKING POWDER (OR MANUFACTURER'S SPECIFIED AMOUNT FOR 1 LB
FLOUR)
GENEROUS 1/4 CUP/70 ML MILK

BUTTER AND FLOUR FOR BAKING PAN
1 EGG YOLK
ALMONDS, FILBERTS, AND CANDIED FRUITS
TO DECORATE

Soak the raisins in lukewarm water, and drain. In a bowl, soak the raisins, figs, chopped filberts and almonds, pine nuts and candied fruits in the grappa.
Mix the baking powder evenly into the flour. Preheat the oven to 350 °F (180 °C). Melt the butter in a bowl over hot water, add the sugar, and beat together until smooth and creamy. Then blend in the eggs, followed by the flour and baking powder. Add milk to soften the mixture. Add the soaked fruit and nuts, and mix well.
Butter a cake pan and coat the inside with flour. Transfer the mixture to the baking pan, and brush the top with egg yolk. Bake for about 45 minutes. Decorate the top of the cake with almonds, filberts, and candied fruits. Serve cold, in thin slices.

PASTA DI STRUDEL CLASSICA
Strudel pastry

GENEROUS 2 CUPS/250 G ALL-PURPOSE
FLOUR
1 EGG
3 TBSP WATER
1/4 CUP/60 G BUTTER
1 PINCH OF SALT
2 TBSP BUTTER, MELTED
CONFECTIONERS' SUGAR

Place the flour in a heap on a clean work surface and make a well in the center.
Separate the egg and set the yolk aside. Soften the butter, and add in flakes to the well in the flour, together with the egg white and a pinch of salt. Mix into the flour, and knead to a smooth, elastic dough. Shape into a ball and leave to rest.
Preheat the oven to 350 °F (180 °C).
Spread a clean kitchen cloth over the work surface, dust it lightly with flour, and place the pastry on top. Roll out the pastry as thinly as possible, pulling and stretching it over the back of your hand until it is so thin as to be almost transparent. Brush it with melted butter, and spread the chosen filling on top. Then carefully roll up the strudel, using the kitchen cloth. Transfer to a greased baking sheet, brush with melted butter, and bake until golden. Sprinkle with confectioners' sugar and serve warm.

RIPIENO PER STRUDEL
Strudel filling

GENEROUS 1 LB/500 G APPLES
1 TBSP/15 G SUGAR
CINNAMON
1 SMALL GLASS OF WHITE WINE
GRATED ZEST OF 1 LEMON

Peel, quarter, core, and slice the apples thinly. Add the sugar, cinnamon, white wine, and lemon zest, and boil until disintegrated. Cool, then spread on the thinly rolled out strudel pastry.

The Vernatsch grapes for St. Magdalener also grow in the steep vineyards of the Bozner Leiten slopes.

FINE WINES FROM THE ALTO ADIGE

Most of the region's winegrowing is located in the valley of the river Adige (Etsch in German), with a small proportion of vineyards along its tributary, the Isarco (Eisack), on steep terraces to the north of Bolzano (Bozen).

Much German is spoken here, and German traditions are still a strong influence on winegrowing. The grape varieties, for example, are Riesling, Silvaner, Müller-

There are tiny country inns called "Buschenschänken" attached to individual farms (above). Many winegrowers make some wine themselves from the grapes they harvest, and sell the wines from their own production in cosy rooms like this (background).

Kalterer See Auslese and Vernatsch Alte Reben

Kalterer See was for many years the Alto Adige's wine lake, producing uncomplicated, quaffable wines, often pale and with a sweet after-taste, and largely responsible for the poor image of the region's wines. The variety used is Vernatsch. Many local producers, including some of the excellent cooperatives, have made great efforts in recent years to turn Kalterer See back into a high quality product. Discredited names are helped toward oblivion by marketing the wines under their variety name, Vernatsch.

Lagrein

Modern Lagrein can be a deeply colored wine, with dark-berried aromas, good body and mouth feel, and even a capacity for aging. Tasting these wines, especially the barrique-aged ones, it seems incredible that winegrowers here so long continued to use this grape only for the rosé wine, Kretzer. It had been thought that only the Gries vineyard in Bolzano was suitable for growing Lagrein, but a number of wineries in the Upper Adige have since proved this idea mistaken.

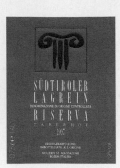

Pinot nero

French in origin, this grape is considered the most difficult of the world's great red varieties. It has not been distinguished by much success in Italy generally, but Alto Adige is an exception. In this region, especially around the village of Mazzon on the left bank of the Adige, magnificent Pinot Noir is grown. With low yields, they produce intensely colored, full-flavored wines with a pronounced bouquet. They make an excellent accompaniment to game.

Südtiroler or Alto Adige (Chardonnay and Pinot Bianco)

Pinot Bianco and Chardonnay used to be confused with each other in the Alpine region and in northern Italy for many years. The wines that feature under the designations *Südtiroler* or Alto Adige have been grown in the region for some one hundred years, but it is only with the advent of modern methods of winemaking and maturation that it has been possible to make of them fruity, yet full and powerful white wines. Barrique fermentation particularly suits the Chardonnay grape, resulting in a very quaffable wine.

Thurgau, Traminer, and Trollinger – here called Vernatsch or Schiava. The way the vineyards are denoted is another, as is the fact that almost all wines are classified as quality wines – here, DOC. Grape harvesting practices too are similar to those followed in Germany, such as the Auslese practice of using selected ripe grapes.

The center of good quality wine production lies along the upper reaches of the Adige, on a mountainside terrace above the river valley between Bolzano (Bozen) in the north and Ora (Auer) in the south. Other, smaller centers of good quality can be found in the Terlan, Meran, and St. Magdalena area and on the left bank of the Adige at Mazzon. Wide as the distribution of German grape varieties is, the best wines are now being made mainly from French varieties such as Cabernet Sauvignon, Chardonnay, and Pinot Noir (also called Pinot Nero and Spätburgunder). This has happened as a result of the leap forward in quality in Alto Adige and other Italian wines during the 1980s. Native varieties have only achieved a share of the limelight in recent years. They have yielded some truly convincing wines that have earned them popularity with consumers. The red wine, Lagrein, has been the star performer here. This grape was previously known mainly for producing a thin, unremarkable rosé, Kretzer. It is a variety that dates back in this region to the 17th century, and its name suggests that it may originate from the Lagarina valley, Valle Lagarina, in the Trentino.

The rise of the modern French varieties had threatened to eclipse Lagrein, but in recent years, a series of winegrowers and winemakers have shown that it is capable of producing powerful wines with an intense color and good balance between soft fruit and hard tannins. Remarkably, one of the best vineyard sites for this variety turned out to be one in Bolzano itself. This is the Gries vineyard, an isolated, flat site in the densely built-up city.

Another interesting feature here in Alto Adige has been the importance of the large houses and cooperatives in developing modern, good quality wine production. Unlike the rest of Italy, where such bodies are still turning out mainly simple, cheap, mass wines to satisfy a demanding market, some of the Alto Adige cooperatives are leaders in the field, with top wines that fetch prices many a renowned winegrower can only dream of.

KALTERER SEE AND ST. MAGDALENER

The most widely grown grape of Alto Adige is the red variety Vernatsch in its various guises: in Trentino, it is called Schiava, and elsewhere – in Germany – Trollinger. Used to make the wine known as Kalterer See, it became the most popular type produced by Alto Adige winegrowers, but simultaneously suffered by becoming a symbol of the decline in quality that took place in the 1970s. When people spoke of the Alto Adige wine lake, what they had in mind were huge quantities of characterless, sweet Kalterer See Auslese wines, which only rarely deserved their designation "quality wine." A striking change has come about in this wine, too. Both Kalterer See – from around the lake of that name – and St. Magdalener – the red wine made from the Vernatsch grape, and grown in vineyards north of Bolzano – are today made by the most modern methods. Both now produce dry wines with pronounced aromas, light but characterized by soft body, and sometimes a slight bitterness in the after-taste, ideal drinking with light, summer foods.

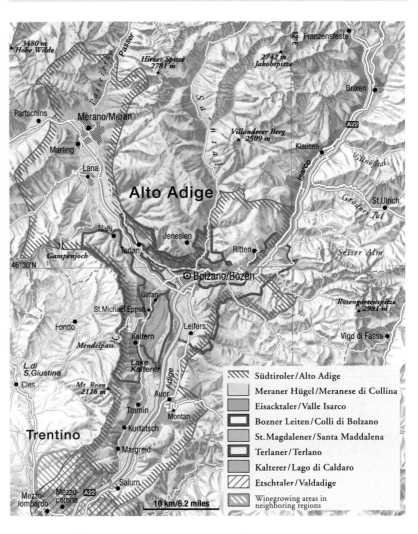

Südtiroler/Alto Adige
Meraner Hügel/Meranese di Collina
Eisacktaler/Valle Isarco
Bozner Leiten/Colli di Bolzano
St. Magdalener/Santa Maddalena
Terlaner/Terlano
Kalterer/Lago di Caldaro
Etschtaler/Valdadige
Winegrowing areas in neighboring regions

Oglio

Passo del Tonale

Val d'Isole

Madonna di Campiglio

3556 m
Cima Presanella

Mt. Adamello
3554 m

Pinzolo

Cima Tosa
3159 m

Molveno

La Paganella
2125 m

Mezzo-
corona

Mezzo-
lombardo

S. Michele
all'Adige

Faedo

Cembra

Lavis

Alto Adige

Salurn

Cavalese

Val di Fiemme

Mt. Croce
2490 m

Cima d'Asta
2847 m

Lombardy

Mt. Care Alto
3462 m

Lago di
Molveno

Vezzano

Civezzano

2383 m

Maso

Strigno

Mt. Frisozzo
3899 m

Stenico

Tione
di Trento

46° N

Trento

Pergine
Valsugana

Levico
Terme

Borgo
Valsugana

Brenta

Lasino

Lago di
Caldonazzo

Trentino

2176 m

A22

Caldonazzo

2336 m
Cima Dodici

3830 m
Cornone di
Blumone

Sarca

Arco

Nogaredo

2059 m

Rovereto

Isera

Lavarone

Folgaria

Riva del Garda

Lago di Ledro

Torbole

Mori

Bagolino

Limone
s.Garda

1977 m
Mt. Caplone

Lago
d'Idro

2235 m

Anto

Idro

Lago
di Valvestino

Lake Garda

Malcesine

Monte Baldo

Avio

Ala

Veneto

Gargnano

2200 m

Mts. Lessini

10 km/6.2 miles

Etschtaler/Valdadige

Casteller

Teroldego Rotaliano

KalererSee / Lago di Caldaro

Trentino

Trento Spumante

South Tyrol /Alto Adige

Winegrowing areas in
neighboring regions

QUALITY WINE PRODUCTION IN THE TRENTINO

The Trentino, southern half of the region Trentino-Alto Adige, is largely mountainous, characterized by the towering peaks of the Dolomites and the Rhaetian Alps. Yet winegrowing is more important than one might think; the valley of the Adige and some of the side valleys offer good vineyard locations. Vines may well have been introduced here by the Etruscans, before the time of the Romans, but until very recently, the Trentino was known only for its trade in casked wine, including that from other regions of Italy. The pergolas that extend to left and right of the motorway present a typical picture of the region's vineyards. They ensure generally high yields, but promise little in terms of quality. Three quarters of the province's grape production is not vinified by the winegrowers themselves, but it goes to the huge tanks of the cooperatives and bulk suppliers. Vineyard land, in sharp contrast to this dismal portrait of the quality and value of the wines, fetches huge sums. The rampant urbanization of the Adige valley puts land at a premium, and stifles any desire to take the risks associated with quality wine production and the low yields it involves.

It is all the more important in the light of this to acknowledge the step taken by those winegrowers who have taken the difficult route, and are pursuing quality in cultivation and winemaking methods – with notable results. The best known of the region's products are its white wines, made from Chardonnay or Pinot Grigio. Many wine-lovers consider the reds of the Adige valley to be better. One in particular carries conviction: the native variety Teroldego – pronounced with the stress on the first "o" – that is grown on the Campo Rotaliano at Mezzocorona and at San Michele, on gravel and alluvial soils. This produces wonderfully complex and powerful wines with aromas of liquorice, plums, cherries, or violets.

Apart from Teroldego, most other wines are sold under the regional name Trentino together with the name of the variety. The best of these are Cabernet and Merlot, but the easy-drinking, slightly rustic native variety Marzemino is also sometimes worthy of attention. Nosiola, the most important white variety, is only grown here. In the Sarca valley, the valley of the lakes that opens onto Lake Garda, this grape is made into a good, sweet Vin Santo. Last but not least, mention needs to be made of sparkling wine production. A number of bulk winemakers in and around the city of Trento specialize in this.

Spumante Trento

Franciacorta and Trentino are the only two classifications of origin applied to sparkling wines. The grapes used are the traditional Champagne varieties, and the best wines made by the bottle fermentation method. Trento Spumante seldom attains the complexity of Franciacorta, but the wines are nevertheless pleasant, fresh, and fruity, and are best suited for drinking as an aperitif.

Trentino (Cabernet)

Trentino is the province's equivalent to the designation Alto Adige (German Südtiroler). Here, too, a number of varietal wines are sold under the common regional name. One of the most interesting developments of recent years has been in Cabernet Sauvignon. The wines may not achieve the greatness of the Bordeaux product, and the growths may not equal those of California, but their fruit character and good structure make them pleasing nonetheless, and a particularly agreeable accompaniment to red meats and game.

Teroldego Rotaliano

Teroldego is one of Italy's most remarkable varieties. It is only on the alluvial plain of the Campo Rotaliano and San Michele that it grows well enough to produce wines worthy of note. Like Lagrein in Alto Adige, it results in full, intensely colored wines with good mouth feel and capacity for aging, suitable for drinking with the whole range of richly flavored meat dishes.

Nosiola

The Nosiola grape was long thought of simply as one for blending or distilling. It does, however, make thoroughly respectable wines. In the Cembra valley, it is often blended with more aromatic varieties. In the Sarcatal, the valley of the lakes, that drains into Lake Garda from the north, it is used to make a wonderful sweet and semisweet Vin Santo.

LOMBARDIA

Lombards, especially those in the bustling city of Milan, stand accused of having contributed little to Italy's stock of culinary specialties, and of being so industriously devoted to their work that they have no time for a long, leisurely meal or a good glass of wine. The secrets of this region's cuisine do seem at first glance less easy to unlock – yet a closer look at the foods bubbling away in its kitchens reveals certain characteristics in common among the nine provinces that make up the region. Rice is popular everywhere, in nourishing soups and in light, separate-grained risottos that are often preferred to pasta. Another feature found throughout Lombardy is the habit of rounding off a meal with a piece of cheese – *robiola* or *grana padano*. Butter is used more often than vegetable oils, and sauces are frequently made with generous amounts of cream. There is, then, a culinary tradition with its own customs and preferences. That might even be said to include the Lombard tendency to spend less time on food – certainly during the working week – than other regions do. Risotto with ossobuco fits this pattern; it saves time, because it is a starter and main course in one. *Casoeula* is another dish that is simple to prepare and quick to eat, as the meat and vegetables are first cut into bite-sized pieces before being cooked together in the same pot.

This sort of "fast food" can be set aside, though, when occasion demands. When the calendar indicates a particular feast day, or when some personal celebration falls due, people spare neither time nor effort in preparing delicious specialties, and delight in enjoying them. The table groans beneath the weight of meat and game, accompanied in Bergamo, Brescia, and Valtellina by polenta. In Mantua, a favorite dish for special occasions is one that used to be served at village festivals – *tortelli di zucca*, ravioli with pumpkin filling, served with melted butter. This is followed by stuffed turkey, stuffed chicken, or a tempting mixture of stewed meats. The accusation is quite mistaken: the people of Lombardy do know how to feast just as well as other Italians.

Previous double page: Christmas would not be the same without panettone. Here, fresh panettone is being offered in the Marchesi bar and *pasticceria*, Milan.

Left: Lago d'Iseo, 40 miles (25 kilometers) long, is one of Italy's most beautiful lakes. The mountainous island of Montisola lies roughly at its center.

ASPARAGUS

Asparagus occupies a significant place in Lombard cuisine. The first tender shoots of spring are eagerly awaited. Whereas places like Bassano del Grappa are committed to white asparagus, green is the preferred type in Lombardy in general. The flavor is delicious, and it is very much easier to grow, as it does not have to be blanched – this is the process of earthing up the young plants or covering them with dark plastic to prevent them from making chlorophyll and becoming green. In contrast, the green asparagus can simply be left to grow in the sunlight. Other nations in history have shared this liking for green asparagus: the ancient Egyptians, Greeks, and Romans.

Asparagus has excellent health-giving benefits. It is low in calories, but rich in vitamins A and B and in minerals; it also has diuretic properties. It tastes best when very fresh, so care should be taken when purchasing to choose smooth, firm, asparagus with clean, unblemished stems, and to avoid any that seems wet. The tips should be compact and straight. If stored at all, it should be kept in cool, dark conditions. A good method is to wrap it in a damp cloth and keep it in the vegetable compartment at the bottom of the refrigerator.

Asparagus can be used to make delicious soup, or as the filling for asparagus omelet. Steamed and tossed in butter, it makes an incomparable vegetable accompaniment. Simply simmering in salted water for 20–25 minutes is an ideal alternative for the calorie-conscious. Asparagus pans are tall and straight.

ASPARAGI AL BURRO
Asparagus with butter

GENEROUS 3 LBS/1.5 KG GREEN ASPARAGUS
1 1/2 CUPS/150 G FRESHLY GRATED PARMESAN OR GRANA PADANO
6 1/2 TBSP/100 G BUTTER

Peel the asparagus if necessary, and cut off the woody part of the stem. Tie the asparagus into a bundle and place upright in a deep saucepan, in plenty of boiling, salted water. Cover and simmer for about 20 minutes. Drain and arrange on warmed plates, and sprinkle with the cheese. Have ready some melted, browned butter, slightly cooled, to pour over the asparagus.

Green asparagus is easier to harvest than white, because it has not been earthed up or covered with plastic sheeting. However, it still demands hard work

A special tool is used to harvest the asparagus – one by one, by hand. First, the spear has to be freed of surrounding earth.

Agricultural standards lay down that the asparagus must be green for at least two thirds of its length if it is to be sold as "green asparagus."

SAINT BERNARD

The history of Bernard of Clairvaux illustrates the power of a single wise man to bring about radical change in the fortunes of a city and an entire region. The year is 1134, and Milan is welcoming the arrival of the abbot Bernard with great pomp. Soon to be declared a saint, Bernard had been sent by Pope Innocent II to settle a theological dispute and to set Milan back on the path of Rome. Every day in the church of S. Lorenzo, he received many citizens of Milan who came begging him to found a monastery. Bernard finally agreed to this request, and set about finding a suitable site. He made the deliberate decision to establish it on a patch of boggy ground outside the walls of the city. This was to become the Cistercian monastery of Chiaravalle.

In the *Legenda Aurea*, the medieval collection of legends of the saints by Jacobus de Voragine, there is an interesting anecdote about the founding of the monastery: "St. Bernard had built a monastery, and it was visited by such a plague of mosquitoes that the brothers suffered greatly. Then St. Bernard spoke and said, 'I will place the church's ban on them.' The very next morning, they were all found dead."

Despite the apparent Divine assistance in matters of combating insects, St. Bernard and his monks found themselves with much other work to do. They carried out their religious duties, and also saw it as their duty to assist the peasants in reclaiming land for the cultivation of crops, regulating water supply and drainage, and establishing large, meticulously organized farms that remain to this day the linchpin of agriculture on the Po plain. The monks of the order helped to create accurately laid out terraced fields, kept under constant irrigation so that they produced vital fresh fodder for cattle-rearing even in the midst of winter frost and ice.

A number of further benefits followed in the wake of the field improvements. The complete draining of parts of the marshes reduced the risk of malaria; the increased crop yields raised the living standards of the local population; and larger herds of cattle could be kept on the new meadows. Cattle farming in its turn brought new opportunities, such as the need for dairy workers to process butter and cheese. One new product was a medium fat cheese made from milk that had been heated. It had excellent keeping qualities. Later, it became known under the name *grana padano*. The range of food being produced in this tract of countryside was soon sufficient to prosper the nearby city of Milan as well.

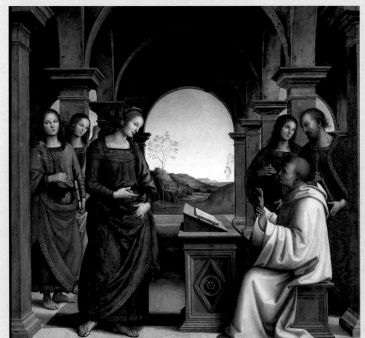

Perugino, *The vision of St. Bernard*, c.1490/94,
oil on canvas, 173 x 170 cm. Alte Pinakothek, Munich.
The Virgin Mary accompanied by angels appearing to St. Bernard.

Asparagi alla milanese

Asparagus with fried egg
(Illustration below)

3 LBS/1.5 KG GREEN ASPARAGUS
SALT
FRESHLY GRATED PARMESAN OR GRANA PADANO
4 EGGS
BUTTER

Peel the asparagus if necessary and cut off the woody ends.
Tie the asparagus into a bundle, and place in a deep
saucepan with plenty of boiling salted water. Cover and
cook for about 20 minutes. Drain and arrange on warmed
plates, or one large serving dish. Sprinkle with the grated
cheese. Fry the eggs lightly in the butter and place carefully
on top of the asparagus.

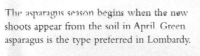

The asparagus season begins when the new
shoots appear from the soil in April. Green
asparagus is the type preferred in Lombardy.

RISOTTO ALLA MILANESE

Rice and rice dishes have an important place in the cuisine of northern Italy, and saffron an equally essential one in *risotto alla milanese*. Milanese chefs prefer to use Carnaroli rice for this dish, whereas Vialone nano is the variety normally used for Venetian risottos. The famous Milanese risotto derives its golden color from the precious spice saffron, still an expensive luxury. This color is also the reason that the dish is sometimes called *risotto giallo* or yellow risotto.

Some historians claim that saffron made its first appearance in the Lombard capital in the 13th century, though it is not known how, or by what route. What is known is that Pope Celestine IV, a native of Milan whose papacy lasted just from October 28 to November 10, 1241, often used the spice. Prepared from the stigmas of the saffron crocus (*Crocus sativus*), it was sent to him from Abruzzi, and used by him not only for cooking, but to mix with the other precious essences of lilies, roses, and lavender with which he scented his daily bath.

RISOTTO ALLA MILANESE
Saffron risotto
(Illustrations right and below)

5 TBSP/75 G BUTTER
2 OZ/50 G BEEF BONE MARROW (OPTIONAL)
1 SMALL ONION, CHOPPED FINELY
2 CUPS/350 G RICE (CARNAROLI OR VIALONE)
1 GLASS DRY WHITE WINE
1 PINCH OF POWDERED SAFFRON OR A FEW STRANDS
ABOUT 3 PINTS/1.5 LITERS MEAT STOCK
SALT AND PEPPER
1/2 CUP/50 G FRESHLY GRATED PARMESAN

Melt 2 tablespoons/50 g of the butter and the bone marrow in a saucepan or large skillet, and sauté the onions until transparent. Add the rice, and turn it constantly in the fat, using a wooden spoon, until translucent. Pour on the wine and cook until completely reduced. Then stir in the saffron. Heat the stock, and add it gradually to the rice, stirring constantly, ensuring that the rice can absorb each addition.

Season with salt and pepper. Just before the rice is cooked, stir in the grated Parmesan and the remaining butter, cover, and leave for a few minutes to rest and develop the right consistency.
The bone marrow is not an essential ingredient, but does give a wonderfully creamy texture.

RISOTTO ALLA MONZESE
Pork sausage risotto

1/2 LB/200 G SALSICCE SAUSAGES
1/2 ONION
1 3/4 CUPS/300 G CARNAROLI RICE
1 GLASS DRY WHITE WINE
2 CUPS/500 ML MEAT STOCK
SALT AND PEPPER
1/2 CUP/50 G FRESHLY GRATED PARMESAN OR GRANA PADANO

Strip the skin from the *salsicce* and slice them. Chop the onion finely, and sauté in the butter until golden. Add the *salsicce* and sauté, and then the rice, turning it with a wooden spoon until coated and translucent. Pour on the wine and reduce. Heat the stock separately, and add it gradually, ensuring that the rice can absorb each addition. Just before the rice is cooked, season with salt and pepper. Stir in the grated cheese, cover, and leave to stand for 2–3 minutes before serving.

RISOTTO AL SALTO
Rice tarts

1 LB/450 G COLD RISOTTO ALLA MILANESE (SEE LEFT)
8 TSP/40 G BUTTER
1 TBSP EXTRA VIRGIN OLIVE OIL
FRESHLY GRATED PARMESAN OR GRANA PADANO

Shape left-over *risotto alla milanese* into 4 roughly equal round, flat portions, and place on baking parchment. Melt the butter in a skillet, and slide the tarts gently into it, without breaking them. Fry the underside until a light crust forms, shifting them during cooking to prevent them from burning. Turn out onto a plate and slide them back to cook the other side, adding a little olive oil. Sprinkle with grated cheese before serving.

Vialone and Carnaroli are the best types of rice for risotto. For Milanese risotto, the other ingredients are bone marrow, butter, stock, wine, onion, saffron, and Parmesan.

Melt the butter and bone marrow in a skillet. Add the onion as soon as the butter becomes frothy. Sauté until translucent but not colored.

Sprinkle in the rice and stir until translucent, but do not allow it to brown. Pour on the white wine and continue stirring to prevent the rice sticking.

The risotto should be creamy and moist but not wet. Leave to stand before serving, to achieve the right consistency.

Tripe

Tripe *(trippa)* – at least in most Italian regions – normally means the fore-stomach of ruminants, but in Lombardy it includes the upper part of the small intestine. Beef or veal may be used. In Lazio, the whole of the small intestine is included, and is called by the local name *paiata* or *pagliata*.

In Lombardy, the intestine is opened out to clean it thoroughly. It has a ridged, wavy surface, full of glands and full of flavor, and is an important ingredient of the classic Lombard dish of mixed tripe called *busecca*. If the idea of preparing it is unpleasant to them, it is possible to buy the tripe ready prepared – even ready parboiled – from a butcher they know and trust. Tripe prepared according to a local recipe can be sampled in one of the region's good restaurants. It makes a delicious starter or main course.

Tripe is rich in mineral content, especially phosphorus and calcium, though it is also high in cholesterol. That need not matter, as it is not eaten every day.

Trippa in umido di mezzanotte della vigilia di Natale
Stew of tripe and vegetables

Generous 4 lbs/2 kg beef tripe
Salt
1/4 lb/100 g bacon, diced
2 cloves of garlic
1 bunch of parsley, chopped
1 stalk of celery
4 carrots
Generous 1 lb/500 g onions
Meat stock or water

Wash the tripe and boil it for 2 hours in salted water. Then cut into roughly 1 inch/3 cm pieces. Crush the garlic and parsley into a paste, then heat this in a saucepan. Slice and add the vegetables, and cook lightly before adding the tripe. Add water or stock to cover, and simmer for 4–5 hours over a low heat. Top up the liquid from time to time. At the end of the cooking time, the liquid should all have been absorbed. Serve with polenta or slices of corn bread. Another suitable accompaniment is boiled garbanzo beans with a little oil, salt, and pepper.

After 15 minutes, add the saffron. This can be dissolved in a little stock, but no more stock is added from this point on.

The gradual, even addition of the stock is the key to making a good risotto. Each time the rice becomes dry, add just enough liquid to cover.

Just before the end of cooking, add the remaining butter and the Parmesan. Leave the risotto to stand, so that the rice can swell and separate while remaining creamy.

91

COTOLETTA ALLA MILANESE

The term *cotoletta* may be a corruption of the southern Italian word *costoletta*, meaning ribs or cutlet, or may come from the French *côtelette*. France is, after all, nearer than southern Italy. Though the origin and the spelling of the name are uncertain, the dish itself is not: it is a portion of meat fried in breadcrumbs, and in its most famous form, it is called *cotoletta alla milanese*. The idea has been extended of late, and chicken, turkey, or even vegetable slices *alla milanese* have been with us for some years now. In dishes like these, the name describes the manner of preparation, and simply tells us that the food has been fried in breadcrumbs.

The origin of the dish is as obscure as that of the name and its spelling, with both Austrians and the Milanese claiming to have invented it. One explanation is that the Austrians passed on to the Milanese the art of preparing meat in breadcrumbs during the one and a half centuries of Austrian rule. The difficulty with this is that the method of preparing Viennese Schnitzel is not the same: the *cotoletta* is dipped first in flour, then in egg and finally in breadcrumbs. Nor is the same cut of meat used: the *Schnitzel* uses leg and not loin. Finally, it is fried in shortening or, today, in oil.

Proof that the *cotoletta alla milanese* is a Milanese invention is in fact provided by two historical documents. The first is a "menu" of 1134, for a meal given by an abbot to the choristers of Sant' Ambrogio. The list of dishes includes *lumbulos cum panitio*, sliced loin in breadcrumbs. This evidence of Lombard specialties is quoted in Pietro Verri's *Storia di Milano*. The second item of proof is a letter written by the Austrian general, Field Marshal Radetzky, to the Imperial staff officer, Baron Attems. After various comments and pieces of information, the general writes of the *cotoletta* and describes the method of preparation, speaking of it as a new discovery. Would he have praised it as a novelty if Viennese Schnitzel had been familiar to him already from home? Perhaps it was the Austrians who learned the dish from south of the Alps – the Milanese at least believe so. Should you put the matter to the test and discuss it with a Lombard chef, you will be assured that this dish is an utterly original Milanese invention.

MONDEGHILI
Meatballs

1 STALE WHITE BREAD ROLL
1/2 CUP/125 ML MILK
1/4 LB/100 G SALSICCE SAUSAGES
1/4 LB/100 G MORTADELLA
SCANT 1 LB/400 G MIXED GROUND MEAT
2 EGGS
1 TBSP CHOPPED PARSLEY
1 CLOVE OF GARLIC, CHOPPED
SCANT 1/2 CUP/40 G GRATED PARMESAN
GROUND NUTMEG
SALT AND PEPPER
BREADCRUMBS
3 1/2 TBSP/50 G BUTTER

Soak the roll in the milk and squeeze out. Chop the *salsicce* and mortadella, and mix well with the ground meat in a bowl. Beat the eggs and add to the meat, together with the parsley, garlic, cheese, and soaked bread roll. Season with nutmeg, salt, and pepper, and mix thoroughly with a wooden spoon. Loosely shape the mixture into small meatballs and toss in the breadcrumbs. Fry them in butter, and serve hot with a salad. The meatballs can also be eaten cold, in summer.

Mondeghili are a traditional way of using leftovers, so the ingredients can be varied to include the remains of a roast, the meat from soups, or sausagemeat. These meats should be ground before making the meatballs.

SCALOPPINE AL LIMONE
Veal cutlet with lemon sauce
(Illustration below)

4 VEAL CUTLETS
2 UNWAXED LEMONS
6 TBSP OLIVE OIL
WHITE PEPPER
1 TBSP BUTTER
SALT

Slice the cutlets in half and beat them out to a thickness of 1/4 inch/0.5 cm. Finely grate the zest of one lemon, and squeeze the juice. Beat together the lemon juice and 4 tablespoons of olive oil, season with pepper, and stir in the lemon zest. Pour over the meat, cover, and marinate for at least 1 hour in the refrigerator, turning once.
Heat 2 tablespoons of olive oil in a skillet. Take out and drain the cutlets, reserving the marinade, and fry for about 2 minutes each side. Lift out, cover, and keep hot.
Pour the marinade into the skillet. Squeeze the second lemon and add the juice to the pan. Boil rapidly, add the butter, and season with salt and pepper. Return the cutlets to the skillet and heat through. Serve immediately on warmed plates, with the sauce poured over.

Ossobuchi alla milanese
Braised knuckle of veal
(Illustration right, behind)

3 1/2 TBSP/50 G BUTTER
4 THICK SLICES OF VEAL KNUCKLE
SALT AND PEPPER
1 GLASS DRY WHITE WINE
1/2 CUP/125 ML CHICKEN STOCK
4–5 TOMATOES, SKINNED AND DICED
1–2 SLICES/20 G RAW SMOKED HAM
1 CARROT
1 STALK OF CELERY
1 SMALL ONION
1 TBSP CHOPPED PARSLEY
GRATED ZEST OF 1 LEMON

Melt half the butter in a shallow saucepan, and briefly fry
the knuckle of veal on both sides to seal. Season with salt
and pepper, then lift out and keep hot.
Heat the chicken stock separately. Pour off the fat that has
collected in the veal saucepan, then replace it on the heat
and pour in the white wine to deglaze, stirring to dissolve
the solidified cooking juices. Reduce almost completely
before adding some of the chicken stock. Add the tomatoes
and knuckle of veal, cover, and simmer for about 1½ hours,
adding more stock from time to time, and seasoning with
salt and pepper. Cut the ham into thin strips. Chop the
carrot, celery, and onion finely. Melt the remaining butter in
a saucepan, sauté the ham briefly, add the vegetables, and
cook gently for 1 minute. Add the parsley and lemon zest.
Then transfer the mixture to the pan with the knuckle of
veal, and continue cooking for 10 minutes. Serve the meat
on warmed plates with the sauce poured over.
This dish is traditionally served with *risotto alla milanese* (see
p. 90). Mashed or duchesse potatoes make a suitable alternative, as do vegetables sautéed in butter.

Arrosto di maiale al latte
Leg of pork in milk

GENEROUS 2 LBS/1 KG LEG OF PORK
1 CLOVE OF GARLIC
2 CUPS/500 ML DRY WHITE WINE
ALL-PURPOSE FLOUR
3 1/2 TBSP/50 G BUTTER
1 SPRIG OF ROSEMARY, CHOPPED
3 CUPS/750 ML MILK
SALT AND FRESHLY GROUND BLACK PEPPER

Place the meat in a large dish, slice and add the garlic,
pour on the wine, cover, and marinate for 2 days in the
refrigerator.
Lift out the meat, carefully pat it dry, and dust it lightly with
flour. Heat the butter in a large saucepan, add the rosemary,
and brown the meat on all sides. Pour on the milk, and
season with salt and pepper. Cover and braise for 2 hours,
until tender.
Place the meat on a warmed dish and keep hot. Boil the
cooking liquid until reduced to a creamy consistency. Slice
the meat and serve hot, with the sauce poured over.

Cotolette alla milanese
Cutlets Milan style
(Illustration above, foreground)

4 THIN VEAL CUTLETS
SALT AND PEPPER
A LITTLE FLOUR
1–2 EGGS, BEATEN
BREADCRUMBS
6 1/2 TBSP/100 G BUTTER
LEMON WEDGES TO GARNISH
PARSLEY TO GARNISH

Carefully beat out the cutlets thinly. Season with salt and
pepper. Dip them first in a little flour, then in beaten egg
and finally in breadcrumbs to coat. Press the breadcrumbs
into place with your hand. Melt the butter in a skillet and
cook the cutlets for a few minutes on each side, until the
coating is golden and the meat inside tender. Lower the
heat and turn the cutlets once more before serving,
garnished with lemon wedges and parsley.

PECK, FINE FOOD MERCHANTS

It would fill an entire book to tell the whole story of Milan's traditional delicatessen store, Peck. Such a book has in fact been written, by author Davide Paolini. His compendium about this gourmets' temple has been published by the Milan publishing house of Mondadori. It will be in order, then, for us to present a rather shorter account.

In 1883, a young man by the name of Peck, who ran a successful sausage business in Prague, opened a branch in Milan to sell mainly German specialties, such as smoked sausage, meat, and ham. He soon reaped the rewards of his enterprise, and his small store became the gastronomic hub of Milan. Peck even became a supplier to the court of Milan and to a

number of the city's noble and respected families. He retired in 1918, handing on the ownership of the store to Eliseo Magnaghi, who moved it to new and very central premises in the Via Spadari. While continuing to sell German sausage and meats in the Peck tradition, Magnaghi also introduced new lines, in particular, fresh, homemade pasta and ready-made meals to take away. The well-heeled soon recognized the advantages of having the Peck ravioli – famous to this day – delivered to their doors, rather than spend time and effort preparing their own. The new management also opened an area to the rear of the store where the specialties of the house could be sampled, and this delightful corner quickly became a meeting place for the intelligentsia of the time. Artists, journalists, army officers, poets, actors, and the great and the good of the city sat around the small tables. Regular customers included d'Annunzio, Bacchelli, Vergani, Monelli, and Marchi. Peck received a further boost to its popularity when the film director, Mario Mattioli, set several scenes of his 1937 film, *Felicita Colombo* in the store. The film told the story of a rich Milanese woman who

ran a grocery business. Following Eliseo Magnaghi's death, the management of the store passed to his daughter Emi, who ran it for 24 years.

The third epoch in the store's history began in July, 1956, with the Grazioli brothers. This was the dawn of the Italian economic miracle that was to make Milan the richest city in Italy, and the firm's new policy took account of that situation. Three further stores were opened: the *casa del formaggio* in Via Speronari (which dealt in cheese), the *bottega del maiale* opposite the main store (dealing in pork and sausage), and the *rosticceria* in Via Cantù (a snack bar, in today's language, selling roast meat). The kitchen and storeroom areas of the building were renovated, and modern technical equipment installed. These changes enabled Peck to introduce a vastly increased range of ready made foods, and its customers responded with enthusiasm. Giovanni and Luigi Grazioli carefully observed the changes in their fellow citizens' eating habits and needs; the demands of work in this booming city meant that people had little time for a protracted lunch with several courses. Peck therefore began to offer tastefully made small snacks –

Peck in Milan is both a delicatessen and a restaurant with a Michelin star. Specialties here include asparagus (in spring), ravioli with red abalone, and sole in curry sauce.

into the main building during the refurbishments. New ventures have been developed: catering by Peck has become an essential feature of every important Milan party, there is a Christmas gift service, and exports are rising constantly. The main countries, in order of sales volume, are Germany, Great Britain, Austria, France, the USA, and Hong Kong.

The Stoppani brothers – four of them – run the business with great energy and devotion. Angelo, the eldest, is responsible for sausage and meat products and for imports; Mario, next in age, takes care of wines and catering; Remo, the third brother, looks after cheeses and exports, and Lino, the youngest, does the management and bookkeeping. Typically for an Italian family enterprise, they are also supported by Mario's sons Andrea, Stefano, and Paolo. There are four grandchildren studying and gaining experience elsewhere before entering the family business. They frequently help out serving food or behind the counter.

It would be impossible to list all the products so attractively and appetizingly set out for sale in Peck's 35,520 square foot (3300 square meter) retail area. It includes sausage, cheese, fruit, vegetables, pasta – both *pasta secca* and *pasta fresca* – bread, fish, seafood, smoked salmon, truffles, mushrooms, caviar, fresh meat, meat products, pastries, ready-made dishes to take away, wines and spirits, all in an incredible range of varieties. In other areas of the store, chefs can be watched at work over sizzling pans, or customers can sit and relax over an ice cream or coffee, to recover from their tour of the counters. Even those who wish to observe rather than buy will find their visit an unforgettable experience. This is a place where customer service is writ large.

open sandwiches and filled rolls – that established a new lunch trend. Employees of neighboring businesses and offices would hurry in to Peck in their lunch break, have a *panino* made up to order from the huge range of fillings and dressings, and hurry out. This venture into fast food did not distract the Grazioli brothers from their trade in quality sausages, hams, and cheeses, nor from an emphasis on good service designed to make the store a welcoming one even for less affluent customers. Peck maintains not only its exclusive image, but a policy of making sure its doors are open to everyone. That policy believes that everyone should feel able to visit the store – even those whose budget only runs to a quarter of ham once a year must never be treated condescendingly. They must know that they are welcome. The Grazioli brothers were well aware that not everyone in the rich city of Milan shared its prosperity, and wanted the delights they sold to be available to them all nonetheless. A further change in ownership occurred on September 1, 1970. The Graziolis chose the sons of the Stoppani family from Corticelle Piave in the province of

Brescia, convinced that only they would be able to continue the business in the established spirit and to the standards that had been set. The Peck enterprise took a further leap forward under the management of the Stoppani brothers. The first step was to modernize the *rosticceria* and the *bottega del maiale*, followed four years later by the main store in the Via Spadari. They also acquired further premises: a wine store in the Via Victor Hugo, where in 1982 they opened a wine and snack bar serving hot and cold food, and the Peck restaurant, also in the Via Victor Hugo, opened a year later. The restaurant's excellent cuisine earned it a Michelin star in 1986. The new building in the Via Spadari was begun in 1988, and the gleaming new gourmets' temple formally opened in 1996.

The elegant, three-story main building is the heart and the control center of the Peck enterprise. Its activities have now extended to include high quality snack bars at the Linate, Malpensa, and Fiumicino airports, six outposts in Japanese Takashi stores, and a restaurant in Tokyo. The *casa del formaggio* and *bottega del maiale* no longer exist as separate stores, but were incorporated

CHEESE AND SAUSAGE VARIETIES

Stracchino or Crescenza

Crescenza cheese derives its other name, *stracchino*, from the way the milk to make it was originally obtained: it was the milk of *vacche stracche*, cows exhausted by the journey back down the mountain from the summer meadows. *Stracco* is local dialect for "exhausted" – and *stracchino* is "little exhausted one."

Small and medium-sized producers of specialist cheeses in the Alpine regions face a difficult struggle to maintain their existence in competition with the varied palette of factory-made dairy products. Unfortunately, European Union regulations often only serve to hasten their demise, by making often contradictory demands, imposing quotas and limits, or fining them for not fulfilling certain norms, despite the fact that theirs are high quality, often imaginative, products. *Stracchino* is one of these threatened products. It is a rectangular cheese made from whole milk. It is a rich cheese, pearly white in color, with a soft, creamy texture and remarkable, delicate flavor.

Taleggio (DOC since 1988)

This is a square cheese weighing about four pounds (2 kilograms). It is a typical Lombard country soft cheese. The rind is brownish and tends to form a mold. Directly beneath this rind, the cheese is soft and soft textured, but in the center, it is whitish and crumbly. The first mention of *taleggio* dates from around 1200, and the method of production has changed little since then, apart from the use of selected enzymes to ensure the quality of the end product. The cheese is still only made from cow's milk. The curd takes 18 hours to form, and the cheese must mature for at least one month before being ready to eat.

Taleggio is mild with a slight sourness, becoming quite piquant as it ages. It should not be kept for long periods because it spoils easily. A slice of *taleggio* rounds off a meal. It also goes well with hot polenta, and tastes delicious eaten with ripe pears.

Gorgonzola (DOC since 1955)

Gorgonzola is a very old cheese specialty, and originates from the town of Gorgonzola in Lombardy. First written records of it are from the 11th and 12th centuries. A blue-veined cheese, it is produced today across a wide area of Piedmont and Lombardy, and is popular both in Italy and abroad. The region produces around three million Gorgonzola cheeses per year, which are exported to the rest of Italy, France, Germany, Switzerland, the USA, and Canada packed as portions in colorfully printed foil wrappers, which must bear the brand figure of the consortium to be genuine. It has a strong, piquant flavor with a hint of bitterness, and is a true all-round cheese. Gorgonzola makes a good partner to eat with polenta, tastes good with egg and with nuts, and can be used for creams and sauces. It is delicious with a robust red wine.

Provolone valpadana (also DOC)

This hard cheese with its characteristic shape – round, pear-shaped, or sometimes cylindrical – originally comes from Basilicata in the south, but is also made in northern Italy today, especially in Lombardy. *Provolone* is sold in various sizes, and is made by a similar *pasta filata* process to mozzarella. The curd is scalded – it is heated until it begins to melt and become stringy (*filata*), and then wrapped around itself until it assumes its round shape. It is dipped in brine and hung up on a cord to ripen, which takes about a year. The rind is coated in wax to protect it from drying out. *Provolone* comes in various flavor categories from *provolone dolce*, which is mild and buttery, to piquant (*provolone piccante*). The mild version makes a good end to a meal, and the piquant one is often used grated. A smoked version is available in Lombardy.

Grana padano

Grana padano is often compared to *parmigiano reggiano*, despite the differences between them in the method of production and region of origin. *Parmigiano reggiano* comes exclusively from Emilia-Romagna, and *grana padano* from the Veneto, Trentino, Piedmont, or Lombardy. *Parmigiano reggiano* may by law only be made from the milk of cows that have been fed on grass or hay, whereas other types of fodder are permissible for *grana padano*. This does not mean that it is in any way inferior. Its manufacture is supervised by a consortium, and only cheeses bearing the official brand mark *grana padano* are the genuine article. The milk from which it is made comes from two consecutive milkings, and is allowed to stand and partially skimmed to produce a cheese with just 30 percent fat in dry matter. The milk is then heated and micro-organisms added. The cheeses are matured for 1–2 years. *Grana padano* has a granular texture, and can become dry and crumbly. It forms a thick, smooth rind. The cheese has a harmonious flavor, not too salty and not too mild, with a slight piquancy and a nutty quality. It can be eaten as an appetizer, or used for grating over pasta dishes or green salads.

Grana Padano

Gorgonzola

Provolone piccante

Stracchino or Crescenza

Taleggio

Salametto

Salame di Varzi

Salame di Varzi

Salame di Milano

Salsiccia luganega

Cacciatorino

Salame di Varzi

Around Pavia, south of the River Po, are a number of villages where sausages are still smoked in the traditional way. This is the area where *salame di Varzi* is made. Only the finest pork is used to make this sausage, and only wine, pepper, salt, and saltpeter are added. The sausage is matured for three to four months. This comparatively long matura-tion brings out the flavor. A whole *salame di Varzi* as sold is a medium-sized, coarse-grained sausage weighing about 2 pounds (1 kilogram). It has been a DOC designated product since 1989.

Salsiccia luganega (or luganiga)

Sausages called *salsiccia* are usually of fresh meat, and cooked or heated in water before serving. The meat is a finely ground mixture of fat and lean pork, flavored with pepper and spices. *Luganiga* or *luganega* is an example of this type. The meat is filled into long casings, divided into sections and sold by length rather than weight. *Luganiga* is often served with polenta in northern Italy. It can be fried, broiled, or braised as well as boiled.

Salame di Milano

This fine-textured salami made from pork, pork fat, beef, and spices is matured for about 3 months and weighs up to about 3 pounds (1.5 kilograms). It has an essential place in any *antipasto misto* starter of mixed sausage, and is popular well beyond its place of origin. It is probably one of Italy's best-known food products, along with Parma ham. The imitations available elsewhere do not necessarily do justice to the original.

Cacciatorino

This small, well-hung variety of salami consists of two thirds lean pork, tender veal, and various types of fat. It was origi-nally devised as a convenient type of sausage for those work-ing out in the forests to take with them as supplies. That may be the source of the name, *cacciatorino*, "small hunter."

Salametto

Salametto is a small, well-hung sausage, similar to *cacciatorino*. It, too, can be taken as provisions for an excursion into the countryside.

DOC OR DOP?

More and more Italian food products in recent years have begun to bear the designation DOP instead of the usual DOC. DOP is a mark awarded by the EU, and stands for *denominazione di origine protetta* (protected designation of origin). All Italian DOC products are recognized as DOP, and the DOC mark continues to be a valid symbol.

COLOMBA PASQUALE

Pavia is the home of a version of panettone, the *columba pasquale*, that is baked in the stylized form of a dove. There is a story behind it, and if this is to be believed, we owe this specialty to a cruel king and twelve beautiful maidens.

Alboin, ruler of the Langobards, had long laid siege to the city of Pavia, and had at last taken it. It is said that he demanded not only the gold and treasure usually paid to the conqueror, but twelve beautiful maidens in addition. The maidens selected were in no doubt of the fate that awaited them and their virtue. They wept inconsolably – all but one, who refused to spend the last hours before her doom in anything as useless as weeping. She sent for honey, flour, and candied fruits, and baked a cake shaped rather like a dove. She then waited with the other maidens for her turn to be called to the royal chamber. When the moment arrived, she presented him with her cake. Filled with suspicion, probably expecting to be poisoned, he demanded that she eat some herself, which she gladly did. He then ventured to try some himself. Perhaps he was all too used to poor food; this cake, in contrast, was delicious, and he ate it all. As a mark of his appreciation, he granted the girl her freedom.

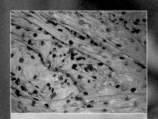

The basic mixture is a yeast dough with candied peel, raisins, and candied fruits.

The paper cake molds are only partly filled. They are baked in these molds.

The wrapper is kept on when the cake comes out of the oven.

PANETTONE

The first indications that a special type of bread was eaten on certain religious feast days – especially Christmas – come from the 11th century. These record how the whole family would gather around the decorated hearth on the feast day, and the head of the household would cut a large loaf. The crust was kept to one side, because it was said to have healing powers, especially for sore throats. This description of the large loaf and the customs associated with its use bears a close resemblance to the cake later to become known as panettone. The name comes from the Milanese dialect, which loves to attach diminutive – or magnifying – endings to words.

At the time of the Milanese Duke Ludovico il Moro (1452–1508), panettone was made just as it is today, as a tall coffeecake. It began as the traditional Christmas cake of Milan, soon endeared itself to the people of Lombardy, and spread to take an essential place on Christmas tables in the whole of Italy. It is now continuing its advance into other parts of Europe and perhaps beyond.

The cake is made from a yeast dough, to which candied citrus peel, raisins, and candied fruits are added. It is baked in paper molds, but only a little of the mixture is filled into each to allow for expansion during baking. It rises well above the top of the mold. It is not turned out of the paper mold once baked; instead, this is left on as a mark of identification, and also to prevent it from drying out.

Until very recently, workers right across industry, whether metalworkers on a huge site, employees of a smaller, specialist factory, or craftsmen in a small workshop, could be observed hurrying home shortly before Christmas with a panettone in one hand and a bottle of Spumante (more often than not a sweet muscat) in the other. These were the Christmas gifts of the factory owners to their workforce.

Another delightful custom associated with panettone has to do with the *panettone di San Biagio*. It is one still observed by many families in Milan, who keep one whole panettone until February 3, the saint's day of St. Blasius. Popular tradition has it that those who eat the stale panettone with its hard crust will be spared from sore throats during the year to come. Bad throats, it must be remembered, are no rarity during the cold, misty northern Italian winter.

SWEET CONFECTIONS

CREMA DI MASCARPONE
Mascarpone cream
(Illustration below)

3 EGGS
1/2 CUP/100 G SUPERFINE SUGAR
1/2 CUP/100 G MASCARPONE
1 SMALL GLASS OF RUM

Separate the eggs, and beat together the yolks and sugar in a bowl. Add the mascarpone, and beat in thoroughly with a balloon whisk. Flavor with rum. Whisk the egg whites until stiff, and fold into the mascarpone mixture. Transfer to dessert dishes, and leave for a few hours in the refrigerator to chill and become firm. Serve with shortbread biscuits.

ROSUMADA
Red wine with egg

4 EGG YOLKS
1/4 CUP/50 G SUPERFINE SUGAR
3–4 GLASSES OF RED WINE (BARBERA OR BARBARESCO)

Beat together the egg yolks and sugar in a bowl until light and frothy and almost white in color. Add the red wine gradually, continuing to beat with a balloon whisk. Pour the creamy mixture into attractive, robust glasses to serve. *Rosumada* is a typical Milanese drink, often taken during the morning or afternoon. In the summer, ice cold water or milk are often used instead of the wine.

SBRISOLONA
Almond cake

Serves 6–8

2 1/2 CUPS/300 G ALL-PURPOSE FLOUR
GENEROUS 3/4 CUP/100 G CORN (POLENTA) FLOUR
6 1/2 TBSP/100 G BUTTER
6 1/2 TBSP/100 G SHORTENING
GENEROUS 1 1/2 CUPS/200 G CHOPPED ALMONDS
1 CUP/200 G SUGAR
2 EGG YOLKS
GRATED ZEST OF 1 LEMON
A FEW DROPS OF VANILLA

Preheat the oven to 320 °F (160 °C). Sift both flours into a bowl. Mix and then knead in the butter and shortening. Add the finely chopped almonds and sugar and mix together. Add the egg yolks, lemon zest, and vanilla, and knead until smooth.
Place the mixture in a greased springform cake pan, smooth over the top, and bake for about 45 minutes. Leave to cool in the tin for about 10 minutes before turning out onto a cake rack. The cake can be kept for several days.
This cake is particularly popular in the province of Mantova. Its Italian name stems from the fact that it crumbles easily when cut (*sbriciolare* means to crumble).

Monte bianco
Chestnut purée with cream

Serves 6

1 1/4 LBS/600 G FRESH CHESTNUTS
2 CUPS/500 ML MILK
1 VANILLA BEAN
SCANT 1 CUP/100 G CONFECTIONERS' SUGAR
1/2 CUP/50 G COCOA
GENEROUS 1 TBSP RUM
3/4 CUP/200 ML WHIPPING CREAM

Preheat the oven to 480 °F (250 °C). Slit the skins of the chestnuts with a sharp knife and bake for about 20 minutes until the shells split open. Rinse briefly in cold water and remove the skins while still hot.
Place the chestnuts, milk, and slit vanilla bean in a saucepan and boil until tender (about 45 minutes). The milk will be almost completely absorbed.
Take out the vanilla bean, and purée the chestnuts. Add the confectioners' sugar, cocoa, and rum, and blend in until smooth.
Whip the cream stiffly. Serve the purée in dessert dishes, topped with cream.

Left above and below: Panettone tastes best when really fresh. The Marchesi bar and *pasticceria* in Milan serves excellent panettone. It is as delicious for breakfast as eaten in the afternoon with a glass of Spumante. The usual way to eat this cake is to break off pieces by hand.

THE LOMELLINA PLAIN

About 19 miles (30 kilometers) south of Milan, between the rivers Po, Ticino, and Sesia, stretches the flat expanse of the Lomellina plain. This area, once nothing but marshland, is the grain and rice field of Italy. Land reclamation by monks around the year 1000 gradually made it cultivable, and rice began to be imported from Spain in the 15th century. The design of the irrigation system for the rice fields is attributed by some to Leonardo da Vinci.

The Lomellina plain is also a center for salami production. The pig industry developed here in tandem with the manufacture of cheese – Grana Padano and Gorgonzola – since the byproducts could be used to feed the pigs. Among the agricultural workers, piglets were in effect a unit of currency, and this enabled them to build up their own breeding herds of pigs. Slaughter day brought a midday meal of pork and onions on a bed of polenta, and an evening feast of pork ribs, salami, risotto, cabbage, and trotters. Sausages of various sorts were made and preserved in fat for months, to be eaten at pre-ordained times. Kidneys were eaten with truffles, and loin hung for a week before being braised in good wine – wine that was also used in making the sausages.

Beef is also widely enjoyed here. It is usually stewed or braised as a ragout. Organ meat (referred to as the "fifth quarter" of the animal) is much in demand. Other meats that often feature in the cuisine of this area are eels and frogs, which frequent the flooded rice fields. Eel in red wine, and eel cooked in the fire in an earthenware pot with parsley and lemon, are both specialties of the region.

OCA FARCITA
Stuffed goose

Serves 6–8

1 CUP/100 G PITTED PRUNES
1 CLEANED, OVEN-READY GOOSE (ABOUT 7–9 LBS/3–4 KG)
GENEROUS 1/2 LB/300 G SALSICCE
2 APPLES (PREFERABLY RENETTE)
2 CUPS/200 G ROASTED, PEELED CHESTNUTS
10 BLANCHED FILBERTS
SCANT 1/2 LB/200 G BACON OR HAM
4 TSP/20 G BUTTER
STOCK OR WATER

Soak the prunes in lukewarm water for half a day. Rinse the goose, and remove the breastbone to make the bird easier to stuff. Preheat the oven to 400 °F (200 °C). Coarsely chop the sausage, apples, chestnuts, prunes, and filberts, and mix by hand. Stuff the goose with the mixture, and sew up the opening with kitchen thread. Lay slices of bacon or ham over the goose, place in a roasting pan, and roast for about 3 hours, turning occasionally, and basting with hot stock or water as necessary.

Right: The Lomellina plain is the center of goose breeding in Italy. Some restaurants offer menus exclusively made up of goose dishes – even the desserts.

Geese cannot be kept indoors like chickens. The farmer must ensure that the birds have sufficient meadowland at their disposal to give them the freedom they need.

THE RISTORANTE

Good home cooking is highly valued in Italy, but it is becoming increasingly fashionable to eat out in restaurants – no more so than in the prosperous cities of the north. Many women in the regions here go out to work, and no longer see the care of the children, the home, and the cooking as their only role. When the industrious men and women of Lombardy return home to find no miraculously produced meal waiting on the table, there is always the restaurant on the corner. Likewise, when a special occasion calls for a celebration, it is to a carefully chosen restaurant – one noted for its good food, or discovered by means of previous visits and "test meals" – that people invite their friends and relations.

In the south of Italy, matters are rather different. Many generations of the same family still usually live together, and if *mamma* has no time to go to the market, *nonna* (the grandmother) will go instead. It is still *nonna* who knows the best recipes and practical cooking tips, and passes them on to the next generation. Celebrations are family occasions, and in the south, this takes place at home. People visit each other, and enjoy a feast together, which may sometimes continue for days.

A visit to a restaurant in Italy requires time. A meal consisting of a single, quickly-consumed course, perhaps followed by a dessert, is largely unknown. Instead, there is a dinner of at least four courses: *antipasto, primo piatto, secondo piatto,* and *dolce* – that is, hors d'oeuvres, first course, second course, and dessert. The meal may be extended by inserting further courses in between these.

It is best to ask the advice of the waiter or wine waiter about the choice of wine. It does not necessarily need to be a bottle, as many Italian restaurants have good regional house wines available by the glass or carafe, which may provide a delicious insight into the wine culture of the area.

The *antipasto* usually consists of smaller items to stimulate the appetite and accompany the aperitif. The popularity of the traditional Italian plate of such delicacies as stuffed mushrooms, preserved or cooked vegetables, juicy olives, sausage and cold meats, called *antipasto misto*, is as great as ever, varying according to taste and season. Restaurant guests can often select their own from a glass counter; elsewhere, the waiter may bring an *antipasto* trolley to the table. On the coast, this course often consists of seafood, *antipasto misto di mare*. It is a mixture of very fresh shellfish and crustaceans in a simple dressing of oil and lemon juice.

The *primo*, or first course, is usually a pasta or rice dish. Half portions can be ordered if an entire plate of spaghetti seems too daunting.

Il secondo, the second course, consists of meat or fish. This is served alone on the plate, apart from the garnish, so it is normal to order an accompaniment, called *contorno*. This is usually lightly cooked vegetables, and, in the north, polenta.

Finally comes the sweet dessert. A selection of cheeses or fresh fruit in season may be offered as an

alternative. Italy has some wonderful regional sweet dishes, so sampling them is particularly recommended if at all possible.

A little help with digestion is welcome following all these delights, and a number of digestive drinks exist – all claimed by their adherents to be most beneficial to the stomach. In the north, a good measure of grappa is usual; traveling south, the choice changes to liquor made with herbs. An espresso is often taken to round off the meal.

Hors d'oeuvres
Usually cold regional delicacies. These are eaten to stimulate the appetite and prepare the palate for the courses to come.

First course dishes
The *primo* almost always consists of pasta, rice, or gnocchi. The intention is the satisfy hunger and set the eater at ease to enjoy the main course.

Fish main courses
For the main course, there is a choice between fish and meat. The two categories are listed separately. The waiter or innkeeper often advises the customer about the options, especially any freshly arrived ingredients. Smaller portions are served if the fish is to be eaten as an additional course before a meat dish.

Meat main courses
Italian menus are often negotiable. If the customer would like the food prepared differently from the options listed, it is possible to consult the waiter about alternatives. The customer's wishes are often met. Meat may be served as the sole main course, or to follow a fish course.

Extras
Complete meals with vegetables are not served in Italy: the fish or meat arrives without any accompaniments, and these are ordered separately.

MENU

Antipasti

Bresaola condita	L. 18.000
Insalata frutti di mare	L. 15.000
Insalata Caprese	L. 13.000
Vitello tonnato	L. 18.000

Primi Piatti

Spaghetti alla trapanese	L. 19.000
Penne all'arrabbiata	L. 15.000
Pappardelle sulla lepre	L. 20.000
Gnocchi con la ricotta	L. 18.000
Risotto nero	L. 18.000

Secondi di Pesce

Baccalá alla vicentina	L. 28.000
Filetti di lavarello in carpione	L. 36.000
Involtini di pesce spada	L. 32.000
Triglie in cartoccio	L. 30.000
Calamari ripieni in teglia	L. 32.000

Secondi di Carne

Cinghiale alla cacciatora	L. 32.000
Scaloppine al limone	L. 33.000
Bue brasato al Barolo	L. 34.000
Saltimbocca alla romana	L. 33.000
Coniglio con olive taggiasche	L. 34.000

Contorni

Radicchio al forno	L. 10.000
Melanzane alla menta	L. 8.000
Puntarelle in salsa di alici	L. 8.000
Insalata mista	L. 7.000

A DAY
IN THE LIFE
OF A CHEF

A strict hierarchy exists in the upper echelons of gastronomy. The regular cooks in the bottom ranks have immediately over them the *demi-chef de partie* and *chef de partie* (senior chefs). They in turn are under the authority of the *sous-chef* (deputy kitchen chef), and above them is the *chef de cuisine* (kitchen chef), or catering manager of a large establishment.

The kitchen chef is the unquestioned authority in the kitchen domain. Only the chef or deputy chef (if the chef is absent) has the right to taste the food and make any decision to adjust the seasoning. On the other hand, it is only the combined skill of the entire team that enables a kitchen chef to reach the highest ranks of international gastronomy, however versatile and gifted that chef may be. Unless the staff includes specialist buyers, the chef's day begins extremely early, with a visit to the vegetable or fishmarkets around three or four in the morning to select the ingredients for the day. During the course of the morning, goods ordered the previous day are delivered. All orders are prefaced by the negotiation of prices and the calculation of the quantities required. Does the chef need a haunch of venison for 20 evening guests, or for a party of 60 businessmen? As the goods arrive, the chef inspects them and checks the quality. Meat and dairy products must be genuinely fresh, and the prices and quantities must tally with the order. The next stage is to discuss the forthcoming menu, and to establish with the service personnel whether there are any guests with special requirements to be catered for. Between eleven and half past, the preliminary cooking begins. Sauces are prepared, and meat put into the roasting ovens. The chef takes part in the preparation, samples the food, and above all, coordinates activities. There is a break after the work of lunch is done.

The chef goes into the restaurant to check that all is in order. In the afternoon, the preparations for the evening are made.

The chef is also responsible for drawing up new menus. This includes decisions about prices and suitable wines to accompany the food. Stocks of drinks, foodstuffs, and kitchen equipment must be maintained. The chef also has the final authority in staffing decisions within the kitchen domain, draws up work rotas, and decides who shall and shall not be allowed to cook in that kitchen.

Below: Complete concentration in the kitchen of Antonio Marangi, chef of the Milanese restaurant Giannino.

GEESE

Ludovico Sforza, called il Moro, Duke of Milan (1452–1508), was not only the patron of Bramante and Leonardo and active in the building of the castle; he was concerned with the problems of agriculture in his territory. He established basic conditions to promote the breeding of geese on the Lomellina plain with the consent and active support he gave to the founding of a Jewish settlement near Mortara. Since the Jews are forbidden to eat pork, but geese were declared to be kosher, these proved an ideal food solution.

With geese (as with pigs) all parts of the creature can be used. The feathers are useful to stuff pillows, their fat as a fine cooking ingredient, their meat is delicious and nourishing, and the livers can be made into pâté. The conditions for keeping them are also similar to those needed for pigs.

From the point of view of cooking, goose is handled much like duck. Goose must always be cooked right through, on account of the high fat content. This fat content gives it the reputation of being heavy and difficult to digest, but the slur is undeserved: goose can be wonderfully light and tender if the fat is properly removed during the cooking process.

Geese on the Lomellina today are bred mainly for their livers. In France, the rich livers of fatted geese, known there as *foie gras*, have always been an acknowledged delicacy; this is being rediscovered in Italy. There are further specialties too, such as a delicious goose salami from Mortara. *Salame d'oca* is made with a mixture of goose meat and fat, with the skin of the neck as the casing.

Like turkey and capon, goose is frequently eaten at Christmas. It may either be roasted whole or jointed and braised.

PETTO D'OCA IN CRESCIONE
Goose breast with watercress
(Illustration below)

1/3 CUP/40 G GOLDEN RAISINS
1/2 GLASS OF BRANDY
2 TBSP/30 ML OLIVE OIL
1/2 BREAST OF GOOSE (ABOUT 1 LB/400 G)
2 CUPS/500 ML VEGETABLE STOCK
4 BUNCHES OF WATERCRESS
1 TSP BALSAMIC VINEGAR
SALT
SEEDS OF 1 POMEGRANATE
SCANT 1/4 CUP/20 G ROASTED PINE NUTS

Soak the golden raisins in brandy for about 3 hours. Preheat the oven to 350 °F (180 °C). Heat the oil in a casserole, and brown the meat on all sides. Pour on the stock, cover, and transfer to the oven to cook. Top up as necessary to ensure that the meat is always one-third covered by the stock. As soon as the goose is cooked, but still slightly pink in the middle, it is ready. The temperature in the center should be 146 °F (63 °C) when measured with a meat thermometer. Wash the watercress and pat dry. Make a dressing by whisking together olive oil and balsamic vinegar, and a little salt. Arrange the cress on plates to serve, and sprinkle with half the dressing.

Slice the goose and lay it on top of the cress while lukewarm. Scatter with golden raisins, pomegranate seeds, and pine nuts, and sprinkle on the remaining dressing.

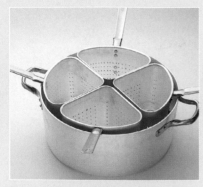

Separator pan (casseruola con 4 cola-pasta a spicchio e coperchio)
For boiling different types of pasta with different cooking times.

Sauté pan (sauté a sponda dritta)
Food inside is kept constantly moving by circular, controlled agitation of the pan. This cooks it evenly and preserves flavor.

Spaghetti saucepan (pentola cilindrica)
For boiling all pasta with a long noodle shape, *bucatini* and *trenette* as well as spaghetti. Also for making stock.

Colander (colapasta sferica 3 piedi)
A freestanding steel colander for draining pasta is more hygienic. Plastic softens and distorts with heat over time.

Non-stick roasting/broiling pan (rostiera antiaderente)
Ideal for oven cooking of meat and vegetable dishes.

Couscous pot (pentola per cous cous)
Used in Sicily and the Sardinian island of Carloforte for the Arab-Sicilian dish *cusucusu* and the Tunisian *cashka*.

Frying and gratin dish (tegame svasato a 2 manici)
For frying small fish, omelets, and foods requiring short cooking times.

Shallow saucepan (casseruola bassa)
Useful for pot-roasting, involving long, slow cooking.

Perforated insert for pasta pot (scalda-pasta a 1 manico con fondo piano)
Enables cooked pasta to be lifted free of the water.

Handled saucepan (casseruola fonda a 1 manico)
For making sauces, cooking polenta, or use as steamer base.

Saucepan (casseruola fonda a 2 manici)
Versatile saucepan for making stock, boiling, braising, and pot-roasting meat.

Nonstick skillet (padella antiaderente)
For low-fat frying on a high heat. Also for sautéing cooked vegetables in olive oil and garlic.

Skillet (padella a sponda obliqua medio peso)
Stainless steel or copper make the best pans.

Fish kettle (romboniera con griglia e coperchio)
This type is for cooking turbot.

Fish kettle (romboniera con griglia e coperchio)
Note the inner steaming platform on which the fish rests.

Deep fryer (padella per fritto alta con paniere)
The frying basket allows fried food to drain.

THE GONZAGAS OF MANTUA

The Gonzaga family had already been rulers of Mantua since the early 14th century. It was not a particularly prosperous region, though it provided an adequate living. The family remained self-contained, little concerned with its neighbors, until the cities of the Renaissance began to flourish, and the Gonzagas started to consider how they in their palace at Mantua could raise their standing with the outside world. They were a family of ancient nobility, but had never enjoyed great riches. A "PR strategy" was called for! The court eventually turned its attention to the cultural approach being developed by Lorenzo il Magnifico in the Tuscan city of Florence. There, the ambassadors of foreign courts and influential merchants received their impression of the city's importance through the artistic and architectural splendors that surrounded them. Around 1470, the Gonzagas acquired the services of the universally acclaimed and innovative painter, Andrea Mantegna (1431–1506). This is the first instance in history of an artist being engaged by a prince, and paid a princely salary to work exclusively for the court.

Above: Andrea Mantegna, Ceiling fresco in the *Camera degli Sposi* with heads of women and putti, 1465–1474, Palazzo Ducale, Mantua.

FAREWELL TO THE MIDDLE AGES

Renaissance effects on Italian cooking are closely linked to the names of two men: Maestro Martino of Como and Bartolomeo Sacchi, called Platina, from Piadena which is near Cremona.

Maestro Martino was personal cook to the bishop of Aquileia at the beginning of the 15th century. He wrote a book called *Liber de arte coquinaria* (On the art of cooking). Bartolomeo Sacchi, called Platina, born 1421, began his career at the court of the Gonzagas. He later spent a few years in Florence, before moving on to Rome, where he took up a post as secretary and scribe at the papal court of Pius II. He was promoted to become the first librarian in charge of the Vatican library when Sixtus IV became pope. Platina put together a compendium on the lives of the popes, but also took an interest in texts about less spiritual and more earthly matters. In this way, he came across Maestro Martino's cookbook. He translated and slightly edited it, and prefaced it with a few chapters of his own. The title was *De honesta voluptate et valetudine* (On honest pleasure and health). The book was published in Rome in 1474, and became in effect the very first bestseller in cooking literature. Language was no barrier to its spread, as Latin was a universal language, and it became known as a culinary classic far beyond Italy. Within a hundred years, it had been reprinted over 30 times, and it was freely translated into other languages, including Italian, French, English, and German.

The book's enduring success can be attributed to the fact that it attempts for the first time to present the culinary and gastronomic knowledge of the second half of the 15th century in a comprehensive and systematic way. This is no mere list of practical instructions on kitchen techniques; the book covers all aspects of cuisine. Dietetics and food hygiene feature in it, and there are useful tips about the composition of certain food products, their nutritional value, and their medicinal uses. The book discusses the ethical aspect of nutrition and the joys of the table. This was a book designed for the middle and higher sections of society, with the moral and intellectual capacity to understand such matters. Taken as a whole, it is a plea for a revolution in taste. People should henceforward, in "the unimportant provision of nourishment," aim for the satisfaction of "the pleasure that comes from honest activity." This, it argues, is the satisfaction that leads to happiness, "just as medicine gives the sick man back his health."

The achievements of Maestro Martino and Platina spelled the end of medieval cuisine, and ushered in a new era. The taste of the Middle Ages was for all that was rare and expensive and able to demonstrate the wealth of the host. Costly spices were used in such great quantity that guests could hardly identify the food at all on first tasting it. This may have been no bad thing, as the food itself was chosen for its rarity value. A dinner of tough eagles or venerable bears emphasized the prestige of the host, but the meat had to be precooked for hours before preparation, and swamped in thick sauces afterwards, simply to make it edible. "Modern" cuisine as promoted by Maestro Martino and Platina placed the emphasis on the use of simple, fresh, widely available ingredients, and on bringing out the true flavors by means of short cooking times, not rendering them ineffective with heavy-handed seasoning. These are the principles that guide Italian cuisine to this day.

BISCOTTI – COOKIES

Biscotti feature prominently on the Italian culinary scene. Every region has its own varieties, shapes, bakers, and, occasionally, factories. The annual production of *tenerezze, mattutini, gocciole,* and other cookies by companies such as Mulino Bianco and Varesi (both part of the Barilla Group) is measured in tons. The basic mix can be variously of the biscuit, yeast, or shortbread type, with or without egg, sweetened with sugar or with honey; it may contain cocoa or chocolate, have a jam or cream filling, or include almonds, filberts, or dried fruit. Cookies are mainly eaten at breakfast in Italy, where it is the custom to eat cake or to dunk one or two *biscotti* into hot milky coffee, or *caffè latte* as it is known there.

LAZZARONI AND AMARETTI

A great variety of different types of amaretti and the smaller amarettini can be found, from the tiny, hard cookies to the large and succulent macaroons with their rounded tops. An espresso ordered in a northern Italian bar will usually arrive accompanied by a cookie of this kind, a special pleasure if it is one of the original Amaretti di Saronno. Amaretti from the town of Mombaruzzo in Piedmont are another type considered to be particularly delicious. They are wrapped by hand in colored paper, like pieces of candy.

The history of amaretti stretches back to the end of the 18th century, to the time when coffeehouses were becoming increasingly popular, and were often meeting places for men of ideas – the scene of lively debate between artists, scholars, and the proponents of various contemporary political causes. Some of the coffeehouses in Milan belonged to the Lazzaroni family. Carlo Lazzaroni (1774–1835), founder of the Amaretti di Saronno dynasty, gradually bought up small bakeries in his home town of Saronno, which had been making almond macaroons for generations, and began to sell their products in his coffeehouses in Milan. His son, Davide (1808–1879), decided to abandon using the small bakeries for production, and built the first cookie factory in Lazzaroni. Here, he manufactured not only the family's established product, amaretti, but also cookies made with an egg-enriched mixture, and panettone. The succeeding generation, the brothers Giacinto, Ernesto, and Piero, founded the company of Davide Lazzaroni & C., but overreached themselves with the construction of a new factory. They were obliged to turn to their cousin, Luigi (1847–1933), to save them from bankruptcy. He was at that time already a successful manufacturer of liqueurs and candied fruits in Monza, so had the means to stage a rescue. Under Luigi's management, the company of Lazzaroni grew into a solid presence in the Italian food industry. He even succeeded in beating back competition from British imports, then dominant in the cookie market. He extended the company's product range, and made attempts to expand exports into Europe north of the Alps. He had to battle against setbacks and disasters, including two factory fires (in 1898 and 1911) and the economic crisis of World War I. Following Luigi's death in 1933, he was succeeded by his sons, Paolo and Mario. They too remained faithful to the family philosophy of making sure only the highest quality goods left the factory, and that the cookies must be packed and presented accordingly. This approach led to the introduction of the beautifully designed tins of the 1920s and 1930s, which have become valuable collectors' items.

Pannocchie

Cinfalotti

Pan di Stelle

Gran Cereale

Primi Raggi

Mattutini

Spicchi di Sol

109

VIRTUOSO DELIGHTS OF CREMONA

The city of Cremona, an important inland port on the River Po, is of course memorable for its contributions in the sphere of music. Antonio Stradivarius, who gave the world his universally famous violins, was a son of Cremona. It has also bestowed the gift of two culinary specialties: *torrone*, a sweet and sometimes sticky candy made of honey and almonds, and a combination of candied fruits in hot mustard, called *mostarda*. Cremona's claim to be the originator of *torrone* does not stand up to scrutiny, however.

TORRONE

The invention of *torrone* is often said to go back to 1441, to the marriage of Bianca Maria Visconti and Francesco Sforza in Cremona. The account claims that, on October 25 of that year, the town's confectioners made an enormous cake of honey and almonds for the wedding breakfast. The cake was in the form of the *torrazzo*, the tall tower on the city's main square. The banquet was held in that very square, which meant that the cake was doubly impressive, because the diners could compare it with the original.

Farther back in time, the Romans used to eat a cake of honey and almonds as a finale to their dinners. There is another early record of this candy dating from the period between 1100 and 1150. A certain Gherardo, citizen of Cremona, was translating a book by a medical doctor, Abdul Mutarrif, whose practice was in Córdoba, Spain. In this work, *De medicinis et cibis simplicibus*, the scholar not only praised the beneficial properties of honey, but spoke of an Arab sweetmeat called *turun*. It seems more likely that this, rather than the *torrazzo* of Cremona, is the true origin of the name *torrone*. Nevertheless, Cremona does produce an extremely delicious *torrone*.

MOSTARDA

The Italian word *mostarda* comes from the French *moutarde* (mustard). This in turn comes from *mour ardent* (hot juice). It used to be the practice to mix mustard seed with grape juice to create a hot seasoning. *Mostarda di Cremona* consists of candied fruits such as cherries, figs, and pears, preserved in a mixture of sugar syrup and white mustard. The result is a highly piquant accompaniment for boiled meat, game, or poultry.

Today, *mostarda di Cremona* is mainly commercially produced. The factories do not use candied fruits, but a stewed fruit mixture that is mixed with mustard sauce. The piquancy of the mustard has been considerably reduced to meet the demands of customers' palates. As with other commercially made mustard products, the flavors and aromas are always best when the *mostarda* is freshly opened, not after it has been kept for any length of time.

Mostarda di Cremona is a piquant accompaniment to other dishes. Tuscany has a similar specialty, called *mostarda all'uso toscano*.

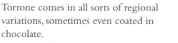

Torrone comes in all sorts of regional variations, sometimes even coated in chocolate.

The imposing campanile and cathedral with its surrounding towers is one of the most famous and impressive sights of Cremona.

Long fish kettle with steaming platform (pesciera con griglia e coperchio)
For poaching or steaming whole, long fish.

Fine-mesh chinois or tammy strainer (chinois a maglia fine)
Conical strainer for soups and sauces at the end of preparation.

Fine-mesh bowl strainer (colino semi-sferico a rete fina)
Sieve for stocks, soups, and sauces.

Flat perforated spoon (schiumarola a rete fine)
Fine-mesh version for lifting and draining a range of deep-fried food, such as vegetables, mozzarella fritters, and fish.

Ladle (mestolo fondo)
For stirring and serving soups cleanly and without drips.

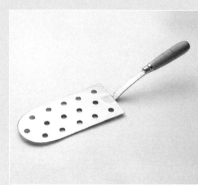

Fish slice (paletta con fori per pesce)
This slotted lifting spatula keeps the fish whole and allows cooking liquid to drain.

Cooking fork (forchettone unipezzo a 2 denti)
For turning roasts and holding meat in place while carving.

Basting spoon (cucchiaione fondo)
A versatile utensil. Useful when making *quenelles*, which are shaped between two oiled spoons.

Perforated spoon (schiumarola)
Has many uses. Can be used to lift cooked gnocchi individually out of the water.

Spatula (palettina senza fori)
Useful for lifting food out of baking dishes without crumbling.

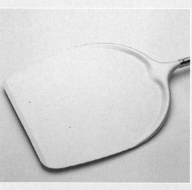

Wooden pizza lifter (pala piatta rettangolare per pizza)
A large, flat, wooden scoop with a handle for reaching into deep pizza ovens.

Mandoline grater (tagliaverdure a mandolino)
For grating vegetables quickly by hand.

Waffle iron (tostatore in alluminio per gauffres e cialde)
For *cialde alla fiorentina* and *brigidini*.

Hand molds for pastry shapes (stampo per crostatine in lega di ottone)

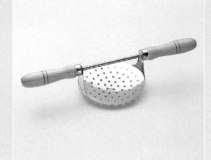

Stamper (stampo per passatelli)
The *passatelli* can be pressed straight into the stock beneath.

Chestnut roaster (padella per castagne)
For dry-roasting chestnuts.

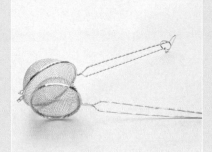

Mesh ladle for nest pasta (paniere per nidi, filostagno)
May be used for preparing nests of tagliatelle, for example.

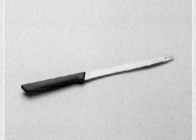

Citrus knife (tagliamino)
A long, thin, serrated knife for cutting lemons. The forked point can be used to lift individual slices.

Nutmeg and lemon zest grater (grattugia per noce moscata e buccia di limone)
Many recipes call for grated nutmeg.

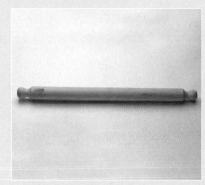

Rolling pin (mattarello)
Used mainly in the preparation of fresh pasta (*pasta fresca*) and the dough for tortellini, ravioli, *quadrucci*, and tagliatelle.

Mortar (mortaio in marmo)
It is better to use a pestle and mortar to make pesto, because the metal blades of food mixers discolor the basil.

Meat grinder (tritacarne)
Ground meat hamburgers or *polpette* and meat balls of all sorts are popular in Italy too.

Mixing bowl (bacinella bombata)
Useful for whisking egg white or cream, and for puréeing fruit.

Lemon press (spremi spicchi per agrumi)
Allows juice to be squeezed over meat and fish without soiling the hands.

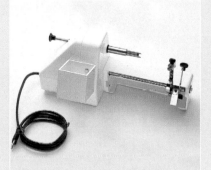

Apple peeler (pela e affetta mele "Kali")
Peels and cores apples neatly in an instant.

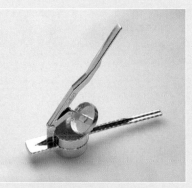

Potato ricer (schiacciapatate professionale)
For crushing boiled potatoes, as when making gnocchi.

Flour scoop (paletta per la farina)
Flour is in constant use in the Italian kitchen, and does not stick to a wooden scoop.

Tomato slicer (affettapomodori "Econo pro")
Instantly cuts tomatoes into even slices.

Spaghetti tongs (molla per spaghetti)
Lifts and serves spaghetti cleanly and easily.

Snail tongs (molla per lumache)
Used to hold the snail and keep the hands clean.

Fish scaling knife (squamapesce)
For removing the scales from fish.

Balloon whisk (frusta)
For whisking egg whites, beating sauces and gravies, and preventing lumps.

Dolci

Macedonia di frutta	L. 10.000
Tiramisù	L. 8.000
Zuppa Inglese	L. 9.000
Frutta varia di stagione	

Formaggi

Ricotta fresca	L. 9.000
Selezione di formaggi	L. 12.000

Vini

Rosso della casa $^1/_2$ lt	L. 4.000
$^1/_4$ lt	L. 2.000
Bianco della casa $^1/_2$ lt	L. 4.000
$^1/_4$ lt	L. 2.000

Bibite

Acqua naturale $^1/_2$ lt	L. 1.000
Acqua gassata $^1/_2$ lt	L. 1.500
Coca Cola 33 cl	L. 3.000

Birre

Nastro Azzurro 33 cl	L. 4.000
Heineken 33 cl	L. 5.000

Digestivi

Grappa	L. 5.000
Amaro	L. 5.000
Coperto e servizio	L. 3.000

Sweet desserts
The meal ends with a sweet dessert or piece of fruit in season (*frutta varia di stagione*), or fruit salad (*macedonia di frutta*).

Cheese
Another popular end to the meal is cheese. The cheese board (*selezione di formaggi*) usually consists of regional specialties, and may feature some new discoveries that are not available in the stores.

Wine
The house wines of many Italian restaurants can be heartily recommended, as these are often good regional wines, and may be more enjoyable than the bottled ones.

Soft drinks
Mineral waters and internationally known soft drinks appear on all Italian menus. The waiter will ask "naturale o gassata?" if mineral water is ordered. This means "still or fizzy?"

Beer
The beers offered usually include some international ones and one or two local varieties. If the quantity is given as 33 cl, bottled beer is meant. Draft beer comes in multiples of 100 centiliters – the choice here is between *birra piccola* (0.2 liters, or just under ½ pint), *media* (0.3–0.4 liters, roughly ½–¾ pint), and *grande* (up to 1 liter, or about 2 pints).

Digestifs
The choice of alcoholic aids to digestion includes marc (*grappa*), anis (*sambuca, mistrà, sassolino, etc.*), regional bitters (*amaro*), and various liquors based on herbs (*centerbe, genepy*).

Cover and service charge
In some restaurants, the prices charged for the food itself exclude the cost of the service and basic table items such as oil and vinegar, bread, olives to nibble while waiting, provision of cutlery, and the like. The service charge (*coperto e servizio*) is levied to take account of these. Other restaurants charge inclusive prices for the food. If the menu does not make clear which is being done, the best solution is to ask the waiter. Even if service is included, the staff are always happy to receive a tip from satisfied customers. The amount is usually five to ten percent of the total bill, though up to 15 percent might be given if service is exceptional.

Michelangelo Buonarotti, *Three lists of foods*, pencil, 21.3 x 14.5 cm, Archivio Buonarotti, Florence.

The Italian menu

In many restaurants, a menu exists, yet the customers hardly look at it. It seems puzzling that anyone bothered to write it. Instead, guests consult the menu of the day, or seek the advice of the waiter or innkeeper. This is regarded as a more reliable way of finding out the best dishes to choose. The freshest options of the day are usually chalked up on a slate, reasonably legibly and interspersed with dialect terms. No-one need hesitate to ask if the information is not clear: extensive discussion with the staff is all part of the accepted proceedings when visiting a restaurant, and some restaurants even dispense with a written menu altogether. Instead, the waiter arrives at the table and lists what is available. Sometimes, the chef will also offer the customers advice at the table, or ask what they would like. Those from outside the area can ask for a description of the regional specialties. The different terms and culinary traditions of the Italian regions make this a necessity, and no customer should feel embarrassed about asking what ingredients or methods of preparation are involved. This will not be seen as indicating a lack of confidence in the cook, but as the guest's natural interest in ensuring an enjoyable evening. If the dishes described do not appeal, it is still no problem. The customers can describe what they want, and can even ask the kitchen whether the necessary ingredients are available. They can say how they would like these prepared: would they like their spinach with onions and garlic, or without? Do they enjoy piquant food, or do they dislike *peperoncini*? These details are matters the cook cannot know, and are not seen as awkwardness on the part of the customers, simply as indications to help ensure satisfaction.

A BRIEF GUIDE TO MENU TERMS

al forno: oven-baked	*brasato:* braised	*in agro:* in lemon or vinegar
alla casalinga: housewife style	*con aglio:* with garlic	*in agro-dolce:* sweet and sour
alla griglia: broiled	*con cipolla:* with onion	*in brodo:* in stock
all'uovo: with egg	*con latte:* with milk	*in marinata:* marinated
al pomodoro: with tomatoes	*con limone:* with lemon	*in padella:* pan-fried
arrabbiato: piquant; with *peperoncini*	*con olio:* with oil	*in umido:* braised or poached in a gravy or sauce
arrosto: roast	*con panna:* with cream	*magro:* lean
bollito: boiled	*cotto:* cooked	*ripieno:* stuffed
	crudo: raw	*sott'aceto:* preserved in vinegar
	fritto: fried	*sott'olio:* preserved in oil
	gratinato: topped with toasted cheese	

BARTOLOMEO STEFANI

A native of Bologna, Bartolomeo Stefani was the kitchen chef at the court of the Gonzagas in Mantua in the second half of the 17th century. The exact dates of his birth and death are not known, but the preface of his book, *L'arte di ben cucinare* (The art of good cooking), seems to indicate that he was the nephew and pupil of Giulio Cesare Tirelli, kitchen chef in the services of the Republic of Venice.

L'arte di ben cucinare is firmly rooted in the traditions of Italian cuisine, and keeps the promise stated in its title. It is also the first cookbook to pay attention to the everyday dishes, *vitto ordinario*, eaten by people of the middle classes, rather than to the feasts of the ruling elite. It is an innovative work in other ways, too: Bartolomeo Stefani not only proposes alternatives to the princely banquets, but deals so minutely with the details that he even offers estimates of the cost of ingredients. The first edition of this work appeared in 1662 in Mantua. This was followed by seven further editions, which continued to appear until 1716.

L'ARTE
DI BEN CVCINARE, ET INSTRVIRE
i men periti in questa lodeuole professione.
Doue anco s'insegna à far Pasticci, Sapori, Salse, Gelatine, Torte, & altro
DI BARTOLOMEO STEFANI
Cuoco Bolognese.
All'Ill.mo, & Ecc.mo Sig. Marchese
OTTAVIO GONZAGA
Prencipe del Sacro Romano Imperio, de'Marchesi
di Mantoua, e Signor di Vescouato, &c.

IN MANTOVA, Appresso gli Osanna, Stampatori Ducali. 1662,
Con licenza de' Superiori,

TORTELLI DI ZUCCA
Pasta with pumpkin filling
(Illustration in background)

Serves 6

1 PUMPKIN (ABOUT 5 LB/2 KG IN WEIGHT)
1 1/2 CUPS/150 G CRUSHED AMARETTI
SCANT 1/2 CUP/50 G SWEET AND SOUR PRESERVED APPLES
OR OTHER FRUITS PRESERVED IN MUSTARD (MOSTARDA)
1 CUP/100 G FRESHLY GRATED PARMESAN
1/4 ONION, CHOPPED
GRATED NUTMEG
PASTA DOUGH (SEE PAGE 191)
SALT
2 TBSP BUTTER

Slice the pumpkin, then peel it and remove the center. Bake it for about 20 minutes at 400 °F (200 °C). Transfer to a bowl and crush the cooked pumpkin with a fork. Chop the mustard fruits and add to the pumpkin, with the crushed amaretti, grated Parmesan, chopped onion, and a little grated nutmeg. Stir together using a wooden spoon, and ensure that the mixture is dry. Roll out the pasta dough thinly, and cut into rectangles 1½ inches/4 cm by 3 inches/8 cm. Place a spoonful of filling on each piece, and fold the pasta over in the middle to enclose the filling. Press the edges together firmly. Cook the *tortelli* in plenty of boiling salted water, and serve with melted butter.

FRESHWATER FISH

Lombardy is a land of abundant lakes and rivers. Tourists swarm to Lago d'Iseo, Lago d'Idro, Lago di Varese and Lake Como, but these lakes are also valuable as a source of freshwater fish. Demand exceeds the naturally available supply, so fish farming is now well established. In the province of Brescia, there is a fish farm that breeds not only the usual freshwater fish, such as salmon trout and rainbow trout, but also has tanks for eels. It even farms sturgeon, and produces small quantities of fine caviar. Environmental problems have all but destroyed the northern Italian sturgeon in the wild, although they did once frequent the River Po and its delta.

FILETTI DI LAVARELLO IN CARPIONE
Marinated whitefish
(Illustration left)

2 ONIONS
2 CARROTS
3–4 TBSP EXTRA VIRGIN OLIVE OIL
I BAY LEAF
I SPRIG OF PARSLEY
I GLASS OF WHITE WINE VINEGAR
SALT AND PEPPER
8 WHITEFISH FILLETS, PREPARED

Chop the onions very finely, and thinly slice the carrots. Cook them gently in a little olive oil. Add the bay leaf, parsley, wine vinegar, remaining olive oil, and a glass of water. Season with salt and pepper, and simmer until the liquid has been reduced by half.
Wash the whitefish fillets, season with salt and pepper, and place in a heatproof casserole. Cover with the marinade, and cook for a few minutes. Cool and leave to marinate for at least 12 hours in the refrigerator.
Other fish, such as carp, tench, and common whitefish can be prepared in the same way. It is important to use very high quality vinegar, for flavor and for keeping qualities.

FILETTI DI TROTA IN COTOLETTA
Trout in breadcrumbs

4 TROUT FILLETS
I CUP/250 ML MILK
SALT
SCANT I/2 CUP/50 G ALL-PURPOSE FLOUR
I EGG
BREADCRUMBS
3–4 TBSP EXTRA VIRGIN OLIVE OIL
A FEW SLICES OF LEMON
PARSLEY

Wash and clean the trout fillets, and marinate in salted milk for 1 hour. Pour off the milk, and pat the fish dry. Beat the egg. Coat the fish lightly in flour, then in beaten egg, and finally in the breadcrumbs.
Heat the olive oil in a skillet, and fry the fish until golden. Drain on paper towels. Garnish with lemon slices and parsley to serve.

Trota (Trout)
Rainbow trout, salmon trout, and brook trout all live in the waters of Lombardy. These delicious freshwater fish are much in demand, and farmed in large numbers, though there are few trout left in the wild. Trout are at their best broiled, but are also good marinated or fried in breadcrumbs.

Coregone, lavarello (whitefish)
This small fish – only 12 inches (30 cm) long – is prized for its delicate flesh. It was introduced to northern Italian waters at the end of the 19th century, where it has increased greatly in number, much to the delight of gourmets. Whitefish are versatile, and can be prepared by any method.

Pesce persico (Perch)
Perch are the amateur angler's favorite fish. Every weekend, the lakes of Lombardy attract many such anglers. The fish can be bought in the local stores, ready filleted, by those who prefer not to line the banks with rod and line. The fish is delicious, but has many bones. It can be fried, or served with *antipasto*.

Temolo (grayling)
Grayling are a rare freshwater fish. They mainly frequent very pure, clean waters. Their flesh has a delicate flavor, reminiscent of thyme. Gentle methods of cooking are best for this fish, to preserve the fine flavor.

Storione (sturgeon)
There are no more sturgeon living wild in the upper Italian lakes, though they are being farmed on a small scale. Sturgeon are mainly treasured for their roe, which is used as caviar. The flesh is very oily, but tastes good broiled or fried, or filleted and cooked in breadcrumbs.

VELTELLINA

The meat products of Valtellina, such as *bresaola*, are widely sought after beyond the immediate region, and another local specialty, buckwheat noodles known as *pizzoccheri*, have increased enormously in popularity. Recently, demand has risen to such an extent that an industrial means of production had to be developed. This in turn increased the requirement for buckwheat beyond what could be grown in the valley itself, and made it necessary to import more from Russia and the former Yugoslavia.

Valtellina is one of the last remaining places where this tasty, health-giving cereal still grows – although it is not strictly speaking a "grain" at all in the botanic sense. Buckwheat, or *grano saraceno*, to give it its Italian name, has always had a place in mountain cuisine, where the land is less fertile. The pasta for *pizzoccheri* is made with two thirds buckwheat flour to one third wheat flour. The wheat flour is needed to provide the gluten that holds the pasta together; buckwheat flour lacks gluten. An excellent way to enjoy *pizzoccheri* is in an oven-baked gratin mixture with potatoes, sage, and Savoy cabbage, using a flavorsome Alpine cheese such as *bitto* or *fontina*.

PIZZOCCHERI
Buckwheat noodle bake
(Illustration below)

1 2/3 CUPS/200 G BUCKWHEAT FLOUR
SCANT 1 CUP/100 G ALL-PURPOSE FLOUR
SALT
2–3 TBSP MILK, 2–3 TBSP WATER
1 EGG
SCANT 1/2 LB/200 G POTATOES
1/4 SAVOY CABBAGE
6 1/2 TBSP/100 G BUTTER
1 CLOVE OF GARLIC, FINELY CHOPPED
3 LEAVES OF SAGE, FINELY CHOPPED
1 1/3 CUPS/100 G COARSELY GRATED SEMIHARD CHEESE (BITTO OR FONTINA)
1 CUP/100 G FRESHLY GRATED PARMESAN

Sift the two flours together with a little salt, and mix with about 2–3 tbsp of milk and of water. Knead together with the egg. Roll out the dough and cut into pasta strips. Cover with a cloth.
Peel and slice the potatoes. Wash the cabbage, and cook with the potatoes in plenty of boiling, salted water for 15 minutes. Then add the pasta, and continue cooking until this is *al dente*. Drain well. Melt the butter in a small saucepan, and add the garlic and sage. Layer the potatoes, cabbage, pasta, the sliced or coarsely grated cheese, the parmesan, and the herb butter in a large casserole dish. Place under the preheated grill for a few minutes. Sprinkle with more parmesan and serve hot.

VALTELLINA WINES

Valtellina used to be the supplier of casked wines for Switzerland, which lies next door. The main grape variety grown in the valley is Nebbiolo, here called Chiavennasca. Small amounts of Pinot nero, Merlot, and local varieties are also used. The Adda valley is so narrow that the sun only reaches its steep vineyard slopes for a few hours a day. This means that grapes grown there do not always achieve maximum ripeness, and it is important to know which precise vineyard produced the wines. The best have achieved DOC recognition. The names of the wines from this region between Sondrio and Montagna are Sassella, Grumello, Inferno, and Valgello. They are sold as Valtellina superiore.

Good Valtellina wines have a fragrance of red fruits and tea leaves, like some Nebbiolo wines from Piedmont. They can be rather hard and unyielding when young, but become round and velvety as they age. The true specialty among Valtellina wines is a *vin de paille* called Sfursat. It is a heavy, dry wine in the style of Amarone, from the Veneto, a wine made by drying the grapes for a time before pressing, in order to increase the concentration of sugar. Only three or four wine growers and wineries produce Sfursat, making it very rare.

VALTELLINA SPECIALTIES

Bresaola

Bresaola first entered the list of gastronomic specialties from the small town of Chiavenna over 100 years ago. It is a cured and air-dried beef, originating from Graubünden in Switzerland. As a product, this means it is related to the Swiss *Bündnerfleisch*.

The meat is cut off the leg, and first cured in salt and pepper before being hung for several months to dry. The microclimate of the Chiavenna caves offer ideal conditions for maturation. Occasionally, light smoking is needed in the latter stages.

Bresaola has a delicately aromatic flavor, not too salty. It is nutritious and easy to digest. It is now made industrially, and has gained so much in popularity that it is to be found even in the far south of Italy. Gourmets slice it thinly and serve it with lemon juice, oil, and freshly milled pepper.

Slinzega

Unlike *bresaola*, which is made from beef, *slinzega* can be made from other meats – horse, donkey, or chamois – though it need not be. These meats are used in the province of Sondrio in particular, where *slinzega* is almost never made from beef. The meat is cured in a brine made to an old recipe. Maturation and smoking are carried out as for *bresaola*.

Violino

Violino is made from shoulder or leg of goat or mutton. The process is the same as for ham. The name *violino* comes from the way it is sliced – by holding it up like a violin, and wielding the knife like a bow. The pieces of meat are selected and flavored with garlic and juniper. Sometimes, they are cured in red wine. The maturation process is the same as for *bresaola*.

Bitto

This cheese is named after the River Bitto, a tributary of the Adda. It is made almost exclusively in Sondrio province. The cheese is cylindrical, 3–5 inches (8–12 cm) high, and weighs 33–55 pounds (15–25 kg). The curd is cooked, molded, and salted, and then ripened for three to six months in cool conditions. The ripening time can be a whole year if the cheese is intended for grating. The paste of the young cheese is fine, but becomes denser and more crumbly as it ages, intensifying in flavor. *Bitto* is enjoyed at the end of a meal with a glass of Sassella, Grumello, Inferno, or Valtellina. It is also an essential ingredient of *polenta taragna* and *sciatt*.

Casera

Casera is a cheese made throughout Valtellina from partially skimmed milk. After adding rennet and heating, the curd has to rest. Then the cheeses are molded, and either dry salted straight away or placed in brine. Ripening takes 30 days.

Casera is a cheese with a medium fat content, whitish in color, and with a thin rind. It is also made by dairies in other parts of Lombardy, outside Valtellina.

SCIATT

Cheese flat bread

Serves 6

1 2/3 CUPS/200 G BUCKWHEAT FLOUR
SCANT 1 CUP/100 G ALL-PURPOSE FLOUR
SALT
1/4 LB/100 G BITTO
2 TSP/10 ML GRAPPA
1 TBSP/15 G BUTTER

Sift the two flours together, and mix in enough luke-warm water to make a moderately stiff dough. Add salt, cover, and leave to rest for about an hour. Slice the cheese thinly, and mix into the dough. Add the grappa. Melt the butter in a non-stick skillet, and cook about a spoonful of the dough at a time, first pressing each portion into a flat cake. Drain on paper towels, and serve hot.

BRESAOLA CONDITA

Bresaola with egg
(Illustration below)

3/4 LB/350 G BRESAOLA, FINELY SLICED
EXTRA VIRGIN OLIVE OIL
2 EGG YOLKS
FRESHLY GROUND PEPPER
OREGANO
JUICE OF 1 LEMON

Arrange wafer-thin slices of the meat on 4 plates, or on a serving platter. Sprinkle with olive oil. Beat the egg yolks, and drizzle over the *bresaola*. Season with pepper and oregano, and leave for a few minutes before sprinkling with lemon juice. Serve with rye bread.

Below: Bresaola with parmesan

CAMPARI, OF COURSE

The Caffè Campari, opened in 1867 in the Galleria Vittorio Emanuele II in Milan, is a distinguished piece of Italian architecture. Soon after opening, it had attracted a large regular clientele. Behind the bar stood the owner himself, Gaspare Campari, and served his customers a creation of his own, *bitter all'ollandese* – bitters in the style of Holland. This drink, with its marked bitterness and striking red color, was enthusiastically received, and was renamed "bitter Campari." To this day, not a soul – apart, of course, from a few privileged employees in Milan – knows the true secret of Campari's ingredients. It is possible to guess, with a little knowledge of alcoholic liquors, that the bitter flavor must be due to cinchona or bitter orange peel, as it is in other bitter aperitifs, but what else? A dignified silence surrounds the matter. All the company will divulge is that the production of these bitters begins with an infusion of herbs, fruits, and various parts of plants. Then the aromas are extracted with alcohol. This flavor concentrate is topped up with alcohol, water, sugar, and a red coloring. What is this coloring? To answer cryptically: the coloring used to be obtained from the body shell of a small beetle, but it is now synthesized chemically.

Milanese bars like the Camparino, shown here, are inviting places for a quick espresso or Campari orange after an exhausting shopping trip.

DRINKS MIXED USING CAMPARI OR FERNET

All recipes serve 1

CAMPARI ORANGE
(Illustration above)

1 MEASURE OF CAMPARI
2 MEASURES OF ORANGE JUICE

Place ice cubes in a glass. Add Campari, top up with orange juice, and stir gently.

CAMPARI SHAKERATO

MEASURE OF CAMPARI
ICE CUBES

Place the ice cubes and Campari in a cocktail shaker. Shake vigorously, and strain into a chilled glass.

THE APOTHECARY

ICE CUBES
1/2 MEASURE OF FERNET BRANCA
1/2 MEASURE OF SWEET VERMOUTH
1/2 MEASURE OF CRÈME DE MENTHE

Place all the ingredients into a cocktail jug, and stir. Pour into a chilled glass.

FERNET

Imagine the end of a wonderful, but slightly heavy meal. Imagine, too, a highly aromatic and soothing drink, the ease of each sip, the relief even in anticipation. Such is Fernet. And it is not only a fine digestif: it is an example of *ben bere alla milanese* – drinking well, in the style of Milan.
This brew of various top secret herbs and alcohol is traditionally matured in oak casks. The first Fernet bottles, which date back to the 18th century, bore a label stating the health claims of the drink: "Benefits the stomach, promotes digestion, strengthens the body, overcomes cholera, reduces fever, and heals those suffering from nervous weakness, lack of appetite, sickness, or tapeworms; suitable for use as a preventative measure for all who are obliged to reside in damp and infectious conditions. May be taken at any time of day as required, undiluted or mixed with water, soda water, wine, coffee, vermouth, or other beverages."
A few of the indications listed are regarded with a little more doubt today: effective against cholera? One thing, though, has not changed. This eminently drinkable medicine is a magnificent remedy for a full stomach after a copious meal.

The Italian bar

Italian bars, unlike those in some other countries, are open throughout the day. This makes them popular meeting places at any hour: perhaps for a *caffè latte* on the way to work, to be sipped standing at the bar, with a small, sweet brioche or a few cookies – or just the coffee on its own. No importance is attached to breakfast in Italy. Tales of bread rolls and jam, of cold meats, even of the astonishing English breakfast with bacon and eggs, have reached the ears of Italians, but are met with something bordering on disbelief or indifference.

Around ten o'clock, the mid-morning break brings a fresh opportunity to return to the bar for a snack, accompanied by an espresso or even a glass of Spumante.

People often go home for lunch, but any who stay can head for the nearest bar to buy a *tramezzino*. These are elaborately filled sandwiches, sometimes toasted on the outside in a sandwich-maker, especially in the regions of the north.

The next flood of bar customers arrive as the stores and offices close. This time, the espresso is often accompanied by an alcoholic drink. If it is time to take an aperitif in anticipation of the evening meal, then visitors to the bar will order one. Italians tend to prefer bitter appetizers like Campari, Aperol, and various herb-based aperitifs, but dry Spumante is becoming just as popular. After the evening meal, the regulars gather at their favorite bar for a *caffè*

corretto, an espresso whose stimulating caffeine content has been "corrected" by the addition of amaretto, grappa, or sambuca. There will usually be some acquaintance to talk to, whether about plans to buy a new car, the political situation in Italy, or just local chitchat.

Lombardy and its capital, Milan, constitute one of the richest regions of Italy. This former stronghold of the mighty Sforza dynasty is the seat not only of the larger banks, but also of the media and the fashion industry. Any enterprise not actually registered here will still try at least to open a showroom or an elegant boutique in the city. Favorite locations are the Via della Spiga, on the Corso Vittorio Emanuele, and other famous streets in Milan's luxury shopping mile.

VAL D'AOSTA

AOSTA VALLEY

Gr. St. Bernhard
2469 m
Aosta
Aosta Valley   Gressoney
                la Trinité
Cogne

How far Italy still is today from having a pan-Italian identity strikes you particularly when you visit the border regions. Often the only evidence that they are politically a part of Italy is the presence of Italian newspapers and television stations, while the dialect, life style, and cuisine appear completely un-Italian. This is also true of the small region of Val d'Aosta. For the inhabitants of the valley, the government in Rome is a long way away, and is seen as a rather too remote figure, since their autonomous status guarantees them a certain political and cultural independence – they speak a Savoy dialect.

In any case, the history of the Aosta Valley belongs in French rather than Italian schoolbooks. After the break-up of the Western Roman Empire, the glacial valley fell to Burgundy in 443, and passed into Frankish hands at the end of the 6th century. In 1025 the Savoyards won control of the area. The new rulers were soon made to realize that the self-willed people of the valley did not like being dictated to, and they changed their strategy accordingly, granting the Valdaostans wide-ranging rights and freedoms. As a result, peace returned to the valley. Even today this policy is still being successfully practiced by Rome.

However, the Valdaostans' striving for independence has nothing to do with any sort of eccentric xenophobia. After all, the valley continued to provide access to important passes, which secured the trade between the boot-shaped peninsula and the economic areas north of the Alps. So travelers today are given the same friendly welcome as they were then, they are fortified before continuing their journey or even encouraged to stay – and above all regaled with delicious specialties. The cuisine of the Aosta Valley is simple and substantial, as befits a mountain region. Hot, wholesome bread soups are just right for snowy winter days, and in pleasant company you can enjoy the *fonduta*, the local version of the cheese fondue so beloved of the Alpine regions. Another time there will be polenta, wholesome rye bread, smoked bacon, tasty sausage specialties, beef and pork, as well as game from the surrounding mountains and forests. Butter and cream are used in stewing, roasting, and braising, since food rich in calories is a tasty and useful weapon against icy temperatures.

Previous double page: Farming the Alpine pastures and the production of cheese play a large part in the Aosta Valley. Young people like Nadir Folget, a budding master cheese-maker in the Casina Folget in Brisogne, see to it that traditions are kept up.

Left: The Aosta Valley is framed by the Valais Alps, the Mont-Blanc massif and the Graian Alps. The castle of Fénis lies between Aosta and St Martin.

RYE BREAD

The traditional rye bread of the Aosta Valley can definitely be described as a specialty. Wonderfully spicy and almost sweet tasting, when lightly spread with butter it makes an excellent accompaniment to the wines of the region.

In the past, even the smallest villages had a communal bakehouse, in which they gathered up to four times a year – mostly in November – to bake bread. To avoid arguments about who owned the bread, each villager cut a distinctive notch in their bread or carved their initials on their loaves. It is true that the bread, which was baked almost exclusively with rye flour, would keep for a whole year, but of course it grew hard with time, so hard that a special tool had to be invented in order to cut it.

BREAD SOUP

As the winters in the Alpine regions are long and cold, a nourishing hot soup is just right for the inhabitants. In the Aosta Valley and its neighboring valleys, bread soup with cheese, cooked slowly in the oven, has always been a favorite food. The simplest version of this dish is *Seupette de Cogne*. It consists only of bread, *fontina*, butter, and stock – all ingredients which could always be found in even the poorest mountain farmhouse kitchen. In comparison, *Zuppa di Valpelline* with its added bacon, Savoy cabbage, and herbs such as marjoram and savory, is almost a luxury version of bread soup.

ZUPPA DI VALPELLINE
Savoy cabbage stew with *fontina* from the Pelline Valley
(Illustrated above)

1 Savoy cabbage
1–2 slices/50 g bacon
1 lb/500 g stale bread
Savory or marjoram
3 oz/150 g fontina cheese, cut into wafer thin slices
6 tbsp/80 g butter
1 3/4 pints/1 liter meat stock
Salt and pepper

Wash and roughly chop the cabbage leaves. Dice the bacon very small. Gently simmer the leaves and the bacon in a casserole until the cabbage colors. Slice the bread and toast in the oven.
Cover the base of a casserole with a few slices of toasted bread. Put a layer of cabbage on top, sprinkle with chopped herbs, place a few slices of cheese and a couple of knobs of butter on top. Then add another layer of bread and so on until all the ingredients have been used up, finishing with a top layer of cheese and butter. Finally, pour over the meat stock and put the casserole to simmer in a preheated oven at 320 °F (160 °C) for about an hour.

ZUPPA DI PANE
Bread soup

3 medium onions/300 g onions
4 tbsp/50 g butter
5 cups/1.2 liters meat stock
4 slices/200 g stale bread
1 1/4 cups/100 g freshly grated gruyère
Freshly milled black pepper

Peel the onions and slice thinly. Melt the butter in a casserole. Add the onions and sauté over a low heat for 20 minutes, without browning. Then pour in the meat stock and boil for about 20 minutes. Meanwhile toast the slices of bread in the oven. Then cover the base of an oven dish with the slices of bread, sprinkle over the grated gruyère and pour in the meat-onion stock. Season the stew with freshly milled black pepper and cook for 20 minutes in a preheated oven at 350 °F (180 °C). Serve very hot!

ZUPPA DI PANE E CAVOLO
Green cabbage soup with bread

1 lb/500 g stale bread
1 clove garlic
1 small green cabbage
2 tbsp/30 g butter
1 small onion
1 1/4 cups/100 g freshly grated grana cheese
6 cups/1.5 liters meat stock
Freshly milled white pepper

First cut the bread in slices and toast lightly in the oven. Then rub the slices of bread with a clove of garlic. Wash the cabbage and simmer the leaves in salt water. Put aside. Peel the onion and chop finely.
Heat the butter in a casserole and gently sauté the onions. Put a layer of cabbage over them and sprinkle with grated cheese. Alternate layers of bread slices, cabbage, and cheese until all the ingredients have been used up. Then pour over the stock, cover, and simmer in a preheated oven for about 2 hours at 320 °F (160 °C). Sprinkle with white pepper and serve hot.

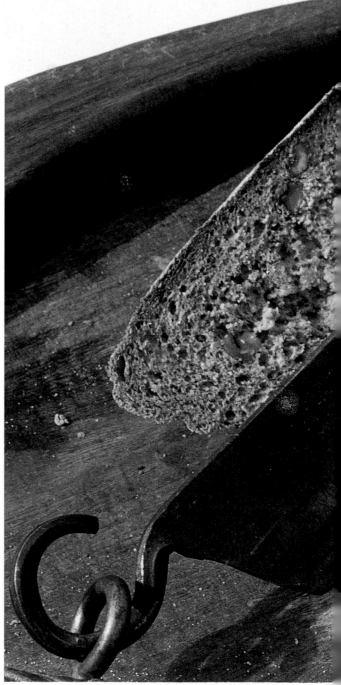

Today the Aosta Valley rye bread is baked with a considerably higher proportion of wheat flour. The round loaves with crosses cut into the tops no longer get as hard as in the old days. On the other hand they do not keep nearly so long, and have to be eaten very quickly.

Typical of the Aosta Valley is the *pane nero* made from rye and wheat flour, which tastes particularly good with the spiced bacon, *lardo*, and the local cheeses.

ALPINE CHEESE

With its lush meadows, the Aosta Valley offers ideal conditions for milk production. No wonder that full-bodied milk, tasty butter, rich cream, and of course the corresponding cheese are right at the top of the Valdaostans' menu. From this point of view, the *fontina*, which is steeped in tradition, is probably the most famous of the valley's cheeses. Its name is derived either from the verb *fondere*, which means to melt, indicating that this cheese is also delicious when melted, or it comes from Alpe Fontin, which is about 15 miles (25 km) from the provincial capital Aosta. Nobody knows for sure. On the other hand, it is a certain fact that the very mild, pale yellow *fontina* is produced from the best, fresh, full-cream milk. The cows which provide this high-quality milk feed exclusively on the grass of the high pastures.

The full-fat *fontina*, which is pale yellow and springy and has a few small holes running through it, has to mature for three to four months at a temperature of 46–53 ºF (8–12 º C). Many cheese factories use special storerooms cut into the rocks for this purpose. Cheeses produced in the summer can be recognized by a particularly buttery consistency and aromatic taste.

While the *fontina* is still young, the locals like to have it on the table for cutting. When it gets a little more mature, it is easy to melt and is therefore also very suitable for cooking. Moreover, the concentrated proteins and fats which it gets from the full-cream milk, make it a valuable part of the daily diet, and the mountain cuisine of the Aosta Valley would be unimaginable without it. It also provides a number of extremely important mineral salts, such as calcium and phosphorus.

In view of all these advantages, it is not surprising that people have tried again and again to copy *fontina*. Probably the best known imitation is *fontal*, which

The protected trademark of the *fontina*.

Like *fontina* and *solignon*, *toma de Gressoney* from the Gressoney Valley is a typical Alpine cheese made from cows' milk.

was created by Danish cheese experts, after they had got to know the merits of the Aosta cheeses during World War II. Production of this industrial version of *fontina* is permitted everywhere, even a long way from Aosta. As a result, the producers of the genuine *fontina* saw the need to protect their product from imitation. First, *fontina* was recognized as a "variety" of cheese. The second step, in 1955, gave it the legally controlled designation of origin DOC. Stamped on the surface of every official, and therefore quality guaranteed, *fontina*, is the trademark of a stylized Matterhorn, and the wording *Consorzio produttori fontina* (Consortium of Fontina Producers).

But the Aosta Valley region has other interesting cheese specialties to offer, for example *solignon*, which comes originally from the Gressoney Valley. *Solignon* consists of a very fatty ricotta, which is mixed with various flavorings: salt, ground paprika, chiles, garlic, juniper, fennel, and caraway seeds. *Solignon* can be eaten fresh or in a smoked version. In the past, the cheeses used to be hung in the chimney flue to dry out. As well as making them keep longer, it gave them a very special individual smoky taste.

Toma de Gressoney, which also comes from the Gressoney Valley, is worth sampling as well. This half-fat cheese is made in the same way as *fontina*. Sometimes it even looks so like it that you could get them mixed up, as the makers use the same shaped molds and also work with the same tools. So if you want a reliable way to distinguish *fontina* from *toma de Gressoney*, only a critical look at the ink stamp will do.

Left: *Fontina* has been produced in the Aosta Valley ever since the Middle Ages.

FONDUTA

There is a long tradition of cheese production in the Alpine valleys. Cheese was on the table throughout the day, in all varieties, young or mature, with bread, with porridge, in soups, or as an accompaniment to meat dishes. As leftover bits of cheese could be melted, the classic cheese fondue was not only seen as a nourishing meal, but at the same time fulfilled all the requirements of a thrifty and sensible use of leftovers. Cheese fondue has always been a favorite "stomach-warmer" throughout the Alps. The Aosta Valley is no exception; people here really enjoy their *fonduta*. Whereas in the classic Swiss cheese fondue the cheese, usually a mixture of Emmental and Greyerzer, is melted together with white wine, herbs, and a little lemon juice, the Brillat-Savarin version of the fondue asks for egg yolk as well. *Fonduta* also includes egg yolk and, in addition, calls for the cheese (in this case *fontina*) to be marinated in milk for at least four hours before melting. The ideal pan for *fonduta* should have a rounded base, to make it easier to mix the melting cheese thoroughly with a whisk.

Fonduta, which, incidentally, is a favorite in Piedmont as well, can be served as a starter or as a main course. It is also served as a cheese sauce with rice or tagliatelle, or used to fill ravioli. If you wish to enjoy your *fonduta* in the classic way, you pour the melted cheese into deep terracotta plates and serve with small pieces of toasted bread. In the autumn, the cheese may sometimes be garnished with a light dusting of white truffles.

FONDUTA VALDOSTANA
Fonduta Aosta style

14 OZ/400 G NOT TOO MATURE FONTINA, WITHOUT THE RIND
1 CUP/250 ML FULL-CREAM MILK
2 TBSP/30 G BUTTER
4 EGG YOLKS
1 WHITE TRUFFLE OR A FEW MUSHROOMS
SALT AND WHITE PEPPER
SLICES OF TOASTED BREAD

Cut the *fontina* into thin slices and marinate in milk for at least 4 hours. Put the butter in a fondue pot and place in a bain-marie. Add the cheese slices and 3 tablespoons of the milk in which they were marinated to the butter. Reduce the heat so the water remains just below boiling point. Melt the cheese, stirring continuously, until it can be pulled out in strings. Whisk the egg yolks with the remaining milk and stir in quickly, to give a smooth, thick cream. Season with salt and pepper. Divide the *fonduta* into small bowls, sprinkle thin slices of truffle or mushroom over it, and serve with slices of toast.

Background: Renato Vollget, owner of the Azienda and Trattoria Vollget in Brisogne, checks the maturity of his homemade *fontina*.

The raw material for the specialty cheeses of the Aosta Valley is of course the fresh, aromatic alpine milk of the Valdaostan cows. Natural untreated milk from their own dairies is used in the production of *fontina*.

The fresh untreated milk for the *fontina* is first heated in a big vat and mixed with rennin. When it has curdled the curd is separated from the whey.

Fontina matures for on average three months. During this time the cheesemaker regularly takes samples of the cheese with a curved scoop.

AOSTA VALLEY SPECIALTIES

Tortino di Riso Alla Valdostana
Rice cake with ox tongue

5oz/150 g salted ox tongue
3 1/2 oz/100 g fontina
2 cups/500 ml milk
Salt and pepper
Grated nutmeg
1 3/4 cups/350 g rice (Vialone)
1 small onion
6 tbsp/90 g butter
Freshly grated parmesan
Breadcrumbs

Dice the tongue and the *fontina* and mix together in a bowl. Pour in the milk and season with salt, pepper and nutmeg. Cover and leave to stand in a cool place for 1 hour. Meanwhile, cook the rice until *al dente*, and drain. Chop the onion and sauté gently until transparent in 3 tbsp/50 g butter, add the rice, sprinkle with parmesan, and mix well. Grease a deep ovenproof dish with butter, and then alternate layers of rice and tongue with layers of *fontina*. Scatter breadcrumbs and knobs of butter over it and bake in the oven until golden brown at 400 °F (200 °C).

Sweet corn and rice

Sweet corn did not arrive in the Aosta Valley until around the end of the 18th century. Rice also arrived here relatively late, and first became known through the region's close connections with Piedmont. However, the Valdaostans soon incorporated both these new ingredients into their cuisine. From the sweet corn they prepared polenta, and there is now a long list of traditional polenta dishes. There is *polenta concia* (baked polenta pudding), *polenta condita* (polenta with sauce), *polenta cùnsa* (polenta with cheese) and *polenta alla rascard* (rustic-style polenta, named after the typical valley farmhouse). *Polenta alla rascard* is made with *fontina* and a stew of ground beef, sausages, herbs, and white wine. The corn porridge is allowed to cool, cut in strips, and put in alternate layers with the stew in a deep casserole. Finally the polenta is covered with thin slices of *fontina*.

There is an equally large selection of rice dishes. Particularly tasty ones are *Riso con la fonduta*, rice with *fonduta*, and *Riso con vino di Donnaz*, rice with Donnaz wine. The *Tortino di riso alla valdostana* is not to be despised either. This is a kind of rice cake with *fontina* and salted ox tongue. The *tortino* is most successful if you use a good quality rice variety such as Arborio or Vialone.

Polenta cùnsa
Polenta with cheese
(Illustrated below)

10 cups/2.5 liters water
Salt
Scant 2 cups/300 g cornmeal
2 cups/180 g fontina, grated
1 1/4 cups/120 g toma, grated
Scant 2/3 cup/150 g butter
Freshly milled pepper

Bring about 10 cups/2.5 liters water to the boil in a copper pan or a large pot. Salt the water and gradually add the cornmeal, stirring the mixture continuously. Add the grated cheese. Boil for about 50 minutes, stirring continuously with a wooden spoon.
Melt the butter gently. Tip the polenta into a big china bowl, and pour over the butter. Sprinkle with freshly milled pepper and serve hot.

Opposite: *Lepre in civet* – Jugged hare
Below: *Polenta cùnsa* – Polenta with cheese

Jugged hare

Anyone who has no ambitions to hunt or is not sure how to dress a fresh hare, would do best to go for an oven-ready animal. The following recipe is also suitable for chamois meat and pheasant. In the Gran Paradiso, you find a rare but tasty variation using marmot, in which the meat has to marinate for at least 48 hours in a mixture of white wine, carrots, celery, onions, and other herbs, so that it loses its strong, unusual flavor.

Lepre in civet
Jugged hare
(Illustrated in background)

1 OVEN-READY HARE, WITH LIVER AND HEART
2 ONIONS
1 CARROT
2 CLOVES OF GARLIC
1 STICK OF CELERY
1 BAY LEAF
2 BOTTLES/1.5 LITERS RED WINE
3 1/2 TBSP/50 G BUTTER
2–3 SLICES/50 G BACON
SALT AND PEPPER
2–3 TBSP WINE VINEGAR

Preferably have the butcher cut the animal into portions. Place the pieces of hare – without the organ meat – in a bowl. Finely chop 1 onion, the carrot, garlic, and celery, and spread over the meat. Add the bay leaf and pour over the wine. Leave the hare to marinate for 1–2 days.

Remove the pieces of hare from the marinade, pat dry with kitchen roll and carefully clean off the remains of skin and sinews. Heat half the butter in a pan and fry the hare on a high heat for about 10 minutes. Remove the meat from the pan, pour off the juices and reserve.

Cut the bacon into small pieces, chop the remaining onion and sauté both in a little butter till the onion is transparent. Put the meat back in the pan, add salt and pepper, and sauté for a further 10 minutes.

Strain the marinade and ladle over the meat. Thicken the liquid over a low heat and continue adding the red wine marinade until the meat is very soft and tender.

Dice the liver and heart finely and sauté briefly in a small casserole with the remaining butter. Add salt and pepper and the wine vinegar. Remove from the heat and stir into the reserved pan juices. Serve the hare with its gravy, and with polenta.

FROM THE KITCHEN AND THE SMOKE-HOUSE

In the past, beef only appeared on the mountain farmers' tables, when an animal had to be destroyed out of necessity. But so that they could live off the stored meat for as long as possible, they salted it to make it keep longer. Even the classic *carbonade* is made from salted beef. Incidentally, stews of this kind are also found in Flemish and Spanish cuisine. The name *carbonade* (from *carbone*, coal) refers to the thick, very dark, almost black, gravy, which forms during the cooking of the meat.

CARBONADE ALL'USO AOSTANO
Beef stew
(Illustrated below)

1 3/4 LBS/800 G BEEF (E.G. SHOULDER)
ALL-PURPOSE FLOUR
3 1/2 TBSP/50 G BUTTER
1 3/4 LBS/800 G ONIONS, CHOPPED
1 BOTTLE/750 ML STRONG RED WINE
SALT AND FRESHLY MILLED PEPPER
FRESHLY GRATED NUTMEG

Cut the beef into pieces, toss in flour, and pan fry in butter over a high heat. Take out the meat and leave on one side. Fry the chopped onions over a high heat, add the meat and simmer gently over a low heat. Gradually pour in the wine. When the meat is ready, (after about 2 hours), season with salt, freshly milled pepper, and grated nutmeg.
In the past *carbonade* was made with salted beef; nowadays they use fresh meat and serve polenta with it.

COSTOLETTA ALLA VALDOSTANA
Veal cutlets with *fontina*

4 VEAL CUTLETS
3 1/2 OZ/100 G FONTINA, SLICED
SALT AND PEPPER
ALL-PURPOSE FLOUR
1 EGG
BREADCRUMBS
1/3 CUP/80 G BUTTER

Without separating them from the bone, cut through the cutlets with a sharp knife to form a pocket. Fill each of these pockets with cheese slices and press the edges together firmly. If necessary, fasten with a toothpick. Salt and pepper them on both sides, then toss them first in flour, then dip in beaten egg and finally coat in breadcrumbs. Fry in the butter until the cutlets are golden brown in color.

Carbonade all'uso aostano – Beef stew

BACON AND SAUSAGES

1 Mocetta

Mocetta and bacon from Arnad are among the most important meat specialties of the Aosta Valley. *Mocetta* or *mozzetta* was originally made from the meat of the ibex. As the numbers of these animals living on the Gran Paradiso massif continue to decline, the ibex has been declared a protected species and hunting it is forbidden. So nowadays the *mocetta* is made with chamois or goat meat. The seasoned meat is first placed in brine and compressed with a weight. After 25 days it is taken out and has to dry and mature for three to four months in an airy place. *Mocetta* should be consumed within one year, as after that it becomes too dry and hard. It is cut into thin slices and served as a starter with butter and rye bread spread with honey.

2 Coppa al Ginepro

This neck-end ham from Arnad gets its special flavor from the juniper berries which are rubbed into the surface while it is maturing.

3 Bacon from Arnad

This bacon, which is famous for its keeping qualities and its tangy flavor, is made from the rind of particularly fat pigs. Boned and cut in pieces, the bacon is decorated alternately with salt and herbs (pepper, bay, rosemary, sage, cloves). After it has been left for a few days, the superfluous salt is removed. Then the bacon has to hang for at least three months. Served with rye bread or chopped nuts it makes an appetizing *antipasto*.

4 Bon Bocon

In the soft, mild, and pasty pork filling of the *salamino* "Tasty morsel" from Arnad, you can already taste how close we are to Piedmont.

5 Pancetta steccata

The *pancetta steccata* is a comparatively rare, but nevertheless very tasty specialty of the Aosta Valley. The piece of belly pork with its thick salted rind is sewn together and clamped between two pieces of juniper wood. This presses the superfluous air out of the bacon, helps the maturing process, and in addition the wood adds a hint of aromatic flavor. After about two months, the *pancetta steccata* can be thinly sliced and served with a good, nourishing bread.

Boudin (not pictured)

The *boudin* is a kind of *sanguinato*, a blood sausage, consisting of pig blood and a mixture of boiled potatoes and bacon. It can be eaten fresh or hung, raw or cooked.

Saucisse (not pictured)

The sausage meat for the *saucisse* or *salsiccia* is made from ground beef and pork and is spiced with pepper, nutmeg, cinnamon, and garlic soaked in wine. This sausage tastes best when it has hung for about six months. After that it can also be preserved in oil, to prevent it from getting hard.

The notable specialty of Aosta Valley charcuterie, *pancetta steccata*, is pressed between two pieces of wood.

TERRACES AT DIZZYING HEIGHTS

From the 9th century onward, the smallest region of Italy was part of the Kingdom of Savoy, and since then has lain in the disputed area between France and the Italian region of Piedmont, resulting in a completely bilingual culture and also, of course, giving its wines their special character. The winegrowing area of the region, which does not even amount to 2500 acres (1000 hectares), extends over 56 miles (90 kilometers) of the long, narrow valley of the Dora Baltea, between the town of Morgex near Courmayeur at the foot of Mont Blanc and Donnas on the Piedmont border. Spectacular, narrow terraces are situated on steep rock faces at heights of up to 4300 feet (1300 meters) above sea level – these are the highest vineyards in Europe. The climate of the Alpine valleys is characterized by extreme winters and occasional very hot summers. Big fluctuations between the daytime and nighttime temperatures during the vegetation period give the grapes a strong flavor. While grapes for white wine with a good acid content are grown in many of the higher vineyards, the terraces in the middle part of the valley near Chambave, which face due south and are generally considered to be the very best sites in Aosta, are also suitable for strong, full-bodied red wines.

About three-quarters of the regional wine production comes under the single DOC Valle d'Aosta, which designates 26 different kinds of wine from 22 registered varieties of grapes – no other region of Italy has a greater variety within so small an area. Particularly outstanding among them are the many local varieties, such as Blanc de Morgex, Fumin, Neyret, Petit Rouge, Vien de Nus, and Premetta, but well-known names like Merlot, Pinot Grigio, or Chardonnay are also grown alongside them.

On the middle and lower slopes even the Nebbiolo ripens, a variety which is usually very demanding and produces interesting light rustic wines in the area around Donnas (or Donnaz). Of the other red varieties, the Petit Rouge and the Gamay are the ones to single out in the upper valley, while Blanc de Morges et la Salle and the sweet Moscato di Chambrave stand out among the white wines.

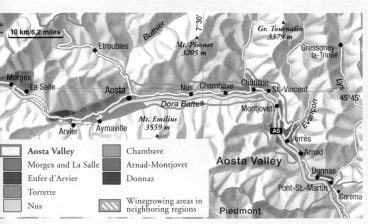

Petit Rouge
Smooth, fruity red wines are made from the Petit Rouge variety, which grows only in the Aosta Valley. The grapes can be pressed as a single variety, but mix well with other varieties – among them Dolcetto, Gamay, and Pinot Noir – to make the red Chambave, Enfer d'Arvier, Novello, Nus Rosso, and Torrette.

Donnaz
The only Nebbiolo wine of the Aosta Valley – Freisa, Neyret, and Vien de Nus can only provide small proportions – is produced close to the Piedmont border and the winegrowing area of Carema. It cannot however be compared with the great Nebbiolo wine of Langa, and at best it can be mellow and fruity, but it never achieves the complexity and lasting quality of Barolo or Barbaresco.

Enfer d'Arvier
This wine comes from the steep vineyards of the Dora-Baltea Valley, which extend up the slopes to a height of 3280 feet (1000 meters). The dry red wine is pressed from Petit Rouge, Dolcetto, Gamay, Neyret, Spätburgunder, and Vien de Nus, and mostly turns out light and low in alcohol.

GROLLA DELL'AMICIZIA

Every family in the Aosta Valley owns a *grolla dell'amicizia*. On important occasions this friendship cup is brought out of the closet to honor a friend or a member of the family. The drinking vessel, carved from a local wood, is round and shallow, closes with a well-fitting lid, and has several spouts coming out of it. People sit together and take turns drinking from the *grolla*. It is traditionally filled with *caffè cognese*; the name doesn't mean a kind of mixed cognac, but refers to the town of Cogne in the Aosta Valley. It's true that every village has a different secret recipe for preparing *caffè cognese*, but it consists mainly of coffee, with a little grappa, sugar, and an orange or a lemon rind. However, the proportions may vary.

Linguists are still arguing over the origin of the term *grolla*. Some maintain that the word goes back to the traditional French *grasal* or *graal*, meaning "dish," and refers to a drinking vessel passed round among the medieval knights. Others think that *grolla* comes directly from the Latin *gradalis*, and is connected with the legend of the Holy Grail, the cup from which Jesus Christ drank at the Last Supper.

DESSERTS

For the simple but very tasty desserts of the Aosta Valley, only the best basic ingredients from the region are used, and these must be left as close as possible to their natural state. *Pere San Martin al vino rosso* are good evidence for this simple but brilliant philosophy. Although the Aosta Valley is not among the major producers of Italian pears, a very special, aromatic variety is grown here: the small, rosy-cheeked St Martin winter pear. Complete with its stalk, it is covered in red wine and baked in the oven – delicious! *Panna cotta* is also an extremely simple yet – if good cream is used – incredibly delicious dessert. It does not exactly come from the Aosta Valley, but is typical of the whole of northern Italy, because there has always been a milk industry here. Nowadays, however, this "baked cream" is made in almost all parts of the country.

PERE SAN MARTIN AL VINO ROSSO
Winter pears in red wine
(Illustrated right)

1LB/500 G SMALL RED PEARS
GOOD RED WINE
CLOVES
SUPERFINE SUGAR
HEAVY CREAM FOR WHIPPING

Wash the pears and place whole – with the core and stalk – in a deep baking pan. Cover the fruit almost completely with red wine, add a few cloves and sprinkle with sugar. Bake for about 1 hour in a pre-heated medium oven. This will give the liquid a syrupy consistency.
Allow the pears to cool and serve with whipped cream and a spoonful of syrup.

PANNA COTTA
Baked cream
(Illustrated below)

Serves 8

1 OZ/30 G POWDERED GELATIN
4 CUPS/1 LITER LIGHT CREAM
1/3 CUP/80 G SUGAR

Soften the gelatin in a little cold water and squeeze out. Bring the cream to the boil with the sugar, simmer for about 15 minutes. Remove the cream from the heat and completely dissolve the gelatin in it, stirring continuously.
Pour the remainder of the sugar into a pan, caramelize it and pour into ramekins.
Fill up with the cream mixture into ramekins and keep in a cool place for a few hours.
Serve with fruits of the forest or raspberry sauce.

HERBS TO KEEP OUT THE COLD

Genepy is possibly the most famous spirit from the Aosta Valley. It is made according to a strictly guarded recipe, using not only alcohol, sugar, and water, but also a great variety of local herbs, among them gentian and Alpine mugwort. There are strict controls on the collecting of the last of these ingredients, which has the botanical name *artemisia glacialis* and grows under the snow cover in the high mountains, so you need a special permit, and even then you are only allowed to pick very few plants.

Fresh or dried herbs can be used in making Genepy. If the plants are fresh, they give the liqueur a beautiful green color. On the other hand, if dried herbs are used, you get a pale yellow variety. Genepy is around 40 percent proof. It is a favorite tonic, but also does good service as a digestive. What's more, it warms up hordes of frozen skiing enthusiasts every season. A very similar herbal liqueur, which could no doubt do the same job, is Alpinista. It too is made with various herbs from the valley.

Alongside the high-alcohol herbal schnapps, marc brandies are also drunk in the Aosta Valley – and particularly, of course, since they started flavoring the grappa with mountain herbs, fruits of the forest, or honey.

GRAND SAINT BERNARD

Back around the time of the birth of Christ, the Romans extended the Grand Saint Bernard or Gran San Bernardo Pass through the Alps. Since then it has connected the Swiss canton of Valais with the Italian Aosta Valley. Today there is no problem crossing the Alps by train, plane, or automobile, and it is now almost impossible to imagine that the road through this mountain range once represented a dangerous, even foolhardy, undertaking. It meant conquering the pass in a coach – as far as the road allowed – on horseback, on a donkey, or at worst even on foot. You were dependent on local guides, some of whom inspired more confidence than others, who might show you the right path, or lead you into disaster. You had to

The basic ingredient of Genepy, *Artemisia*, grows at a height of 6500 to 9750 feet/2000 to 3000 meters, and is picked at the end of August.

think carefully about where you could have the animals taken care of and find a place to rest when night fell. Moreover, there were robbers lying in wait in the ravines, who would take the last penny from travelers and pilgrims. Travelers crossing the Alps were often helpless victims of those sudden changes in the weather for which the high mountains are feared, not to mention the constant danger of avalanches. In summer it meant you had to beware of landslides and screes, in winter, you could easily be buried under a blanket of snow.

To provide shelter, food, and emergency help for travelers, in the middle of the 11th century Saint Bernard of Menton, who was then Archdeacon of Aosta, founded a hospice high up on the pass, which was at the time the most important trade and pilgrim route through the Alps. The first written mention of a dog comes from the early 18th century. The monastery chronicle reports that the hospice was open to travelers day and night. All visitors received a free meal of

Above and right: In the distillery of the famous producer of spirits and delicatessen La Valdotaine in St. Marcel, very unusual specialties are produced and, of course, "herbal" grappa. The large selection ranges from raspberry grappa to liquorice grappa and chili grappa.

meat and bread. Big portions of meat were roasted on a spit – an arduous task for the cook. In 1701, the master cook Vincent Canos built a treadmill and put a dog in it, so that it turned the spit as it moved. Around 1750 the *marronniers*, the mountain guides from the hospice, began to take the dogs out on the road with them. The big sturdy St. Bernards had to go ahead of the walkers in order to make a path through the snow with their broad chests. In addition, the dogs proved to have an extraordinary sense of direction, so they could safely guide the *marronnier* and his travelers down to the valley or back to the hospice, even in darkness or fog. The St. Bernards also worked as avalanche dogs. They did not have to be specially trained for this, as it is in their nature to scratch for things they can scent through the snow. The number of buried and frozen travelers did, in fact, fall drastically at that time. The little barrel of brandy, which the St. Bernard supposedly carries on its collar, should be consigned to the realms of legend. Of course, the big dogs did occa-

sionally carry loads up to the hospice as well, but their rescue work consisted of tracking missing people, not providing the rescued with alcohol. There is no mention of these mysterious little barrels anywhere in the hospice chronicles.

Today travelers still come to visit the hospice. It is still run by monks, though they no longer see searching for the buried and reviving exhausted travelers as being their most urgent tasks; now they offer their guests a peaceful retreat, away from the hectic rush of the outside world. St. Bernards are no longer employed in mountain rescue either; now there are helicopters and rescue teams equipped with sonar.

The dog with the little barrel is part of the Alpine myth, but such a burden would be a hindrance during a rescue, and accident victims should not drink alcohol anyway.

The clear herbal schnapps of the Aosta Valley is called Genepy. It is flavored with various herbs and plants, including Alpine mugwort.

PIEMONTE

The "land at the foot of the mountains," which is how Piedmont translates, is at its most magical in the autumn, when the leaves change color and thick swathes of mist drift over valleys and hills. This is the time to look out for truffles and other delicious fungi in the woods, to collect nuts, gather cardoons, go hunting, or admire the selection of fresh game in the shops. In the evening people sit around the fire, hold long conversations and open a bottle of wine. The Piedmont cuisine may have certain refinements, but it is deeply rooted in a tradition of simple wholesome cooking, which relies on first class, very tasty ingredients. Truffles, garlic, game, and crisp vegetables, together with cheese and rice, are the basis of Piedmont specialties.

Autumn is also the time of the wine harvest. Piedmont has earned a worldwide reputation for a series of outstanding wines. Barolo, Barbaresco, and Barbera are only three of the names, but they all stand for the highest quality. But there are other treasures to be discovered in Piedmontese cellars. Fine sparkling wines, which can compare with the best champagne, are also produced in the region. Of course it is often claimed that Piedmontese cuisine is closely related to the French, but this is a culinary half-truth. You get closer to the facts, if you speak of French influence on Piedmontese cooking – and conversely of Piedmontese influences on French cooking. This flourishing exchange of gastronomic ideas has a history going back some 800 years, as during all that time Piedmont was part of Savoy, a kingdom which included areas that now belong to France, Switzerland, and Italy. The Savoy dialect, which was spoken there, was influenced by French – so many technical terms of French origin are still found in Piedmontese cookbooks today. *Fumèt* means smoked, *civet* means meat stock, and *cocotte* describes a cast iron casserole. But – as we said before – this is a long way from saying that Piedmontese cuisine is a branch of traditional French cookery, since it has completely independent specialties in store: *bagna caoda*, delicious raw Piedmontese vegetables with a tangy anchovy dip, rice dishes such as *risotto alla piemontese*, *paniscia di novara* or world-class cheeses like Gorgonzola or *castelmagno* – these are delights you absolutely must taste.

Previous double page: When it comes to truffle hunting, you don't just need human intelligence, a dog's good sense of smell is even more important.

Left: Lago d'Orta is the most westerly lake on the North Italian side of the Alps. Wooded shores alternate with quiet villages. In the middle of the lake is the island of San Giulio.

CASTELMAGNO

Castelmagno is a Piedmont specialty. This blue cheese of legally controlled origin (DOC) is produced exclusively in the communities of Castelmagno, Pradleves, and Monterosso Grana in the province of Cuneo. It is easy to recognize the true Castelmagno by its trademark, a little triangle in a stylized letter C on the top side. Like its more famous relative Gorgonzola, Castelmagno can look back on a proud tradition, as the cheese was specifically mentioned in the record of a legal arbitration settlement as long ago as 1277. This paper says that an annual charge was made for the use of a pasture about which the communities of Castelmagno and Celle di Macra were arguing at the time – and it was payable to the Margrave of Saluzzo in the form of Castelmagno cheese. Thanks to the cheesemakers' sense of tradition, today's Castelmagno tastes almost exactly the same as it did in the 13th century. The semisoft cheese has only 34 percent fat in the dry mass. It is usually made only from cow's milk, but may additionally contain small quantities of semiskimmed sheep's or goat's milk. The milk is first allowed to curdle, then hung in a cloth for the whey to drain off. After that the curd stays for a few days in wooden vats before being pressed into molds. The cheeses have to mature for two to five months in well-ventilated caves in the rocks.

A young Castelmagno has a reddish rind and is ivory colored. It tastes slightly salty, with a delicate hint of nuts. Mature Castelmagno has a dark red to gray rind and the blue-green veins of the mold can be clearly seen running through its ocher curd. It tastes strong and tangy. Young or mature, Castelmagno is an outstanding cheese for the table, and is particularly good served with acacia honey and a fortified wine.

After curdling, the cheese curd is emptied into cloths and hung up to allow the remaining whey to drain off.

Castelmagno matures for four to six months, which gives it a full, tangy taste. Cheese-buffs let it get even older.

WHAT DOES THE DOC LABEL MEAN ON A CHEESE?

The abbreviation DOC stands for *Denominazione di origine controllata* and means the origin is legally controlled. In this way high quality cheese varieties – like good wines – are protected from inferior quality imitations. In order to produce a particular cheese, the makers usually join together in a *consorzio di tutela*, a kind of cooperative, to draw up an exact description of the area of origin, the method of production and the finished product. Through a control-system, which they set up themselves, they ensure that these regulations are adhered to. They also apply for the cheese and its area of origin to be officially recognized. If the cheese has received state approval, it can have the letters DOC added to its name from then on, but it must be submitted to regular critical testing by independent experts. Now there are not only DOC standard cheeses in Italy, but also ham, vinegar (Aceto balsamico di Modena DOC), and other specialties, which can boast a protected origin.

GORGONZOLA

Gorgonzola is one of Italy's most famous exports. The little wedges, usually wrapped in silver paper, can be found on cheese boards all over the western world. Like many other kinds of cheese, Gorgonzola is a DOC protected product, but the area in which it is produced is much bigger than, for example, that of Castelmagno. Gorgonzola may come from provinces lying partly in Lombardy and partly in Piedmont, namely Bergamo, Brescia, Como, Cremona, Cuneo, Milan, Novara, Pavia, and Vercelli. Nowadays the

The milk is heated to about 86 °F (30 °C), and rennin is added to make it curdle. Spores of the mold *Penicillium glaucum* are also added.

majority of Gorgonzola producers are based in Piedmontese Novara.

With its 48 percent fat in dry mass, Gorgonzola is a full-fat cow's milk cheese. It used to be made from unpasteurized milk, but now, for reasons of hygiene, pasteurized milk is used, and the mold *Penicillium glaucum* is added to aid fermentation and produce the blue veins. Gorgonzola matures for two to three months in temperature-controlled conditions in natural caves in the rocks or similar storerooms.

Gorgonzola is an outstanding cheese for the table. It can be served as an appetizer or, with bread and a strong red wine, it can finish off a meal. It also has its uses in the kitchen. Risottos, sauces, fillings, and stuffings will all taste wonderful, if flavored with crumbled Gorgonzola.

After the whey has been separated, the cheese curd is compressed in molds of 10 to 12 inches (25 to 30 cm) diameter. Then the cheese is allowed to set. Later on, the master cheesemaker will keep taking the cheese out of the mold, in order to salt the surface.

Gorgonzola is available in various stages of ripeness. The more mature it is, the more piquant the flavor.

Left: To ensure that the mold spreads evenly throughout the cheese, the spores are distributed by boring into the cheese with long stainless steel needles, first from one side, then a week later from the other side.

RICE GROWING

There are various theories about how rice came to Italy. While some say that the Romans were already acquainted with rice, others think that it was brought to Sicily by the Arabs about the turn of the first millennium. The preferred version in Venice is that traveling Venetian merchants brought rice back with them from their journeys to the Levant. However, true rice cultivation only started to develop in the 15th century, after plague and famine had devastated vast areas of Europe in the Middle Ages. In Italy, they were also looking for new foods at that time, and they remembered rice. The Cistercian monks of the monastery at Luciedo, near Trino Vercellese, soon discovered that conditions in the well-watered plains of the Po valley were favorable for rice, and that the plants grew very well there. But at first, the inhabitants of the surrounding villages wanted nothing to do with it. They were skeptical about a plant which grew only in water, because they thought that this method of cultivation would encourage the spread of serious diseases like the plague. However, the persuasive skills of the monks, coupled with the need for food, overcame these fears.

In the 19th century, large-scale rice growing began in the Po valley, because it became apparent that the rice trade had significant economic potential for this rather poor region. Great canals were built, such as the Canale Cavour, opened in 1852, and ingenious and efficient irrigation systems were set up, so that increasingly large areas could be opened up for rice growing. Italian rice soon began to enjoy great popularity abroad and exports flourished. Even Thomas Jefferson, the third President of the United States, took a few grains of rice home from his journey through Italy, because the rice grown in the Po valley could withstand the heat better than the rice Jefferson knew from his homeland. So he simply "imported" this firm variety from the Old World, and it quickly gained acceptance in the rice growing areas of the United States.

In the 20th century, rice growing had reached such a stage of perfection that Italy was way ahead of other European producers. But in the fifties, the Po valley was still paying for the presence of the huge rice industry and the prosperity it brought to some people with the immense poverty of the lower strata of the population, who worked in the fields for starvation wages. The fate of the *risaroli*, the seasonal workers, and the *mondine*, the girls who weeded the rice, is recorded in many folksongs and plays, but the most vivid account of the hard labor in the fields is probably that given in the 1949 Italian film *Riso amaro* (Bitter Rice) by the neo-realist director Giuseppe de Santis.

Rice growing today is, of course, largely mechanized – modern machinery has taken over the strenuous work of planting, weeding, and harvesting – but it is still a challenging agricultural occupation, because the fields require a slow but constant flow of water, so they have to slope at a particular angle in order to prevent the water from running away too fast or standing too long, either of which would damage the plants.

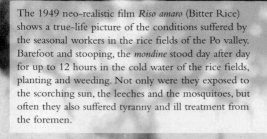

The 1949 neo-realistic film *Riso amaro* (Bitter Rice) shows a true-life picture of the conditions suffered by the seasonal workers in the rice fields of the Po valley. Barefoot and stooping, the *mondine* stood day after day for up to 12 hours in the cold water of the rice fields, planting and weeding. Not only were they exposed to the scorching sun, the leeches and the mosquitoes, but often they also suffered tyranny and ill treatment from the foremen.

After sowing in March, the rice fields are flooded and the area between Vercelli, Novara, and Pavia looks almost like one big lake.

Rice is harvested in September, by which time the plants are brown and dry.

Big mills separate the grain from the husks, and then the rice is polished.

VARIETIES OF RICE

The most commonly grown rice variety in Italy is *oryza sativa japonica*, whose grains remain firm when boiled. By contrast, the long-grain rice *Oryza sativa indica*, which cooks quickly and turns to mush, is hardly grown at all. Italian rice is monitored by the National Rice Institute, which regularly checks the quality, purity, and nutritional content of the different varieties. Rice offered for sale is divided into four categories, which must be shown on the packaging: *riso commune* (household rice), *riso semifino* (round grain rice), *riso fino* (medium grain or standard rice), and *riso superfino* (superfine rice).

As rice dishes may call for varieties with different consistencies and cooking qualities, cooks in northern Italy pay particular attention to the selection of rice. Varieties which take a long time to cook, like Razza 77 and Ribe, have big, almost transparent grains, containing little starch. These are suitable for rice salads and boiled or baked rice dishes. Varieties with semisoft grains, like Arborio, Carnaroli, and Vialone, have large grains with a high starch content. They remain moist and juicy, so they are particularly suitable for risotto. Soft varieties, like Maratelli and Balilla, have very small starchy grains, which cook quickly without breaking up. They are particularly suitable for rice soups.

Riso commune (Household rice)
The Balilla, Americano 1600, Elio, Selenio, and Originario varieties belong in this category. *Riso commune* has small, short, round or semicircular grains. It takes 13–14 minutes to cook, gets very soft, and is suitable for desserts, soups, and *timbale*.

Riso semifino (Round grain rice)
This group includes the Maratelli, Vialone nano, Padano, Lido, Argo, Cripto, and Rosa Marchetti varieties. *Riso semifino* has thick, medium length, round or semicircular grains. It takes 15 minutes to cook and is suitable for minestrone and other soups, but also for *timbale* and as a side dish.

Riso fino (Medium grain or standard rice)
This group is subdivided into Fino medio (varieties Europa, Loto, Riva) and Lungo A (varieties Ariete, Cervo, Drago, Ribe, R.B., Rizzotto, Sant'Andrea, Ringo, and Vialone). *Riso fino* has long, spindle-shaped grains (except for Vialone, which has round grains). It takes 16 minutes, cooks evenly, remains firm, and is suitable for risotto, rice salads, soups, and as a side dish.

Riso superfino (Superfine rice)
This group is subdivided into Lungo A (Arborio, Baldo, Roma, Razzo 77, Koral, Volano, and Carnaroli) and Lungo B, which includes Graldo Panda, Pegaso and Thaibonnet. *Riso superfino* has long, thick, half spindle-shaped grains. It takes 18 minutes to cook and is very suitable for risotto. Carnaroli in particular, which is often twice as expensive as other varieties, makes a splendid risotto, and it can also be used for starters – salads, *timbale*, and side dishes.

1 R.B.
2 Riso brillato
3 Riso sbramato
4 Roma
5 Riso parboiled
6 Balilla
7 Vialone nano
8 Arborio

RISOTTO AL BAROLO
Risotto with Barolo
(Illustrated above)

6 TBSP/100 G BUTTER
1 SMALL ONION
2 CUPS/400 G RICE
1 CUP BAROLO (WINE)
ABOUT 4 CUPS/1 LITER MEAT STOCK
2/3 CUP/50 G GRANA CHEESE, GRATED
FRESHLY MILLED BLACK PEPPER
WHITE TRUFFLES, ACCORDING TO TASTE

Heat half the butter in a wide, fairly shallow casserole. Chop the onion finely and sauté in the butter, without browning. Add the rice and sauté briefly, stirring continuously. Then pour over the wine and bring to a boil. Gradually add the preheated stock. Allow to boil gently until the rice has absorbed the liquid and is cooked through.
Remove the casserole from the heat and carefully stir in the remaining butter. Sprinkle with cheese and freshly milled pepper and serve. If desired, the flavor of the risotto may be enhanced with a few shavings of truffle.

Superfine Carnaroli rice makes a splendid risotto. It takes up liquids evenly, but the grains nevertheless remain firm and separate.

RISOTTO AGLI SPUGNOLE
Risotto with morels

1/2 CUP /120 ML LIGHT CREAM
1 CUP/250 ML WATER
GENEROUS CUP/25 G DRIED MORELS
2 SHALLOTS, CHOPPED
2 TBSP/30 G BUTTER (FOR SAUTÉING)
1 CUP/200 G VIALONE RICE OR OTHER HIGH QUALITY RISOTTO RICE
1 CUP/250 ML WHITE WINE
SALT AND PEPPER
3 CUPS/750 ML HOT CHICKEN STOCK
4 TBSP/60 G BUTTER (FOR THE RISOTTO)
3/4 CUP/60 G FRESHLY GRATED PARMESAN
FINELY CHOPPED PARSLEY

Bring the cream and the water to a boil, pour over the morels, and leave them to soak in the cream and water for about 15 minutes. Pour the liquid into a bowl and reserve. Wash the mushrooms under running water and chop roughly. Sauté the shallots lightly in 2 tablespoons butter. Add the mushrooms and rice, pour over the wine, and season with salt and pepper. Gradually pour in first the reserved liquid, then the chicken stock, until the rice has absorbed all the liquid and is cooked. Then mix in butter, Parmesan, and parsley, and serve hot.

RISOTTO AI PORCINI
Risotto with boletus

Serves 4–6

5 1/2 TBSP/85 G BUTTER
1 LARGE ONION, CUT INTO THIN RINGS
3/4 LB/300 G FRESH BOLETUS MUSHROOMS, SLICED
SALT
2 CUPS/400 G CARNAROLI RICE
7 CUPS/1.75 LITERS HOT CHICKEN STOCK
3/4 CUP/60 G FRESHLY GRATED PARMESAN
FRESHLY MILLED PEPPER

Heat half the butter in a pan and sauté the onions and mushrooms until soft. Salt, and add the rice. Gradually pour over the stock, until the rice has absorbed the liquid and is cooked (about 20 minutes). Remove from the heat and add the remaining butter and the parmesan. Season with pepper and serve immediately.

RISOTTO ALLA ZUCCA
Pumpkin risotto

6 TBSP/90 G BUTTER
1 ONION, FINELY CHOPPED
3/4 LB/300 G PUMPKIN, DICED
SALT
2 CUPS/400 G ARBORIO RICE
7 CUPS/1.75 LITERS HOT VEGETABLE STOCK
FRESHLY GRATED NUTMEG
PEPPER
3/4 CUP/60 G FRESHLY GRATED PARMESAN

Heat 4 tablespoons of the butter in a pan. Sauté the onion until translucent, add the pumpkin, and cook until tender. Mash with a potato masher and salt. Add the rice and cook for 1 minute, stirring all the time. Gradually pour over the hot stock, until the rice has absorbed the liquid and become white and creamy. Continue to stir. Remove the pan from the heat, and add the remaining butter, nutmeg, pepper, and Parmesan.

PANISCIA DI NOVARA
Vegetable soup with rice

1/2 LB/200 G RIPE TOMATOES
2 STICKS CELERY
2 MEDIUM SIZED CARROTS
1 SMALL SAVOY CABBAGE
1/2 LB/300 G FRESH BORLOTTI BEANS
2 OZ/50 G PORK FAT
SALT
1 SMALL SALAMI D'LA DUJA (A SAUSAGE PRESERVED IN OIL)
1 MEDIUM SIZED ONION, CHOPPED
2/3 CUP/50 G BACON, CHOPPED
2 TBSP/30 ML OLIVE OIL
1 2/3 CUPS/300 G ROUND GRAIN RICE
2/3 CUP/150 ML BARBERA (WINE)

Skin the tomatoes and remove the seeds. Clean the celery, peel the carrots and cut both into small pieces. Remove the outer leaves of the cabbage and cut the inner leaves into strips. Shell the beans. Put the vegetables and the pork fat into a large pot, cover with water, and a little salt, and cook for about 2 hours. Skin the salami and cut up small. Fry the onion, bacon, and salami in a casserole in olive oil. Add the rice and stir. Pour over the wine and allow the liquid to boil away. Pour over the vegetable soup and finish cooking over a low heat (about 20 minutes). Allow to stand for a few minutes and serve.

RISOTTO ALLA PIEMONTESE
Piedmontese-style risotto

1 3/4 CUPS/350 G RISOTTO RICE
4 CUPS/1 LITER HOT MEAT STOCK
4 TBSP BUTTER
1/2 CUP/40 G FRESHLY GRATED PARMESAN
SALT
GRATED NUTMEG
1/4 CUP/40 G GRAVY
TRUFFLE

First boil the rice in the meat stock over a high heat for 15 minutes, stirring occasionally. Remove the pan from the heat, add butter, parmesan, salt, and a little nutmeg. Leave to stand for a few minutes, then pour the rice into a deep, prewarmed bowl. Pour the gravy into the middle of the risotto, garnish with thin slices of truffle, and serve.

MEAT AND POULTRY

Piedmontese cuisine is very varied and sometimes even lavish. For instance, instead of using one or two kinds of meat to make one of the most famous of northern Italy's favorite dishes, *Bollito misto*, the Piedmontese always make it with four or more different meats.

Beef and chicken always go into the pot, but even this simple version of *Bollito* is enriched by adding capon and ox tongue. On the other hand, if you are aiming for a prestigious variant, calf's tongue and leg of veal are also essential ingredients. In addition to the meats already mentioned, genuine *Bollito misto* calls for calf's head, pig trotters, and *cotechino*, a spicy pork sausage. *Bollito* is comparatively easy to prepare. The pieces of meat are put in a pot, either one after the other or, depending on kind and size, all at the same time, and boiled until they are soft and tender. Only the sausages go into a different pot. The pieces of meat are sliced, garnished with the sausages, and the whole thing is served with *Bagnet verd*, a green sauce made from parsley, garlic, anchovies, and oil, or *Bagnet d' tomatiche*, a sweet and sour tomato sauce, or *Mostarda di Cremona*, tart candied fruits in mustard syrup.

However, braised as well as boiled meat dishes are very popular in Piedmont. *Bue brasato* is a typical north Italian dish, consisting of beef slowly braised in strong red wine with vegetables and herbs. Incidentally, this dish owes its name to the method of preparation. *Brasato* comes from the north Italian expression *brasa*, meaning coal, as the pot used to be placed on a coal-fired range and, to ensure the heat is evenly distributed, glowing coals were also placed on the lid of the pot.

Manzo brasato al Barolo
Braised meat in red wine
(Illustrated below)

For the marinade:
1 CARROT
1 MEDIUM ONION
1 STICK CELERY
2 BAY LEAVES
BLACK PEPPERCORNS
1 SMALL PIECE OF CINNAMON STICK
RED WINE (BAROLO)

3 1/2 LBS/1.5 KG RIB OF BEEF
6 TBSP/100 G BUTTER
SALT AND PEPPER
1 SMALL GLASS BRANDY

Cut the carrot, onion, and celery into small pieces and put in a large pot with the bay leaves, peppercorns, and a small piece of cinnamon stick. Add the meat, pour over the wine, and leave to marinate for 24 hours in a cool place. Remove the meat from the marinade, drain, and pat dry with kitchen paper.

Heat the butter in a casserole, brown the meat over a high heat, and salt. Strain the marinade and ladle over the meat. Cover and simmer for several hours over a low heat, until the gravy has almost boiled away.

Take out the meat, cut into slices, and arrange on a prewarmed serving-dish. Strain the gravy into a small pan, and continue cooking for a short time over a low heat. Add salt, pepper and the brandy, allow to thicken, and pour over the meat. Serve with mashed potatoes.

Bollito misto
Mixed stewed meats

Serves 8–10

1 SALTED CALF'S TONGUE, WEIGHING ABOUT 1 1/4 LBS/600 G
SALT
PEPPERCORNS
2 1/4 LBS/1 KG BEEF (SHOULDER OR NECK)
1 OVEN-READY CHICKEN, WEIGHING ABOUT 3 1/2 LBS/1.5 KG
3 CARROTS
4 STICKS CELERY
1 SMALL LEEK
2 ONIONS
1 LB/500 G VEAL (TOPSIDE)
1/2 LB/300 G FRESH PORK SAUSAGE, FLAVORED WITH GARLIC

Put the tongue in a pan with just enough water to cover it and bring to the boil. Reduce the heat, and cook the tongue for about 1½ hours until tender.

While it is cooking, boil 12 cups/3 liters water in a large casserole and add the peppercorns and the beef. Reduce the heat and simmer the meat for about 30 minutes. Then add the chicken.

Dice the carrots, celery, leek, and onions, and add them with the veal to the large casserole with the beef and the chicken. Continue to simmer for about 1 hour.

Prick the sausage several times and heat slowly in water. Rinse the tongue, which has now finished cooking, insert a kitchen knife into the tip, and remove the skin. Add the skinned tongue to the casserole with the other meat, and heat.

Cut the various meats into thin slices, divide the chicken and the sausage into portions, and arrange them all on a prewarmed serving dish. Garnish with the vegetables. Serve with *Bagnet verd* (Green sauce, see p. 149).

Serve with *Bagnet verd* (Green sauce, see p. 149).

VEGETABLE FONDUE

The classic Piedmontese dish *Bagna caoda* is a kind of vegetable fondue. Crisp raw or quickly blanched vegetables (cardoons, celery sticks, artichoke hearts, strips of bell pepper, spring vegetables, etc.) are dipped in a hot sauce of garlic and mashed anchovies and eaten with crusty bread.

BAGNA CAODA
Hot sauce

4 TBSP/50 G BUTTER
5 CLOVES OF GARLIC, THINLY SLICED
1 CUP/250 ML EXTRA VIRGIN OLIVE OIL
1/4 LB/100 G ANCHOVY FILLETS

Melt the butter in a pan and sauté the garlic. Gradually pour over the olive oil and stir in the anchovies, until a creamy consistency is obtained. Simmer for about 30 minutes and pour into a terra cotta bowl placed over a spirit burner.

To make the sauce more digestible, it is recommended that the hearts are removed from the garlic cloves, or that the garlic is marinated in milk for a few hours before use.

Vitello tonnato
Veal in tuna fish sauce (Illustrated in background)

1 1/2 lbs/700 g veal (fillet or leg)
Extra virgin olive oil
2 cups/500 ml dry white wine
Salt and pepper
2 bay leaves
2 sticks celery
1 clove garlic
1 scant cup/200 ml olive oil
2 egg yolks
Juice of 1 lemon
6 oz/200 g tuna fish in oil
2 anchovy fillets, finely chopped
2 tbsp capers and paprika

Brown the meat well in a casserole with some oil. Pour over the white wine, and add salt and pepper. Add the bay leaves, celery, and garlic, and braise for about 50 minutes over a medium heat. Allow to cool completely.
Prepare a mayonnaise from the egg yolks, olive oil, and the lemon juice. Rub the mayonnaise, together with the tuna fish, anchovies, and capers through a sieve. Cut the cold meat in thin slices and arrange on flat plates. Cover with the mayonnaise and keep in a cool place for about 2–3 hours. Garnish with capers and paprika, and serve with red wine. This dish is one of the classic starters from Piedmont, and was already famous by the beginning of the 19th century.

The battle and the chicken ragout

There are various and to some extent contradictory theories about the origin of *Polla alla Marengo*. The famous chef Auguste Escoffier (1846–1935) mentions this dish in his book *Le Livre des Menus* (The Book of Menus), and the historian Massimo Alberini, who provided a foreword to this work, gives the following introduction to the recipe: "Marengo is one of the few historical names which are linked to a particular event. On the afternoon or evening of June 14, 1800, the cook of the then First Consul, Napoleon Bonaparte, hastily prepared *Pollo alla Marengo* – probably with hens stolen from a Piedmontese farmer. The cook carved up the birds and braised the pieces in olive oil, white wine, and parsley, while the battle of Marengo raged outside. Escoffier, who was one of the most important chefs of recent times, later made this dish more elaborate by adding tomatoes, freshwater shrimps, bread, and fried eggs, all ingredients which Napoleon, who always remained loyal to 'his' chicken, would never have allowed."

Pollo alla Marengo
Chicken Marengo
(Illustrated left)

1 oven-ready chicken
All-purpose flour
2/3 cup/120 g extra virgin olive oil
Salt and pepper
1 lb/500 g ripe plum tomatoes, with skin and seeds removed
2 cloves garlic, pressed
A few leaves of basil
2 cups/500 ml dry white wine
1/2 lb/200 g fresh mushrooms, sliced
6 freshwater shrimp
6 slices white bread
6 eggs
Juice of 1 lemon
Large handful of parsley, finely chopped

Wash the chicken, cut in pieces, and toss in flour. Heat the olive oil in a pan, brown first the thighs, then the remaining pieces of chicken over a low heat, turning occasionally, and season with salt and pepper. Remove the breast portions from the pan and keep warm. Cut the tomatoes in pieces and add to the pan, together with the garlic and basil. Pour over a glass of white wine, cover, and braise for about 15 minutes over a low heat. Replace the chicken breasts in the pan, add the mushrooms, and braise for a further 20 minutes over a low heat. Heat the remaining wine in a casserole, add the shrimp, and cook for 4–5 minutes. Strain and keep warm. In another pan, fry the bread slices in a little olive oil, so that they remain soft inside. Fry the eggs in the same oil, without allowing them to run together. Drizzle the lemon juice over the chicken, sprinkle with parsley, and salt and pepper. Arrange the chicken pieces with the pan juices in the center of a serving dish. Put a fried egg on each slice of bread and arrange in a circle round the meat, garnish with the shrimp and serve.

Prosciutto baciato

Prosciutto baciato – also known as *Filetto baciato* – is an exquisite Piedmontese specialty. It is made from pork fillet or another lean part of the pig. The piece of meat, which should weigh about 1½–1¾ lbs (700–800 g), is marinated for a week in white wine and herbs. Then a salami paste is made, using plenty of *lardo* (bacon fat), and the fillet is covered with a layer about ⅜–⅝ inch (1–1.5 cm) thick. Then it is all stuffed into natural sausage skins by hand and stored for six months. When cut, the *Prosciutto baciato* looks lovely. The bright red of the fillet contrasts with the pale, almost white, layer surrounding it. Only a very few butchers produce this specialty; annual production is around 20,000.

Bagnet verd
Green sauce

1 small bunch parsley
1 clove garlic
A few capers
2 small pickled gherkins
2 anchovy fillets
1 stale bread roll
3 tbsp wine vinegar
1 hardboiled egg
Extra virgin olive oil
Salt and pepper
1 tsp sugar

Chop the parsley, garlic, and capers finely and cut the gherkins and anchovies in small pieces. Soak the bread roll in vinegar.
Put everything into a mortar and grind. Pass through a sieve and stir in the olive oil. Season with salt, pepper, and sugar. Serve as an accompaniment to beef or *Bollito misto*.

Gianduiotto

CONFECTIONERY

Since the Conquistadors returned from their journeys of exploration in the West, bringing not only news of a New World, but also cocoa, chocolate fever has been rife. Cortez and his men could not have known, at the beginning of the 16th century, what enthusiasm those unprepossessing beans would arouse. Within a few decades, they had already radically changed European traditions, fashions, and the whole culture of enjoyment. Cocoa had become so widespread in the 17th and 18th centuries, that hot chocolate was obtainable in any inn in Venice or Florence.

At that time, Piedmont and its capital Turin were developing into an important center for chocolate and confectionery. Around 1800 even Swiss confectioners like François Cailler came to the area, eager to learn. We owe the invention of the famous Turin hazelnut praline *gianduiotto* to the best-known Italian confectioners, Peyrano, Streglia, Feletti, Talmone, and Caffarel. It was created during the carnival of 1865 in honor of the traditional theatrical mask Gianduja, a symbol of the city. Genuine *gianduiotto* consists of cocoa, sugar, vanilla, and hazelnuts.

Below: 30–50 whitish seeds, the so-called cocoa beans, are hidden in each of the fruits of the cacao tree (*Theobroma cacao*). Before use, they have to be fermented, roasted, and ground into powdery brown cocoa mass.

Package design from the first half of the 19th century – the three pretty little girls, in their special aprons, are advertising the three major products of the Caffarel firm: cocoa, chocolate, and pralines.

How chocolate is produced

The evergreen cacao tree grows up to 25 feet/8 meters high. Its reddish flowers are surprisingly small in relation to the big, cucumber-like red or yellow fruits, which sprout directly from the trunk or the main branches. Cacao trees certainly need warm to hot temperatures, but they cannot tolerate direct sunlight. The shoots in particular are dependent on other plants to give them shade. Cacao trees also demand a high moisture content in the atmosphere. The tree must grow for about ten years before it really bears fruit. The fruits ripen at irregular intervals, so they have to be harvested every 4–6 weeks. Beneath the semihard, ribbed shell is a sugary flesh surrounding the cocoa beans. The freshly picked fruits are broken open, and the 30–50 whitish seeds removed. Then the cocoa beans are put into a tub, where the surrounding flesh begins to ferment. This is when the flavors first begin to develop. Then the beans are dried and the raw cocoa is shipped out. The beans are roasted, peeled, and ground, forming a sort of mushy pulp – the cocoa mass. To extract the oil and produce weak or strong cocoa powder – for drinking or cooking – the mass is pressed until the cocoa butter has separated out, and the pressed cakes are ground. Basic chocolate recipes include cocoa mass, sugar, cocoa butter, milk products such as condensed milk or milk powder, and flavorings such as vanilla or cinnamon. The ingredients are first thoroughly mixed in a melangeur, a kind of crusher. At the same time the mass must ripen for 24 hours at 77–120 °F (25–50 °C), which gives it a doughy consistency. This raw chocolate can be used for basic chocolate products, but for fine chocolate bars, the mass must be put into a machine called a *conche*, where it is compressed by rollers at 140–175 °F (60–80 °C) for several days, so that the flavorings mix and emulsify. Then the pulp is cooled to about 78 °F (28 °C) and poured into bars.

Ferrero and Nutella

The history of chocolate specialties from Piedmont would be incomplete without the brothers Giovanni and Pietro Ferrero from Farigliano near Cuneo. Born one at the end of the 19th century, the other at the beginning of the 20th, they survived both world wars and the ensuing set-backs. But the family, who owned a little cake store in Alba, were not discouraged. Shortly after the end of World War II, the Ferreros began producing a new kind of nut and cocoa cream, which they christened Nutella and sold at a very favorable price. The appetizing aroma of chocolate and the high quality of Piedmontese hazelnuts soon made this reasonably priced, nutritious spread a success. Lovers of Nutella must have remained loyal to Ferrero, as today the company is Europe's leading confectionery manufacturer and has also been producing other sweet delicacies for a long time.

But Nutella is more than just a chocolate spread – it is a highly addictive passion. On September 27, 1998, a meeting took place in a hotel outside the gates of Alba, where 350 *nutellomani* together indulged a passion, which they share with millions of fellow addicts throughout the world. Alba was, of course, the only possible venue for the celebrations – even the mayor attended, publicly confessing his own passion – because the Ferrero factory, which is still producing several million tonnes of Nutella today, is situated there. The man behind the Nutella party is – coincidentally – called Davide Ferrero, but he is not related to the "genuine" Ferreros. Apart from that, the young lawyer is president of the *Ciococlub*, the umbrella organization for Nutella fans. The club now has its own Internet site, which has been visited by around 10,000 initiates to date. Admission to the Nutella party cost the guests a minimum contribution of the equivalent of about 5 dollars. Part of the proceeds of the party were intended to go to charity, but some of the money was spent on buying 120 pounds/50 kilograms of chocolate spread and the 14 gigantic loaves of bread (each 8 feet/ 2 ½ meters long) consumed by the lucky guests. Incidentally, the Nutella party and the *Ciococlub* are not advertising or PR stunts, and the president emphasizes that they were not sponsored by Ferrero or any other chocolate firm. The "genuine" Ferrero family had previously made it clear that they wanted nothing to do with the event. But the chocolate-covered enthusiasts didn't give a cocoa bean for that, and it certainly didn't spoil their fun.

Hernando Cortez (1485–1547)
Copper engraving by Isabella Piccini, active around 1665/92, colored after a contemporary portrait.

153

ALESSI – DESIGN IN THE KITCHEN

In Piedmont there is a tradition of good knives, pots and pans, scissors, and other kitchen equipment. The Strona valley has always offered ideal conditions for the metal-processing industry. Fast-flowing torrents rushing down from the mountains used to provide the necessary water power – an important factor in the days before the invention of our present energy systems. On the north shore of Lake Orta there are still a few manufacturers making household and kitchen wares of stainless steel and other materials. One of these is Alessi. The grandfather of the current company president, Alberto Alessi, from the third generation of the family, founded a small workshop in Omegna in 1921. In 1928, it moved to Crusinallo, where the company still has its headquarters.

Of course Alessi has always been famous for clean, functional design, but in the eighties the company wanted more. In the boardroom, they dreamed of producing kitchenware whose form and function were geared to providing active support for the cook, thereby contributing to the success of the meals. So the creative team, in collaboration with designers, cooks, and historians, developed new products, which not only found their way into Italian kitchens, but soon enjoyed great popularity in the rest of Europe as well. Very few customers are scared off by the relatively high prices, since anyone who knows anything about cooking realizes firstly that good utensils are essential, and secondly that high quality kitchenware is virtually indestructible, and for that reason alone is worth a few lire, dollars pesetas, pounds, drachmas, or marks.

COMPANY HISTORY

Giovanni Alessi

1921
Giovanni Alessi Anghini founds a metal-processing business in Omegna and starts by taking in orders.
1928
The Alessi Company moves to Crusinallo.
1932
Carlo, the founder's eldest son, who had studied industrial design, joins the business. Among the most influential of his designs were the Bombé tea and coffee services.

1955
In the years following the second world war, the company is successfully transformed into a modern industrial undertaking. Carlo moves into management. His brother Ettore begins working with designers like Luigi Massoni, Carlo Mazzeri and Anselmo Vitale.

Alessi Company headquarters in Crusinallo

1970
Alberto, a grandson of the founder with a law degree, joins the firm. His goal is to abolish the distinction between mass production and craftsmanship quality.
1972
Alberto commissions Ettore Sottsass to design some oil and vinegar sets.
1977
Richard Sapper is entrusted with the design of the first *caffettiera*. It is the start of a collaboration, which will produce many classic designs of coffee-maker.
1980
Achille Castiglione works with Alessi and designs Dry, the first Design-Smiths cutlery set. It comes onto the market in 1982.
1983
The Piazza Tea and Coffee Project is brought to life. The idea: famous architects should design a tea and coffee service, without having to consider the limitations of mass production. The result: objects made of high quality materials in limited editions designed by architects like Michael Graves, Hans Hollein, Aldo Rossi, Robert Venturi, and Richard Meier.
1986
Philippe Starck works for Alessi and achieves immediate success with a postmodern classic, the Juicy Salif juice press. It comes onto the market in 1989.
1989
Designers Stefano Giovannoni and Guido Venturini, working as the design duo King Kong, design the amusing Girotondo collection.
1993
Start of the Family Follows Friction Project, a series of utensils by young designers, in shapes inspired by comic figures and toys.
1997
Enzo Mari joins the ranks of famous designers working for Alessi. New designs are produced, but Alessi also reissues some old designs from the sixties, which were produced for Danese.

Right hand page: Juicy Salif juice press Philippe Starck, 1989

Cruet set for oil, vinegar, salt, and pepper
Ettore Sottsass, 1978

La Cupola espresso machine
Aldo Rossi, 1989

9090 cafetière
Richard Sapper, 1979

La Conica coffee pot
Aldo Rossi, 1984

Dry
Achille Castiglioni, 1982

Bread basket
Enzo Mari, 1997

"Singing" kettle
Richard Sapper, 1983

Nonno di Antonio garlic press
Guido Venturini, 1996

Corkscrew Anna G
Alessandro Mendini, 1994

Tea and coffee service Piazza
Hans Hollein, 1983

Bombé tea and coffee service
Carlo Alessi Anghini, 1945

Toast rack from the Girotondo series
King Kong, 1996

Il Conico kettle
Aldo Rosso, 1986

Sugar bowl
Michael Graves, 1992

A Law for wine

There can hardly be another wine law in the world as controversial as the Italian one. When it came into being in 1963, the legislature was above all concerned with protecting the winegrowers from unfair competition. Legally designated origins are important for consumers too, of course, because they guarantee that the wine they have bought really comes from the area shown on the label – which was not necessarily true before. But the wine law does not only define the winegrowing area, but also regulates the varieties of grapes individual wines are made from, and even how they are to be made. In order to classify the different qualities, the legislature created a quality pyramid with four tiers. The majority of wines are sold as simple *vino da tavola*, table wine of no designated origin. Above them are the *vini con indicazione geografica (Igt)*, wines with a simple geographical indication of origin. Quality wines are categorized as DOC, *Denominazione di origine controllata*, controlled designation

of origin, and the highest level as DOCG, *Denominazione di origine controllata e garantita*, that is controlled and guaranteed wines. There are in total only 18 designations of origin altogether in this most prestigious category. In practice, the almost 300 labels of designated origin in Italy only rarely guarantee a high quality wine – sadly there are wines of only average quality in many DOC and even DOCG areas, and even whole winegrowing areas which do not actually deserve the title of quality winegrowing area. As a result, many wine-lovers choose their wines exclusively by the name of the producer, not by the legal category, and so it happens that today – paradoxically – even table wines may be among the most expensive and sought-after in Italy.

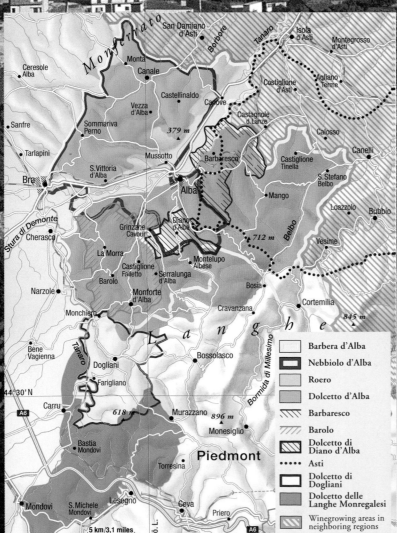

- Barbera d'Alba
- Nebbiolo d'Alba
- Roero
- Dolcetto d'Alba
- Barbaresco
- Barolo
- Dolcetto di Diano d'Alba
- Asti
- Dolcetto di Dogliani
- Dolcetto delle Langhe Monregalesi
- Winegrowing areas in neighboring regions

PIEDMONT – KINGDOM OF THE NEBBIOLO

Piedmont lies tucked between the northwestern curve of the Alps and the Apennines, which determine its climate – very hot summers and almost continental cold winters. Wine is grown in almost all parts of the region, but especially in the hilly countryside of the southern half, which is made up of the provinces of Cuneo, Asti, and Alessandria. Of almost 123,550 acres (50,000 hectares) of grapes, 60 percent is designated for the production of quality wines, which represents a very high proportion for Italy.

The most widely grown grape in Piedmont is – one might almost say of course – red, and is called Barbera. The former mass-grown variety, which was at the center of the country's biggest wine scandal in the eighties, has become something of a star over the last decade. Its wines have achieved a quality which has won the respect of wine-lovers throughout the world. But the region owes its prestige almost exclusively to the Nebbiolo, or more precisely the Nebbiolo wines Barolo and Barbaresco, which are produced on the hills of Langa or Langhe right next to the truffle-capital Alba. In a way, the emergence of the famous Nebbiolo wines in the 19th century marks the birth of modern Italian quality wine production as a whole, as well as that of the Piedmont region as a traditional and dependable producer of fine wines.

"King of wines and wine of kings" – that is what they called Barolo, which is today the most important of the Nebbiolo wines, not least because its "discovery" by the French enologist Oudart in the castle of the Marchesa Giulietta Falletti was actively supported by the House of Savoy. It is an ideal combination of the characteristics of the Nebbiolo grape: strength, elegance, and good keeping quality. As it ages, good Barolo develops hints of truffle, tar, undergrowth, roses, tea, and spices and, when mature, tastes full, round, and velvety in the mouth.

NOT ONLY IN PIEDMONT

Although today Nebbiolo is considered to be one of the best varieties of grape in the world, it has not become widespread, unlike famous French grapes, such as Cabernet Sauvignon or Merlot. In Italy, outside Piedmont, it is cultivated almost exclusively in Lombardy. In the Valtellina valley, where it is the main variety used in the DOC Valtellina, it is known by the name of Chiavennasca, and it makes up a small part of the blend used for the still, red wines of the DOC Terre di Franciacorta, from the Franciacorta area. Apart from that, this variety is occasionally planted in the United States – especially in the Californian winegrowing areas of Sonoma, Paso Robles, Santa Maria, and Santa Barbara – and experimentally in a few Australian vineyards. Most recently, even one German grower has been experimenting with Nebbiolo grapes.

Before Oudart's time, Nebbiolo from Barolo and the surrounding villages was mostly made sweet. Later they allowed the must or the wine to ferment so long on the skins, that, when young, the finished product often seemed harsh and off-putting, with an exaggerated taste of tannin, only developing a certain charm with age. In the eighties, a group of younger Piedmontese winegrowers took it upon themselves to give Barolo a more modern face. They changed the methods of pressing, and allowed the wine to mature in small casks made of new wood, which gave its bouquet an even greater variety, and made it mellower and more attractive when young. As so often in the world when something is revolutionized, in Piedmont, too, modernists and traditionalists argued over who made the genuine, true, and unadulterated Barolo. But basically this argument was unnecessary, since the best adherents of both sides produce outstanding wines which mature well – just in a different style.

From right next to Barolo – on the opposite side of the small town of Alba – comes Barbaresco, a wine which is reputed to be less strong but even more elegant, and to have a certain "femininity." Once the more famous and successful of the two wines, it nevertheless suffered during its time of great commercial success, which led many winegrowers and sellers to produce it in increasing quantities and increasingly dubious quality. It is only in recent years that a handful of growers from Barbaresco and the surrounding area have restored the wine to its former greatness.

Other Nebbiolo wines from the area around Asti, which are no doubt only second rank, but are rising in quality, are Nebbiolo d'Alba, and the red Roero. By contrast, the Nebbiolo wines of Northern Piedmont, Gattinara, and Ghemme – where the grape is known as Spanna – suffered a similar fate to that of Barbaresco, but with far more serious consequences. Even the recently successful application for DOCG status could not breathe new life into them. In Piedmont, Nebbiolo is used in a further 14 DOC wines, which are for the most part (still) fairly unimportant. These include old, traditional, but forgotten names like Boca, Bramaterra, and Fara, as well as the new labels Langhe, Monferrato, and Piemonte, and among them are a series of high-quality former table wines. In some of these, the variety is well supplemented by adding larger or smaller quantities of Barbera.

In summer Nebbiolo needs a lot of light and warmth. The cold Piedmont winters, seen here near Ivrea, provide the optimum conditions for the vines to regenerate.

WORMWOOD AND VERMOUTH

The herb-flavored wine vermouth was once scarcely ranked as a valued or prestigious drink. Although it seems to have a long tradition behind it, the name probably goes back to the Old High German word *werimouta*, which describes a kind of vegetable bitters that stimulate the digestion, but which nobody liked drinking. This was to change abruptly in 1786, when Antonio Benedetto Carpano presented the customers in his bar in Turin with his own creation, which he called vermouth.

The new drink was immediately taken up with enthusiasm. Carpano had not only managed to improve local white wine by adding a particularly refined and strictly secret mixture of herbs, he had also succeeded in polishing up the hitherto mediocre image of wormwood and selling it as a luxury wine. Carpano's competitors were also convinced by this concept. Other manufacturers of spirits, particularly Cinzano, began to produce the aromatic fortified wine. Martini & Rossi came on to the market in 1863 with their version of vermouth. Other Piedmontese firms such as Gancia and Cora followed.

Piedmont is still the home of vermouth, and Carpano, Cinzano, and Martini & Rossi are still synonymous with this aromatic drink. The only difference is that now they no longer make it in little witches' kitchens, but with the aid of the most modern technology. The basic ingredient is white wine. While the pioneers of vermouth relied on Moscato d'Asti or Moscato di Canelli, today they use white wines with very little distinctive flavor of their own. They add sugar, alcohol, and a mixture of various herbal extracts, among them mugwort, wormwood leaves, marjoram, nutmeg, thyme, sage, cinnamon, aniseed, fennel, and cloves. The "seasoned" wine is then heated and distilled. Sweet vermouth is colored with caramel. The alcohol content of a dry vermouth must be around 18 percent.

MANHATTAN
(Illustrated left)

1 MEASURE OF CANADIAN WHISKY
1/2 MEASURE OF SWEET VERMOUTH
DASH OF ANGOSTURA BITTERS
ICE
COCKTAIL CHERRIES

Pour the whisky, vermouth, Angostura, and ice into a cocktail shaker, mix, and strain into a chilled cocktail glass. Decorate with cocktail cherries and, if desired, with a twist of lemon peel.

Martini, Carpano, Gancia, Cora, Cinzano – these are the great names of vermouth, which should be found in every well-stocked bar. The two classic Italian cocktails Americano and Negroni both contain vermouth. Negroni apparently owes its name to a certain Count Camillo Negroni, who invented it.

Dry Martini

1 1/4 MEASURES OF GIN
1/4 MEASURE OF VERMOUTH
EXTRA DRY
ICE
1 OLIVE WITH PIT

Pour the gin, vermouth, and ice
into a cocktail shaker, mix, and
strain into a chilled cocktail
glass. Garnish with an olive.
Only use olives with pits, never
stuffed olives. Olives should not
be preserved in oil but in brine.
A twist of lemon may be added.

All recipes for 1 drink

Extra Dry Martini

1 1/2 MEASURES OF GIN
DASH OF VERMOUTH EXTRA DRY

Pour the gin and a suggestion
of very dry vermouth into a
cocktail shaker, mix, and strain
into a chilled cocktail glass.
Purists insist that the gin should
merely be shown the vermouth
bottle.

Americano

ICE
3/4 MEASURE OF CAMPARI
3/4 MEASURE OF SWEET
VERMOUTH
SODA WATER
SLICES OF LEMON

Put the ice into a glass. Add
Campari and vermouth. Top up
with soda water and stir briefly.
Garnish with lemon peel.

Negroni

1/2 MEASURE OF CAMPARI
1/2 MEASURE OF SWEET
VERMOUTH
1/2 MEASURE OF GIN
ICE
ORANGE AND LEMON PEEL

Pour the Campari, vermouth,
gin, and ice into a cocktail
shaker, mix, and strain into a
chilled cocktail glass. Garnish
with orange and lemon peel.

opular tradition accuses the Ligurians of being unrecep-tive to strangers, feeling happiest at home, and preferring to do everything for themselves. In their cuisine, too, they like to use those trusted products which come from the 220 mile (350 kilometer) long stretch of coastline, with its rough, mountainous hinterland or are fished out of their own waters. The tangy herbs, the crisp vegetables, the sea creatures, the eggs for the *Torta pasqualina* – everything is *nostrano*, that is, local produce, as it says on the notices in the markets. Even the wine, which is grown with great effort on the rough, steeply terraced slopes, and lovingly made into small vintages of the highest quality, seems to have been invented in Liguria, it suits the local food so well. Savory cakes and pies are a Ligurian specialty. As well as *Torta pasqualina*, they still serve the traditional *Torta marinara*, which is not – as the name might lead you to think – a pie filled with fish, but a splendid savory flan. It was made with Swiss chard, ricotta, fresh mush-rooms, and parmesan by the seamen's wives, because they knew that husbands on leave after months at sea at the mercy of a ship's cook – who might have been competent if they were lucky, but was usually only capable of serving dried fish and ship's biscuit – always came ashore with a hearty appetite for savory herbs, earthy mushrooms, and fresh cheese. It is not surprising that Ligurian cuisine is nicknamed *cucina del ritorno*, or "homecoming" cooking. A more modest, but no less tasty version of the *Torta salata* or savory cake is Ligurian *focaccia*. In many areas, this thin bread is also filled with cheese, copiously sprinkled with oil, and garnished with onions. The addition of onions was particularly sensible in the harbor towns, because their bactericidal effects and high vitamin C content helped to protect the population against the diseases the men brought back from overseas.

Because the Ligurians like to make everything for themselves, they have also invented a pizza of their own. The focaccia-like specialty, topped with onions and anchovies, comes from Oneglia, now called Imperia, and is known as *Pizza all'Andrea*. It was invented at the end of the 15th or beginning of the 16th century – by the ingenious statesman and naval hero Andrea Doria, at least so the legend goes.

Previous double page: Tasty vegetables such as freshly picked artichokes are a part of the Ligurian cuisine. Here the grower Giampiero Navone is checking his stock.

Left: The steep, inaccessible, terraced vineyards of the Cinqueterre, pictured here near Corniglia, do not permit the use of machinery. The grapes must be tended and harvested by hand.

Alice (sardelle or anchovy) and sardina or sarda (sardine)

With cries such as "Wonderful anchovies for sale, as fresh and lively as if they had quicksilver in their bodies!" or "I sell the silver from the sea!" the fishermen advertise their freshly caught wares. Like the sardine, the sardelle, now better known as the anchovy, is a member of the herring family. They were traditionally caught in the seas outside the Gulf of Genoa. But now – probably on account of their comparatively firm flesh – both

Sardelle

Sardine

sardines and anchovies find their way less often into the cooking pot, which is a real shame, because they taste very piquant and spicy. Sardines and anchovies are nice freshly cooked, but can also be tasty when preserved in oil, salt, or marinade. Sardines, which are good value, are often sold smoked, if they do not end up in oil, in a can on the supermarket shelves of the rest of Europe.

Aguglia (garfish)

This valuable fish actually belongs to the cod family, but is very different in appearance. The garfish has a long, slender body and grows up to three feet (one meter) long. Salt water gar can be caught all year round, but the best time is between September and January. Its fine, firm flesh is good when braised, and this tasty fish is an essential part of a *fritto misto alla ligure*

Tonno (tuna)

Though the tuna found in Ligurian waters is obviously smaller than its relatives on other shores, its flesh tastes just as good, if not better. Fresh tuna can be cut in wafer-thin slices and served as a *carpaccio*, but it is also a delicacy when grilled. Tuna preserved in vinegar or oil is good for savory sauces or as a filling for pasta.

Sgombro (mackerel)

The mackerel, which is related to the tuna, is one of the commonest fishes throughout the world. Italians are particularly fond of this tasty, healthy, good value fish. Mackerel must always be eaten very fresh, because it quickly goes off.

HUNTING THE BLUE FISH

The seas of the Gulf of Genoa are restless waters. Countless whirlpools, shallows, storms, and other horrors lurk between the Ponente and the Levant, turning the daily tasks of fishermen and sailors into a dangerous adventure. Fishermen in particular always had to struggle to earn a living – and it is still the same today – because the waters are not especially rich in fish. If they are to catch anything at all, they must venture far out to sea, and hope to find the *pesce azzurro*. These fish get their name from the blue-green sheen of their skin and the fact that they live far out in the deep blue waters of the open sea. The "blue fish" group includes herring species like sardines and anchovies, as well as certain others, such as mackerel, tuna, and swordfish.

LIGURIAN FISH DISHES

Stuffed sardines are not really difficult to prepare, but they take a bit of work, because stuffing the tasty mixture into the little bodies is tricky. But it is well worth the effort, as this typical Ligurian specialty tastes absolutely delicious.
Cappon magro, on the other hand, is a rather complicated dish and takes a little time to prepare. The appeal of the "lean capon" lies in the perfect combination of ingredients from the seas with those from the fields and gardens. Originally a simple sailors' dish, its preparation on land has become ever more elaborate, because it had the advantage of fitting neatly into the requirements for fasting. As capons – roosters which have been castrated and fattened up – are very fatty, they were not allowed to be eaten during Lent. So the resourceful Ligurians changed to "lean capon," which – strictly according to Church law – consists of various kinds of fish, but in the cooking can incorporate all kinds of delicious bits of chicken. By contrast, *burrida* is a fairly simple, nutritious fish dish which in former times appeared every day on tables in the fishing villages.

CAPPON MAGRO
Lean capon (Illustrated right)

1 CLEANED AND GUTTED GURNARD
1 SMALL CRAYFISH
12 SCAMPI
ASSORTED SEAFOOD
HERB AND ONION STOCK
OLIVE OIL
JUICE OF ONE LEMON
SALT
1 CAULIFLOWER
1/2 LB/200 G GREEN BEANS
1 LARGE POTATO
1 CELERY HEART
2 CARROTS
1 BUNCH SALSIFY
4 ARTICHOKES
VINEGAR
4–6 SLICES/200–300 G ZWIEBACK
1/2 CLOVE OF GARLIC
6 HARD-BOILED EGGS, QUARTERED
15 GREEN OLIVES
4 OZ/100 G MUSHROOMS IN OIL

For the sauce:
2 STALE ROLLS
VINEGAR
6 SALTED ANCHOVIES
BASIL LEAVES, CHOPPED
1 CLOVE GARLIC, MINCED
1 BUNCH PARSLEY, CHOPPED
1/3 CUP/50 G PINE NUTS
2 TBSP/20 G CAPERS
2 EGG YOLKS
1 CUP OLIVE OIL
1/2 CUP QUALITY VINEGAR

Wash and fillet the gurnard. Clean the crayfish, scampi, and other seafood. Cook them all together in the herb and onion stock. Marinate in oil, lemon juice, and salt.
Boil the prepared cauliflower, beans, potato, celery, and one carrot in a saucepan until tender. Cook the salsify and the quartered artichokes separately. Cut the cooked vegetables into small pieces and dress with oil, vinegar, and salt.
For the sauce, soak the rolls in vinegar. Wash the anchovies and grind in a mortar. Add the basil, garlic, parsley, pine nuts, capers, egg yolks, and rolls, and grind to a fine paste. Sieve the paste into a bowl, and mix well with one glass oil and ½ glass good vinegar. Rub the zwieback slices with garlic and cover the base of a large soup bowl. Drizzle a little oil onto them, and pour over a few spoonfuls of sauce. Arrange vegetables, gurnard, and four hard-boiled eggs in layers. Finally place the crayfish in the middle and arrange the seafood around it. Chop the two remaining hard-boiled eggs and sprinkle over.
Slice the remaining raw carrot and place on small skewers with the shrimp, olives, and mushrooms, and place in the bowl, so that the various colors contrast with one another.

ACCIUGHE RIPIENE AL FORNO
Stuffed anchovies

1 1/4 LB/600 G FRESH ANCHOVIES
1 STALE ROLL
MILK
2 EGGS
1/2 CUP/40 G PARMESAN, GRATED
MARJORAM
1 CLOVE GARLIC, CHOPPED
SALT AND PEPPER
OLIVE OIL
BREADCRUMBS

Left: Steeply rising cliffs are so much characteristic of the Ligurian riviera.

Clean and gut the anchovies, cut off the heads and tails, and allow to drain. Soak the roll in milk, and chop up a few anchovies. For the filling, mix the eggs, cheese, the softened roll, marjoram, garlic, and chopped anchovy in a bowl, and season with salt and pepper. Fill the anchovies with the mixture. Brush a fireproof dish with oil, and sprinkle with breadcrumbs. Place the stuffed anchovies in it, with the filling uppermost, and bake in a preheated oven at 400 °F (200 °C) for 12–15 minutes until the filling is golden brown.

BURRIDA
Fish soup

2 LB/1 KG ONIONS
2 CLOVES GARLIC
5 TBSP OLIVE OIL
1 LB/500 G TOMATOES
SALT
2 LB/1 KG ASSORTED SEA FISH
1 LB/500 G SEAFOOD (SCAMPI, BABY SQUID)
PEPPER
1 BUNCH PARSLEY, CHOPPED
1/2 TSP DRIED OREGANO
1 GLASS DRY WHITE WINE

Cut the onions in thin rings and the garlic in wafer-thin slices. Slowly heat a little olive oil in a pan, and sauté half the onion rings and garlic. Blanch and skin the tomatoes, remove the seeds, and dice small. Add half to the onions and salt.
Gut and clean the fish and seafood. Fillet the fish, peel the scampi, cut the heads off the squid. Add the fish and seafood to the pan, and season with salt and pepper. Cover with the remaining onions, tomatoes, and garlic, and salt and pepper once more. Sprinkle the top with parsley and oregano. Pour over the white wine, and drizzle over the remaining olive oil. Cook over a low heat, until the soup has thickened to a creamy consistency.

OLIVE OIL

After Spain, Italy is now the second largest producer of olive oil in the world. Apart from Lombardy and Piedmont, where the climate is not suited to olive growing, different kinds and sizes of olives grow throughout Italy, and the oils they produce are very varied. Liguria is the home of a particularly fine oil. Unlike the sometimes very tangy and rather bitter Tuscan, or the sharp, fruity oil from Apulia, Ligurian olive oil is very light, with a delicate, aromatic flavor. Unfortunately it is rarely obtainable outside the region, as it is only produced in small quantities. In this mountainous region, with its many steep slopes, it is just as difficult to grow and harvest olives as wine, because the olive trees have to be planted on narrow, and rather inaccessible terraces.

The main varieties grown in Liguria are Taggiasca and Lavagnina, but most of the oil comes from Taggiasca olives. The relatively small fruits are picked in December and January, when they are almost ripe. The whole family is involved in the harvest, as they are forced to pick in the traditional manner here, because the steep, narrow strips of land are unsuitable for the modern machinery that is normally used in flat areas. The team of pickers sets off for the olive grove with big nets and long poles and ladders. First of all, they spread the nets out under the trees, then they carefully strike the branches with the poles, so that the ripe fruits fall. Any that remain are stripped off by hand. This method of harvesting is very labor-intensive, and this is later reflected in the price of the oil. But hand-picked olives have one big advantage. The fruits are not damaged in the gathering, so the oily flesh does not oxidize with the air, which would considerably detract from the taste and quality of the oil later on. Oxidation, an increase in the free oil acid content, and the threat of fermentation are the chief dangers to which the fresh crop is exposed, so the olives must be brought to the oil mill as quickly as possible. To shorten the way to the nearest main road, or even to the provincial capital, which may be very long in those parts of Liguria

which are not highly developed, most villages have installed their own oil mills – known as *gumbi*. These small mills are often found in the cellars of private houses, and were often turned by donkeys. If the village was near a stream or a river, the mill might also be water-powered. Small oil mills are still working in some parts of Liguria today, producing excellent oil in the traditional way.

The olives are first ground to a brownish pulp between massive millstones. Then the oily mass is spread out on round mats, which are piled on top of one another, and the oil is pressed out of this "tower" with constantly increasing pressure from above. The juice which is pressed out contains not only oil, but also water and fruit residue. Formerly – and you can still see some smaller producers using this process today – the emulsion was just left alone, because the oil and fruit juice separate automatically, and the heavier water is left at the bottom of the barrel. But nowadays centrifuges are mostly used to separate the oil and water, as the fruit juices can easily start to ferment. Finally the oil is put into large containers so that the sediment can settle. In Liguria, these traditional containers are called *giare*. Many oil mills even had purpose-built storage tanks lined with ceramic tiles, but now clarification usually takes place in modern stainless steel containers.

CONIGLIO CON OLIVE TAGGIASCHE
Rabbit with olives

3 LBS/1.5 KG OVEN-READY RABBIT, WITH ORGAN MEAT (LIVER, HEART, AND KIDNEYS)
1 SMALL ONION
3 CLOVES GARLIC
1 SPRIG ROSEMARY
1 SPRIG THYME
2 BAY LEAVES
1 SMALL PEPERONCINO
EXTRA VIRGIN OLIVE OIL
SALT
3 CUPS/750 ML DRY WHITE WINE
1/2 CUP/70 G BLACK OLIVES IN BRINE

Cut the rabbit in medium pieces, wash, and pat dry. Wash the liver, heart, and kidneys, pat dry, and leave aside. Finely chop the onion, press the garlic, and chop the herbs. Sauté all together with the bay leaves and small peperoncino in olive oil in a casserole. Add the rabbit pieces, and brown on all sides over a high heat. Cut the organ meat into small pieces and add to the casserole. When the meat has colored, add salt, and pour over the wine. Cover, reduce the heat, and allow the wine to boil away slowly. If the meat should get too dry, pour over a little lukewarm water. After about 45 minutes, add the black olives and simmer for about 15 minutes, until the juices have thickened.

The different colors of the freshly picked olives indicate different degrees of ripeness. The darker the fruit, the riper it is.

Background: In many parts of Italy, the landscape means that the olives still have to be gathered with nets, which involves a lot of effort. Modern machinery is difficult to use on steeply terraced ground.

Ceppo antiquo – Extra virgin olive oil

Gaziello – Extra virgin olive oil

Trucco – Extra virgin olive oil

Amoretti Carlo – Extra virgin olive oil

Ranzo imperia – Extra virgin olive oil

Podere L'Alpicella – Extra virgin olive oil

Amoretti Carlo – Extra virgin olive oil

Trucco – Extra virgin taggiasca olive oil

The annual basil has leaves of various sizes. The stems grow up to 20 inches (50 cm) high.

PESTO AND OTHER SAUCES

Pesto alla genovese or *Battuto alla genovese* is certainly one of Liguria's most famous specialties. This spicy green paste of basil, olive oil, garlic, pine nuts, and cheese has recently become very popular in the rest of Europe, although there it usually comes straight out of a sterile jar onto the pasta. But it is definitely worth getting to know the flavor of freshly-made pesto.

Whether the traditional Ligurian sauces absolutely must be made in a mortar is arguable – but it is certain that good results can only be obtained by using good ingredients.

Opinions on the ingredients of pesto and theories concerning the only proper way to make it are many and varied. Some insist on the inclusion of pine nuts, while the purists say this is a variation from the district of Savona and has no connection with the original *Pesto alla genovese*. They also argue about whether the basil leaves should be washed, and whether it is permissible to make pesto in a blender, instead of in a marble mortar. All you can say about it is that the metal blades of the blender really can affect the taste of the basil. On the other hand, the machine only takes a short time to produce an even paste, which would have taken a cook, using traditional utensils such as a mortar and a wooden pestle, quite some time to achieve. At any rate, the experts are agreed on two points: the aromatic taste of the pesto is absolutely dependent on the quality of the olive oil and the basil. Only the best Ligurian extra virgin olive oil should be used. Cheap olive oil ruins the pesto, just as surely as limp herbs, which have never seen genuine sunlight in their short life. Even the very strong flavored basil from southern Italy distorts the taste, as it often has a slightly minty aftertaste. Small-leafed Ligurian basil, which has been grown in a tiny herb garden where a strong sea breeze sometimes blows, is undoubtedly the best. Leaves picked while the plant is in flower have the strongest flavor. For anyone unwilling to believe this, a trip to the pesto stronghold of Genoa is recommended. Sampling it here will confirm once and for all that Ligurian pesto simply could not taste as good anywhere else in the world.

The splendid Ligurian pasta creations would also be inconceivable without the delicious local sauces. The pale, creamy *Salsa di noci*, made from walnuts, pine nuts, garlic, butter, and cream, is almost as much of a favorite in Liguria as the green pesto. The combination of nuts and cream or yogurt might suggest that the recipe originated in the Orient. As an important port, Genoa traditionally provided a forum for culinary influences from all over the world. Other Ligurian sauces, too, such as *Sugo di carciofi*, which is made from artichokes, mushrooms, onions, garlic, concentrated tomato paste, and white wine, taste wonderful with *trenette* or *trofie*. Only *Bagnun di acciughe*, a particularly tangy sauce of anchovies and tomatoes, is not used for pasta. Instead, it is spread on slices of toasted white bread.

PESTO ALLA GENOVESE
Genoese pesto (basil sauce)
(Illustrated right)

1 BUNCH BASIL
1 CLOVE GARLIC
2 TBSP/20 G PINE NUTS
COARSE SALT
SCANT 1/3 CUP/25 G NOT TOO STRONG PECORINO, GRATED
SCANT 1/3 CUP/25 G FRESHLY GRATED PARMESAN OR GRANA
2–3 TBSP EXTRA VIRGIN OLIVE OIL

Wash the basil carefully and allow to drain. Chop in a blender, together with the garlic, pine nuts, and a pinch of coarse salt. Gradually add the grated cheese, and work into an even paste. Finally, slowly mix in the olive oil, until a creamy consistency is achieved.
Before pouring over the pasta – *trenette* are the best kind – mix the pesto with a little of the hot water in which the pasta was cooked.

Minestrone alla genovese

Genoese vegetable soup
(Illustrated pp. 178/179 front left)

1/4 LB/100 G WHITE CABBAGE
SMALL HANDFUL/50 G GREEN BEANS
2 POTATOES
2 CARROTS
2 LEEKS
2 TOMATOES
2 ZUCCHINI
1 ONION
1 CLOVE GARLIC
1 BUNCH PARSLEY
A FEW BORAGE LEAVES
1/4 LB/100 G FRESH OR PRESOAKED RED BEANS
1/2 CUP OLIVE OIL
1 PIECE OF PARMESAN RIND
6 OZ/150 G SHORT NOODLES
1 TBSP PESTO
SALT
FRESHLY GRATED PARMESAN

Clean all vegetables and herbs, and chop in small pieces. In a large pan, bring a good 8 cups/2 liters water to a boil. Add the beans and vegetables, with the exception of the onion, garlic, and herbs and cook until tender in fiercely boiling water. Then add the onion, garlic, and herbs, reduce the heat, cover, and simmer for just under 2 hours, stirring occasionally. After 1 hour, add the oil and the cheese rind, and salt the vegetables. Mash the potatoes and beans with a wooden spoon or a soup ladle, to give the soup a velvety consistency, but do not purée the vegetables. When the vegetables are cooked to a pulp, add the noodles and cook until *al dente*.

Remove the soup from the hob, stir in the pesto, and salt to taste. Pour into soup plates and serve with a dash of olive oil and freshly grated parmesan.

Salsa di noci

Walnut sauce

18 WALNUT KERNELS
1/3 CUP/50 G PINE NUTS
1/2 CLOVE GARLIC
1 BUNCH PARSLEY
1 CUP/250 ML LIGHT CREAM
SALT AND PEPPER
3 TBSP FRESHLY GRATED PARMESAN
1 1/3 TBSP BUTTER

Blanch the walnut kernels and remove the skins. Chop the walnuts, pine nuts, garlic, and parsley finely in a blender, and pour into a bowl. Slowly add the cream, stirring constantly. Season with salt and pepper.

Pour over the pasta, cooked until *al dente* with grated parmesan and melted butter.

Bagnum di acciughe

Anchovies in tomato sauce

1 3/4 LBS/800 G FRESH ANCHOVIES
2 CLOVES GARLIC, FINELY CHOPPED
1 ONION, FINELY CHOPPED
4–5 TBSP OLIVE OIL
3/4 LB/300 G RIPE TOMATOES, SKINNED AND SEEDED
1 GLASS DRY WHITE WINE
1 BUNCH PARSLEY, CHOPPED
SLICES OF WHITE BREAD, TOASTED

Clean and gut the anchovies, and pat dry. Sauté the onion and garlic in olive oil. Dice the tomatoes small, add them to the pan, with salt and pepper, and simmer for 10 minutes. Pour over half the wine, and simmer over a low heat. Place the prepared anchovies in the pan, pour over the remaining wine, cover the anchovies with a little sauce, and sprinkle with parsley, salt, and pepper. Depending on their size, the anchovies will be ready in about 10 minutes. Rub the slices of toast with a little garlic, put them on plates, and arrange the anchovies in their "bagnum" on top.

Bagnum di acciughe was in times gone by the fishermen's breakfast, when they had returned from fishing and were waiting for their nets to dry. There were little cooking stoves on the boats, on which the men could prepare this simple dish for themselves.

Harvest time in the vegetable covered plains of Albenga in the province of Savona.

VEGETABLES

Vegetable growers in Liguria struggle with the same difficulties as wine and olive growers. Large stretches of level ground suitable for long, flat beds are comparatively rare; in many places, the Ligurians must instead tend and care for small market gardens, split over several terraces. But this does not frighten them off; on the contrary, they love young, crisp vegetables, and they are proud of the regional dishes which they make from them. Artichokes, asparagus, leeks, and tomatoes, as well as olives for the table and dwarf beans, are among their favorite vegetables.

Carciofo, the Italian word for artichoke, probably comes from the Arabic *kharshuf* – an indication that the plant was also grown in the Near East. Today artichokes grow all around the Mediterranean, but very diverse varieties have become naturalized in Italy. In Liguria, the most commonly grown variety is Spinoso di Liguria, which can be harvested in autumn and winter. Artichokes are not only delicious and easily digestible but also healthy. Whether they are sautéd, stuffed, or dipped in sauce a leaf at a time, they contain a lot of mineral salts and roughage, their bitter constituents stimulate the digestive system, they invigorate the liver, detoxify the body, and lower the cholesterol level. Alongside countless recipes for their beloved artichokes, the Ligurians also have in *condijun* a fitting counterpart to the *salade niçoise* of the neighboring French Riviera. And in the winter, *mesciua*, a tasty soup made from dried beans and chickpeas, is a great favorite. According to legend, this specialty was invented in one of the ports. Apparently poor women used to run to the harbor when grain or bean sacks were about to be taken on board or unloaded from the hold of a ship, because some of the sacks would always split while they were being moved, so the women could collect the grain and beans to make soup for their families in the evening.

As well as Spinoso di Liguria, the wonderfully delicate variety Violetto d'Albenga is also grown in Liguria.

SALAD DELIGHTS

In summer on the Riviera, they like crisp salads, smelling of gardens, the sea, and olive oil. Whereas in France you order a *salade niçoise* for lunch, a few miles further east you ask for a Genoese *condiggion*, also known in other areas as *condijun*. Despite the linguistic differences, all these salads are made from fresh vegetables like tomato, cucumber, bell pepper, and onion, dressed with basil, garlic, and a sauce made of vinegar, oil, and salt. This crisp summer salad is garnished with a hard-boiled egg cut into eight and black olives.

CONDIJUN
Colorful salad
(Main illustration, center back)

1 CLOVE GARLIC
4 BEEF TOMATOES, NOT TOO RIPE
2 YELLOW BELL PEPPERS
1 CUCUMBER
2 SPRING ONIONS
1 HANDFUL BLACK OLIVES IN BRINE
2 ANCHOVIES
A FEW BASIL LEAVES
OLIVE OIL
VINEGAR
SALT
1 HARD-BOILED EGG

Rub the inside of a salad bowl with the clove of garlic. Remove the seeds from the tomatoes and peppers. Chop tomatoes, peppers, cucumber, and onions into small pieces. Put everything into the bowl, and add the olives, cleaned anchovies, and basil. Dress with oil, vinegar, and salt. If desired, add a hard-boiled egg cut in eight.
Mix well and allow to stand for about 10 minutes before serving.

MESCIUA
Pulse stew

1 1/2 CUPS/300 G CHICKPEAS
1 1/2 CUPS/300 G DRIED WHITE BEANS
1/2 CUP/100 G BUCKWHEAT GRAINS
BAKING SODA
SALT
BLACK PEPPER
OLIVE OIL

The evening before, soak the chickpeas, beans, and buckwheat in plenty of lukewarm water in three separate bowls, to each of which has been added 1 teaspoon of baking soda.
Drain the chickpeas and beans, put in a pan of slightly salted cold water, and boil for about 3 hours. Half an hour before the end of the cooking time, put the buckwheat in a separate pan of slightly salted water and boil for 30 minutes. As soon as they are all ready, pour the buckwheat with its water into the pan with the chickpeas and beans. There should be about 6 cups/1½ liters of liquid in the pan altogether. Salt, and cook for a further 15 minutes.
Pour the stew into a bowl and serve. Have black pepper in a mill and olive oil on the table, for everyone to help themselves.

FRICASSEA DI CARCIOFI
Fricassee of artichokes

12 ARTICHOKES
2 TSP/10 ML LEMON JUICE
3 EGGS
1/3 CUP/30 G GRANA, GRATED
1 CLOVE GARLIC
1 1/2 TBSP/20 ML OLIVE OIL

Clean the artichokes, break off the stalks, and remove the hard outer leaves. Cut in pieces and remove the hairy bits from inside. Place in a bowl of water and lemon juice, and leave aside.
Break the eggs and stir in the cheese. Heat the oil in a pan, and sauté the artichokes with the garlic. Add the egg and cheese mixture to the artichokes in the pan and mix thoroughly. Serve immediately and very hot.

CARCIOFI RIPIENI
Stuffed artichokes
(Main illustration, far right)

8 ARTICHOKES
LEMON JUICE
2 CLOVES GARLIC
1 BUNCH PARSLEY
A FEW SPRIGS OF MARJORAM
OLIVE OIL
SALT AND PEPPER
1 TBSP ALL-PURPOSE FLOUR
2 BAY LEAVES

Remove the outer, woody leaves of the artichokes and trim the bases. Bang the ends of the leaves on the chopping board a few times to loosen them. The artichokes should be the shape of a sawn off skittle. Loosen the leaves and remove the hair. Put the artichokes in a bowl with water and lemon juice and leave aside.
Finely chop the hair, garlic, parsley, and marjoram. Mix them all together, then mix in a bowl with oil, salt, and pepper. Fill the artichokes with the mixture, and dust with flour. Heat oil in a deep pan, and fry the artichokes head downward, until the filling is golden brown. Then add hot water, salt, and bay leaves, and turn the artichokes. Cook for a further 30 minutes in an open pan. When the liquid has boiled away, the artichokes are ready. Serve hot.

WINEGROWING IN THE LAND OF THE SEAFARERS

Long ago, the Greeks and the Etruscans brought grapes to this narrowest and most attractive part of the Italian coast, which is tucked in between the peaks of the Apennines and the shores of the Riviera, and stretches from the French border to the white marble cliffs of Carrara. Although grapes have been grown here since ancient times – for instance, the existence of the Dolcetto grape, known as Ormeasco in Liguria, was documented as long ago as the 14th century – viticulture plays a minor role in this land of seafarers, as a branch of the economy which has been supplemented by heavy industry and tourism.

Even the general boom in Italian winegrowing since the end of the sixties is only beginning to have an effect in Liguria. Old, local grape varieties continue to disappear from the scene, because they are no longer being cultivated by the younger generation. Not even five percent of the wine production has quality wine status, and the majority of the wines are still sold directly to tourists and locals. It is probably unfair to suggest that the growers should take better care of their varieties and the diversity of the vineyards, since the work is often so strenuous, and the returns are usually small in relation to the expenditure. Yet it is nonetheless regrettable when a fascinating part of the Italian wine scene continues to waste away or is threatened by progressive urbanization.

The truly recommendable Ligurian wines come from the growing area of Riviera Ligure di Ponente and Rossese di Dolceacqua in the west, Cinque Terre to the north of the port of La Spezia, and Colli di Luni on the border with Tuscany. The last named extends into the neighboring region – which is rare on the Italian wine map.

UNKNOWN GRAPE VARIETIES
Despite the unfavorable conditions, delicious and interesting wines can be found in Liguria, but their names are often almost unknown. One of the best is Rossese di Dolceacqua, from the area round Ventimiglia. The Rossese variety comes originally from France, and produces medium strength red wines, though many growers still make wines from it that are too pale and thin. From the immediate neighborhood comes Ormeasca. It seldom achieves the fullness and intense fruitiness of its various Piedmontese cousins but, especially in the mountains around Pieve di Teco, it can produce lovely round, mellow wines.

The most interesting of Liguria's white wines is made from the variety Pigato. These wines can be really strong, and are perfect with the tangy fish dishes which are served here by the sea. Occasionally they are even stored in wooden casks, which adds even more to their strength and fullness. Finer and fruitier are the wines from the Vermentino grape, which are sold under the DOC labels Riviera Ligure di Ponente and Colli di Luni. But the really famous ones, though not always better than the Vermentino wines, are the whites from Cinque Terre, especially in their sweet version, Schiacchetrà.

FIVE VILLAGES AND A FORGOTTEN SCIACCHETRÀ
Cinque Terre, five villages or five territories, is the name of by far the best-known winegrowing area in Liguria. No bigger in all than a single average Bordeaux establishment, it has one of the most dramatic vineyards in the world. Narrow, almost threatening terraces cover the slopes, which fall steeply down to the sea. Many of these vineyards can only be reached on foot, and cultivating grapes here is an arduous task. If it were not for tourism, which still guarantees a swift trade in the local wines, most would have been given up long ago. However, the small direct sales of wine to uncritical consumers have often prevented the local winemakers from paying enough attention to quality. Sciacchetrà, the most famous specialty of the Cinque Terre, has been almost forgotten. The intense, straw to amber colored, aromatic and balsamic sweet wine, made from the Albarola grape, which may be expected to have a surprisingly spicy taste, is now obtainable in acceptable quality and worthwhile quantities from only a very few winemakers. Let us hope that this ancient monument among Italian wines can be saved, before it dies out completely.

Right: On the narrow terraces of the Cinque Terre, seen here near Levanto, the growers struggle against difficult conditions.

Vermentino Riviera Ligure di Ponente
Like the Vermentino wines from southeastern Liguria, those of the western Riviera Ligure from the slopes of the Apennines between Genoa and Ventimiglia are usually pleasantly fruity. The vintages from the Riviera dei Fiori, Albenga, and Finale are particularly good.

Colli di Luni
The white and red wines with this label originate from the border area between Liguria and Tuscany. The whites are dominated by the fruity Vermentino variety, and the reds by Sangiovese, as are most of the wines from neighboring Tuscany.

Piedmont

Fossano

Mt. Monegosa
1355 m

Mt. Antola
1597 m

Mt. Maggiorasca
1799 m

Ovada

A26

A7

Torriglia

Emilia Romagna

Cuneo

Demonte

A6

Tanaro

Ceva

Millesimo

Arenzano

Genoa

Nervi

Recco

Rapallo

A15

Pontremoli

Borgo
S.Dalmazzo

Mondovì

Varazze

Albisola Marina

S.Margherita
Ligure

Chiavari

Lavagna

Savona

Spotorno

LIGURIA

Portofino

Tuscany

A12

Limone
Piemonte

Mt. Galero
1708 m

Ormea

Finale Ligure

Pietra Ligure

Loano

Gulf of Genoa

Sestri
Levante

Levanto

La Spezia

Sarzana

Mt. Saccarello
2200 m

Maritime Alps

FRANCE

Pieve
di Teco

A10

Albenga

Riomaggiore

44°N

Diano Castello

Alassio

Portovenere

Lerici

Dolceacqua

Camporosso

Taggia

Imperia
Porto Maurizio

San Remo

Ventimiglia

Bordighera

25 km/15 miles

Rossese di Dolceacqua

Riviera Ligure di Ponente

Cinqueterre,
Cinqueterre Sciacchetra

Colli di Luni

Winegrowing areas in
neighboring regions

EMILIA-ROMAGNA

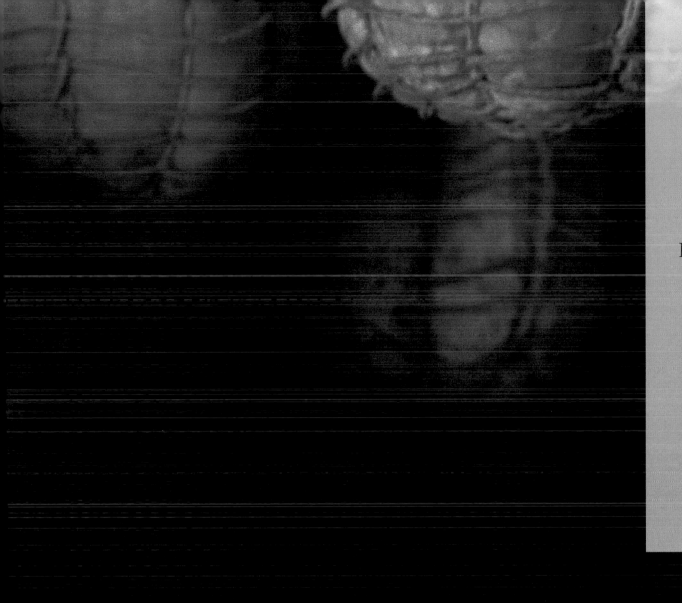

EMILIA-ROMAGNA

The delicatessen stores and cuisine of Emilia-Romagna offer everything the palate could desire: splendid hams and fresh mortadella, tasty parmesan, an endless variety of homemade pasta served with irresistible sauces, sumptuous meat dishes, tangy game, sweet or savory cakes and pastries, delicious desserts, light, sweet wines and, not least, the most splendid vinegar in the world, *aceto balsamico tradizionale*, which is only made by a handful of old-established producers. One reason for the incredible variety of its cuisine is that the region is made up of two different areas: Emilia, the area between the Po valley and northern Tuscany, and Romagna, the mountainous country with the Adriatic coast to the east. The fertile Emilia contributes pasta, dairy produce, and fine meat, while the sometimes rough and inaccessible Romagna offers aromatic herbs, tangy game, and fish dishes from the coast. The menu is completed by specialties from the cities. Parma is proud of its ham and *culatello*, Bologna offers the most exquisite mortadella, the best lasagne, and the most delicious tortellini in the world. Piacenza is the home of tortellini, Reggio Emilia is famous for its braised meat and *erbazzone*, Ferrara is the sausage capital, and in Modena they serve the incomparably tasty *zampone*, or stuffed pig trotters. In Emilia-Romagna they live off good food in two senses. Local specialties end up on their own plates – but have also long been produced for export, thus contributing to the wealth of the region. In the Middle Ages, the rest of the world already held Parma ham and parmesan cheese in high esteem, and no other corner of Italy is so densely packed with small, medium, and large food companies.

Although specialties from Emilia-Romagna are now obtainable all over the world, it is best to get to know them on the spot. Over a glass of Lambrusco and a *piadina*, a traditional dough cake cooked over an open fire, you can have a cozy chat with the Emilians and the Romagnoli about the only disputed subject in the region's cuisine: which is the tastiest pork crackling – the rather dry version from Emilia or the fat, juicy one they prefer in Romagna?

Previous double page: Fernando Cantarelli tests the ripeness of his Culatello ham with the traditional horse bone.

Left: The marshes of the Po delta represent the typical landscape of Emilia, whereas Romagna, which lies to the east, is characterized by its mountains.

PASTA

Emilia-Romagna is a pasta paradise. Apart from the innumerable varieties of *pasta secca* made from durum semolina, homemade *pasta fresca* made from wheat flour and egg is available everywhere for you to try. Connoisseurs maintain that the fresh pasta dough here is smoother and more elastic than in any other region. In the kitchens of Emilia-Romagna, both large and small, *pasta fresca* is made in a huge variety of forms. It can come in strips, diamonds, squares, or rectangles. You can have it filled with meat or cheese, like ravioli, tortellini, tortelli, or steaming lasagne. It can come in the form of *anolini, agnolotti, cappelletti,* or *cappellacci* with *sugo* or with *ragù*. There is no limit to the makers' imagination.

The dough is always prepared according to the same recipe, carefully kneaded, and either pulled out by hand or rolled out thin with a rolling pin. Every *rasdora* – as the housewives were once known in the local dialect – has her own technique and knows the secret regional recipe which affects the "inner life" of the pasta. *Tortelli di primavera*, filled with fine herbs and ricotta, come from around Parma. In other areas they fill the pasta with pumpkin, and in the mountains of Romagna they use chestnuts. Tortellini, for which there are around 110 different recipes, were apparently invented in Bologna. The shape is supposed to symbolize the navel of Venus!

But it is not only tasty varieties of pasta, which can be made from dough, there are also pastry specialties like *torte salate*, savory tarts, and crispy dough cakes like *piadina, tigella,* and *crescentina*. In Reggio Emilia they bake *erbazzone*, a savory cake filled with spinach and Swiss chard, and in Modena they serve *tigella* with pure lard, seasoned with rosemary and garlic.

TORTELLINI ROMAGNOLI
Tortellini filled with turkey
(Illustrated below)

For the dough:
3 1/2 CUPS/400 G ALL-PURPOSE FLOUR
1/2 TSP SALT
4 EGGS

For the filling:
1 TBSP BUTTER
3/4 LB/350 G TURKEY BREAST, CUT SMALL
2 OZ/50 G RICOTTA
2 OZ/50 G BEL PAESE
1/4 CUP/25 G FRSHLY GRATED PARMESAN
GRATED RIND OF 1/2 LEMON
2 EGGS
GRATED NUTMEG
SALT AND FRESHLY MILLED BLACK PEPPER

MELTED BUTTER
FRESHLY GRATED PARMESAN FOR SPRINKLING

For the dough, sieve the flour onto the working surface, and make a well in the middle. Add the salt and eggs and knead to a smooth dough. Shape into a ball, wrap in a damp cloth and leave for 30 minutes.

Melt the butter in a heavy pan, add the turkey meat, and sauté for 15–20 minutes over a low heat. Put the turkey pieces through the food processor and mix with the other ingredients for the filling. Season with nutmeg, salt, and pepper.

Roll the dough out thin and cut circles about 2 inches/5 cm diameter. Put a little filling in the middle of each and fold over into a half moon shape. Wind each one round your finger like a ring and press the ends together.

Cook the tortellini in plenty of vegetable or fish stock until they rise to the surface. This will take about 5 minutes. Take them out, using a draining spoon, and put them in a prewarmed bowl.

Pour over melted butter, and sprinkle with grated parmesan if desired.

ERBAZZONE REGGIANO
Spinach cake
(Illustrated in background)

Serves 6

For the dough:
2 1/2 CUPS/300 G ALL-PURPOSE FLOUR
1/2 TSP SALT
2 TBSP BUTTER, MELTED
1 TBSP VEGETABLE OIL

For the filling:
2 LBS/1 KG LEAF SPINACH OR SWISS CHARD
4 TBSP OLIVE OIL
2 SLICES/50 G SMOKED HAM, DICED
1 TBSP CHOPPED PARSLEY
1 CLOVE GARLIC, CRUSHED
1 EGG
2/3 CUP/50 G FRESHLY GRATED PARMESAN
SALT
2 TBSP/25 G BUTTER

Sieve flour and salt into a bowl and knead with the melted butter to form a crumbly mixture. Work in the vegetable oil and enough lukewarm water to give a smooth, workable dough. Leave in a cool place.

For the filling, wash the spinach (or Swiss chard), blanch briefly, drain well, and chop fine or puree in the blender. Heat olive oil in a pan, and sauté the diced ham for 2 minutes over a low heat. Stir in the spinach and continue cooking gently for a further 2 minutes. Add the parsley and the crushed garlic, and sauté for a further 2 minutes. Whisk the egg until frothy. Remove the pan from the heat, and stir in the egg and parmesan. Season with salt and leave in a cold place.

Roll two-thirds of the dough out flat, and shape into a thin round. Brush the inside of a 10-inch/25-cm diameter springform pan with a little melted butter, and cover the base and sides with the dough. Fill with the spinach mixture and press down the edges of the dough. Roll out the remaining dough to make a lid, place over the filling, and press the edges down firmly. Prick the lid several times with a fork, and brush with the remaining melted butter. Bake in a preheated oven for 1 hour at most at 400 °F (200 °C). Serve hot or cold.

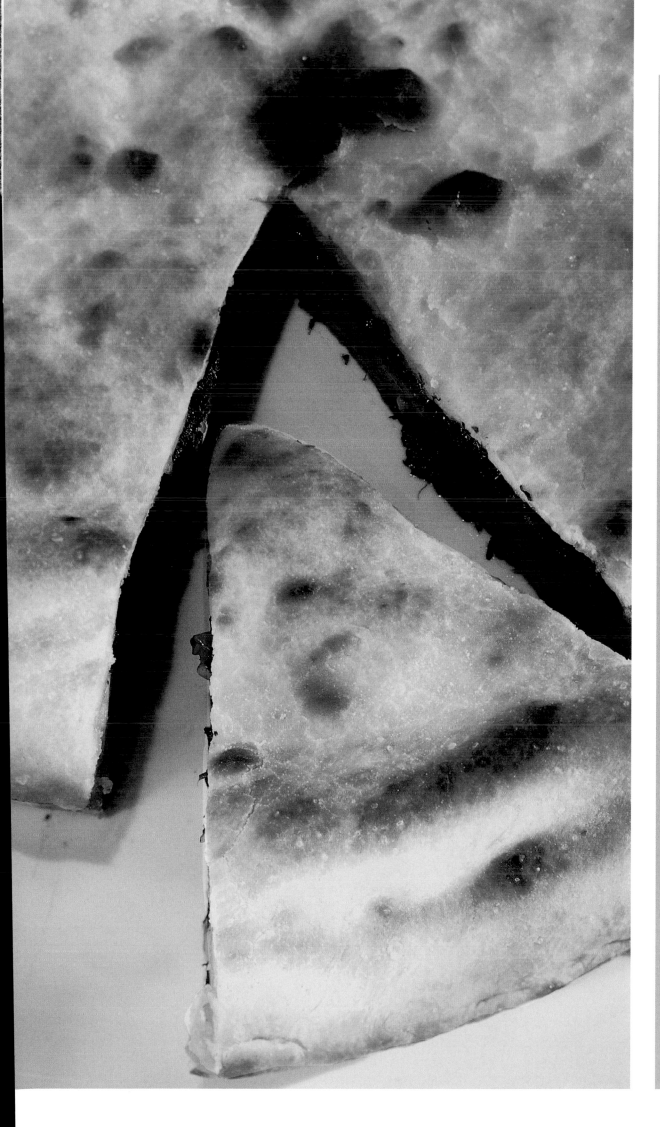

Here *piadina* is being served as a *panino*, a roll or sandwich, filled with tomato and mozarella.

Tigella
Tigella is a traditional bread from the Modena area. It is made by mixing wheat flour, water, and salt to form a soft dough. When the dough has rested for 30 minutes, it is cut into round portions and rolled out. The loaves are baked in special shallow forms. The word *tigella* originally meant the flameproof terra cotta dish it was baked in but, in the course of time, the name was transferred to the bread itself.

Piada or Piadina
In Romagna, instead of being called *tigella*, the round, flat loaf is known as *piada* or *piadina*. The dough consists of wheat flour, water, salt, and a little oil or fat, according to taste. It is rolled out to the size of the round baking dish. These plate-sized baking forms are available in stainless steel or terra cotta, but you can also use a cast iron pan. The *piada* only takes a few minutes to bake, and tastes delicious with Parma ham, cheese, or briefly cooked vegetables.

Crescentina
Crescentina differs from *tigella* and *piada* in the proportion of sour dough it contains. Otherwise the dough is prepared as for the other flat loaves from wheat flour, water, salt, and a little fat. To sour the dough, it must be left to stand for an hour. After that it is cut into small, round slices, and baked on a flat sheet. *Crescentina* can be served instead of bread with any kind of dish, but people mostly like to eat it with ham, cheese, and vegetables.

Gnocco fritto
The dough is made from wheat flour, water, fat, salt, and a pinch of baking powder. It is left to stand in a warm place, then rolled out flat and cut into rounds, which are pierced with a fork. The rounds are deep-fried in oil, and taste best if served very hot.

Erbazzone
Like the Ligurian *torta pasqualina*, *erbazzone reggiano* is a *torta salata*, a piquant, savory tart. But unlike the Ligurian Easter cake, *erbazzone* from Reggio is made not with eggs but with ham or bacon. In many mountain areas it can also be filled with Swiss chard or spinach and boiled rice.

189

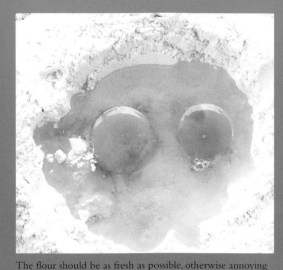

The flour should be as fresh as possible, otherwise annoying holes may form in the dough. As a rule, you can reckon on one egg to ⅞ cup/100 grams flour, but this is only a rough indication.

In many parts of Italy, they make pasta with only the egg yolk, or only the white, or sometimes no egg at all, but just wheat flour, water, and a pinch of salt.

First the eggs are mixed with a little flour in a well in the middle. Then the dough is kneaded well and long enough for it to become smooth and workable, so it can be rolled out very thin.

ALL ABOUT PASTA...

Almost all the regions of Italy have their own theory about the origin of pasta. The Ligurians assume that Genoese merchants saw the recipe of the nomadic peoples of Mongolia and brought it back home. The Venetians believe Marco Polo imported noodles from China; they do not care about the suspicion, voiced by certain historians, that in reality the famous traveler never left his native city. In Rome they claim that the ancient emperors and senators ate pasta. The Sicilians insist that pasta arrived on the island with either the ancient Greeks or the medieval Arabs. In Naples, on the other hand, they will have nothing to do with this story, as the Campanians think that the original Greek and Arab pasta consisted of nothing more than rough pieces of dough, and it was the inventive cooks of the Neapolitan macaroni kitchens who made pasta what it is today: a passion all over Italy.

However this may be, it is a fact that today pasta comes in more than 300 varieties, and is one of the favorite courses on the Italian menu. Two different kinds can be distinguished: *Pasta secca* describes pasta made from durum semolina and water, which is sold dried and rarely made at home. *Pasta fresca* or *pasta fatta in casa* means the fresh, homemade pasta, with a dough consisting of wheat flour, egg, and possibly a little water or white wine. There are, however, homemade *pasta fresca* which do not include egg.

Pasta secca is a manufactured product which, because of its impeccable tradition, elegantly overcomes the arguments for and against "ready-made" foodstuffs. Even the most hardworking housewife or the most ambitious chef would leave the making of *pasta secca* to the *pastaio*, that is the pasta-maker, or recently also the pasta factory. *Pasta secca* can be split into two groups: *pasta lunga* and *pasta corta*. *Pasta lunga* includes all varieties over four inches (ten centimeters) long, such as spaghetti, spaghettini, or tagliatelle. Shorter pasta creations, like the splendid penne, medium length farfalle, or the tiny noodles used in soup, fall into the category of *pasta corta*. *Pasta secca* is generally distinguished by its reliable *tenuta di cottura*; this means that the pasta holds together well in the cooking and does not fall to pieces in the bubbling water. Although most manufacturers state the exact cooking time on the packaging of their pasta, a good *tenuta di cottura* also becomes apparent if pasta, which have inadvertently been cooked a little too long, do not become soft or mushy, but still keep their shape and firm consistency, even after a few minutes over the recommended cooking time.

In contrast to most industrially produced *pasta secca*, *pasta fresca* is the personal creation of each individual. There are countless tricks for making the dough particularly smooth and ways of rolling it out especially thin, but the basic recipe is almost always the same. For every ⅞ cup (100 grams) flour, you take an egg and a pinch of salt. *Pasta fresca* comes *a strice*, in strips cut from the smooth dough, or *ripiena*, that is, filled. The fillings are as varied as the shapes of the pasta itself – from pumpkin, via ricotta, to meat and fish, virtually anything finds a place inside little pasta envelopes.

In many parts of Italy, the fresh pasta dough is colored, to make *pasta colorata*. The secret of the *pasta nera* (black pasta) made in coastal regions is cuttlefish ink. Puréed spinach gives *pasta verde* its green color, a spoonful of tomato purée turns the dough light red, and a drop of beetroot juice dyes the pasta a delicate shade of pink. In Sardinia, saffron is used to give *malloreddus* its golden yellow sheen. Nowadays, colored *pasta secca* is also obtainable in the shops. These varieties are colored either with artificial dyes or with the same natural substances that are used for *pasta fresca*. It is just prejudice to say that pasta makes you fat, as 4 oz (100 grams) uncooked *pasta secca* contains only 325 calories, and the same amount of *pasta fresca* around 365 calories. Pasta also provides valuable carbohydrates, contains important mineral salts, and supplies vitamin B1, B2, and niacin. If pasta is not served with a very heavy sauce, it can even appear on a diet sheet.

Tagliatelle are one of the traditional kinds of pasta from Emilia-Romagna, and are made fresh almost every day.

Anyone who does not want to spend time rolling out dough can invest in a pasta machine, which may be hand-cranked or electrically operated. With different attachments, you can produce every imaginable shape.

THE PROPER WAY TO COOK PASTA

Pasta is quick to cook and is always successful, if you follow a couple of basic rules. The pan it is cooked in should be as big and deep as possible. You should reckon on at least 4 cups (1 liter) water to 4 ounces (100 grams) pasta, because the pasta needs room to move, to prevent it from sticking together. For every liter of water, you should add up to ½ teaspoon (10 grams) salt.

Before putting in the pasta, the water must be brought to a rolling boil, and it must keep bubbling throughout the whole cooking time. An occasional stir will ensure the pasta cooks evenly. Filled pasta must be cooked with care, as if the water boils too violently or you stir too roughly, the pasta may be damaged and the filling may leak.

The cooking time is calculated according to the size of the pasta. Very small or thin noodles cook more quickly than the bigger, thicker kinds. Pasta made from fresh dough generally has a shorter cooking time than *pasta secca*. You can only tell if the pasta is ready by trying it. Italian pasta is cooked *al dente*, that is, soft on the outside, but with a firm center. If the pasta is just right, tip the contents of the pan through a strainer.

BASIC PASTA RECIPE

Serves 6–8

GENEROUS 4 CUPS/500 G ALL-PURPOSE FLOUR
5 EGGS
1/2 TSP SALT
FLOUR FOR DUSTING

Sieve the flour onto the working surface. Make a well in the middle and add the eggs and salt. Work in the flour around the edges of the well, and form into a coarse dough. Knead for 15 minutes until smooth. Wrap in kitchen foil and leave for 1 hour.

Dust the work surface with flour, and roll out thin, using a floured rolling pin. Keep turning the dough, so that it is spread evenly.

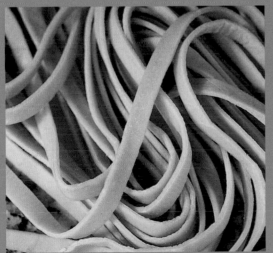

Long, wide, flat pasta ribbons are usually called tagliatelle. In Parma, they make a version with wheat and chestnut flour.

KNOW YOUR PASTA

Pasta di semola di grano duro secca
This dried pasta made from durum semolina and water keeps for a very long time, if stored correctly.

Pastina or Pasta corta mista
These small noodles made of durum wheat are very good in consommés and soups.

Pasta glutinata
This durum wheat pasta with added gluten is often used for children's meals.

Pasta corta or Pasta tagliata
In this category you find almost all medium-sized durum wheat pasta, which is eaten as *pasta asciutta*, dry pasta, with just a little tomato sauce.

Pasta lunga
Long durum wheat pasta, like spaghetti, is also eaten as *pasta asciutta*.

Pasta di semola fresca
Not dried, but freshly made from durum wheat and water, this kind of pasta is a specialty of the southern regions. Sardinian *malloreddus* is just one example of this kind.

Pasta all'uovo secca
This dried pasta made from durum wheat and egg is often produced in strips. Ready-made, filled ravioli or tortellini also consist of egg dough, but are not as tasty as homemade pasta.

Pasta all'uovo fresca
Homemade pasta of wheat flour (type 00) and egg do not keep long, and should therefore be eaten as soon as possible.

Pasta speciale
This category includes colored pasta, *pasta colorata*, and varieties that have flavorings mixed into the dough (mushrooms, truffle, wine) or contain extra kinds of flour added (wholemeal flour, buckwheat).

PARMIGIANO REGGIANO

To make parmesan, milk from the evening and morning milkings are mixed.

The milk is heated and curdled by adding rennin.

The curd is broken up until it is fine and crumbly.

When the curd has been heated again, the young cheese sets.

A linen cloth is pulled under the cheese mass. The first whey drains off.

Two strong men are needed to lift the cheese from the vat.

The cheese is pressed into a mold, so that more whey can drain off.

Young cheese, starting to form a rind, is stored in brine for 3–4 weeks.

Back in the Middle Ages, the big cheeses stored in the dairies of Parma were already considered a tourist attraction. Around 1500, pilgrims and travelers were offered bite-sized pieces of the local specialty cheese as an appetizer. The trademark of Parmigiano Reggiano, which is still valid today, was probably designed in 1612 by a certain Bartolomeo Riva, Treasurer of the Farnese estates under Duke Ranuzzio I. Parmesan – now a DOC product – is still made according to traditional methods, which are just as strictly laid down as the area in which it may be produced. It is only allowed to bear the name Parmigiano Reggiano if it is produced in the provinces of Parma, Reggio Emilia, Modena, Mantua (on the right bank of the Po), and Bologna (but here on the left bank of the Reno). In addition, the milk must come from free-range cows, which have only been fed on green fodder.

In the dairy, the milk is first left to stand overnight, so that the cream can be skimmed off the next morning. Then fresh morning milk is added to the skimmed milk. The mixture is heated in a big copper vat. When it has reached about 86 °F (30 °C), the cheese-master stirs in rennin from calves' stomachs. Fermentation starts immediately, and the milk has curdled within 15 minutes. The curd, the *cagliata*, is then broken up into pieces the size of grains of wheat – which is where the name *grana* (corn) comes from. Then the mass is heated again, at first slowly to 113 °F (45 °C), then finally to 131 °F (55 °C), to separate the cheese from the whey. This curd, weighing up to 132 pounds (60 kilograms), is heaved out of the vat by strong men using a big linen cloth, halved, and pressed into a wooden or metal mold.

Each cheese is stamped by the dairy which produces it.

The man in charge of storing the cheeses tests their condition and aging at regular intervals.

To reach its final maturity, Parmigiano Reggiano must be stored for a long time. The oldest varieties spend three years in the wooden stands.

The route followed by Parmigiano Reggiano from the milk vat to the ripening store is determined by men, not machines.

THE RIPENESS OF PARMESAN

The production season for genuine Parmigiano Reggiano begins on April 1 and ends on November 11. The ripening time must last at least until the end of the following summer. So a cheese made late in the autumn can theoretically leave the storeroom after nine months, but is generally allowed much longer to develop its delicate, tangy, but never sharp flavor. There are three categories of ripeness:

Parmigiano Reggiano fresco
Young parmesan is ripened for less than 18 months.

Parmigiano Reggiano vecchio
Medium to old parmesan has 18 to 24 months' ripening time behind it.

Parmigiano Reggiano stravecchio
Very old parmesan has undergone a ripening time of 24 to 36 months.

The mold has already been lined with a cloth so that later on the fresh cheese can be safely lifted out. Now the remaining whey is gently pressed out of the soft mass. As soon as the cheese has developed some consistency and started to form a rind, the trademark, consisting of the words "Parmigiano Reggiano" and the date of production picked out in small dots, is stamped on. Then the cheeses have to stand in brine for three to four weeks, after which they dry off for a few days in the sun, to allow the rind to firm and develop further.

Parmesan reaches its final maturity not in the dairy, but in gigantic storerooms, which are maintained by the community or by a sponsor. These so-called "cathedrals" can hold 50,000 to 100,000 cheeses. But the cheese still needs to be looked after while it is ripening. During the first half year, it needs to be turned every four or five days, and in the following months every ten days. At the end of this long process, it must still undergo rigorous testing and – if it passes – be branded with the seal of quality.

Externally, and from the point of view of production technique, genuine parmesan is not very different from the varieties Grana Padano, Grana Vernenga, or Grana Lodigiano. But grana may come from a wide range of areas in northern Italy, and the milk it is made from may come from cows which have been fed on lower quality fodder.

CHIZZE
Filled pasta
(Illustrated above)

For the dough:
3 1/2 CUPS/400 G ALL PURPOSE FLOUR
4 TSP/20 G BUTTER
4 TSP/20 G SHORTENING
4–5 TSP BAKING POWDER
1 PINCH SALT

3 CUPS/200G FINELY GRATED PARMESAN
OIL OR SHORTENING FOR FRYING

Slowly knead the flour, butter, shortening, baking powder, and salt, if necessary adding a little warm water. The dough must not be so moist that it will stick when being rolled out, or so dry that it will break.

Roll the dough on a floured work surface to about ⅛ inch/ 3mm thick, and cut in 3–3½ inch/7–8 cm squares. Sprinkle the squares with parmesan, and fold into triangles. Press the edges firmly together, and fry the *chizze* in hot oil or shortening.

CROSTINI AL PARMIGIANO
Parmesan toasts

2 EGGS
2/3 CUP/150ML MILK
6 CUPS/400G FRESHLY GRATED PARMESAN
PEPPER
GRATED NUTMEG
1 BAGUETTE
1 TBSP/30 G BUTTER
1/3 CUP 100ML RED WINE

Mix the eggs, milk, and cheese, and season with pepper and nutmeg. Slice the bread, and spread each slice with the cheese paste. Heat the butter in a pan, and lightly brown the bread slices. After a few minutes, pour over the wine, and cover the pan. Cook until the cheese has melted.

PORTAFOGLI DI PARMIGIANO
Parmesan wallets

6 THIN SLICES OF VEAL OR PORK
GRATED PARMESAN
6 SLICES PARMA HAM
ALL-PURPOSE FLOUR
2 TBSP/30 G BUTTER
1 GLASS WHITE WINE
3 1/2 TBSP/50 ML LIGHT CREAM
SALT AND PEPPER

Sprinkle each slice of meat with parmesan, cover with a slice of ham, fold in half, and fasten with a toothpick, and toss in flour. Heat the butter in a pan, and brown the meat over a medium heat. Pour over the wine a little at a time, then finally pour over the cream, and cook for a few minutes more. Season with salt and pepper.

PROSCIUTTO DI PARMA

It is not so easy to explain how Parma ham acquires its incomparable taste. Some say it is a result of the particularly favorable climatic conditions in and around Parma; others consider that it is entirely due to the healthy diet of the pigs. Not to mention other important factors, such as using the correct cut from the haunch, expert curing, and allowing sufficient time for it to mature.

"From young pigs which, if possible, should come from the mountains, cured without too much salt, a deliciously fragrant meat" – this description of Parma ham, which sounds almost like an advertisement, was written in the 16th century by Bartolomeo Scappi, Pope Pius V's personal chef. In the past it was quite usual for meat to be salted and dried in order to preserve it. But it was not until the end of the 19th century that there was a real boom in these "preserves." Suddenly everyone was eating this aromatic ham as a starter. Demand rose swiftly, and around 1870 a high quality ham industry quickly grew up in Langhirano, a little village near the provincial capital of Parma.

There are still huge storehouses in Langhirano and the surrounding villages today. Behind their high walls, millions of Parma hams are maturing, and receiving precisely the right amount of air through louvered windows, which are opened or closed according to the weather. Prosciutto di Parma is a DOC controlled product; that means its origin is legally protected and monitored. There is a consortium which supervises adherence to the quality guidelines. Even the pigs, whose hams will later be stamped with the coveted trademark of the crown of Parma, are subject to strict regulations. They must come from inspected pig-houses in northern and central Italy, and during their lifetime must have fed on nothing other than the whey left over from the production of parmesan, forage barley, sweet corn, and fruit. They are slaughtered at the age of ten months, but only if they are nice and fat, and have reached the prescribed minimum weight of 350 pounds (160 kilograms). The fat layer is absolutely necessary, because it will surround the delicate, firm, rosy meat while it is maturing, and protect it from drying out.

In the first production phase, the fresh ham, weighing 22–24 pounds (10–11 kilograms), is continually salted and kept in a cold room at 32–39 °F (0–4 °C). The salt and the cold draw the water out of the meat. From time to time the ham is beaten, so that the salt penetrates right to the innermost fibers. When enough water has been drawn out of the ham, it is washed, and the part of the meat which is not covered by the natural skin and fat is thickly smeared with a fatty paste of lard, rice flour, and pepper, to prevent it from drying out. Then the ham must mature for a few months, to allow the natural biochemical processes to turn the raw, salted meat into an aromatic Parma ham. By the time it has finished maturing, the weight of the ham will have been reduced by about 15 pounds (7 kilograms). A genuine *prosciutto di Parma* takes 10–12 months to mature, but it can be given even longer, to make it taste even more delicate and refined.

Half of all Parma ham goes for export. As people outside Italy prefer their ham off the bone, the hams are carefully boned, and wrapped in foil to seal in the flavor. The other half of the production is eaten by the Italians themselves. *Prosciutto di Parma* may be served as an *antipasto* with just white bread or grissini, but it can also be served with fresh melon or ripe figs. Of course it also goes well with buttered asparagus. However it is presented, it is always important to slice it very thin, otherwise it will not develop its full flavor.

A hollow horse bone can be used to check how the ham is maturing. It works something like an apple-corer.

During the months when the hams are hung in stores under suitable microclimatic conditions (below), the special flavor develops as a result of natural biochemical processes.

Quality ham should be sliced shortly before being served.

A special consortium monitors the quality of Parma ham.

Fernando Cantarelli is not only a master ham-maker, but also the enthusiastic owner of the Trattoria Cantarelli in Samboseto. His customers, who include prominent people, appreciate the quality of his wares.

CULATELLO

Culatello undoubtedly represents the quintessence of Parma ham. The whole haunch of the pig is not used to make this kind of ham, only the heart, the precious center, which consists of soft, tender muscle meat. When they are slaughtered in autumn, the pigs, which have been fed on natural foods like whey, bran, sweet corn, and barley, must be at least 14 months old, and weigh over 396 pounds (180 kilograms). The haunches weigh about 33 pounds (15 kilograms), but more than two-thirds is cut away, so that a *culatello* tips the scales at a bare 8.8 pounds (4 kilograms).

Culatello comes originally from Zibello, a small town near Modena. It is still produced here by hand. The small, pear-shaped, trimmed "hearts" of the haunch are first treated with brine, and put into a breathable, intestine-like skin. Then the 14-month drying and maturing process begins. *Culatello* is very tender and has a pleasantly mild taste. A few wafer-thin slices and a little bread make a simple but very tasty starter. To increase the enjoyment, remove the skin, and marinate in wine for 10 days. Experts are still arguing over whether red or white wine brings out the flavor best.

Background: Genuine *Culatello di Zibello* has been a protected trademark since 1996.

TOSCANA

Tuscany

Carrara
Massa   Pistoia
Viareggio   Lucca   Mugello Prato
Pisa   Arno   Firenze   magano
Ponte-   San   Arezzo
Livorno dera   San Miniato
         San Gimignano   Siena   Cortona
Tuscany   Montepulciano
Piombino   Mte. Amiata
                 1738 m
                        Grosseto
         Maremma
      Orbetello

Well-balanced, simple, rooted in the soil, and yet refined – this describes the cuisine of Tuscany. It creates little fuss, it is straightforward, honest, but full of wit and irony – just like the people who live here. The gently rolling hills, olive groves, and still mountains are filled with the scent of foliage and herbs. The smell of freshly chopped, resinous wood is already in the air before the fire is lit for the broiled or spit-roasted meat and game specialties. Although in the large towns the gastronomic culture proves more luxurious than rural cuisine, sumptuous dishes like those of neighboring Emilia-Romagna are not served here. In Florence, for instance, a luxury consists simply of a particularly good piece of meat, the *Bistecca alla fiorentina* (Florentine beefsteak), or a *Spiedino toscano*, meat on a skewer seasoned with olive oil and rosemary. Otherwise, Florentines also subscribe to Tuscan ideals still held in high esteem, of simplicity, clarity, and naturalness that owe a great deal to the Italian Renaissance. Overly sophisticated dishes are scarcely to be found, and even in the best restaurants the obligatory soup course is served in rustic earthenware bowls. It is in the country, in particular, that cookery without frills comes into its own. Here legumes, bread, cheese, vegetables, and fresh fruit dominate the menu. *Ribollita, Panzanella, Pappa col pomodoro* – these are all dishes that are typical of remote, agricultural Tuscany. The bread, deliberately baked without salt, which tastes just as good as a neutral accompaniment to delicious sausage specialties as it does with strong-flavored pecorino cheese, remains a true staple food here, eaten by Tuscan people throughout the day. Yet in spite of the fact that the ingredients are so modest, no-one would describe Tuscan cuisine as plain, or even boring, for the patience and skill of the cooks are legendary. Preparation of even the most time-consuming specialties is carried out with loving care and always in the traditional manner. Despite being down-to-earth, Tuscan gourmets nevertheless permit themselves one small vanity: they openly claim that Italian ice cream, famous throughout the world, was invented here. The idea is supposed to have occurred to Renaissance architect Bernardo Buontalenti, while he was planning the Forte Belvedere fortifications, as a means of enhancing the banquet. In other parts of Italy, it is believed that the Arabs introduced ice cream to Sicily, from where it spread through the entire peninsula. This theory falls, however, upon deaf ears in Tuscany.

Previous double page: *Panforte senese* is an old and venerated specialty from Siena. The first references to this sweet, spiced bread date back to the 13th century.

Left: The Tuscan landscape is characterized by gently rolling hills, olive trees, and grapevines.

BREAD

Because he was a member of the Ghibelline faction that was loyal to the Holy Roman Emperor, the great 13th-century writer Dante Alighieri was banished from Florence in 1302 by the Guelph faction, loyal to the pope, which had regained power. The exile eventually found refuge in Ravenna, where he remarked upon "the saltiness of other people's bread." If one ignores the possible hidden metaphor in this statement, the student of culinary history will immediately recognize a reference to the difference between Tuscan bread and other central Italian bread. Back in the Middle Ages, the Tuscans were evidently baking their rustic bread, *pane sciocco*, without the addition of any expensive salt. The Tuscan people were no doubt making the point, even then, that there is no need whatsoever to add salt to bread, since its ultimate function is to accompany inherently salty specialties such as sausage, cheese, or meat dishes.

Today, bread remains a staple food in Tuscany. Noodles and rice were once served only on special occasions, and the situation has not changed a great deal. Until recently it was customary in rural areas to heat the large, free-standing ovens once a week to bake bread for the entire village, while families in the towns took their dough to the baker. Payment for this essential service was even fixed by law.

Bread is eaten by Tuscans throughout the day. In the morning, at breakfast time, it is dipped in coffee made with milk, and it serves as an appetizer before lunch in the form of toasted *bruschetta* or daintily garnished *crostino*. Crusty bread with a few drops of the best olive oil makes a wonderful snack. But bread is also used for cooking: it appears as an ingredient in *Cacciucco*, the traditional fish soup; it is found in vegetable dishes; it is crumbled on top of *pinci*, or home-made spaghetti; and it forms a rustic accompaniment to beans and cabbage. At the end of a meal, it tempts one to eat it with a little pecorino cheese, and it also tastes good with dried figs, nuts, and fresh grapes. In the afternoon bread is dipped in wine, spread with butter, or sprinkled with sugar.

The range of different types of bread is correspondingly great. Rustic loaves, whole wheat bread, fine wheat bread, corn bread, and many other specialties are baked using an extremely wide variety of flour blends. Bread appears in the shape of *rondeggiante* (round flat loaves), *bozza* or *pagnotta* (tall, round loaves), or *filone* (long bread sticks). The delicate *semella* is suitable for breakfast or a light snack, the *fiorentina* is a tasty pretzel, and the *schiacciata all'olio* refers to a flat loaf of bread sprinkled with oil. *Bozza* and *filone*, the two most common types, must have a crisp crust and a loose-textured crumb containing lots of holes if they are to be judged a success. In Tuscany there is indeed a saying, *pan bucato e cacio serrato*, "bread needs holes, cheese doesn't."

Pasta secca or *pasta fresca*, which are universal throughout the rest of Italy, play a more subordinate role in Tuscan cuisine. Consequently, *grano-tenero* wheat (soft wheat for the bread that is omnipresent in Tuscany) is the main variety grown in Crete, the granary of the region.

Bruschetta
Toasted bread with tomatoes
(Illustrated below)

4 SLICES TUSCAN BREAD (WHITE BREAD)
2 TOMATOES
1 BUNCH OF BASIL, COARSELY CHOPPED
SALT AND PEPPER
1 CLOVE OF GARLIC
3 TBSP EXTRA VIRGIN OLIVE OIL

Toast the slices of bread in the toaster or under the broiler. Cut the tomatoes into small cubes and mix with the coarsely chopped basil in a dish. Season with salt and pepper. Rub the toasted bread slices with garlic, spread the tomato and basil mixture on the slices of bread, and sprinkle generously with olive oil.

CROSTINO
Toasted bread with chicken livers

1 SMALL ONION
3 TBSP OLIVE OIL
1/2 LB/250 G CHICKEN LIVERS
1 GLASS DRY MARSALA OR VIN SANTO WINE
SALT AND PEPPER
3 1/2 TBSP/50 G ANCHOVY FILLETS
3 1/2 TBSP/50 G CAPERS
3 1/2 TBSP/50 G BUTTER
TUSCAN BREAD (WHITE BREAD), SLICED

Chop the onions finely and sauté gently in the olive oil.
Cut the chicken livers into pieces, add to the onions, and
fry for a few minutes. Pour in the Marsala or Vin Santo and
simmer until the liquid has almost evaporated. Season the
chicken livers with salt and pepper, and sauté for another 5
minutes. Leave to cool slightly, then place in a food
processor with the anchovy fillets, the capers, and the butter,
and blend to a very fine purée. Toast the slices of bread in
the oven and spread thickly with the chicken liver paste.

PANZANELLA
Bread salad

1 LB/500 G STALE TUSCAN BREAD (WHITE BREAD)
SALT
5 RIPE TOMATOES
1 RED ONION
1 CUCUMBER
1 BUNCH OF BASIL
3–4 TBSP EXTRA VIRGIN OLIVE OIL
PEPPER
1–2 TBSP WINE VINEGAR

Cut the bread into small pieces and soak in cold water with
a pinch of salt. When the bread is saturated, squeeze it out
and place in a salad bowl. Dice the tomatoes, cut the onion
and cucumber into small pieces, and add to the bread.
Coarsely chop the basil and stir this into the bread mixture
too. Sprinkle generously with olive oil, season to taste with
salt and pepper, and place in the refrigerator. Before serving,
add the wine vinegar and mix thoroughly again.
This simple, summery dish is very frequently prepared in
the country to use up leftover bread.

PAPPA AL POMODORO
Tomato soup with croutons

4 TBSP OLIVE OIL
1 ONION
3 CLOVES OF GARLIC
1 3/4 LBS/750 G TOMATOES
4 CUPS/1 LITER CHICKEN STOCK
SALT AND FRESHLY GROUND BLACK PEPPER
1/2 LB/250 G STALE TUSCAN BREAD (WHITE BREAD), WITH
CRUSTS REMOVED
A FEW BASIL LEAVES

Heat half the olive oil in a large pan. Peel the onion and
garlic, chop finely, and sauté gently in the hot oil until soft
and transparent. Blanch the tomatoes, skin, and cut into
cubes. Add the tomatoes to the onion and garlic mixture in
the pan and saute for 5 minutes. Then add the stock
gradually. Season with salt and pepper and cook for
30 minutes.
Heat the remaining oil in a shallow pan, cut the bread into
small cubes, and brown in the hot fat. Chop the basil leaves.
Pour the soup into soup dishes and sprinkle with the
croutons and the basil leaves. Serve immediately.

Pan di granturco
Pan di granturco like *ciaccia* from the Maremma, is made
from maize flour.

Pane classico integrale
Unsalted *classico integrale*, made
from semolina, has a very crisp
crust

Schiacciatina
Schiacciatina, like *spolettina*, is made from salt
dough, and, like *treccina*, it is made from fine flour,
yeast, and olive oil. It is a small, flat loaf.

Filone
Filone is the classic Tuscan
unsalted loaf.

Pan de ramerino
Pan de ramerino, rosemary bread, used to be baked during
Holy Week. The loaves were decorated with a cross and
sold in church porches by the *semellai*, the traveling bread
sellers. The dough is enhanced by the addition of sugar,
raisins, and chopped rosemary leaves. As this bread is very
nourishing, it soon began to be eaten throughout the year,
rather than exclusively at Easter. It remains very popular
throughout Tuscany today.

Pane con i grassetti
This bread is typical of the Garfagnana area. The dough has
pork crackling mixed into it.

Pane con l'uva
In Lombardia, *pane con l'uva* is the term used to describe small loaves
or rolls that are eaten mainly at Easter. In Tuscany, by contrast, this
grape bread is made by rolling out the dough on a baking sheet in
the manner of a classic *schiacciata*, adding a generous layer of red
grapes, and sprinkling it with sugar. This bread is typically eaten here
in the autumn. At harvest time it is often served instead of desserts.
In many areas, Tuscans eat it as an accompaniment to fresh figs.

TUSCAN BREAD

Tuscan enthusiasm for bread and bread
specialties is quite inexhaustible. In addition
to the varieties already mentioned, there is
pane pazzo, or "mad" bread, containing
pepper; *pane di Radicofani*, with grapes,
honey, and pepper; *pan co santi*, the bread of
the saints, containing nuts, raisins, almonds,
honey, pepper, and oil; *pane dicembrino*, or
December bread, with raisins, nuts, honey,
and pumpkin; *ciambella di quaresima* or
quaresimali, a pretzel for fasting periods, as
well as various cookies and *panforte*.

Carsenta lunigianese
This bread, from Lunigiana, is baked in a
pan on a layer of chestnut leaves. It is
served on Good Friday.

Ciaccia
This bread, from the Maremma, is made
from maize flour.

Donzelle
In order to make *donzelle*, the dough is
rolled out with a rolling pin, then cut into
diamond shapes, and finally fried in olive
oil. In the area around Prato these small
loaves are known as *ficattole*, and in the
Lunigiana area they are sold as *sgabei*.

Fiandolone
Fiandolone was the bread eaten by the
forest workers and miners of Mount
Amiata. The dough is made with sweet
chestnut flour and is baked in the oven,
strewn with finely chopped rosemary
leaves.

Pan maroko
Pan maroko contains equal parts of wheat
and maize flour. The dough is made with
oil, water, and yeast, and has raisins and
pine nuts added to it.

Panigaccio
Panigaccio is a specialty of the *Lunigiana*
area. The dough, made from flour, water,
and salt, is baked in glowing red-hot

crucibles, and is served with grated cheese
and a hint of oil.

Panina gialla aretina
This yellow bread from the Arezzo area is
eaten at Easter time, like *panina unta* with its
very high fat content. It is often enhanced
by the addition of raisins, saffron, and spices,
and is served with eggs that have been
consecrated in church beforehand.

Panini di San Antonio
These sweet rolls are eaten in the country
on January 17, the feast day of St. Antony,
although not until they have received a
blessing, alongside the livestock and the
fields, in church that morning.

Schiacciata
Schiacciata is made from bread dough that is
rolled out on a baking sheet, brushed with
olive oil, and generously salted. Imaginative
variations on this loaf include added pork
crackling, herbs, potatoes, and tomatoes.

HARVESTING OLIVES

The fruit of the olive tree is harvested during the weeks between the beginning of November and the middle of December. The exact time of the harvest must be carefully chosen, for the olives must neither be too unripe, nor completely ripe. Harvesting is still frequently done by hand, even today. The olives, which are picked or carefully "combed off" with a special rake, fall on to nylon sheets laid out beneath the trees before harvesting begins. Many olive growers, however, rely on technology rather than manual work, and use a machine that shakes off the olive crop. An articulated arm grasps the olive tree, shakes it, and catches the fruit in a container shaped like an inverted umbrella, from which the olives are extracted and the stalks and leaves removed. This method of harvesting can only be used in specially adapted olive groves, however. Regardless of whether the harvest is mechanical or manual, olives must be gathered as quickly as possible and taken to the oil mill, since oxidation and uncontrolled fermentation are a threat, as they are in white wine production. In the oil mill the stalks and leaves are removed from the fruit,

Below: Although harvesting by hand is tedious, it has the advantage that the fruit is not damaged.

which is then washed. It is then crushed by the rolling motion of heavy granite millstones. Although far more modern equipment exists, Tuscan growers are attached to these stone monsters, since they make light work of even the hardest olive stones, thus guaranteeing a very uniform olive pulp. After milling, the pulp is "kneaded," in other words stirred slowly and carefully. After this, the oil miller spreads it in layers, just under an inch (two to three centimeters) thick, on the waiting press mats, which are then stacked in a suitable frame. A hydraulic press now begins the pressing operation. The mixture of oil and water emerges from the sides of the mats, and is collected. The water is separated out in a centrifuge. The fresh oil is poured into terra cotta jugs or, in the case of modern mills, into steel tanks, and then takes between 30 and 40 days to clear, protected from the effects of light and temperature fluctuations, after which it is again filtered.

Some oil mills nowadays do not operate entirely in accordance with the traditional system. Although, in such a modified production system, the olives are also crushed first, the pulp is not then placed in the traditional press, but is instead spun at high speeds. Processing of the resulting mixture of oil and water then continues in a centrifuge, until the pure oil is separated out.

The young olives ripen through summer and fall on the tree. Harvesting does not begin until winter.

Huge granite millstones crush even the hard stones.

LEVELS OF QUALITY

Olio d'oliva extra vergine
Extra virgin olive oil from the first pressing, of the best quality.

Olio d'oliva vergine
Virgin olive oil from the second and third pressings, still of very good quality.

Olio d'oliva
Olive oil (also pure olive oil), blended from native and refined oil.

Olio di sansa d'oliva
Olive pomace oil, obtained almost exclusively from the pomace residues left after pressing, extracted with the aid of solvents.

Next the olive pulp is spread on circular mats and the stack of mats is compressed. The oil emerges as soon as the press exerts force on the stacked mats.

Many types of olive are grown in the Marche region. The well-balanced oil is among the best in Italy.

The sharp, fruity oil from Apulia is obtained from olives that are fully ripe, and therefore is extremely acidic.

Tuscan oils – depending on their place of origin – taste spicy, nutty, or sometimes peppery.

Sicilian olive oil, like that from Apulia, has a strong and sharp, yet fruity flavor.

The fine olive oil from Umbria has a delicate scent of herbs and a pronounced green color.

The olive oil from Molise is greenish in color, with yellow accents. It has a mild flavor.

The emerald-green olive oil from Abruzzi has a fruity aroma and a strong flavor.

Florence c. 1480, copy of the Carta della Catena (detail), Museo di Firenze com'era, Florence

CATHERINE'S COOKS

In September 1533, when Catherine de' Medici boarded the ship in Portovenere that was to take her to her marriage to Henry II of France, she clearly had more than an overnight case with her. For reasons of security, Catherine, a native of Florence, took numerous containers full of provisions as well as her chests of clothes and jewel boxes. Her royal entourage included, in addition to those who repeatedly came under suspicion of preparing poison, cooks' apprentices, cup bearers, bakers, confectioners, and some very capable chefs.

Catherine's skepticism regarding French cuisine was nevertheless quite justified, for gastronomic culture on the banks of the Seine was in a sorry state at the beginning of the 16th century. The French court clung to the medieval precepts of Lucullus, according to which a meal was supposed to reflect the wealth of the household, an ingredient which was exotic by virtue of its cost was held in higher esteem than a fresh local product, the foodstuffs were subjected to the most tortuous preparation methods and veritable orgies of seasoning, and the meal would conclude with a guessing game as to what ingredients the dishes might have contained. Although the seminal work on Italian gastronomic and culinary matters, Bartolomeo Sacchi's revised version of the *Liber de Arte coquinaria* by Maestro Martino, had been translated into French a few years previously, and although the humanist, who was also known by the name Platina, was, moreover, genuinely at pains in his treatise *De honesta voluptate et valetudine* to explain the rules that were fundamental to good food, the French seemed to have great difficulty in grasping them. This state of affairs changed abruptly as Catherine entered the political and culinary arena. Her marriage to the French king, cleverly engineered by the diplomatic skill of Pope Clement VII, finally brought a lighter touch to the gloomy sauces of the French chefs. Catherine, who was herself fond of eating, and whose reforms were far removed from asceticism, abolished the bad habit of serving sweet and sour, or piquant and salty dishes at the same time, and instead arranged for dishes to be served that really went well together. Inelegant, structureless, and gluttonous feasts became a thing of the past thereafter, and banquets became ceremonial, characterized by fine dishes, elegance, and refined table manners. Heavy goblets gave way to elegant glassware from Venice, and glazed earthenware, known as faience, was imported from Faenza in Italy. Catherine even introduced the use of the fork, but was more successful in this respect with her son, Henry III, than with her husband, whose table manners continued to leave much to be desired.

Furthermore, Catherine improved the reputation of "cheap" staple foods such as oil or beans, and favored dishes and specialties such as guinea fowl with sweet chestnuts, fricassée, pot-roasts, pies, sorbets, and a liqueur that was prepared from the recipe of the monastery at Murate. She made spinach cooked in the Florentine style fashionable, ordered vast amounts of artichokes to be prepared for her husband, and, if various claims are to be believed, was even responsible for introducing the Trebbiano grape. Other sources, by contrast, claim that the daughter of the house of Medici smuggled the Cabernet grape into Tuscany from France.

In short, any aspiring Parisian was at pains to adopt Catherine's precepts and to dine *à la mode de la Reine Catherine*. Centuries later, she was still being given credit for the new initiatives in culinary techniques. No lesser a figure than Antoine Carême (1784–1833), gifted chef of both the emperor Napoleon and Talleyrand, held the opinion that French chefs had first to learn the arts of cooking and baking from Catherine's Italian cooks before they could develop them into great French *cuisine*.

Santi di Tito (1536–1603), *Portrait of Catherine de' Medici, Queen of France*, 1585/86, oil on wood, 56 x 46½ inches (142 x 118 cm), The Uffizi, Florence

THE CUISINE OF THE RENAISSANCE

The culinary Renaissance in Italy also has its roots in the rediscovery of antiquity. In the kitchens of monasteries and aristocrats' palaces, where by that time a measure of affluence had been attained, attention was given to the products of Greek and Roman culinary arts, and the author Apicius, in particular, was frequently studied. Cooks and banquet organizers now attempted to apply the ideals espoused by the Renaissance – of order, proportion, harmony, and balance – to culinary matters as well. Influences from the Levant, an area with which trade was flourishing, as well as from the Arabian-occupied Sicily, were welcomed and assimilated without prejudice. Whereas, in the Middle Ages, people still retained a marked preference for prestigious dishes that were first boiled, then roasted, and finally submerged under a sauce containing the largest possible amount of expensive spices, Renaissance cooks were at pains to develop straightforward recipes and gentler cooking methods intended to emphasize, rather than grossly alter, the taste of the ingredients themselves. Opulent mixtures of spices and food that had been skillfully changed beyond all recognition gradually fell out of fashion, therefore, and instead any gourmet could for the first time identify, without too much guesswork, what was on his plate.

Although Italians henceforth strove to achieve simple and noble dishes, only very sparing use was made of regional peasant cookery. Cooks preferred to adapt new dishes from distant foreign countries. Tuscan peasant dishes such as polenta (porridge made from grain) or vegetable purée with hot onions or sharp-flavored garlic were considered unrefined – and were to remain so for a long time to come, for the cookery revolution passed the less privileged by, leaving practically no trace in their cooking pots.

The Renaissance is also the period in which a connection was first made between pathology and day-to-day nutrition. What had previously been considered self-evident was suddenly discussed, commented upon, analyzed, and ultimately viewed from a completely new angle by doctors and physiologists: namely, that food can bring health, but can also precipitate illnesses or exacerbate existing complaints. So, in the same way that man, who had become the focus of interest, was classified as choleric, melancholic, phlegmatic, or sanguine, depending on whether his bodily humors were hot or cold, sweet or sour, thick or thin, green, black, or yellow, scholars now examined the special properties of foodstuffs and ingredients using similar criteria, in order to recommend strongly that certain groups of people eat a particular dish or ingredient, or alternatively advise them against doing so if at all possible.

Torta di zucca
Pumpkin tart
(Illustrated in the background)

1 LB/500 G PUMPKIN
SCANT 2 1/2 CUPS/600 ML MILK
1/2 CUP/100 G SUGAR
1/8 TSP GINGER
1/8 TSP CINNAMON
3 EGGS
1 PINCH SAFFRON
BUTTER
1 LB/500 G PUFF PASTRY
1 TBSP ROSEWATER

Peel the pumpkin. Cut the flesh into pieces, grate finely, and cook for 15 minutes in 2 cups (500 ml) milk. Drain, pressing the pumpkin to remove excess liquid, and mix with the sugar, ginger, cinnamon, eggs, saffron, 3½ tablespoons (50 g) butter, and the remaining milk. Roll out the puff pastry into two thin circles and place one of them on a baking sheet greased with butter. Spread the filling over and cover with the second pastry circle. Bake at 350 °F (180 °C) for about 50 minutes. When the filling has risen, sprinkle with rosewater and serve.

Pesce impanato
Fish in batter
(Illustrated below)

For the batter:
1 3/4 CUPS/200 G ALL-PURPOSE FLOUR
1 TSP SALT
1 CUP/250 ML FLAT BEER
2 TBSP OLIVE OIL
3 EGG WHITES

2 LB 5 OZ/600 G FISH FILLETS (E.G. SOLE, PLAICE, HADDOCK, ETC.)
SALT AND PEPPER
2 TBSP LEMON JUICE
OIL FOR DEEP FRYING

To make the batter, mix together the flour and salt, and stir in the beer. Then incorporate the olive oil and leave the batter to stand for 30 minutes. Next beat the egg whites until stiff and carefully fold into the batter.
Wash the fish fillets, cut in half, season with salt and pepper, and sprinkle with lemon juice. Coat the fillets in the batter and fry in hot oil for about 5 minutes until they are crisp.

Tortellini rinascimentali
Tortellini with pork filling

For the dough:
5 CUPS/600 G ALL-PURPOSE FLOUR
6 EGGS
1/2 TSP SALT

For the filling:
2 TBSP/50 G SALT PORK, CHOPPED FINELY
1 1/2 CUPS/300 G GROUND PORK
3/4 CUP/50 G PARMESAN, GRATED
1/2 CUP/50 G PROVENTURA CHEESE, SLICED
1/2 TSP CINNAMON
1/8 TSP PEPPER
1/8 TSP GROUND CLOVES
1/8 TSP GRATED NUTMEG
1 PINCH SAFFRON
1 TBSP RAISINS
1 TBSP PARSLEY, FINELY CHOPPED
2 EGGS
8 CUPS/2 LITERS MEAT STOCK
PARMESAN
SUGAR AND CINNAMON

To make the dough, place the flour in a heap on the work surface and make a hollow in the center. Pour the eggs into this and knead slowly into a dough. Dissolve the salt in 3 tablespoons lukewarm water and add gradually, a drop at a time. Cover the dough and leave to stand for about 1 hour.
To make the filling, mix the chopped salt pork with the ground pork, parmesan and *proventura* (a type of smoked Mozzarella) and fry for a few minutes. Add the spices, raisins, parsley, and eggs, mix well, and leave to cool slightly. Roll out the dough on a floured work surface and stamp out small circles. Heap some of the filling on each circle, lay another circle on top, and press the edges together tightly.

Cook in the stock, which should be boiling but not bubbling fiercely, for approximately 10 minutes. Remove with a skimming spoon and serve hot.
Serve grated parmesan, sugar, and cinnamon separately, to sprinkle on according to taste.

Zuppa di funghi
Mushroom soup

1/2 LB/200 G FRESH GOOD-QUALITY MUSHROOMS (PREFERABLY WILD)
2 CUPS/500 ML SWEET WHITE WINE
1/2 TSP PEPPER
SCANT 1/2 CUP/100 ML OLIVE OIL
1/3 CUP/80 ML UNFERMENTED SOUR FRUIT JUICE OR CIDER
SALT
SUGAR
4 SLICES OF WHITE BREAD, TOASTED
1 CUP ORANGE JUICE
1/2 TBSP CINNAMON
5 CLOVES

Remove the stalks from the mushrooms, place in cold water and wash several times. Bring the mushrooms to the boil with 1 cup (250 ml) wine and the pepper, drain, and cut into bite-sized pieces. Pour the oil into a shallow pan, add the mushrooms and braise slowly. Add the unfermented fruit juice or cider and simmer for at least 15 minutes. Season with salt, and a little sugar if desired. Place the mushrooms in bowls with a generous helping of stock.
Place the toasted slices of bread in a pan with 1 cup (250 ml) of wine, the orange juice, cinnamon, cloves, and 5 teaspoons sugar, and bring to a boil. Carefully remove the soaked slices of bread and lay on top of the mushrooms. Serve hot.

CHEESE

When one thinks of pecorino, one associates it first with the southernmost regions of Italy, but this aromatic ewe's milk cheese is just as typical of central Italy and Tuscany, where no larder is without *cacio*, as it is known here. It used to be regarded as a coarse peasant's specialty, often eaten as a snack with a chunk of bread and strong Tuscan wine, but now it is once more to be found in the finest kitchens. The best known varieties of pecorino toscano are produced in the heart of the region, in Chianti, near Cortona and Casentino, Pietrasanta and Lucardo, near Siena, and in the Maremma. Pecorino is available in varying degrees of ripeness. Very new pecorino is on sale after two to four weeks, while medium mature pecorino is ripened for two months. Mature pecorino, which is used instead of parmesan for grating, takes six months to ripen, but is often stored for longer.

Tuscans claim that the fragrant herbs for which the region is famous impart an incomparable flavor to this ewe's milk cheese. For this reason, the cheesemakers make sure that the animals can graze undisturbed on extensive pastures. Pecorino is produced from December to August. First, rennet is added to full-fat ewe's milk. After half an hour the coagulation process is complete, and the curd can be pressed. The resulting mass, which resembles quark, can now be left to stand in a warm place before being put in molds. The new cheese has to be carefully salted and turned by hand every day so that it can develop a rind. In many areas the rind is treated with tomato concentrate, so that it assumes an orange appearance. Other procedures involve using edible charcoal to impart a gray color, or placing the cheese on walnut leaves while it ripens to turn the rind a brownish color. *Marzolino*, a small egg-shaped pecorino, which is made from the first milk in spring (usually in March, hence its name – is a particularly remarkable specialty. It tastes best when it is still quite new.

There are so many different types of pecorino that Tuscan cuisine hardly needs any other kind of cheese. Occasionally, however, *raveggiolo*, a fine, mild cheese, is served, quite new and preferably with a little olive oil. To make savory tarts and robust fillings of all kinds, as well as sweet dishes and desserts, Tuscan cooks (like their counterparts elsewhere in Italy) use ricotta, which is made from whey and resembles cream cheese.

PECORINO CON I BACCELLI
Pecorino with broad bean pods
(Illustrated above)

BOILED BROAD BEANS IN THE POD
FRESH PECORINO

This dish can be served as a snack in the afternoon, or to follow the second course. Boil the beans in their pods in lightly salted water, then drain off the water. Arrange in an attractive wicker basket, put the cheese on a wooden board, and place in the center of the table. The beans are shelled, the skins are removed, and then they are dipped in salt and eaten with a small piece of pecorino, accompanied by homemade bread and a glass of Chianti.

A modern alternative is to shell the cooked beans, cut the pecorino into small cubes, and place in a ceramic dish. A sauce is prepared using sparkling white wine, salt, olive oil, and freshly milled pepper, in which the cheese and beans are marinated. This is a delicious starter for a wholesome country meal.

MUSHROOMS

The people of Central Italy are passionate about mushrooms. In Umbria, in Marche, in Lazio, and also in Tuscany and the Maremma, mushroom pickers zealously comb the wooded areas from late summer to the end of autumn. The popular *porcino* mushroom, or *boletus edulis*, is just one of the many varieties that find their way into the baskets of mushroom fanciers every year. Chanterelles, morels, saffron milk cap, honey agaric, and numerous other kinds can be found beneath trees and in the meadows. In some areas the enthusiasm for gathering autumn mushrooms reached such a pitch that the authorities were obliged to place an official restriction on the amount that could be collected per person per day of six and a half pounds (three kilograms).

FUNGHI MISTI
Mushroom ragout

2 LBS/1 KG MIXED FRESH WOODLAND MUSHROOMS
1 SMALL BUNCH OF PARSLEY
2 CLOVES OF GARLIC
5 TBSP OLIVE OIL
3 TBSP WHITE WINE

Clean the mushrooms, wash and chop the parsley, peel and quarter the garlic cloves. Heat the olive oil in a heavy pan, add the garlic, and sauté for a few minutes. Add the mushrooms and fry briefly. Reduce the heat and pour in the white wine. Braise the mushrooms until they are soft. Serve sprinkled with parsley.

Porcino mushrooms
(Illustrated in the background)
The porcino mushroom (edible *boletus*) is by far the favorite Italian mushroom. Its large, round caps are stuffed, thinly sliced to accompany meat dishes, or finely chopped and added to sauces. The porcino mushroom can even be pickled in vinegar or preserved in other ways without losing much of its natural flavor.

THE WHITE TRUFFLES OF SAN MINIATO

Jean Anthelme Brillat-Savarin, the great French gourmet and author of *The Physiology of Taste*, published in 1825, described the truffle as the "diamond of cuisine," a view that is willingly shared in many regions of Italy. The aroma of this noble mushroom, therefore, is just as well-loved in Tuscany as the scent of forests, meadows, and herbs. Truffle lovers make their pilgrimage to San Miniato every year. The white truffles from this region were once sold in various Tuscan markets, or even disappeared via dubious channels, only to re-emerge in Alba in the Piedmont, where they were sold at top prices as coveted Alba truffles. In order to combat this, the truffle hunters of San Miniato, Montopoli, and Pontedera banded together. In October and November they organize their own market, for which the romantic alleyways of San Miniato, bathed in gentle autumn sunlight, provide the ideal backdrop. Compared with those from other regions, the white truffles of San Miniato are relatively large, and have a very intense flavor. In the kitchen they are grated raw over the top of dishes, or used as an aromatic filling for specialties such as *Fagiano tartufato*, pheasant with truffles.

San Miniato is the Tuscan fortress that is the home of the white truffle. A truffle market is held here in October and November.

Honey agaric
The honey agaric mushroom (*chiodino* or *famigliola buona*) must always be cooked, because, like other members of its family, it is poisonous when raw. If properly prepared, however, it is a mushroom that is full of flavor and very versatile. The honey agaric mushroom has a wonderfully sweet taste, and is perfect for making mushroom risotto.

Field mushrooms
The field mushroom (*prataiolo*) has far more flavor than the white button mushroom, which is artificially cultivated and has a lonely upbringing in a dark cellar or grotto. Mushrooms should never be peeled, but should be cleaned by careful brushing, which is the only way in which they retain their delicate flavor.

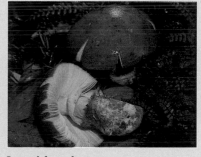

Imperial mushrooms
The imperial mushroom (*fungo imperiale* or *amanita cesarea*) is one of the most sought-after mushrooms in Italy. In a warm climate it thrives particularly well. Caution is nevertheless advisable for private collectors, for this family of mushrooms also includes some poisonous specimens such as the notorious deadly amanita.

Morel mushrooms
The morel mushroom (*spugnola* or *eleta*) is an extremely interesting mushroom, which is also frequently used in cookery when dried. The delicate, spongy cap is especially prized by gourmets. It is advisable not to gather morels oneself, however, as it is extremely easy to confuse them with their poisonous relatives.

Chanterelle mushroom
The chanterelle mushroom (*cantarello* or *finferlo*) is one of the most popular and most common mushrooms worldwide. It has a delicate flavor, an appetizing fragrance, a good texture, an attractive appearance, and is a perfect accompaniment to rice or light meat dishes. It is also wonderful on its own, especially with parsley, mild onions, and a butter sauce.

Saffron milk cap
The saffron milk cap (*agarico delizioso*) is gathered on account of its nutty flavor. Caution is advisable, however, for it must not be confused with its poisonous relative, the sharp agaric. It is also susceptible to attack by pests, so it should be carefully inspected before purchase or thoroughly cleaned before preparation.

Oyster mushroom
Although the popular oyster mushroom (*gelone, fungo ostrica* or *pleuroto*) is grown commercially on a large scale, it does not then taste nearly as good as specimens allowed to grow on the stumps of fallen trees. It is very good fried or broiled, and, when finely sliced, can even be used raw as an ingredient in a cold salad.

BEEF FROM THE CHIANA VALLEY

Some scholars are of the opinion that Chiana cattle are descended from *bos primigenius*, the cattle that can be seen in prehistoric cave paintings. These cattle were held in high esteem by Etruscans and Romans, not only because of their meat, but also on account of their porcelain-colored white hide, and consequently these beautiful animals were often shown in carnival processions and then sacrificed to the gods.

Today, the Chianina breed is one of the most sought-after and valuable in Italy. Given optimal conditions, such as those in the Chiana valley, the cattle grow rapidly, attaining a comparatively large size. They can be recognized by the pale coloring, the light, short-horned head, and the elongated rump with broad back and loin sections. Meat from the Chiana valley is low in fat without being dry, and is particularly spicy and flavorsome as a result of the natural grazing available to the animals. Tuscans say it has a salty taste. The young animals, which reach weights of up to 1540 pounds (700 kilograms), provide large cuts of meat, including the huge T-bone steaks for *Bistecca alla fiorentina*. The meat is so tender that it needs only to be laid on a charcoal grill for a few minutes, and can almost be eaten raw. The writer Aldo Santini calls *Bistecca alla fiorentina* the "Giotto of good cooking." The word *bistecca* comes from the English *beefsteak*. Legend has it that in 1565, during a feast in the Piazza San Lorenzo in Florence, spit-roasted beef was served to the populace. The guests included some Englishmen, who, when they caught sight of the juicy meat, began chanting "Beefsteak, beefsteak" to emphasize their desire for a piece of meat. The Florentines immediately translated the cry into "bistecca." Before this feast, steaks had been called *carbonate*, literally carbon steaks, since they were broiled on charcoal, but the new name soon replaced this. This method of preparation was known even in ancient times: the Etruscans were already cooking T-bone steaks.

BISTECCA ALLA FIORENTINA
Florentine T-bone steak
(Illustrated below)

Serves 3–4

1 BEEFSTEAK ON THE BONE, TWO FINGERS THICK, AT LEAST
1 LB 12 OZ/800 G IN WEIGHT
SALT
FRESHLY MILLED PEPPER

In Italy a bewildering array of expressions and names is currently in use for the various parts of cattle. Although state guidelines exist regarding the correct terminology, hardly anybody takes any notice of them. Since both the butchers and their customers prefer to keep using the names to which they are accustomed, which are often in dialect, the terms listed below serve merely as a guide.

Quarto anteriore (forequarter)
1   *Costata:* cutlet, chine
2   *Sottospalla:* forerib
3   *Pancia:* thin flank
4   *Fesone di spalla:* thin rib
5   *Reale:* thick rib
6   *Petto:* skirt
7   *Muscolo anteriore:* shank
8   *Polpa di spalla:* brisket
9   *Girello di spalla:* shoulder
10 *Copertina:* chuck
11 *Copertina di sotto:* blade
12 *Collo:* neck

Quarto posteriore (hindquarter)
13 *Lombata:* sirloin
14 *Filetto:* fillet
15 *Scamone:* top rump
16 *Fianchetto:* piece of loin from head of bone
17 *Noce:* tender cut from lower head of bone and thick flank
18a *Fesa:* tender cut of topside
18b *Sottofesa:* tender cut of silverside
19 *Girello:* round
20 *Campanello:* shank
21 *Muscolo posteriore:* hind shank

Classification of animals:
Vitello: veal, very pale meat, also
Vitello di latte: milk veal.
Vitellone: young animal, one to two years old, heifers must not have calved.
Manzo: three-year old animal; bulls have been castrated, heifers have not yet calved.
Bue: castrated bull (bullock), four years old or more.
Toro: fully grown bull.
Vacca: fully grown cow that has calved.

The meat should be at room temperature before broiling. Lay the steak on a grid and broil over red-hot charcoal, glowing but without flames, until a good crust has formed. This takes approximately 5 minutes. Then turn, without piercing the meat with the fork. Season the side that has already been broiled with salt. Broil the other side for a similar length of time until a crust has formed. The meat inside should still be red. Remove from the heat, season with salt and pepper, and serve immediately. White beans or lamb's lettuce are a suitable accompaniment.

OSSIBUCHI ALLA TOSCANA
Osso buco, sliced veal shank, Tuscan-style

4 SLICES OF VEAL SHANK, WITH MARROWBONE
ALL-PURPOSE FLOUR
4 TSP/20 G BUTTER
3–4 TBSP EXTRA VIRGIN OLIVE OIL
1 ONION
2 STICKS CELERY
1 CARROT
1 GLASS RED WINE
1/2 LB/200 G SIEVED TOMATOES
SALT AND PEPPER
MEAT STOCK IF REQUIRED

Coat the pieces of shank in flour and then fry in butter and olive oil until they are browned evenly on all sides. Remove from the pan and set aside in a warm place. Cut the onion, celery, and carrot into small pieces and sauté in the same pan. Add the red wine and stir in the tomatoes. Lay the pieces of meat in this sauce, adding enough water to cover them completely. Cover with a lid and braise for about 1 hour. Turn the pieces of veal after 30 minutes and season with salt and pepper. If the sauce thickens too much, add a little stock.

Above: Tuscan meat has an outstanding reputation. In order to safeguard it, the Chiana and Maremma cattle breeders have formed a consortium for their protection, watching carefully to ensure that the breeds retain their characteristics and are kept in the traditional way, roaming freely in their natural environment. This results in healthy, well-bred animals that provide lean, tasty, juicy meat. These top-quality products are sold in selected butchers' shops. Look for the mark of the consortium, stamped in ink or branded on the meat, then you will surely have the best.

BEEF FROM THE MAREMMA

The conclusion can be drawn from the archaeological finds at Cere and the bull's head in the museum at Vetulonia that cattle were already being bred in the Maremma in Etruscan times. They are descended from the so-called wild oxen mentioned by Pliny. Maremma cattle are strong, robust animals that were used by farmers for working in the fields before the advent of agricultural machinery.

Today, the gray cattle with their prominent horns – those of the bulls are half-moon-shaped and can grow to a length of three feet (one meter), while those of the females are curved like a lyre – are bred almost exclusively for their tender, tasty meat. In order to refine the species further, they have been cross-bred with Chiana and French Charolais cattle.

PORK

Pig-rearing has been an important economic factor in Italy since the time of the Langobardi in the 7th century. The medieval custom of measuring the size and value of a forest, not by the acre or hectare, but instead by the number of pigs it could sustain, shows how important this source of meat and fat must have been. Indeed, a family could live off a pig for a whole year, and the undemanding creature had the advantage of being easy to keep, since it could be fed on kitchen scraps and other waste. In addition to this, every part of the pig could be used: the meat either came directly to the table, or was made into robust sausages and ham; the lard and fat were important sources of energy; the skin could be tanned; and the bristles were used to make brushes.

Tuscans traditionally enjoy eating pork. Cold cuts and a *crostino* are rated equally highly as an *antipasto* or as a light snack between meals. And in rural areas, as recently as a few years ago, a plate of sausage was served in between the main course and the dessert as the high point of the meal and as a mark of esteem. Two different groups of products result from the processing of pork. On one hand there are the specialties consisting of "whole" meat, such as ham, shoulder cuts, belly, bacon, chuck, neck, and loin, and on the other hand there are the sausage products that are made from ground meat with the addition of salt, preservatives, and spices, such as *salsiccia* (sausage), *soppressata* (brawn), *buristo* (blood sausage), *salame* (salami), *finocchiona* and the crumbly *sbricciolona* (two typically Tuscan fennel sausages). Between Pisa and Arezzo, Prato, and Grosseto, there are still many small family businesses where pigs are slaughtered in the traditional manner, and where the meat is processed to make high-quality products. A number have specialized in maturing sausages carefully in order to develop their own characteristic flavors. And because Tuscany is a vast region with the most diverse climatic conditions, there is a correspondingly wide variety of local specialties. Furthermore, every butcher here is the proud possessor and guardian of his own secret recipe, often inherited from his grandfather, according to which he seasons the sausagemeat or smokes the ham.

Tuscan pork is of especially high quality, and bears no resemblance to the watery cutlets that shrink in the frying pan to half their original volume, which are on sale all too frequently at the meat counter in supermarkets north of the Alps. The indigenous breeds, which once populated the gently rolling Tuscan hills, feeding on acorns, beechnuts, and the fruits and berries in the undergrowth, are nevertheless under threat of extinction. One of these endangered species is the Cinta senese, which was originally a native of the heavily forested areas around Siena. These animals cannot be kept in pigsties, since they would put on too much fat too quickly, and water would be stored in their tissues. It is too expensive for the breeders to keep them under free-range conditions. In recent years, however, the demand for meat from free-range animals has risen.

A number of Tuscan breeders have now joined together to form an association, the *Compagnia della Cinta senese*. They all breed pigs in the proper manner, rearing the piglets quite naturally without the use of any fattening feed. The breeders know that at present they are offering a niche product, but experience has

As in the case of beef, different names for the various cuts of pork are in circulation, depending on the region, so the terms below can serve only as a guide.

1 *Capicollo, Coppa:* chine, neck
2 *Guanciale:* pork cheek
3 *Spalla:* shoulder
4 *Geretto anteriore:* foreleg
5 *Costine di petto, Puntine di petto:* forerib
6 *Pancia, Pancetta:* belly, lean
7 *Geretto posteriore:* hindleg
8 *Cosciotto, Prosciutto:* ham, hindquarter
9 *Lonza, Lombo:* loin
10 *Nodino:* pork cutlet with fillet
11 *Filetto:* fillet
12 *Costoletta, Costina, Braciola:* cutlet
13 *Zampetto, Piedino:* foot
14 *Puntine:* middle pork rib
15 *Lardo:* lard, pork fat (the fat lies above the cutlets)

also taught them that customers appreciate the special flavor of products from free-range pigs, and are quite prepared to reach a little deeper into their pockets to buy it. The best example of the legendary Tuscan concern for quality is provided by the Chini family, which not only runs a butchery but also rears its own pigs in a forest near Gaiole, in Chianti. The father, Vincenzo Chini, for the most part concentrates on slaughtering pigs and preparing sausages, while his son Lorenzo is responsible for rearing the pigs. For centuries, since 1682 to be precise, the Chini family have adhered steadfastly to the traditional production methods for regional sausage specialties – and as a consequence have been repeatedly rewarded with numerous medals and prizes.

TONNO DEL CHIANTI

Tonno del Chianti, Chianti tuna fish, is made with the meat from suckling pigs. The *lattonzoli* (the Tuscan name for a suckling pig) weigh between 88 and 110 pounds (40–50 kilograms). In Tuscany, superfluous young animals, which the farmers had been unable to feed, were traditionally slaughtered during June and July. Because of the intense summer heat, however, it was impossible to salt the meat to preserve it, and so it was cooked in Vin Brusco. To a certain extent, Vin Brusco can be described as a "by-product" obtained from pressing Chianti: it is the wine made from the remaining white Trebbiano and Malvasia grapes.

Afterwards the meat was stored in olive oil. For some reason, this method of preparation imparted a flavor of tuna fish to the meat, and the Tuscans, who used not to catch tuna fish, thereby discovered an extremely tasty substitute.

For years, production of *Tonno del Chianti* was completely neglected. Today, thanks to Dario Cecchini of Panzano in Chianti, there is once again a single butcher's shop in Chianti – and worldwide – where *Tonno* is produced.

ARISTA ALLA FIORENTINA
Florentine roast pork
(Illustrated below left)

Serves 6

3–3 1/2 LB/1.5 KG PORK ROASTING JOINT, WITH BONE
2 CLOVES OF GARLIC
1 SPRIG OF ROSEMARY
SALT AND PEPPER
OLIVE OIL
2 LB/1 KG POTATOES

Loosen the meat from the bone. Finely chop the garlic and rosemary and mix with salt and pepper. Spread half the mixture on the bone. Replace the meat on the bone, and rub the other half of the herb mixture into the meat, using the hands. Sprinkle with oil and braise in a preheated oven at 350 °F (180 °C) for approximately 1 hour 20 minutes, basting repeatedly with the juices from the meat. Peel the potatoes and cut into large pieces. Add to the roast after 30 minutes.
Leave the roast to stand for at least 10 minutes after it comes out of the oven. Remove the bone, cut the meat into pieces and serve.

CREMA PARADISO
Tuscan creamed bacon

2 LB/1 KG FIRM BACK BACON
2 TBSP/20 G SEA SALT
BLACK PEPPERCORNS, CRUSHED
WINE VINEGAR
5–6 CLOVES OF GARLIC, CRUSHED
A FEW SPRIGS OF FRESH ROSEMARY, CHOPPED

Grind the bacon in a food processor. Add the salt, peppercorns, a few drops of wine vinegar, the garlic, and the rosemary. Knead the bacon on a marble slab until a light, delicate cream is formed. Spread on hot toast and serve with Chianti.

LUMACHE AFFUMICIATE CON CAPICOLLO LARDELLATO
Smoked snails with bacon and pork chine

24 SNAILS
1 STICK CELERY, COARSELY CHOPPED
1 SHALLOT, COARSELY CHOPPED
1 SMALL CARROT, COARSELY CHOPPED
3/4 CUP/200 ML WHITE WINE
SALT AND PEPPER

For the filling:
6 1/2 TBSP/100 G BUTTER
1 SLICE BROILED PORK CHINE, 1/4 LB/100 G IN WEIGHT
2/3 CUP/50 G BACON, COARSELY CHOPPED
2 OZ/50 G SMOKED SCARMORZA CHEESE, COARSELY CHOPPED
1 CLOVE OF GARLIC
SALT AND PEPPER

Wash and clean the snails and place in a pan with the celery, shallot, carrot, wine, and plenty of cold water. Boil for about 4–5 hours, occasionally adding a little water if necessary; do not season with salt and pepper until the end of the cooking time.
To make the filling, put the butter, pork chine, bacon, cheese, and garlic in the food processor and process until smooth. Season to taste with salt and pepper. Leave the snails to cool in the cooking liquid, drain, and prepare as follows: first place some of the filling in a dish, lay the snails on top, then cover with filling, but not to the top of the dish. Cook in the oven at 400 °F (200 °C) until the top is brown, and serve very hot.

FEGATELLI DI MAIALE
Pig's liver in a pig's stomach

1 LB/500 G PIG'S LIVER
1/2 LB/200 G LEAN PORK
1 CLOVE OF GARLIC
SALT AND PEPPER
1/2 LB/200 G PIG'S STOMACH
5–6 BAY LEAVES
2–3 TBSP EXTRA VIRGIN OLIVE OIL
RED WINE OR MEAT STOCK

To make the filling, cut the liver, pork, and garlic cloves into small pieces, and season with salt and pepper. Place the pig's stomach in boiling water for a few minutes, drain, and pat dry. Cut into pieces big enough to hold a portion of filling about the size of a fist. Stuff the pieces of pig's stomach with the filling, place a bay leaf in each, and secure with a cocktail stick.
Cook in olive oil in the oven for approximately 20 minutes, adding a little red wine or meat stock if necessary.

FILETTO DI MAIALE GRATINATO
Pork fillet au gratin with herbs

1 CUP MIXED/100 G THYME, ROSEMARY, MARJORAM, AND SAGE
2 1/2 CUPS/300 G BREADCRUMBS
1 CUP/100 G MONTASIO STRAVECCHIO, GRATED
3 1/2 TBSP/50 ML EXTRA VIRGIN OLIVE OIL
1 PORK FILLET, ABOUT 1 1/2–1 3/4 LB/700 800 G IN WEIGHT
SALT AND PEPPER
2 EGGS
SCANT 1/2 CUP/100 ML SUNFLOWER OIL

Finely chop all the herbs. Add the breadcrumbs, cheese, and a little olive oil, and mix. Season the pork fillet with salt and pepper. Beat the eggs, then dip the fillet in the egg and turn to coat it. Spread with the herb mixture. Fry in sunflower oil in a preheated pan for approximately 3 minutes on each side. Cook in the oven at 320 °F (160 °C) for about 10 minutes. Cut the fillet into thin slices, and serve with Savoy cabbage and smoked bacon.

FEGATELLI DI MAIALE AGLI AROMI
Pig's liver in herb stock

Serves 6

1 LB/500 G PIG'S LIVER
8 SAGE LEAVES
1/2 LB/200 G PIG'S STOMACH
1 CUP/100 G BACON, FINELY DICED
1 ONION, CUT INTO RINGS
8 ROSEMARY LEAVES
LARGE HANDFUL FRESH PARSLEY
SALT AND PEPPER
3/4 CUP/200 ML DRY WHITE WINE

Cut the liver into 8 evenly sized pieces and wrap individually with a sage leaf in pieces of pig's stomach. Fry the bacon with the onion rings, rosemary, and coarsely chopped parsley in a shallow pan for several minutes. Add the liver and cook for at least 20 minutes over a low heat, adding the salt, pepper, and wine.
Arrange the liver on a toasted slice of polenta, and serve with braised beans.

WINEGROWING IN ITALY

The history of winegrowing in Italy begins in about 800 B.C., when Greeks planted vines they had brought with them when they colonized Sicily. For a long time, southern Italy remained the Greeks' most important winegrowing center. In the year A.D. 79, however, the wine world was shaken by a catastrophe: the masses of lava from Vesuvius not only buried Pompeii, but, by destroying the most important port in the empire, also destroyed the foundations of the trade in wine with other countries in the Mediterranean region. From that point onward, winegrowing advanced farther and farther north, at first into the hills near Rome, and later, especially during the reign of the emperor Probus (276–82), even reached the most remote provinces beyond the Alps. The foundations for the present-day winegrowing regions of Bordeaux, Moselle, and Wachau had been laid. With the eventual fall of the Roman empire in the 4th century A.D., Italian viticulture also went into decline. It was not until Renaissance times, when Tuscan merchants began to take an interest in the wine trade, that cultivation of vines regained its economic importance. Grape juice was a perfectly natural product and was at that time seldom considered a luxury as had been the case in ancient Rome. In the second half of the 19th century, the country experienced a genuine winegrowing revolution. Under the influence of the modernists, the followers of Garibaldi and founders of the Republic, winegrowing and cellar techniques were significantly improved, and wines were created that have remained popular to this day: Chianti and Barolo, Valpolicella and Brunello. However, the first half of the 20th century saw a setback. Until well after World War II, many producers laid more emphasis on large-scale production than on growths that were superior in quality. This state of affairs did not change until the 1970s and 1980s, since when the quality of Italian wines has improved so much that the best products can be compared on equal terms with the great names in international winegrowing.

TUSCAN ARISTOCRACY SUPPLIES THE WORLD

While the central European winegrowing areas of Rheingau, Moselle, Burgundy, and Bordeaux were blossoming for the first time in the Middle Ages, winegrowing in Italy was descending into a deep crisis. It was not until the 13th and 14th centuries that it began to recover a little. In Tuscany, aristocratic families such as those of the Marchesi Antinori and Marchesi Frescobaldi – families that today still number among the leading Tuscan winegrowers – began to devote themselves to the wine trade in addition to their various banking and commercial activities. The extent of their influence is demonstrated by the fact that, from time to time, the Frescobaldi family financed the English court, and acted as a tax collector for the Vatican.

In winter, when the vines are in their resting phase, the foundations for the next season are already being laid. This is when the shoots are pruned and the soil is ploughed.

Harvesting takes place in September and October. The grapes should be picked as quickly as possible.

FROM DIONYSUS TO THE BACCHANALIA

Like the Greeks, the Romans also had a god of wine. In ancient Athens, Dionysus was the god of fertility, wine, and ecstasy. Because such things were definitely regarded as "women's matters" in ancient times, it was mainly the women who commemorated "their" god every winter by means of long, relaxed feasts, during the course of which wine and all kinds of intoxicants imaginable were consumed in great quantities. These rites continued in the Roman Empire as bacchanalia, feasts in honor of Bacchus, the god of wine. The excesses were sometimes so great that the feasts were forbidden due to fears for public order. It was not until Christianity was established as the official state religion in the 7th century in our calendar that the bacchanalia came to an end.

Background: At the end of May the flowering stems can be seen in all their glory. They are growing especially quickly at this point. In order to ensure optimal conditions for the grapes later on, the new shoots are again tied in.

The buds break in March and April. The vintner ties the quickly growing shoots to a framework of wires that has been erected previously.

It is still difficult to tell whether this is a white or a red grape variety, since most grapes look much the same until they ripen in July.

Quality control in the vineyard is achieved by means of the refractometer, an optical device used to ascertain the specific gravity of the must.

Now there is no time to lose, for uncontrolled fermentation or decay jeopardize quality.

After the fresh must has been clarified and any cloudiness removed, fermentation is started.

Racking, transferring the wine to another container, is necessary to separate the new wine from the yeast.

When maturing quality red wines in wooden casks, both large barrels and small barrique-type containers are used.

The vintner checks at regular intervals to ensure that the wine is maturing in the barrels according to plan.

Unlabeled bottles are temporarily stored in the cellar.

After labeling, the bottles are ready for sale.

CHIANTI – A SUPERSTAR

Tuscany ranks alongside Piedmont as the most famous winegrowing region in Italy. Though it provides a contrast with Piedmont, where the wine industry is characterized on one hand by rural production methods that are still quite antiquated, and on the other hand by the very elitist image of its top wines, Tuscany also enjoys great popularity. Wines with names such as Chianti, Brunello, Nobile di Montepulciano, Vernaccia di San Gimignano, Galestro, or Sassicaia are famous throughout the world, and every wine-lover knows what to expect from them. Tuscany can also be considered the perfect embodiment of the unity between wine and culture, and there have been few great artists in the past who have not sung the praises of its wine in one form or another to hand down to succeeding generations. The history of Tuscan winegrowing has always been determined by the interplay of the major landowners – especially the clergy and the nobility – and the

Wines from the Chianti-Rufina area have an astonishing capacity for aging.

In the center of Tuscany, nestling between Chianti, Brunello, and Nobile, lies the spectacular countryside of Crete Senesi.

mezzadri, or sharecroppers, tenant farmers allowed to live on the land and cultivate it in return for half the crop. When the big estates were broken up after World War II, and many of the *mezzadri* migrated to the towns, there was a danger that winegrowing in the region would be forgotten. Many of the neglected properties were acquired at that time by businessmen and migrants from the rich cities of northern Italy and from abroad, who invested heavily in their restoration. In order to process the grapes they had harvested, they were obliged to rely on the help of learned oenologists. If the wines were to be sold, they had to meet the more exacting standards of wine connoisseurs all over the world. Experiments were conducted with new pressing methods, with the maturing process, in other words storing the wine in small barrels made from new wood, with French grape varieties, and with unusual combinations of varieties. Modern Italian wine had been born, and bore a Tuscan name.

Unfortunately, these revolutionary wines often failed to comply with the regulations, some of which were very rigid, of the system governing designation of origin, and as a result the region, which was one of the first in history to use protected designations of origin – Carmignano is one of the oldest ever – was obliged to sell its top wines as mere table wines. However, even this anomaly could not halt the trend to high-quality products. The Sangiovese grape variety in particular, which is suited to the almost universally hilly landscape of the region, and which needs both the intensive sunshine of the terraced vineyards and the pronounced fluctuations between day and night temperatures that occur at altitude, became an absolute superstar here.

The Sangiovese grape was not only responsible for the famous Brunello di Montalcino wine, but also accounted for an increasingly large proportion of the blend of grapes used to make Chianti, which today, following a corresponding change in the law in the 1990s, may now be pressed exclusively from the Sangiovese grape. It guaranteed the quality of Nobile di Montepulciano and Morellino di Scansano, of Carmignano and some of the great table wines, known as the *Super-Tuscans*, according to the apt name coined for them by the Anglo-Saxon world. Among the other red grape varieties, which continue to deliver outstanding results here, the varieties of French provenance – Cabernet Sauvignon, Merlot, and to a lesser extent also Shiraz and Pinot Noir – are particularly noteworthy.

Tuscany's white wines, however, are less compelling. Although Galestro was a successful, fresh, uncomplicated branded wine made from Trebbiano grapes in the 1980s, although Vernaccia di San Gimignano and white Montecarlo wine enjoy a very good reputation, and despite the fact that the occasional interesting Chardonnay can now be found in the very heart of the Chianti region, white Tuscan wines have never approached the prestige and class that has been achieved by the reds.

Right: The Castello di Brolio near Gaiole in the Chianti region dates back to the year 1141. It was here that Baron Ricasoli "discovered" modern Chianti in the 19th century.

VIN SANTO

Vin Santo, or holy wine, is a soft, medium-dry to sweet, straw-colored dessert wine, containing 15 to 16 percent alcohol by volume. In the autumn, the freshly harvested grapes are hung up to dry and pressed only when they are almost completely transformed into raisins. The resulting must has a correspondingly high concentration and sugar content. After fermentation, small oak or chestnut barrels are half-filled with the wine and then hermetically sealed. Because of the residual yeast from previous vintages, a secondary fermentation starts in the barrels. These are stored beneath the roof, so that the wine develops in the summer heat and the winter cold, which accounts for its rich flavors of nuts, apricots, honey, spices, and blossom. It takes two to six years for the wine to mature. After a meal, Tuscans like to dip hard almond cookies, *Biscotti di Prato* or *cantuccini*, in small glasses of this wine. However, a good, old Vin Santo wine is also exceedingly suitable as a "meditation wine," as the Italians call it, in other words a wine for moments of reflection between mealtimes.

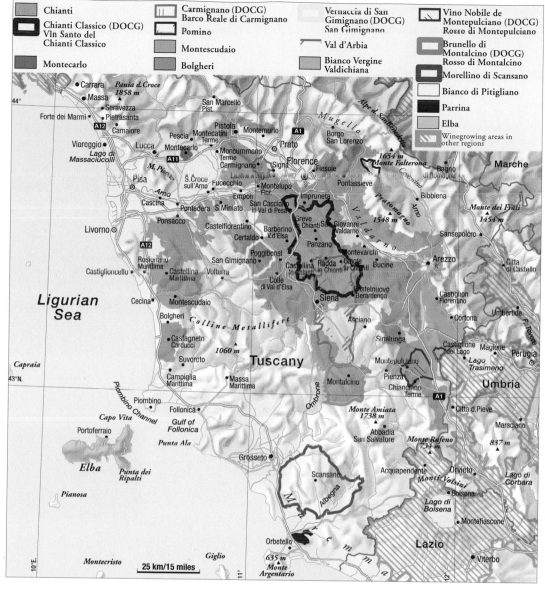

Map Legend

- Chianti
- Chianti Classico (DOCG) Vin Santo del Chianti Classico
- Montecarlo
- Carmignano (DOCG) Barco Reale di Carmignano
- Pomino
- Montescudaio
- Bolgheri
- Vernaccia di San Gimignano (DOCG) San Gimignano
- Val d'Arbia
- Bianco Vergine Valdichiana
- Vino Nobile de Montepulciano (DOCG) Rosso di Montepulciano
- Brunello di Montalcino (DOCG) Rosso di Montalcino
- Morellino di Scansano
- Bianco di Pitigliano
- Parrina
- Elba
- Winegrowing areas in other regions

25 km/15 miles

CHIANTI – ITALY'S MOST POPULAR WINE

Chianti, in addition to being one of the oldest wines, is above all one of the quality wines that Italy produces in the greatest quantity – by far outstripping Asti, Soave, Prosecco, or Valpolicella. In years when the yield is good, almost 26.42 million U.S. gallons (one million hectoliters) of Chianti are bottled and exported all over the world. However, Chianti does not describe one single product: it is a generic term, encompassing very different wines produced in various parts of Tuscany. At the heart of the Chianti region is the most famous area, Chianti Classico, recently singled out by a separate law of designated origin – the historic central area of Tuscany between Florence in the north and Siena in the south. It was here, over 150 years ago, that Baron Ricasoli developed his recipe for Chianti at Castello di Brolio. He specified that the wine should

consist of a blend of 70 percent Sangiovese, 15 percent Canaiolo nero, 10 percent white Trebbiano Toscano and Malvasia del Chianti grapes, and 5 percent of other grape varieties. The purpose of this blend was to give the Sangiovese grape a more intense color and more flavor, and to make it more accessible, even while still new, by adding other grape varieties.

Only as a result of the winegrowing revolution of the past 30 years has Ricasoli's recipe become obsolete. Talented winemakers have managed to crystallize all the desired properties from the Sangiovese grape, without needing to compromise its unmistakable character by adding other varieties of inferior quality. As a result, more and more vintners are pressing their Chianti exclusively from Sangiovese grapes, while others are dispensing with the majority of the traditional blending varieties, and, especially as regards the white grapes, are instead substituting small quantities of finer, imported varieties

such as Cabernet, Shiraz, or Merlot. Modern, well-made Chianti Classico is characterized by the marriage of great finesse and elegance with good strength and aging properties. It not only goes extremely well with most Tuscan dishes, but also successfully complements the cuisine of other countries. Although the name and the grape varieties used are identical, the wines produced from the legally defined zones of the Chianti region are sometimes very different. The most famous of them is Chianti Rufina, from a small winegrowing area east of Florence. When new, these wines have more pronounced acidity than the Classico, but they have better aging properties. Wines produced in the Chianti zones of Colli Fiorentini (near Florence), Colli Aretini (near Arezzo), Colli Senesi (a huge area south of Siena), Colline Pisane (near Pisa), Montalbano (the area west of Florence, in which Carmignano is also produced), and Montespertoli (a new part of the region, near the town of the same name) are lighter and less complex in character than those of the Classico and Rufina areas.

BRUNELLO AND OTHER WINES

If Chianti is regarded as the most popular Italian wine, then Brunello is surely one of the most renowned. By contrast with Chianti, it is pressed exclusively from the Sangiovese grape. Feruccio Biondi-Santi is credited with the creation of this wine. Not only did he fill the first bottle, officially called Brunello di Montalcino, in 1888, but had also carefully selected especially suitable vines for his production beforehand. For a long time it was thought that the grape, referred to by the vintners of Montalcino as Sangiovese Grosso, was a special variety of Sangiovese, but the grapes chosen by Biondi-Santi were probably just the best specimens of the vines that were normally grown in the Chianti region.

Good Brunello is immensely strong, characterized by strong tannins when new, and after a long maturing process develops a wonderfully aromatic bouquet reminiscent of spices, game, hide, and sweet tobacco. For a long time, unfortunately, the DOC regulations forced the vintners to mature the wine for four or even five years in huge wooden barrels, which was simply too long for weaker vintages – after this period maturing in the wood they seemed thinner and more drained than before, and during the course

of the aging process they quickly lost their luster and charm. Today, a shorter period of storage in the cask and the use of small barrique-type barrels have given even Brunello a more modern appearance. The wine of secondary quality, which is drunk when newer, from this wine-producing area is sold under the name Rosso di Montalcino. Last but not least, the wine Moscadello di Montalcino is pressed here from Muscat grapes.

A NOBLE WINE

Prugnolo gentile is the name given to the Sangiovese grape in the area around the small town of Montepulciano, where the main wine produced is the Vino Nobile di Montepulciano. This small medieval town stands in solitary splendor high above the Chiana valley – famous for its cattle – and above the Lago Trasimeno. Stronger than the second-quality wine of the region, the Rosso di Montepulciano, it nevertheless has a flowery bouquet and leaves a firm, substantial impression on the palate that falls somewhere between Chianti and Brunello. It is, of course, best when drunk with a good Chiana beef steak.

THE OLDEST DESIGNATION OF ORIGIN IN THE WORLD

Carmignano is grown on the hills to the west of Florence, protected as long ago as 1716 by Cosimo III by means of a statutory designation of origin – possibly the first DOC wine in Italy, and perhaps even the first *appellation* in the world. It was also the first Tuscan wine in which the French grape variety Cabernet Sauvignon was officially permitted. In terms of strength and substance, the wine is

comparable with the Nobile di Montepulciano. Wines from good vintages made by top producers can be aged for several decades. In the Carmignano area there is also a wine of secondary quality with DOC status, the Barco Reale di Carmignano, which contains no Cabernet, but only Sangiovese and Canaiolo grapes.

A SECOND TUSCAN REVOLUTION

For a long time the Tuscan coast between Livorno and Grosseto was a no-man's land in terms of winegrowing. There was practically only one DOC wine, the rosé wine from Bolgheri.

Since the 1970s, however, great advances have been made by a table wine from this area, Sassicaia. This was destined to become the most famous Italian wine

San Gimignano, with its famous towers, is the birthplace of the first Italian DOC white wine.

Cypresses, vines, meandering roads, and typical farmhouses – this is the image of Tuscany that is known and loved the world over.

produced from a single grape variety, and was pressed entirely from the Cabernet grapes from vines imported directly from the Bordeaux region by Count Incisa della Rochetta.

In due course, Sassicaia was much imitated, and the resulting wines included Sassicaia's neighbor Ornellaia, for which Cabernet Sauvignon, Cabernet franc and Merlot grapes were blended, and Grattamacco, which contained a large proportion of Sangiovese grapes. In

the meantime, however, the designations of origin of the region have been changed, with the effect that these famous table wines can also be labeled as DOC wines, thus acquiring a recognized seal of quality. They are enjoyed at their best with red meat dishes, such as *Osso Buco*.

WHITE WINE AND THE TOWERS OF SAN GIMIGNANO

The most famous white wine from Tuscany comes from San Gimignano, the city famous for its many towers rising high into the sky. Vernaccia grapes have been cultivated in this area since the 13th century, and Vernaccia was the first Italian white wine

to be accorded DOC status. The dry, slightly aromatic wine is an outstanding accompaniment to many pasta dishes and fish. The red wines from San Gimignano have also recently obtained DOC status.

SMALLER DESIGNATED REGIONS

Currently the most dynamic winegrowing area in Tuscany is the southern province of Grosseto, in other words the coastal region of Maremma. Wines

produced here from the Sangiovese grape include Morellino di Scansano, a fruitier wine than Chianti, Nobile or Brunello. Bianco Pitigliano, by nature a more neutral,

lighter white wine, is pressed quite close by. Of more interest is the white Montecarlo from the province of Lucca in the north of the region.

Finally, mention must be made of the Pomino DOC area, situated in the mountains above Chianti Rufina. Excellent reds are pressed here from Sangiovese, Cabernet, and Merlot grapes, and a modern white wine is created from white Burgundy, Chardonnay, and Trebbiano grapes, which goes exceedingly well with the fresh, aromatic specialties of the region. It is a particularly good accompaniment to fish dishes, such as *Pesce impanato*.

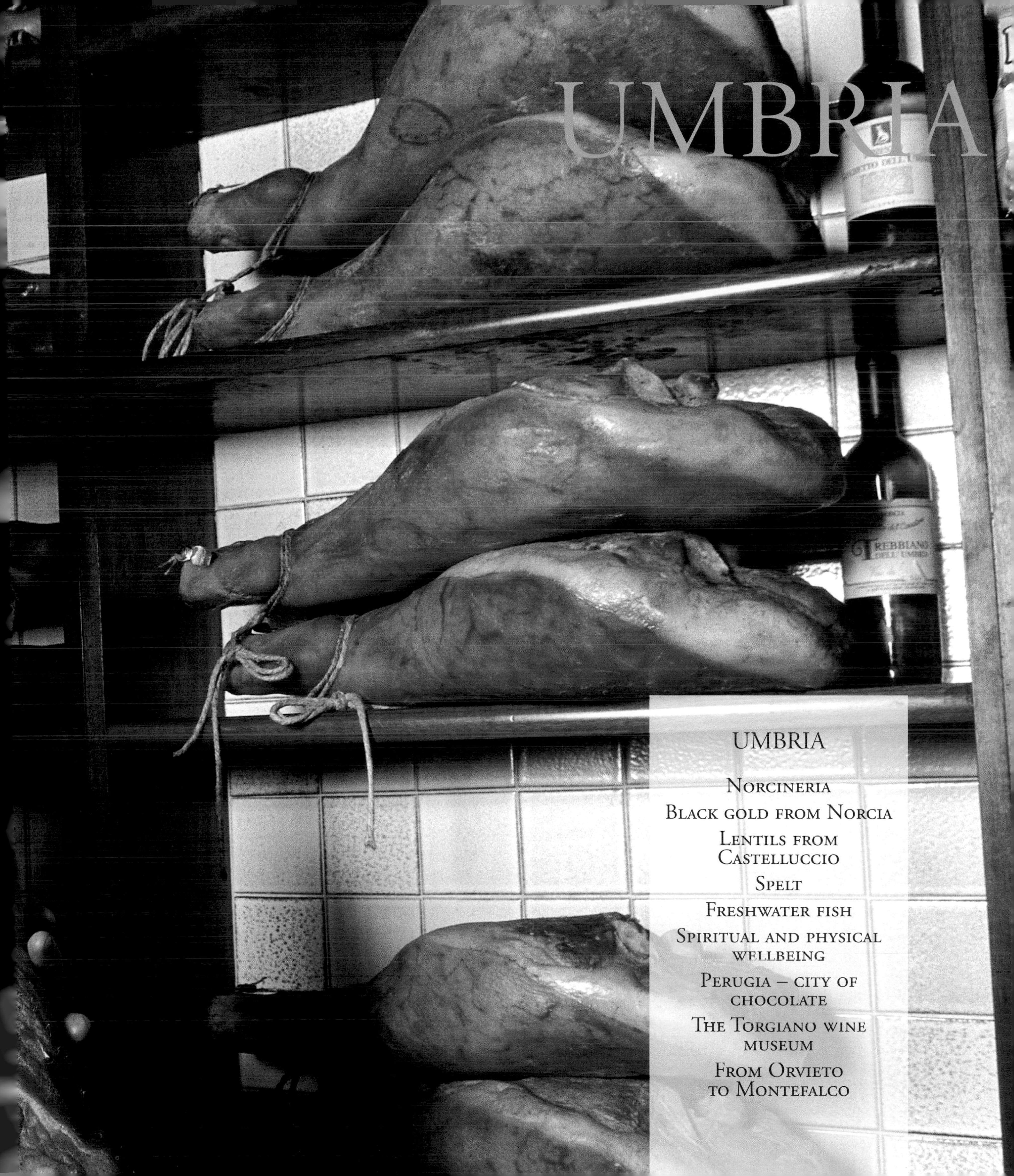

UMBRIA

UMBRIA

Norcineria

Black gold from Norcia

Lentils from Castelluccio

Spelt

Freshwater fish

Spiritual and physical wellbeing

Perugia – city of chocolate

The Torgiano wine museum

From Orvieto to Montefalco

Umbria – the very name is redolent of shady forests and still lakes. The landscape appears overlaid with gold, especially in the fall. Echoes of long-forgotten fairy tales can be heard in enchanted groves, and, in the still retreats and monasteries, the visitor can understand what may have inspired St. Francis of Assisi to compose his ode to the sun. Umbrians have had a mystic, and at the same time very respectful, relationship with nature since time immemorial. The simple "Franciscan" dishes of Umbrian cuisine also appear natural, or left in their natural state. Complicated fillings, pies, or stuffings are just as difficult to find here as heavy cream sauces. Food here is boiled, roasted, flavored, and embellished using the local light olive oil, with its delicate scent of herbs, that is one of the best in Italy and is sometimes as green as Umbria itself.

The food served is whatever happens to be in season. Vegetable dishes predominate in spring and summer, while in the autumn and winter the focus is on the spoils of the hunting season and the famous black truffles from Norcia. This picturesque little medieval town is justifiably regarded as a culinary stronghold in the region. It is worth a visit, not just in late autumn, when the "black gold" is in season, for the art of butchery and sausage-making has been perfected here to the extent that the butchers have been closely identified with their native town. As a result, the word *norcino* signifies not only an inhabitant of Norcia, but also – and this applies throughout Italy – a pork butcher and sausage producer.

In Umbria the manner in which expensive ingredients, specialties, and delicacies are handled is refreshingly casual. It is taken completely for granted that the best natural ingredients should be used in this simple, down-to-earth cuisine. Nutritious soups, spit-roasted meat, home-made noodles – all are prepared with a great deal of love and care. And this relaxed approach even applies to the famous truffles. Umbrian chefs dice them, pound them in a pestle and mortar with anchovies and garlic, use them to add a lingering flavor to a meat sauce for pasta, beat generous quantities into the eggs used to make omelets, and even use these noble mushrooms in their *Torta di pasqua*. The Umbrian philosophy is that things have always been done this way, and anyway the results taste good.

Previous double page: The Norcineria Ansuini in Norcia is famous for its handmade sausage and ham production.

Left: The quiet town of Assisi lies on the slopes of Mount Subasio. It was here that St. Francis founded his order at the beginning of the 13th century.

BLACK GOLD FROM NORCIA

Above and in the background: The black Norcia truffle (*tuber melanosporum*, also known as the Périgord truffle) can be eaten raw, but is also used to flavor other food.

The natives of Piedmont have Alba, the Tuscans have San Miniato, and the Umbrians travel to Norcia to buy truffles. Whereas white truffles predominate in Piedmont and Tuscany, Umbria is known for its black truffles, although light-colored varieties are also found here. The dispute among chefs and truffle lovers as to which type is tastier will probably never be settled. All that is certain is that the black truffle is more versatile than its white sister, for it can be eaten raw and is also a suitable ingredient or addition for flavoring sauces, pies, and pasta, without losing its aroma when it is heated. The Umbrian truffle areas extend along the rivers Nera, Corno, and Sordo, as far as the Monti Martani and the mountains near Trevi and Subasio. The knobby black mushroom is gathered mainly in the area around Norcia and Spoleto, white varieties are found around Gubbio, and one comes across black winter truffles, as well as both black and white summer truffles, throughout Umbria.

TIPS FOR COOKING TRUFFLES

- White truffles should always be prepared and eaten raw.
- Never boil black truffles, but heat them gently.
- It is not always necessary to combine truffles with cheese.
- Salt and the best extra virgin olive oil are essential.
- Only use truffles for dishes that do not have their own strong characteristic flavor.
- Before preparing truffles, remove any remaining soil using a soft brush, and then soak them for a few minutes in lukewarm water. The outer skin of the truffle is edible as well as the flesh.

BLACK TRUFFLE VARIETIES

Black Norcia truffles
The black Norcia truffle (*tuber melanosporum*) is gathered mainly in the area around Norcia and Spoleto. It thrives at altitude on hills and mountains, and prefers the company of oaks, holm oaks, and walnut trees, among which it forms circular, smooth areas devoid of grass, known as *pianelli*. The Norcia truffle has a black skin covered with small, slightly indented wart-like bumps. Its flesh is a purplish black with distinct white veining. It has a delicate, pleasant scent. Hunting for this delicacy is permitted only during the period between December 1 and March 15.

Black winter truffles
The black winter truffle (*tuber brumale Vitt.*) (illustrated below) grows in various regions and is not particularly demanding as regards its habitat. Its skin is dark and has wart-like protuberances, but these are

not prickly when touched. Its gray flesh has sharply contrasting white veins, and its aroma is strong and pervasive. The season for winter truffles lasts from December 1 to March 15.

Black Muscat truffles
The black Muscat truffle (*tuber brumale Vitt. Var. Moscatum, De Ferry*) is a close relative of the black winter truffle. It also has a black wart-covered skin, but its flesh is blackish with broad white veins. In addition, the Muscat truffle appears to have practically no scent. It is gathered between December 1 and March 15.

Black Bagnoli truffles
The black Bagnoli truffle (*tuber masentericum Vitt.*) is a variety of Norcia truffle, found mainly in Campania. However, it also thrives in the mountains and beech groves of other regions. It has a black, wart-covered outer skin, and its flesh is gray with white veins. This truffle is not to everyone's taste, as it has a rather unpleasant smell of tar or carbolic acid, but its devotees gather it between November 1 and March 15.

Right: The olive oil is heated in a heavy cast iron pan and the mixture of egg, cream, and truffles is poured in.

The eggs are beaten with the cream and seasoned with salt and pepper. The diced truffles are then added.

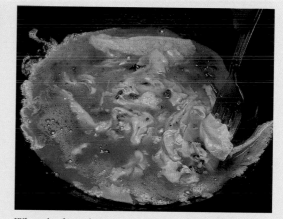

When the *frittata* begins to set, it is loosened from the sides and bottom of the pan with a fork.

FRITTATA AI TARTUFI
Truffle omelet
(Illustrated above)

1 MEDIUM-SIZED BLACK TRUFFLE FROM NORCIA
6 EGGS
4 TBSP CREAM
SALT AND PEPPER
1–2 TBSP OLIVE OIL
JUICE OF 1 LEMON

Brush any earth off the truffles, clean with paper towels, and cut into thin slices. Reserve the two best slices and dice the remainder. Beat the eggs, cream, salt, pepper, and add the truffles. Heat the olive oil in a cast iron pan, add the egg mixture, and allow it to set. Turn over carefully and cook on the other side until it turns golden brown. Slide the *frittata* on to a plate, sprinkle with lemon juice, decorate with the two truffle slices, and serve immediately.

SPAGHETTI ALLA NORCINA
Spaghetti Norcia-style

14 OZ/400 G SPAGHETTI
4–5 TBSP EXTRA VIRGIN OLIVE OIL
2 CLOVES OF GARLIC
3 ANCHOVY FILLETS, CUT INTO SMALL PIECES

5 OZ/150 G BLACK TRUFFLES, THINLY SLICED
SALT AND PEPPER

Boil the spaghetti in plenty of salted water until it is *al dente*. Heat the olive oil in a small pan and sauté the cloves of garlic. Remove the garlic, add the anchovy fillets to the oil, and allow them to disintegrate slowly over a low heat. Remove the pan from the stove and mix most of the thinly sliced truffles into the anchovy paste. Season with salt and pepper, then spread over the spaghetti. Garnish with the remaining truffle slices.

CROSTINI UMBRI
Toasted bread with truffle paste

1/4 LB/100 G BLACK TRUFFLES FROM NORCIA
2 ANCHOVY FILLETS
4–5 TBSP EXTRA VIRGIN OLIVE OIL
SALT
4 SLICES WHITE OR BROWN BREAD

Brush the truffles well under running water, pat dry, and grate finely. Crush the anchovy fillets and mix with the olive oil to form a smooth paste. Stir in the truffles and add a very small amount of salt. Spread the paste on the freshly toasted slices of bread.

LENTILS FROM CASTELLUCCIO

Lentils are a very ancient cultivated plant that reached the Mediterranean region from the Orient. Although cultivation of lentils is not common in Umbria, the few plants that are grown are of extraordinarily high quality. The famous lenticchie di *Castelluccio*, the most sought-after lentils in Italy, grow on the high plain of Castelluccio, at an altitude of 4600 feet (1400 meters). They are small and green, and very healthy, due to the large amount of proteins and mineral salts they contain – and at the same time so tender that they do not need soaking and are tender after cooking for only 20 to 30 minutes. Unfortunately, only very limited quantities appear on the market. Only a few tens of thousands of pounds can be produced on the high plain, and the Annifio and Colfiorito plantations contribute approximately another 20,000 pounds. Those who have the opportunity to try these legumes, now protected by a designation of origin, should jump at the chance.

BEANS, ONIONS, AND CELERY

Tender lentils are not the only field-grown specialty that Umbria has to offer. A great deal of time, patience, and care has always been devoted to the cultivation of vegetables in general here.

Cave belongs to the Foligno district and lies in the center of the "fruit garden" on the banks of the river Topino. Beans flourish here on the alluvial soil, which is extremely fertile and rich in minerals, and the ideal soil conditions enable them to be grown completely organically. Two large and 15 smaller agricultural businesses produce the two main varieties. Both the green and yellow beans have a soft shell and a very delicate flavor. They are suitable for soups and starters, but also taste good steamed, embellished only with a little delicate Umbrian olive oil.

The "onion growers' country," as it is called here, is near Cannara. Onions have always been an indispensable feature of Umbrian cooking. Historical documents show that they were served in the 17th century with beet, leeks, cabbage, and beans. The summer and autumn varieties grown in the region today can be eaten raw, but can also be steamed, oven-baked, eaten cold in salads, as an accompaniment to deep-fried food, or in soups and sauces. Those cooks who are sensitive to onions should slice them and leave them to stand in cold water for a few hours before handling them further. As a result, Umbrian onion soup, or *cipollata*, becomes an unadulterated pleasure.

Black celery has been cultivated in Trevi since the middle of the 18th century. This vegetable could be found in all the markets until it was largely ousted by the American celery that was imported increasingly often after World War II. In Trevi, though, there are still a few indomitable growers who cling to "their" celery. Genuine Trevi celery, with its strong aroma, has no unpalatable tough fibers, is very tall, dark green on the outside, and consists of a single bulbous heart from which the leaf-shaped sticks grow. An attempt to make *Parmigiana alla Trevi*, the oven-baked celery soufflé with a cheese topping, using a different variety of celery may be successful, but will never taste as good as the original.

Furthermore, celery is extremely healthy – it is a valuable source of minerals, and also provides a great deal of Vitamin B and Provitamin A.

LENTICCHIE DI CASTELLUCCIO CON SALSICCE
Lentil stew with sausages
(Illustrated left)

1 1/2 CUPS/300 G CASTELLUCCIO LENTILS
SALT
4 STRIPS/80 G BACON
2 TBSP EXTRA VIRGIN OLIVE OIL
1 TBSP BUTTER
1 ONION
1 STICK CELERY
2/3 CUP/150 G SIEVED TOMATOES
4 CUPS/1 LITER MEAT STOCK
4–8 FRESH SALSICCE
PEPPER

Soak the lentils the night before in lightly salted lukewarm water. Cut the bacon across into pieces and fry gently in a pan with 1 tablespoon olive oil and 1 tablespoon butter. Chop the onion and celery finely and fry gently for a few minutes. Add the well-drained lentils and the sieved tomatoes and pour in the hot meat stock. Cover the pan and cook the lentils for 1 hour over a low heat. Fry the *salsicce* in a pan with 1 tbsp olive oil. When they are nearly cooked, season the lentils with salt and pepper and add the *salsicce*. Serve on soup plates.

SPELT

Spelt was used long ago by the ancient Romans as an ingredient in their *puls latina*, a dish comprising a mixture of cereal and legumes cooked in water. Every family possessed a special mill to separate the grain from the hard, bearded husks.

Botanically speaking, Umbrian spelt belongs to the variety *Triticum durum dicoccum*, and is cultivated primarily in the region around Monteleone and Spoleto. Following the introduction of wheat, which was easier to process, the importance of spelt, which has to undergo a special process to remove the husk after threshing, declined rapidly. This undemanding cereal plant continued to be grown only in regions where nothing else would grow. In recent years, however, spelt has been rediscovered – not least because of its dietary and nutritional value – and consumption is steadily increasing.

Spelt contains more essential amino acids, in other words the protein building blocks necessary for life, than many types of wheat. It also provides more vitamins and trace elements. Since spelt also contains a considerable amount of silicic acid, it not only ensures a good complexion and shining hair, but is also reputed to stimulate the mental faculties. As a rule, spelt needs soaking for between 12 and 48 hours, and then requires several hours' cooking. Nowadays, cooking time can be halved with the aid of the pressure cooker. If the grain is coarsely ground before it is prepared, soaking can be eliminated entirely. The time required for cooking is then only 20 to 30 minutes, as long as is necessary to swell the spelt over

a low heat. *Minestra di farro*, spelt soup, is one of the most traditional spelt dishes, which is also familiar in Lazio. The popular and wholesome *imbrecciata* is a stew made from various types of cereal and legumes.

Above: Unlike other cereals, in which the grain and husk are separated by threshing, spelt grain has to be released using special mills. The spelt grain accounts for one-third of the total weight of the harvest.

IMBRECCIATA
Legume and cereal stew
(Illustrated right)

1/4 CUP/50 G EACH OF PEARL BARLEY, WHEAT, AND SPELT
1/3 CUP/50 G PINTO BEANS AND LENTILS
1/2 CUP/50 G EACH OF CORN, GARBANZO BEANS, AND FAVA BEANS
5 TBSP EXTRA VIRGIN OLIVE OIL
1/4 LB/100 G BACON, CUT INTO STRIPS
2 ONIONS, CHOPPED
1 BUNCH OF MARJORAM, COARSELY CHOPPED
2/3 CUP/150 G TOMATO PASTE
SALT AND PEPPER
4 CUPS/1 LITER WATER OR STOCK

Soak the cereal and legumes separately overnight. Next day, drain off the water and cook each variety separately, noting the difference in cooking times.
Heat the olive oil in a large pan and sauté the bacon strips and the chopped onions. Add the coarsely chopped marjoram and the tomato paste, and simmer over a low heat for about 15 minutes. Add the legumes and the cereal, and mix together thoroughly.
Add the water or stock, and simmer for a few minutes longer.

MINESTRA DI FARRO
Spelt soup

1 HAM BONE WITH A LITTLE MEAT, COARSELY CHOPPED
1 BUNCH OF SOUP VEGETABLES (2 CARROTS, 1 LEEK, 2 CELERY STALKS, PARSLEY)
1/4 LB/100 G SMOKED HAM, DICED
3/4 CUP/150 G SPELT, COARSELY GROUND
SALT AND PEPPER
1/4 LB/100 G PECORINO, GRATED

Boil the ham bone in plenty of water for about 15 minutes. Remove the bone and discard the water. Clean the soup vegetables and cut into small pieces. Boil with the diced ham and the bone for about 2 hours in 12 cups (3 liters) water. Add the spelt, season with salt and pepper, and allow to swell over a low heat for about 15 to 20 minutes. The spelt grains should not be completely soft, but should retain a little of their bite. Season to taste with salt and pepper. Serve with grated pecorino.

FRESHWATER FISH

Although Umbria has no sea coast, this does not mean fish is absent from the menu here. This stretch of countryside has numerous lakes and rivers running through it, the most important of which is Lake Trasimeno, which lies half an hour's drive west of Perugia. Covering nearly 50 square miles (128 square kilometers) in area, Lake Trasimeno is one of Italy's largest inland lakes.

The sparse population of Umbria and the largely unspoiled natural environment guarantee clean fishing grounds, in which enthusiastic anglers have free choice. There are roach, eels, freshwater perch, trout, grayling, barbel, whitefish, tench – and, it is claimed, the fattest carp south of the Alps. The catch is broiled, baked in the oven, or made into a splendid freshwater fish soup, which is more than equal to any saltwater versions from the coast.

REGINA IN PORCHETTA
Carp in fennel sauce
(Illustrated below)

1 CARP, APPROX. 2 1/2 LBS/1.2 KG IN WEIGHT
1/4 LB/100 G SMOKED HAM OR BACON
2 SPRIGS OF FRESH ROSEMARY
1 TBSP FENNEL SEEDS
4 CLOVES OF GARLIC
JUICE OF 1/2 LEMON
1/2 GLASS OLIVE OIL
SALT AND PEPPER
1 LEMON

Gut the fish, remove the scales, and wash. Pull the rosemary leaves off the stems. Combine the ham, fennel seeds, garlic cloves, and rosemary in a food processor. Stuff the carp with this mixture and place in a flameproof dish. If there is any stuffing left over, this can be spread on top of the fish. Cook in a preheated oven at 400 °F (200 °C) for approximately 30 minutes. Beat the lemon juice with the olive oil and baste the carp with this mixture occasionally. Finally, season with salt and pepper. Decorate with slices of lemon and serve.

Right: Lake Trasimeno, with its abundance of fish, attracts many fishermen, especially on weekends.

Carpa (carp)
Anglers claim that the largest carp in Italy are found in Umbrian waters. They are often oven-baked.

Lasca (roach)
This fish tastes rather like pike, but its flesh is not quite so firm and it has slightly less flavor.

Trota (trout)
This popular little fish is very frequently served in Umbria as *Trota al tartufo*, trout with truffles.

Pesce persico (freshwater perch)
The firm, tasty flesh of freshwater perch can be deep-fried, but it is also suitable for pickling.

Temolo (grayling)
The tender, aromatic flesh of the grayling has a delicate flavor of thyme, and seasoning should therefore be used sparingly.

Anguilla (eel)
Freshwater eels grow much fatter than their marine counterparts; Umbrians grill them or serve them in sauce.

Barbo (barbel)
Barbel must never be eaten raw, since their uncooked flesh is poisonous. They taste very good boiled or fried.

Alborella (whitefish)
This outstanding fish tastes sweet and is extremely suitable for almost all methods of cooking.

Tinca (tench)
The tender, sweet flesh of this fish, a relative of carp, tastes very good fried or else baked.

FISHING

Those who consider that fishing is a typical northern European pastime should just take a walk in an Italian town or along an Italian lakeside. In the towns the keen observer will find many specialist shops for this relaxing sport, selling rubber boots and fly boxes, while on the weekend thousands of fishing enthusiasts drive to the inland waterways, prepare their bait, and wait patiently for a fish – the size of which is almost always irrelevant – to bite.
Artificial lakes have already been constructed in many regions, and are stocked at regular intervals with freshwater fish to make weekend expeditions worthwhile. In Umbria, however, such measures are unnecessary, since the lakes of the region contain fish in extraordinary abundance. In particular, many anglers drive to Lake Trasimeno, for it is here – as is proudly claimed on the shores of the lake – that the fattest carp in Italy are landed. However, the other types of fish offered by the lake are also well worth waiting for.

THE TORGIANO WINE MUSEUM

This wine museum, opened in 1974 on the estate of the Lungarotti family, lies at the heart of Umbria, to be more accurate in Torgiano. Situated close to the Umbrian capital of Perugia, this quiet, medieval village with its defending walls and towers has just the right atmosphere for tasting a few good wines and touring the museum to glean information about the history of winegrowing. The museum owes its existence to the doyen of winegrowing in the region, Giorgio Lungarotti, and his wife, Maria Grazia, a couple who were also responsible for arranging the rooms of the Palazzo Graziani Baglioni, an old 17th-century nobleman's residence.

The rooms of the museum, which are also of architectural interest, and which originally belonged to the *pars agricola*, the part of the estate used for agricultural purposes, invite the visitor to travel in time through the world of wine. One wanders through the Middle East, where the first vines were cultivated 2500 years ago, follows the land and sea trade routes, via which the grape spread through the Mediterranean region, and discovers what methods were used to make wine at the time of the birth of Christ.

The wine culture of Umbria is worthy of special attention, and, in addition to early examples of wine produced in the region, the museum also houses an impressive collection of antique and modern wine containers. These are a reminder of the pottery industry that flourished well into the 18th century in many central Italian towns. In one of the adjacent rooms there is an old Umbrian wood-fired kiln, which is still occasionally heated so that visitors can fire their own wine goblets. Emerging from this fine little museum, one feels that one understands why there is more to wine than a glass of fermented grape juice – it is a culture that makes changes and leaves a lasting impression, not only on its native countryside, but also on people.

Above: The Lungarotti family has made Torgiano wine famous.

Below: In the Torgiano wine museum, which is run by the Lungarotti foundation, one can learn about historic methods of making wine.

FROM ORVIETO TO MONTEFALCO

Although Umbria is commonly called the green heart of Italy, in winegrowing terms it has long stood in the shadow of neighboring Tuscany. Despite this, wines such as Orvieto were well known, despite a less than outstanding reputation for quality.

The region first began attracting the attention of wine connoisseurs throughout the world when Giorgio Lungarotti from Torgiano instituted his annual wine competition, the Banco d'Assaggio, which has been highly regarded for some time. Admittedly, Torgiano wine, which was recognized with a controlled designation of origin, or DOC, and in the case of Torgiano Riserva even a DOCG, a controlled and guaranteed designation of origin, did not enjoy any particular international success, which was probably due to the fact that Lungarotti remained its only producer. From that time on, however, nothing was to stand in the way of the development of quality wine production in the region. The best known wine in the region prior to this, the white Orvieto, which still accounts for two thirds of the region's DOC wine production, led the field, and was transformed from a generally unprepossessing, thin white wine, even drunk as a sweet wine by the natives, into a bold, dry wine, suitable for serving even with robustly-flavored dishes. Although most of the wine is produced by no more than three large cooperatives, a handful of smaller and medium-sized vintners have been able to make their mark with surprising experiments and strikingly good wines. During the course of these experiments, which focused primarily on Orvieto Classico, the geographical heart of the winegrowing area, some excellent table wines emerged, the producers of which had pulled out all the stops in terms of modern Italian winemaking — for example, using international grape varieties, storing the wine in small, new wooden barrels, regulating fermentation temperature, and employing the most up-to-date cellar technology. Most other parts of the region now have their own designations of origin too, including wines of a quality ranging from good to very good. The most famous of these come from the region around the Umbrian capital, Perugia, and from the borders with Tuscany. Bottles labeled Colli del Trasimeno and Colli Perugini contain fresh white and red wines, which are pressed from the same grape varieties as many famous Tuscan wines: Sangiovese, Merlot, and Cabernet among the reds, Trebbiano, Grechetto, and Chardonnay among the whites.

The wines of Montefalco, in the north of the region, have also made an impressive leap in quality, especially in the case of the reds, which are made from Sangiovese and the indigenous Sagrantino grapes. Sagrantino di Montefalco, the wine made from a single grape variety that has been elevated to DOCG status, has great strength and fullness, combined with an intense bouquet of fruit and spices, and is comparable with the really great wines of Italy. Passito, the sweet version of Sagrantino di Montefalco, is sumptuous, fruity, and full-bodied — a genuine Umbrian specialty.

In front of the impressive silhouette of the Orvieto Cathedral grow the grapes for the city's favorite white wine.

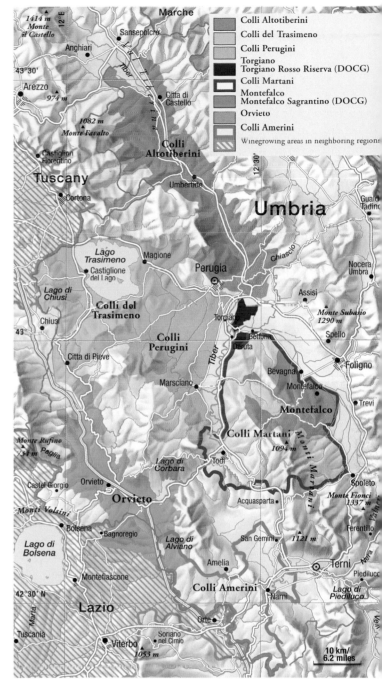

Torgiano Riserva
Umbria's most famous wine is Torgiano Riserva, made from Sangiovese and other indigenous grape varieties. This elegant wine is not excessively strong or alcoholic, is an excellent accompaniment to red meat, and can age very well, but unfortunately it is offered by only one top producer.

Colli Martani
Colli Altotiberini, Colli Amerini, Colli del Trasimeno, Colli Martani, and Colli Perugini are Umbrian designations of origin from the northern part of the region. The white wines are mostly pressed from Trebbiano toscano grapes, while the reds

are pressed from Sangiovese, blended with Montepulciano, Merlot, or other varieties. These wines are largely unassuming and rather light, and are not particularly prestigious.

Sagrantino di Montefalco
Sagrantino is a variant of the red Montefalco, pressed exclusively from grapes of the same name. These are mostly processed when they have dried slightly, producing a very strong red wine with a high alcohol content.

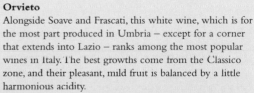

Orvieto
Alongside Soave and Frascati, this white wine, which is for the most part produced in Umbria — except for a corner that extends into Lazio — ranks among the most popular wines in Italy. The best growths come from the Classico zone, and their pleasant, mild fruit is balanced by a little harmonious acidity.

These white wines, which are produced around the city with the famous cathedral, are occasionally also fermented and matured in small wooden barrels, or barriques. However, this method of maturing the wine is successful only if the strength and concentration of the grapes used are well above average.

MARCHE

The sea, dense forests containing oak trees that are hundreds of years old, churches, monasteries, and fortresses rising up from the medieval towns perched high up in the delightful ranges of hills, and hospitable people, who love their native land more than anything – all these are typical of Marche, a region still largely undiscovered by the tourist industry. From a culinary point of view, too, the character of this region is quite unique. Whereas the cuisine in neighboring Umbria is for the most part simple, even spartan, the people of Marche have expensive and sophisticated tastes, though they do not indulge these to excess. Even the most sumptuous stuffing for suckling pig is invariably rooted in the traditions of robust, country cooking.

Even in Gioacchino Rossini's time, cooking and eating well were considered important. It is no wonder that the composer devoted at least as much attention to questions of the *buona tavola* as to his virtuoso music. Not without good reason is the aristocratic tag *alla Rossini* still attached to the names of numerous dishes of variable authenticity. Above all, the cuisine of Marche is one of great variety that unfolds as one progresses from the Adriatic to the Apennines. On the coast, fish and seafood are transformed into fantastic dishes. They may be grilled on a spit, or made into the traditional *brodetto*, a creamy-textured fish soup consisting of no fewer than 13 types of fish. In the hills and mountains inland, gourmets swear by the wild and domestic pigs, the succulent haunches of which are transformed by dedicated butchers and sausage-makers into products such as tasty ham, which, by contrast with other parts of Italy, is served not in thin slices, but cut into bite-sized chunks. The natives of Marche claim to have invented roast suckling pig, and if one watches the men sitting by the fire, turning the spit reflectively, and indulging in technical talk about cooking times, one might almost believe them. Meanwhile, the women can be found in the kitchen, preparing silky smooth tagliatelle. This delicious pasta, made from eggs, flour, and a little semolina, is either served with a thick, reduced sauce, or alternatively filled with a robust meat sauce, for the natives of Marche have a real passion for fillings. Suckling pig, chicken, and fish are almost always stuffed, and if one takes the trouble to pit it properly, there is room for stuffing in even the smallest olive.

Previous double page: The delicious stuffed olives from Ascoli Piceno are known as *olive ascolane*. Although time-consuming to produce, they are well worth the effort.

Left: Many festivals are held on the Piazza del Popolo in Pesaro, shown here with the town hall in the background.

FISH SOUPS AND OTHER DELIGHTS

The fish caught off the coast of Marche cover ten percent of Italy's requirement for fish and seafood. On board the cutters that dock every day in the ports of San Benedetto del Tronto, Fano, Porto San Giorgio, and Civitanove Marche are sardines, large and small octopus, turbot, squid, and scorpion fish. Crustaceans such as lobster, crayfish, mantis shrimp, and spider crabs are also caught in the rich fishing grounds of the Adriatic. In addition, cockles, mussels, sea dates, and razor fish can also be found in the frequently rocky coastal waters.

Originally, the dish known as *brodetto* was born of necessity. Because every fishing boat always has its complement of fish and seafood that cannot be sold due to poor quality or inadequate size, the fishermen of Marche invented a creamy-textured fish soup, a delicious way to use up all the "B class" produce. This simple dish could also be prepared straight away on board ship, using a little seawater, vinegar, and olive oil. In due course, landlubbers also came to appreciate *brodetto*, and transformed the simple fishermen's fare into a delicacy by adding a careful blend of spices and by choosing superior quality fish. *Brodetto* always tastes different, depending on the season and what fish the catch yields – and this fish stew is a constant challenge for every cook, for the ingredients must always be combined in an imaginative way, as well as being appropriate for the season.

Almost every town and every settlement on the coast has its own basic recipe for *Brodetto*, and the inhabitants all believe their particular recipe to be the best in the whole region. However – if one disregards the many variations – it is possible to identify two approaches to the art of making *Brodetto*. On one hand there is *Brodetto all'anconitana*, which comes from the area

between Pesaro, Monte Conero, and Ancona, while the other school is represented by *Brodetto portorecanatese*, which is cooked between Porto Recanati and San Benedetto del Tronto, in the south of Marche. *Brodetto all'anconitana* is regarded as the original and the most traditional version. Between nine and 13 different varieties of fish and seafood are used to make it, and it is flavored with tomatoes, onions, parsley, garlic, vinegar, and oil.

However, there are also recipes that specifically exclude vinegar, and in Ancona itself a pure, very aristocratic *Brodetto* made from sole is often served. *Brodetto portorecanatese* is *giallo dorato*, golden yellow, as it is colored with saffron. Porto San Giorgio *Brodetto*, on the other hand, contains chili pepper, turning it into a really fiery soup for palates that are not accustomed to it. These are just a few examples – it would be quite impossible to give all the recipes here. Nevertheless, the natives of Marche are so proud of their classic fish soup that they have founded an association specifically for the purpose of preserving it: the *Accademia del Brodetto*.

Salinge are a very unusual specialty, found only in this region. They are crustaceans, particularly well known in the area around Ancona. In Marotta they are called *garagoj*, and in the local dialect they are called *murici*. These gastropods were known in antiquity, for reasons other than their culinary qualities. They secrete a substance that was used as a dye in ancient times and from which the crimson dye industry originates. Today, these shellfish, which are usually cooked with bacon in restaurants, are just eaten as a choice seafood, and a festival devoted to them is held annually in the town of Marotta.

BRODETTO ALL'ANCONITANA
Fish stew, Ancona-style
(Illustrated right)

Serves 6

3 1/2 LBS/1.5 KG PREPARED MIXED SALTWATER FISH AND SHELLFISH
3–5 TBSP EXTRA VIRGIN OLIVE OIL
ALL-PURPOSE FLOUR
3 CLOVES OF GARLIC
1 ONION, CHOPPED
2 BAY LEAVES
1 PIECE PICKLED CHILI PEPPER
1 LB/500 G TOMATOES
1 TBSP CHOPPED PARSLEY
SALT AND FRESHLY MILLED BLACK PEPPER
2 TBSP WINE VINEGAR
6 SLICES WHITE BREAD

Place the shellfish with 2 tablespoons olive oil in a pan and sauté until the shells have opened: discard any that haven't. Remove the meat from the shells and set aside. Clean the fish, cut into small pieces, and coat in flour. Heat the remaining olive oil in a casserole and add the peeled garlic cloves, the chopped onion, the bay leaves, and the chili pepper. Sauté for 10 minutes, then remove the garlic cloves. Skin the tomatoes, dice and add with the parsley to the casserole. Season to taste with salt and pepper, and simmer for 20 minutes. Strain the sauce through a sieve, return to the casserole, and add the pieces of fish. Cover with a lid and simmer gently for 15 minutes until the fish is tender. Add the shellfish and vinegar and simmer for 5 minutes. Place a slice of bread in each bowl and pour the soup over.

CROCETTE ALLE ERBE
Shellfish with herb sauce

4 1/2 LB/2 KG *salinge* (SHELLFISH)
1 HANDFUL OF DILL
2 CLOVES OF GARLIC
1 SPRIG OF ROSEMARY
1/2 GLASS OLIVE OIL
SALT AND PEPPER
1/2 GLASS DRY WHITE WINE
1 TBSP TOMATO PASTE

Wash the shellfish and remove from the shell at both ends. Finely chop the dill, garlic, and rosemary. Place the olive oil in a pan and sauté the chopped herbs. Add the shellfish, season with salt and pepper, and pour in the wine. When the wine has evaporated, dissolve the tomato paste in a little water, add to the pan, and continue cooking over a low heat until the shellfish are tender. Serve hot.

The fishing port of San Benedetto del Tronto also supplies markets inland, such as that of Ascoli Piceno.

Calamari ripieni in teglia
Stuffed squid
(Illustrated left)

Serves 6

4 CLOVES OF GARLIC
1 BUNCH OF PARSLEY
A FEW MINT LEAVES
3/4 LB/300 G LEAN VEAL
2 TBSP BREADCRUMBS
EXTRA VIRGIN OLIVE OIL
SALT AND PEPPER
1 3/4 LBS/800 G PREPARED SQUID
2 TBSP TOMATO PASTE
JUICE OF 1/2 A LEMON

Heat a pan of salted water with 3 garlic cloves, half of the parsley, and the mint leaves, add the veal and cook for approximately 40 minutes until tender. Grind the meat in a food processor with the breadcrumbs, add a little oil, and season with salt and pepper. Wash the squid, season with salt and pepper, stuff with the ground meat mixture, and secure with a cocktail stick or thread. Chop the remaining clove of garlic and sauté briefly with the rest of the parsley in a large pan. Add the tomato paste, and season to taste with salt, pepper, and lemon juice. Place the stuffed squid in the pan, cover with the tomato sauce, cover with a lid, and cook over a low heat for approximately 15 minutes until tender. Serve hot.

Brodetto di San Benedetto del Tronto
Fish stew, San Benedetto del Tronto-style

Serves 8

1 3/4 LBS/1.5 KG PREPARED ASSORTED FISH AND SEAFOOD (IF POSSIBLE SQUID, CALAMARI, SCORPION FISH, MONKFISH, RED MULLET, GRAY MULLET, JOHN DORY, COCKLES, AND MUSSELS)
OLIVE OIL
1 ONION, CHOPPED
1 SMALL PIECE CHILI PEPPER
1 1/2 LBS/700 G TOMATOES
1 PINCH SALT
FISH STOCK (MADE USING FISH HEADS, FISH BONES, AND VEGETABLES)
1 GLASS WHITE WINE
8 SLICES TOASTED CRUSTY BREAD

Clean the fish and seafood. Heat some olive oil in a pan and sauté the onions gently. Add the chili pepper, tomatoes, salt, fish stock, squid, and calamari, and cook for 15 minutes. In another pan, layer first the scorpion fish, then the monkfish, followed by the red mullet, gray mullet, and John Dory. Pour some of the stock containing the seafood over each layer. Add the cockles and mussels, pour in the wine, and cook in a covered pan for approximately 25 minutes. Serve on toasted slices of bread.

Left: *Brodetto all'anconitana* – fish stew, Ancona-style (in the foreground) and *Calamari ripieni in teglia* – stuffed squid (to the rear).

BEATRICE'S FAVORITE DISHES

Beatrice Sforza (1475–1497), daughter of the house of Este, Duchess of Urbino, and wife of Duke Ludovico il Moro, in addition to her patronage of artists such as Bramante and Leonardo da Vinci and her involvement in building the castle at Milan and the Charterhouse at Pavia, also had a penchant for gastronomic pleasures, and was even reputed to be a good cook herself. However, the dishes bearing her name today are not necessarily the result of the ingenuity and culinary skill of the duchess, having instead been created by various cooks in accordance with her tastes. The dish dedicated to her, for example, mixed vegetables "à la Beatrice," was invented by a French cook, who liked to serve his creation, consisting of morel mushrooms, glazed carrots, artichoke hearts, and new potatoes, as an accompaniment to roast meat.

The snail-shaped pasta stew enriched with chicken livers, known as *Lumachelle all'urbinate*, is also called

Giovanni Ambrogio de Predis (1455–1508), *Portrait of Beatrice d'Este*, second half of the 15th century, Pinacoteca Ambrosiana, Milan.

Piatto alla Beatrice Sforza Duchessa d'Urbino, and apparently has its origins in the dukedom of Urbino in its heyday. It is now suspected, however, that the dish owes its name to the simple fact that only the rich and powerful could afford this specialty, rather than to Beatrice herself.

LUMACHELLE ALL'URBINATE
Vegetable soup with pasta
(Illustrated below)

2 MEDIUM-SIZED CARROTS
1/4 WHITE CABBAGE
2 SALSICCE
2 CHICKEN LIVERS
1/4 CUP/60 G BUTTER
3/4 LB/300 G TOMATOES, SKINNED AND DICED
4 CUPS/1 LITER MEAT STOCK
SALT AND PEPPER
3/4 LB/300 G SMALL PASTA SNAILS (*lumachelle*)
1 1/2 CUPS/100 G PARMESAN, FRESHLY GRATED

Dice the carrots finely, and cut the cabbage into strips. Squeeze the *salsicce* out of their skins and chop coarsely, and cut the chicken livers into small pieces. Sauté all these ingredients in butter, then add the diced tomatoes and leave to simmer over a low heat until the sauce has thickened. Add the meat stock, and season to taste with salt and pepper. Add the pasta to the soup and cook until *al dente*. Sprinkle with grated parmesan before serving.

URBINO

After Urbino was declared a dukedom in the middle of the 15th century, the city swiftly developed to become the center of a dynamic and flourishing state. By contrast with the princely courts of Tuscany or Emilia-Romagna, however, splendid banquets seem to have been held only on rare occasions in the Palazzo Ducale, one of the most beautiful architectural works of the Italian Renaissance. The ducal influence on the culinary traditions of the region was therefore correspondingly slight, and only a few dishes were named in honor of the court. The natives of Marche were again to demonstrate their continuing immunity to external influence later, when even the opulence of the 18th century passed them by, leaving no trace.

Nevertheless, there is one specialty with a "grand" history. *Vincisgrassi*, a sumptuous dish of baked pasta with a spicy meat filling, similar to lasagne, was originally eaten only by rich noblemen. At that time it was called *Princisgrassi*, a reference to the corpulence of those who could afford to consume this expensive dish. In 1849, when Austrian troops marched into Marche, their general, Prince Windischgraetz, enthused so much about the sheets of pasta with their meat sauce filling that the inhabitants of Marche, who naturally felt honored, promptly decided to change the name of the dish to "Windischgraetz." Unfortunately, however, since scarcely anyone could pronounce the prince's name properly, the name *Vincisgrassi* seems to have been coined instead.

The Palazzo Ducale in Urbino was probably built as a result of the marriage of Federigo da Montefeltro and Battista Sforza in 1460. It was constructed by Luciano da Laurana, and with its magnificent façade and superb interior decoration it is among the most artistically important architectural works in Italy.

VINCISGRASSI
Lasagne with meat sauce

Serves 6

For the sauce:
3–4 TBSP OLIVE OIL
3 1/2 TBSP/50 G BUTTER
1 ONION, CHOPPED
3/4 LB/350 G GROUND BEEF
1 CUP/100 G RAW HAM OR BACON, FINELY CHOPPED
4 TBSP WHITE WINE
4 TOMATOES, SKINNED AND DICED
GRATED NUTMEG
SALT AND FRESHLY MILLED BLACK PEPPER
3/4 LB/350 G VEAL SWEETBREADS

For the pasta:
3 1/2 CUPS/400 G ALL-PURPOSE FLOUR
1 PINCH SALT
1 CUP/150 G SEMOLINA
4 EGGS
3 1/2 TBSP/50 G SHORTENING
3–4 TBSP WHITE WINE

BUTTER
1 1/2 CUPS/100 G PARMESAN, FRESHLY GRATED
2 1/2 OZ/75 G MOZZARELLA

To make the sauce, heat the oil and butter in a pan and fry the chopped onions until they are soft and transparent. Add the ground beef and the finely chopped ham, and continue to fry for 10 minutes over a low heat. Pour in the wine, add the tomatoes, season with nutmeg, salt, and pepper, and cook for approximately 1 hour over a low heat. Boil the veal sweetbreads in water for 10 minutes, then remove the outer skin and cut the sweetbreads into small cubes. Add these to the meat sauce and braise for 5 minutes.

To make the pasta, sift the flour on to a work surface, sprinkle the salt and semolina on top, and make a hollow in the center. Add the eggs, shortening, and wine, and knead into a smooth dough. Roll into a ball, wrap in a damp cloth, and leave to stand for 30 minutes. Roll the dough out thinly and cut into wide strips, approximately 4 inches (10 cm) long. Boil the lasagne in plenty of salted water until it is just tender and drain well.

Grease a flameproof dish with butter, and arrange a layer of lasagne in the bottom. Pour over some of the meat sauce, sprinkle with grated parmesan, and place a few slices of mozzarella on top. Cover with another layer of lasagne. Repeat the process until all the ingredients have been used, finishing with a layer of cheese. Melt 3½ tablespoons (50 g) butter and drizzle over the top. Bake the lasagne in a preheated oven at 400 °F (200 °C) for approximately 40 minutes.

POLLO IN POTACCHIO
Roast chicken with onions and chili pepper

3–4 TBSP EXTRA VIRGIN OLIVE OIL
1 SMALL ONION, CUT IN RINGS
2 CLOVES OF GARLIC, CRUSHED
1 OVEN-READY CHICKEN
1 SMALL CHILI PEPPER
SALT AND FRESHLY MILLED BLACK PEPPER
1 TBSP TOMATO PASTE
1 GLASS DRY WHITE WINE
A FEW SPRIGS OF ROSEMARY
6–8 TBSP CHICKEN STOCK

Heat the oil in a casserole and sauté the onion rings and the crushed garlic for 5 minutes. Cut the chicken into pieces and add, followed by the finely chopped chili pepper.

Season to taste with salt and pepper, and brown the chicken on all sides over a moderate heat.

Mix the tomato paste with a little warm water and add to the chicken, together with the wine. Reduce the temperature, cover with a lid, and braise the chicken for approximately 30 minutes. Finely chop a sprig of rosemary and sprinkle over the pieces of meat. Braise the chicken for a further 30 minutes until tender, occasionally adding a little stock. Scatter over the remaining sprigs of rosemary as a garnish and serve.

PASSATELLI ALL'URBINATE
Spinach and meat dumplings

SCANT 1/2 LB/200 G SPINACH
10 1/2 OZ/300 G FILLET OF VEAL
1 OZ/30 G BEEF BONE MARROW
2 TBSP/30 G BUTTER
2 3/4 OZ/80 G FRESH BREADCRUMBS
4 EGGS
GRATED NUTMEG
SALT
1 1/2 CUPS/100 G PARMESAN, FRESHLY GRATED
6 CUPS/1.5 LITERS STOCK

Wash the spinach, tear into small pieces, and heat for a few minutes without adding any water. Cut the veal fillet into small pieces, grind finely in a food processor, and purée with the beef bone marrow, spinach, and butter in a pestle and mortar. Place this mixture in a dish. Add the breadcrumbs, eggs, a pinch of nutmeg, salt, and at least half of the grated parmesan, and mix well. The meat mixture should be quite firm. Form into short, fat dumplings (*passatelli*), and cook these in the stock until they float to the surface. Serve in a soup tureen with the stock, and sprinkle with the remaining parmesan.

GIOACCHINO ROSSINI

In 1829, Gioacchino Rossini wrote his last major opera, "William Tell." After this, at the height of his popularity, the 37-year-old composer and maestro of Italian opera buffa went into voluntary retirement, in order to have sufficient time and leisure in the next 39 years to devote to his hobby, the *buona tavola*. When Rossini died in Paris in 1868, he left several recipes he had invented himself. Furthermore, many cooks had dedicated their own creations to him, with the result that today there are more than a hundred dishes with names bearing the tag *alla Rossini*.

Rossini was born on February 29, 1792 in Pesaro, a port in the north of Marche, but – owing to his profession – spent most of his life in Paris, where he

assembled menus consisting not just of French delicacies, but of a combination of these with Italian specialties that he arranged to have despatched to his residence from his homeland on a regular basis. It seems that he had a particular weakness for Marsala, but supplies of risotto rice, truffles, and sun-ripened tomatoes were also received for the maestro himself to combine with the specialties available locally.

One of the composer's original recipes is for *Maccheroni siringati*, piped macaroni. This owes its name to the laborious method of preparation, which involves introducing a stuffing made of foie gras, creamed York ham, and truffles into cooked pasta tubes using a tiny silver syringe. Today, there is a slightly modernized version of this recipe known by the name *Maccheroni alla pesarese*.

There are countless anecdotes concerning Rossini the gourmet. For example, in a letter to the soprano Maria Colbran, following the scintillating première of the "Barber of Seville," instead of enthusing about his

Above: The hand-written notation is from Gioacchino Rossini's "The Barber of Seville" ("Il Barbiere di Siviglia"). The first performance of this opera buffa was given in Rome in 1816.

successful opera buffa, he wrote about a new recipe for truffles that he had discovered: "Take oil from Provence, English mustard, French vinegar, a little lemon juice, pepper, and salt, mix everything together well, and add a few truffles cut into small pieces, the wonderful smell of which will transport the connoisseur into a state of ecstasy." It appears that Maria Colbran liked it – she later became Rossini's wife. And the apostolic secretary, a cardinal whose acquaintance Rossini had just made, insisted on blessing this recipe for sensual pleasure.

Cannelloni alla pesarese
Cannelloni Pesaro-style

1/4 LB/150 G COOKED HAM, NOT TOO LEAN
I SMALL ONION
1/4 LB/100 G LEAN VEAL
6 1/2 TBSP/100 G BUTTER
I CUP MEAT STOCK
SALT AND FRESHLY MILLED BLACK PEPPER
1/4 LB/100 G CHICKEN LIVERS
I BLACK TRUFFLE
I CUP FRESH CREAM
10 OZ/300 G CANNELLONI
I 1/2 CUPS/100 G PARMESAN, FRESHLY GRATED

Chop the ham, onion, and veal very finely and fry for a few minutes in 8 teaspoons (40 g) butter over a low heat. Pour in the meat stock, season with salt and pepper, and simmer over a low heat for approximately 30 minutes.
Pass the chicken livers and finely chopped truffle through a sieve, stir with a wooden spoon, and season to taste with salt and pepper. Gradually fold in two-thirds of the cream. The stuffing should be smooth, but not too soft.
Half cook the cannelloni in salted water. Rinse with cold water, drain, and lay on a cloth to dry.
Grease the base of a wide, flameproof dish with butter. Put the stuffing in a piping bag and fill the cannelloni with it.

The port of Pesaro, birthplace of the composer Gioacchino Rossini, is in northern Marche.

Place half the pasta in the dish. Cover with some of the veal and onion sauce and sprinkle with parmesan. Then place a second layer on top, cover with the remaining sauce, and sprinkle with the rest of the parmesan. Pour over the remaining cream, and dot the rest of the butter over the top. Bake in a preheated oven at 400 °F (200 °C) for approximately 15–20 minutes, until golden brown and crisp on top.

Filetto alla Rossini
Fillet of beef Rossini-style
(Illustrated below)

2 TBSP EXTRA VIRGIN OLIVE OIL
8 TSP/40 G BUTTER
4 FILLET STEAKS
I TBSP ALL-PURPOSE FLOUR
1/2 GLASS MARSALA
SALT AND PEPPER
4 SLICES GRUYÈRE
4 SLICES RAW HAM
1/2 CUP BÉCHAMEL SAUCE
4 SLICES WHITE BREAD
WHITE TRUFFLES

Heat the olive oil and butter in a heavy pan and fry the fillet steaks. When the meat starts to brown, dust with flour, sprinkle with the Marsala, and boil until the sauce thickens. Season on both sides with salt and pepper. Braise the meat until it has absorbed the liquid, then remove and place in a flameproof dish. Lay the slices of cheese and ham on top, pour over the béchamel sauce, and bake for a few minutes in a preheated oven at 400 °F (200 °C) until the top is brown. Fry the slices of bread in butter, arrange the fillet steaks on them, and top with wafer-thin slices of truffle.

Vincenzo Camuccini (1773–1844), *The composer Gioacchino Rossini*, first half of the 19th century, Museo Teatrale alla Scala, Milan.

279

CHEESE

Pecorino, a ewe's milk cheese, is produced in Marche as well as throughout the rest of central and southern Italy, but as well as eating it, the natives of Marche also used it for the purpose of sport. Today, the *gioco della ruzzola* event is held in only a few communities, and a wooden replica is used instead of a cheese. Originally, the idea was to roll a large, well-matured pecorino cheese along the street, usually with teams from neighboring villages competing against one another. Each cheese roller had three attempts, and the team that rolled the pecorino the furthest was the winner. This sporting competition was reminiscent of the legend of the devil's bridge at Tolentino.

After the river bridge at Tolentino had collapsed for the umpteenth time, because of the simple fact that it was unable to stand firm in the silt of the river bed, the builder, one Mastro Bentivegna, made a pact with the devil in desperation. In return for building a stable

bridge, the devil was promised the soul of the first person to cross it. The devil agreed and built the bridge in a single night. When St. Nicholas arrived on the scene to bless the new structure, accompanied by a little dog, he suddenly removed a small pecorino cheese from his habit and rolled it across the bridge. The dog chased eagerly after the cheese, and was therefore the first to cross the bridge. The devil was left with nothing.

Below: Antonio Budano runs a cheese business in the port of Ancona. This store is famous for its specialties, and is a veritable treasure trove for lovers of cheese. Antonio Budano is one of the few dealers who are concerned with preserving and marketing regional cheese specialties that have now become rare.

CHEESE

1 Casciotta d'Urbino
As early as 1545, *casciotta* is mentioned in a document concerning the statutes of the duchies of Urbino and Solone di Campiello. The Renaissance painter Michelangelo Buonarroti is said to have been so fond of the mild, buttery cheese that he bought estates in this region. *Casciotta* consists of between 70 and 80 percent ewe's milk, and the color of the porous cheese varies from whitish to straw yellow. In the area around Castel Durante and Urbino, where there were traditionally many potteries, new cheese was pressed in special ceramic containers, while presses made from maple or beech wood were used elsewhere.

2 Ricotta
Ricotta is not a type of curd cheese, as is frequently supposed, but a cheese made from whey. It can be made using cow's or ewe's milk, and has a mild or sharp flavor depending on the degree of ripeness.

3 Cagiolo
Cagiolo is now produced in only a few cheese-producing dairies in the Osimo area. It is a cross between a hard cheese and a firm ricotta. Children, in particular, used to eat it with their fingers, as a snack between meals.

4 Slattato
Slattato resembles *crescenza* from Lombardia and *squacquarone* from Romagna. It is a soft cheese made from full-cream milk, which is stored in dark, warm rooms.

5 Pecorino in Fossa
Pecorino in fossa can be translated roughly as "trench pecorino". First, a ewe's milk cheese with the greatest possible fat content must be produced in spring, and air-dried until the summer. In the middle of August the "trenches" are prepared. Only the districts of Talamello and Sogliano have the tuff, a type of volcanic rock, that is suitable for storing the cheese. A deep shaft is dug in the ground, the trench walls are scorched with a torch, and the floor is covered with straw. Then the cheeses,

SAUSAGE AND HAM SPECIALTIES

Ham

Ham has always been produced with particular care and attention by craftsmen in Marche. Before food technologists and experts on smoking techniques were available to dispense advice, people relied on their experience, and to a certain extent this is still true today. Farmers in the area around Porto Recanati, who smoke ham over their fires for their own consumption, are convinced that a glow-worm in the house is a bad omen for the ham, and will spoil it.

The trade in ham and pecorino dates back to medieval times. The annual market at Pistia, on the border between Marche and Umbria, was not just the scene of lively trading: it also attracted many minstrels, who serenaded courting couples with verses that were supposed to bring good luck.

Ciauscolo

Ciauscolo is made from the belly and shoulder of the pig. The meat is supplemented with half its weight in fat and is flavored with salt, pepper, garlic, fennel, and orange peel. The mixture is then passed through the meat grinder until a very fine-grained mass is obtained. The meat is used to fill lengths of intestine, the sausages are dried in a smoking chamber, and then hung up to mature for a period of about three weeks. *Ciauscolo* tastes good spread on bread, but can also be used whole as a substitute for a *cotechino*.

Coppa

In the area around Ascoli Piceno the term *coppa* is used to describe a boiling sausage made using meat from the head, bacon, pepper, nutmeg, and orange peel. Sometimes pine nuts or almonds are also added. The meat is used to fill lengths of thick intestine, and the sausages can be eaten the next day. *Coppa* should not be kept for more than 30 days, or it loses its flavor.

Salame lardellato

The sausage meat of *salame lardellato* consists of lean pork shoulder or leg meat, diced bacon, salt, pepper, and whole peppercorns. The sausage meat is used to stuff the pig's large intestine and is initially dried for a day and a half, followed by three or four days in a warm room with an open fire, then two days in a cold room, and finally two months in a well-ventilated storage area.

Prosciutto di Montefeltro

The spicy, pear-shaped *prosciutto di Montefeltro* ham is made from the meat of free-range, black pigs. Before it is hung in the smoking chamber, it is washed with vinegar and rubbed with ground pepper.

Salame del Montefeltro

Salame del Montefeltro is a piquant-flavored sausage made from the leg and loin meat of free-range black pigs. It is produced with the addition of generous quantities of ground pepper and whole peppercorns.

Salame da Fabriano

Salame da Fabriano is made in the same way as *salame lardellato*, except that the sausage meat consists exclusively of leg of pork, seasoned with salt and pepper.

Fegatino

Fegatino is a liver sausage. Like *ciauscolo*, it consists of pork belly and shoulder, but liver is added instead of fat.

Soppressata da Fabriano

Soppressata da Fabriano consists of a mixture of meat, passed through the meat grinder several times, flavored with diced bacon, salt, and pepper. The sausage meat is used to stuff skins made from natural intestines, and the sausages are smoked before maturing.

Mazzafegato da Fabriano

Mazzafegato da Fabriano is a mortadella made from fat and lean pork, to which organ meat (liver and lungs) is added. The fine-grained sausage meat is seasoned to taste with salt and pepper, stuffed into intestines, and smoked. *Mazzafegato* is typically eaten at carnival time.

---

wrapped in walnut leaves and cotton sacks, are laid in the trench. In order for the maturing process to begin, the trench must have an airtight seal. After a minimum of three months, the *pecorino in fossa* is brought to the surface, like buried treasure.

6 Biagiotto or pecorino nostrano

This is a soft cheese resembling Casciotta d'Urbino that is very common in Marche. It is also known as *Pecorino di Senigallia*, after the area in which it is made. It can consist either of a mixture of cow's and ewe's milk, or purely of ewe's milk, like the example illustrated. It tastes best after it has matured for two months.

7 Barzotto di Grotta

Barzotto di grotta is a soft cheese made from ewe's milk or from a mixture of cow's and ewe's milk. The qualification *di grotta* is a reference to the fact that this cheese is ripened in a ventilated cave.

8 Pecorino tartufato

Black and white truffles are ground and mixed into this ewe's milk cheese when it is new, before it is matured for two to three months.

9 Ricotta secca

A lot of salt is added to this cheese, made from the whey of ewe's or cow's milk, to help it mature. It is then left to drain and dry out, and hardens after four to five months. It can either be crumbled over fresh summer salads or, when it has hardened and thus acquired a sharper flavor, grated over hot pasta dishes.

10 Pecorino alle Vinacce

After maturing for seven to eight months in a cave, this ewe's milk cheese is sealed for a further three months in a bed of dried marc in old, obsolete red wine barrels. The temperature rises, and the cheese begins to ferment again. At the end of the process it has a violet-colored rind and a spicy flavor, slightly reminiscent of wine must.

Stuffed olives – how it's done

The pit of the olive is removed using a sharp, pointed knife. Only the large varieties with small stones, such as tenera ascolana, are suitable for stuffing.

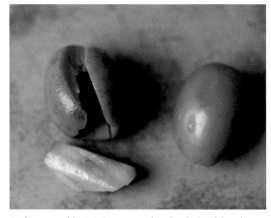

As far as possible, it is important that the flesh of the olive should remain undamaged and intact when it is pitted.

The filling consists of beef and pork, tomato paste, chicken livers, egg, parmesan, and breadcrumbs.

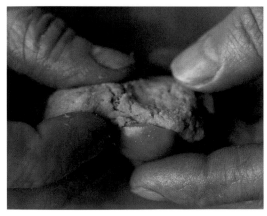

The fine-textured mixture, which has been passed through a meat grinder, is carefully stuffed into the cavity, and the olive is pressed back into shape.

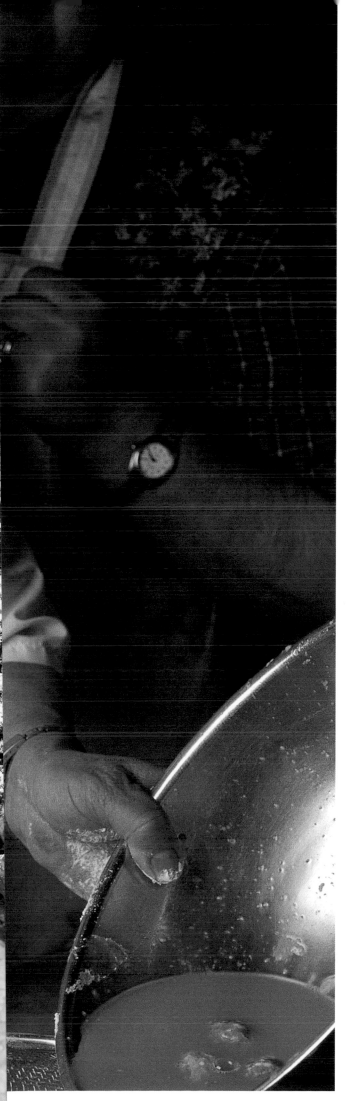

STUFFED OLIVES FROM ASCOLI PICENO

Olives are the culinary emblem of Ascoli Piceno. The ancient Roman writer Martial describes how olives from Ascoli were served at every banquet, as an appetizer at the beginning and to clear the palate at the end. Pliny considered this variety of olive to be the best in Italy, and the satirist Petronius describes Trimalchio gossiping about a banquet at which Nero and his entourage were apparently offered the olives in question as a first course. In the 18th century, the resourceful cooks from this small town in southern Marche hit upon the idea of stuffing the olives and then deep-frying them. A delicacy was born.

This costly specialty can really only be prepared using olives of the variety tenera ascolana, which grow all around Ascoli in very chalky soil on a small plantation of just under 250 acres (100 hectares). The harvest is comparatively modest, but because tenera ascolana olives have particularly soft, mild-tasting flesh and an extremely small pit, they are especially suitable for stuffing. Those who have sufficient patience, however, can also try using larger-pitted varieties.

Whether or not they are stuffed, the olives must ferment for about ten days under controlled conditions. They are then marinated in brine (3½ tablespoons (70 grams) of salt to 4 cups (1 liter) of water), enhanced by the addition of fennel. This is what gives them their mild, yet delicate flavor, and at the same time makes them suitable for keeping.

Left: In the Villa Cicchi, on the Azienda Agraria Conca D'Oro near Ascoli Piceno, the stuffed olives are served very fresh and very hot, for this is when they taste best.

Below: The olives must be deep-fried in plenty of hot olive oil. They are then drained briefly on kitchen towels.

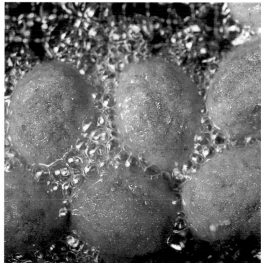

OLIVE ALL'ASCOLANA
Stuffed olives
(Illustrated above and below)

Serves 6

BREADCRUMBS
1 CUP STOCK
1/4 LB/100 G BACON, FINELY CHOPPED
2 TBSP OLIVE OIL
1/4 LB/100 G PORK
ABOUT 6 OZ/150 G BEEF
1 TBSP TOMATO PASTE
3–4/50 G CHICKEN LIVERS
1 EGG
3/4 CUP/50 G PARMESAN, FRESHLY GRATED
CINNAMON
GRATED NUTMEG
SALT AND PEPPER
APPROXIMATELY 50 LARGE, GREEN OLIVES IN BRINE
2 TBSP ALL-PURPOSE FLOUR
2 EGGS
OIL FOR DEEP FRYING

Soak 3 tablespoons of breadcrumbs in stock. Fry the bacon in olive oil, add the pork and beef, and fry these as well. Dilute the tomato paste with lukewarm water and add to the meat. When the meat is tender, add the chicken livers and fry for a further 5 minutes. Then grind all these ingredients in a food processor. Add the egg, parmesan, and the soaked breadcrumbs to the meat and mix well. Season to taste with cinnamon, nutmeg, salt, and pepper. Pit the olives and stuff with the mixture. Coat in flour, beaten egg, and breadcrumbs, and deep-fry in plenty of hot olive oil until crisp. Drain on kitchen towels and serve hot.

Emilia-Romagna
Rimini
Riccione
Cattolica
SAN MARINO
San Marino
A14
Pesaro
Fano
Montefeltro
Adriatic Sea
44°N
25 km/15 miles
13°E
Colli Pesaresi
Mondolfo
Senigallia
Tuscany
Urbino
Fossombrone
Falconara
Marittima
Ancona
Urbania
Chiaravalle
Marche
1454 m
Mt. dei Frati
Sansepolcro
Pergola
Barbara
Jesi
Osimo
Castelfidardo
Mt. Catria
1701 m
Sassoferrato
Cupramontana
Loreto
Città
di Castello
Fabriano
Cingoli
Recanati
Civitanova
Marche
Matelica
San Severino
Marche
Macerata
Gualdo
Tadino
Tolentino
Porto
San Giorgio
Nocera
Umbra
1571 m
Camerino
Maceratesi Hills
Grottammare
43°
Monte
Pennino
Falerio dei
Colli Ascolani
San Benedetto
del Tronto
Amandola
Mt. Sibilla
2176 m
Ascoli
Piceno
Martinsicuro
Umbria
Norcia
Spoleto
Mt. Piselli
1676 m
A14
Abruzzi
Teramo

Colli Pesaresi
Bianchello del Metauro
Verdicchio dei
Castelli di Jesi
Lacrima di Morro d'Alba
Rosso Piceno
Esino
Rosso Conero
Colli Maceratesi
Verdicchio di Matelica
Vernaccia di Matelica
Vernaccia di Serrapetrona
Falerio dei Colli Ascolani
Winegrowing areas in
neighboring regions

ADRIATIC WINES FROM NORTH TO SOUTH

Marche constitutes a kind of natural, southern extension of Romagna, or, viewed from a different angle, the northern continuation of Abruzzi. Its wine shares a whole range of features with that of its neighbors, including Umbria and Tuscany, from the best grape varieties to the various types of soil and the climate. Situated only a few miles from the tourist beaches of Rimini, the region has long enjoyed the privilege of straightforward, lucrative marketing. However, this has not necessarily helped the region to achieve labor-intensive and capital-intensive quality wine production.

Vineyards cover large areas of the hills inland from the long Adriatic beaches, and occasionally extend right down to the sea, for instance around the rocky outcrops of Ancona. Because of the sea, it is noticeably mild here, in stark contrast with the cooler, harsher climate of the Apennine or Abruzzi valleys penetrating deep inland, which brings out particular characteristics in the wine. For a long time, the most famous wine from Marche was white Verdicchio, sold since the

1950s in a green bottle, shaped like an amphora that is its trademark. The fact that this bottle is not actually a traditional one, but was invented by a marketing specialist in Milan, has not detracted from its commercial success. In recent decades, however, there has been a definite shift in the quality spectrum from white to red wines, based on the Montepulciano and Sangiovese grape varieties – one of the greatest and most famous of Italian red wines is produced in Tuscany from Sangiovese grapes.

RED WINE FROM ANCONA

The best-known, and perhaps also the best, red wine from Marche is Rosso Conero. It should only be made using Montepulciano grapes, but a little Sangiovese probably finds its way into some wines. It originates from the coastal area around the city of Ancona, and

has developed over the past two decades into a really good product, which can, moreover, still be obtained very cheaply – an advantage

Left: Every year, approximately 9,504,000 US gallons (360,000 hectoliters) of DOC wine, such as white Verdicchio and red Rosso Conero, are produced from vineyards in Marche.

that, unfortunately, has often been lost by most renowned wines from other regions of Italy.

Rosso Piceno, on the other hand, its counterpart from the south of the region, is officially a blend of Sangiovese and Montepulciano grapes, although there

are vintners and wine-making experts who maintain that the Monte-pulciano grape is simply a variety of the Sangiovese. It is said that in wines made from a blend of

both types, the Sangiovese grapes are responsible for the finesse and complexity, while the Montepulciano grapes give body and fullness.

CHANGE OF STYLE FOR VERDICCHIO

As far as the white wines of Marche are concerned, Verdicchio wine from the two DOC regions of Castelli di Jesi and Matelica is really the only wine with a role to play. Until very recently, Verdicchio was a decidedly rustic, strong white wine, frequently lacking the elegance, fruitiness, and freshness needed to satisfy the wine connoisseurs of Italy and the world. However, since the vintners of Marche stopped the practice of leaving the must to stand on the crushed grape skins and instead started pressing it straight away, and since they dispensed with the old Governo procedure, in which dried grapes were added to the finished wine to restart fermentation, Verdicchio has become a pleasantly fruity white wine of light to medium strength, a real pleasure when drunk as an

accompaniment to an excellent fish dish.

Last but not least, it should also be mentioned that the most famous winemakers of Marche turned their backs on their homeland several decades

ago: the winemakers in question, the Mondavi family, have been producing wine in the Napa valley in California since the 1960s, and are now among the best-known names in wine production worldwide.

LAZIO
ROMA

Rome and Lazio constitute a vast region. The flavor of their cuisine is impossible to sum up in a couple of words – the culinary traditions of Rome, the Eternal City, and its rural surroundings are far too diverse. Hospitality, such as was practiced in ancient times, is considered very important here, as is the cuisine, which relies heavily upon the butcher, and features robust organ meat dishes. Refined Jewish specialties share equal status with simple dishes that originate from the Sabine mountains.

Rome, the capital of Christendom, has always had many guests to accommodate. In the inns and taverns, pilgrims and travelers were served nourishing meals, consisting of pasta, broccoli, beans, rocket, and ewe's milk cheese, accompanied by strong country wine. *Bavette alla carrettiera, spaghetti alla puttanesca,* and *spaghetti alla carbonara* are still found on the menus of the unspoiled eating houses. Specialties obtained from what is known as the "fifth quarter" of the animal are produced in the great slaughterhouses in the heart of the city. When the enticing aroma of *coda alla vaccinara* or *rigatoni alla paiata* streams forth from the kitchen, one would not think that these were the less popular, mostly cheaper cuts of beef or pork. The dishes of modern Roman haute cuisine, on the other hand, are derived from a completely different tradition: residents in the Jewish quarter have long since ceased cooking just for themselves, but instead prepare *pizza ebraica d'erbe* or endives with anchovies for visitors from other parts of the city as well. Rome is also a city of bars, cafés and restaurants. Even the morning cappuccino is drunk in a local bar, and Romans go out to eat with family or friends whenever they can. There may well be historical reasons underlying the lack of enthusiasm for cooking in the private kitchens of Rome: owing to the dense population of the city and the fear of a catastrophic fire, people living in the rented apartments of ancient Rome were not permitted to light a fire for the purpose of cooking. As a result, the average Roman was already eating cold food at home over 2000 years ago – and, if he felt like something hot, he had recourse to one of the numerous hot food stalls. Even in affluent households with their own fireplaces, people preferred to leave the preparation of everyday meals, as well as the creation of opulent banquets, to experts engaged for the purpose. It would appear that modern caterers and party organizers may well have originated from ancient Rome.

Previous double page: The large coffee machine, dispensing espresso and cappucino, is an indispensable feature of every Italian bar.

Left: There are magnificent views of the landscape from the autoroute between Terni and Rome, like this one near Magliano Sabina, in the border region between Umbria and Lazio.

ROMAN HOSPITALITY

Rome is a hospitable city. Christian pilgrims, worldly businessmen, Church officials, commercial travelers, art-loving tourists, artists, literary folk, and pleasure-seekers of whatever kind – the Eternal City has been positively overrun by such visitors since time immemorial. Even in ancient times, life on the seven hills attracted curious people from all the Roman provinces. It was when Christendom emerged as a world power that Rome, the navel of the world, became a really popular travel destination. In 1300, when Pope Boniface VIII invited guests to a gigantic millennial celebration, around two million pilgrims streamed into the city. This huge volume of visitors presented a major challenge, both for the Roman infrastructure and the hotel and innkeeping business. Where were all these people to be accommodated? Which staging posts and courtyards would they be able to use to change horses, and by which routes would they enter the city? What was to be offered to the guests by way of food and drink, and where would the necessary quantities of food be obtained? In the early days of tourism, as travel became more common, monasteries and convents assumed responsibility for the spiritual and physical well-being of travelers, and, in most parts of the Christian world, weary travelers or those who had been caught unawares by bad weather, illness, or injury, could always count on the help and hospitality of monks and nuns in the monastic orders. In Rome, however, the number of visitors far

Historic painting of pilgrims in a tavern, a miniature from the manuscript *Tacuinum Sanitatis*, Italy, late 14th century, Nationalbibliothek, Vienna.

exceeded the capacity of ecclesiastical shelters. Private hotels and inns sprang up out of the ground like mushrooms, for business with the foreigners was profitable. Bars and taverns flourished, and, during the period between 1500 and 1800, Rome was the city with the best and cheapest gastronomy.

In the middle of the 19th century there were over 200 restaurants, 200 cafés, and around 100 inns and lodging houses. In those days, of course, one could not speak of these as "hotels" as we know them today. Single rooms in guest houses were very rare, and the more affluent travelers spent the night in crowded dormitories, while the servants were obliged to bed down in the stables with the horses. The catering, too, was extremely simple. The owner's wife often did the cooking, serving robust traditional Roman or Latin fare with a tankard of table wine.

In order to ensure a continuous supply of drink for the thirsty guests, the coachmen usually broke their journey in the *castelli* during the night, and delivered new wine barrels on a daily basis to the innkeepers at the crack of dawn.

In order to put a damper on the competition between landlords, various corporate bodies of innkeepers and hoteliers were formed. These enforced the ban on sending employees to intercept approaching pilgrims or commercial travelers outside the city gates, in order to direct them to their own particular establishments. Since the majority of the potential guests was illiterate, entrepreneurs were obliged to advertise with the aid of striking signs or attractive pictures on the doors and walls of their premises. As a result there were inns called "The Bear," "The Crossed Swords," "The Twin Towers," and also the "Osteria del Gallinaccio," which means giant cockerel (near what is now the Via del Tritone), which was famous for its roast turkey. In order to convey the message that drink was also available, bars and taverns were decorated with vine leaves or branches. This foliage, or *frasche*, gave the name *frasca* or *fraschetta* to the genuine Roman restaurant. Today, however, these charming establishments must take care that they are not ousted by the increasing numbers of fast-food chains, for competition to attract the paying guest is just as fierce now, at the beginning of the third millennium after the birth of Christ, as it was in olden times.

ABBACCHIO AL FORNO CON PATATE
Lamb with potatoes

Serves 6

4 1/2 LBS/2 KG SHOULDER OR LEG OF LAMB
3 CLOVES OF GARLIC
2 SPRIGS OF ROSEMARY
4 TSP/20 G BUTTER
1 1/2 LBS/700 G POTATOES, CUT INTO CUBES
SALT AND FRESHLY MILLED BLACK PEPPER
3–4 TBSP EXTRA VIRGIN OLIVE OIL

Rinse the lamb under running water, pat dry, and spike with
the cloves of garlic, halved lengthways, and the sprigs of
rosemary. Brush the butter over the meat and place in a
casserole with the potato cubes. Season with salt and
pepper, sprinkle with the olive oil, and bake in a preheated
moderate oven for at least 45 minutes, occasionally basting
the lamb with the meat juices.

SALTIMBOCCA ALLA ROMANA
Veal cutlet, Roman-style
(Illustrated on facing page, below)

8 SMALL VEAL CUTLETS
8 SLICES RAW HAM
8–12 SAGE LEAVES
3 1/2 TBSP/50 G BUTTER
7 TBSP DRY WHITE WINE OR MARSALA
SALT AND FRESHLY MILLED BLACK PEPPER

Place a slice of ham on each veal cutlet, with the sage leaves
on top, securing with a wooden cocktail stick. Heat the
butter in a wide pan and fry the cutlets gently on both
sides. Pour in the wine, season to taste with salt and pepper,
and simmer for 6–8 minutes, until the meat is tender.
Arrange the cutlets on a warmed plate, and remove the
cocktail sticks. Add 1 tablespoon water to the meat juices,
stir, and pour over the meat.

CODA ALLA VACCINARA
Oxtail ragout

Serves 8

4 1/2 LBS/2 KG OXTAIL
SALT
1 LEEK
2 STICKS CELERY
1 CARROT
1 BAY LEAF
1 SPRIG OF THYME
GENEROUS 1/4 LB/150 G RAW HAM
1 ONION
1 SPRIG OF MARJORAM
3 TBSP EXTRA VIRGIN OLIVE OIL
1 GLASS DRY WHITE WINE
2 LBS/1 KG SIEVED TOMATOES
PEPPER
1 OZ/30 G SEMISWEET CHOCOLATE
GROUND CINNAMON
NUTMEG
1 TBSP RAISINS
1 TBSP PINE NUTS

Cut the oxtail into pieces, pour boiling salted water over
them, and leave to stand for 10 minutes. Place the pieces of
meat in a casserole, cover with cold water, add some salt,
and bring to the boil. Chop the leek, 1 stick of celery, and
the carrot. Add with the bay leaf and the sprig of thyme to
the meat, and simmer for about 2½ hours.
Finely chop the ham, onion, and marjoram, and fry in olive

The genuine *osteria* is threatened with extinction
today. Only a few of these traditional bars, like this
one at Frascati, are able to survive.

Nowadays, *osteria* often means a restaurant with a wine cellar. The old, traditional bars, however, had no kitchens or cooks and
only served drinks. The guests had to bring their own food, such as bread, pizza, or cheese. Nevertheless, the *osteria* was an
ideal place for a convivial gathering of friends and workmates.

oil. Remove the oxtail pieces from the stock, drain well, and
add to the ham. Pour in the white wine and boil rapidly to
reduce. Add the sieved tomatoes, season with salt and
pepper, mix well, and simmer for 1 hour.
Remove a little of the sauce from the frying pan, mix with
the grated chocolate, and stir back into the sauce in the pan
to thicken it.
Cut the remaining celery into pieces, blanch in salted water,
and add to the oxtail. Season to taste with a small pinch of
cinnamon and grated nutmeg. Add the raisins and pine nuts,
and remove the pan from the stove. Serve the oxtail ragout
hot with the celery.

CAPITONE MARINATO
Marinated eel

2 LBS/1 KG EEL
OIL FOR FRYING
2 CUPS/500 ML RED WINE VINEGAR
1 CLOVE OF GARLIC
1 BAY LEAF
A FEW BLACK PEPPERCORNS
SALT

Cut the eel into pieces and fry, with the skin on, in hot oil.
Heat the wine vinegar in a casserole with the peeled and
finely chopped clove of garlic, the bay leaf, and the whole
peppercorns.
Lay the fried pieces of eel in a ceramic dish and pour over
the hot marinade.
Leave the eel to stand in the marinade to absorb the flavors
for some time, preferably 2 weeks.

THE ESPRESSO MACHINE

In around 1937, after some initial experiments, Achille Gaggia succeeded in producing a machine using piston technology that functioned in accordance with a combined pump and pressure principle. Thanks to this process, espresso coffee henceforth acquired its characteristic *crema*. Series production of this machine began after World War II.

The large espresso machines found in every Italian bar and restaurant from the Alps to the toe of Sicily basically operate on the same principle as the *moka per il caffè*, in which water is also forced through coffee grounds under high pressure. From a purely technical point of view, the process can be described as follows: water at a temperature of 194–203°F (90–95°C) is forced through a few grams of powder under pressure of 9 bars in 25 to 30 seconds, resulting in 25 milliliters (less than two tablespoons) of coffee. However, this utterly fails to describe the essence of espresso coffee. It should be deep black, and the foam, or *crema*, on its surface must be a delicate, shimmering light brown. It is then that the coffee is at its best, refreshing the mind,

cheering the spirit, and disposing the drinker both to dream and to reflect.

Italian coffee – and espresso in particular – is commonly held to be exceptionally strong. The opposite is the case, however. In reality, the beans for the Italian market are just more heavily roasted than the varieties destined for sale in northern European countries. In Italy, as in other countries, the coffee varieties are blended. Up to seven varieties are used in coffee bars, of which arabica is the finest. Although the special roasting process in Italy enhances the aromatic substances, the process simultaneously removes most of the caffeine from the beans. Italian *caffè*, provided it is drunk in moderation, is therefore perfectly suitable even for people suffering from circulatory disorders.

Right: Gaggia's historic levered machine was made in 1948. Achille Gaggia had attempted to develop a new type of coffee machine as long ago as 1937. Series production of his machine, which uses piston technology and employs a combined pump and pressure process, began after the end of World War II.

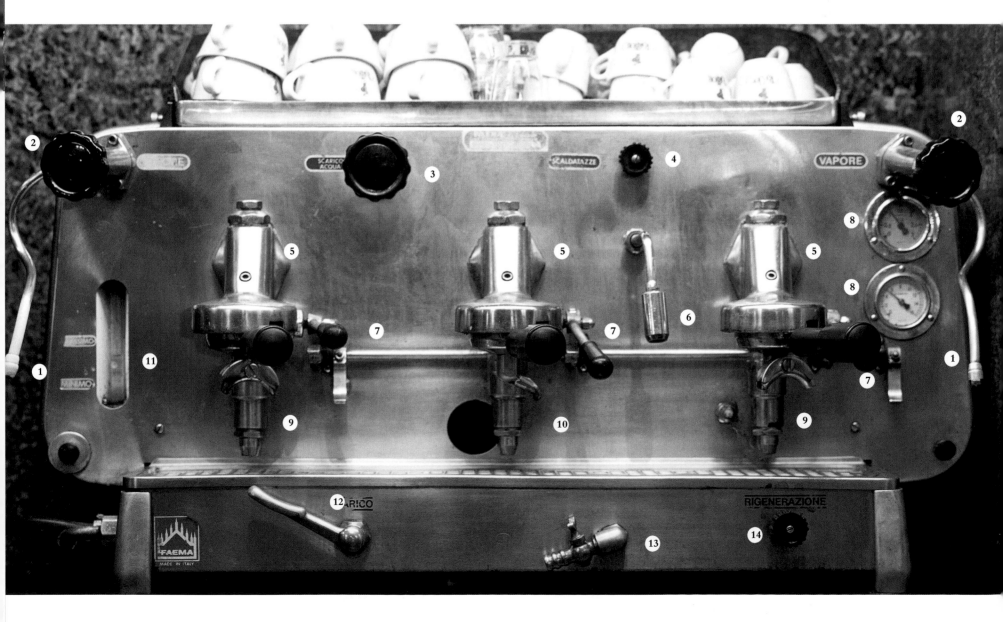

THE DOMESTIC ESPRESSO MACHINE

Espresso machines for domestic use work in accordance with the same principle as the large machines in restaurants and bars. They also produce coffee under pressure, and most of them also have a nozzle to make frothy milk for cappuccino. In domestic machines it is important – whether or not they are in constant use – that the nozzle for the milk is continually cleaned, otherwise milk residues might turn sour or even block the nozzle. In addition, care should be taken to ensure that the equipment does not become furred with limescale. If the mains water supply is very hard, it is advisable to use still mineral water to make coffee. The manufacturer's instructions should be followed to descale the espresso machine, should this become necessary at any time.

Although machines without a brand name are an attractive proposition due to their low prices, and though most of them function for a time, the consumer would be better advised to buy a branded product. Interestingly, and perhaps significantly, domestic espresso machines have never met with as much success south of the Alps as in the north. This may be connected with the dense concentration in the south of bars and cafés, in which espresso of outstanding quality is available.

PREPARING ESPRESSO

Coffee is prepared using three different methods in Italian households: on kitchen stoves the *napoletana* or *moka per il caffè* methods are used, while in rather more modern kitchens the task is performed by a small espresso machine of modest dimensions, designed for domestic use. In the numerous bars and cafés, by contrast, there is always a large, powerful machine made by a reputable firm such as Gaggia, for this is the only way in which to meet the enormous demand for this popular black drink.

The coffee grounds, preferably freshly milled, are loosely packed in the filter, without pressing down hard.

Milk can be made frothy with the aid of the steam nozzle if the espresso is to be turned into a cappuccino.

The metal filter is suspended in the espresso machine and screwed tightly into the thread.

The espresso machine (left) and its working parts

1 Steam nozzles, on the left, for heating and frothing milk; on the right, for heating water for tea
2 Pressure regulator
3 Knob for regulating the overflow valve (6)
4 Steam outlet to keep the cups on the machine warm
5 Filter holder
6 Overflow valve
7 Lever for regulating the flow of water
8 Manometer above measures water temperature; manometer below measures pressure for water pump
9 Twin spouts for two cups
10 Single spout for one cup
11 Water level indicator
12 Water inlet
13 Additional tap for connecting alternative water supply (for descaling)
14 Circulation of water for cleaning (e.g. for descaling)

A BRIEF LESSON ON COFFEE

The two varieties of coffee that are important on the global market are arabica and robusta. Arabica (mountain coffee, or *Coffea arabica*) is of higher quality and is now cultivated primarily in Brazil. Whereas arabica requires altitudes of between 1300 and 4250 feet (400 and 1300 meters) and requires particular soil conditions, the second most important variety, robusta (Congo coffee, *Coffea canephora*), though less temperamental, produces coffee of lesser quality. Robusta is cultivated in West Africa, Indonesia, and India. A coffee tree can grow to a height of 13 to 20 feet (4 to 6 meters), but on the coffee plantations it is grown only as a low bush so that the ripe coffee cherries can be harvested easily. To obtain the coffee beans, the cherries are dried and the flesh is peeled away mechanically. The beans are then fermented, washed, and dried. It is the wholesaler who assumes responsibility for roasting the beans. Lightly roasted coffee is pale, with hardly any bitterness. It is, however, more acidic, and also has a proper coffee flavor. At the same time, it is high in caffeine. Although the more heavily roasted beans are darker, they are less acidic and less flavorsome, and contain a smaller proportion of caffeine.

La Napoletana

The *caffetiera napoletana* consists of four parts: the kettle, the filter section, the holder for the coffee grounds inside the filter, and the can with its small spout that screws on top. The holder inside the filter is filled with loosely packed coffee grounds and the kettle is filled with water. As soon as the water begins to boil, the *napoletana* is removed from the stove and inverted. Assisted by gravity, the bubbling hot water then passes through the coffee grounds, dripping into the can as espresso coffee.

Moka per il caffè

The mocha machine works according to a rather different principle. Although the coffee grounds must be loosely packed in the filter and not compressed, the *caffetiera* is not inverted. Instead, the pressure generated in the kettle when the temperature rises causes the water to rise through the filter containing the coffee grounds into the can. As soon as the first drops of coffee appear in the can, the *moka per il caffè* should be removed from the stove, otherwise the espresso may have a slightly "scorched" flavor.

A PASSION FOR PASTA

In Rome there is a passion for pasta that seems to break all records. Even such icons of the Italian film industry as Gina Lollobrigida and Sophia Loren have always publicly acknowledged their love of pasta, and have provided the most compelling evidence that noodles do not make one at all fat or ugly. Sophia Loren's husband, film producer Carlo Ponti, is said to have told his wife quite categorically to eat as much pasta as often as she wished, since the occasional periods of abstinence from pasta that the *grande dame* of Italian cinema had imposed on herself resulted only in bad temper and domestic strife.

Rome – at least according to the Romans – is the birthplace of world-famous creations such as *spaghetti alla carbonara* (spaghetti, with bacon, egg, and Parmesan), *bavette alla carrettiera* (bavette with pork, tuna, and mushrooms), *spaghetti all'amatriciana* (spaghetti with bacon, tomatoes, and chili pepper), and *spaghetti alla puttanesca* (spaghetti with anchovies and olives). Rome is a city full of contrasts, in which rich and poor sometimes live no more than a stone's throw away from one another. Although all Romans are united by their love of pasta, for the less well-to-do it provides a cheap, satisfying, healthy, and tasty meal.

MEALS FOR FAST DAYS

Much as the Romans enjoy the high life, and despite the fact that they can never have enough of their specialties, many citizens still observe the culinary rules laid down by the Church when a period of fasting begins. Many meat-free dishes have been invented in Roman cuisine for fasts, for ultimately even periods of fasting should not be completely devoid of pleasure. Most of these *piatti da magro*, or "lean" vegetarian dishes (for the Catholic Church forbids consumption of meat and meat products at such times) were therefore usually served as fast day meals or as traditional fare for Good Friday.

On Good Friday, when, as is well known, the most stringent fasting rules apply, Romans first visit their family graves and then attend mass. As soon as darkness begins to fall, housewives hurry into their kitchens and begin making preparations for the classic Good Friday evening meal: there is a choice of the famous *zuppa del Venerdì santo* (Good Friday soup), the sumptuous *luccio brodettato* (pike cooked in stock), nourishing *zuppa di aragosta* (lobster soup), or *pasta e broccoli in brodo di arzilla* (pasta and broccoli in ray stock).

PASTA E BROCCOLI IN BRODO DI ARZILLA
Pasta and broccoli in ray stock

2 CLOVES OF GARLIC
1 SMALL ONION
1 BUNCH OF PARSLEY, COARSELY CHOPPED
SALT

2 LBS/1 KG FRESH RAY, READY TO COOK
1 SALTED ANCHOVY
2 TBSP/30 ML OLIVE OIL
SCANT 1/3 CUP/75 ML DRY WHITE WINE
1 SMALL PIECE HOT CHILI PEPPER
1/2 LB/200 G TOMATO FLESH
GENEROUS 1/2 LB/300 G BROCCOLI FLORETS
7 OZ/200 G SPAGHETTI

Place 6 cups (1.5 liters) water with 1 clove of garlic, the onion, half of the chopped parsley, and a little salt in a pan large enough to hold the ray, and boil for about 10 minutes.

Clean the ray, add to the pan, and boil for a further 20 minutes. Remove the fish from the water, bone the fish, and set aside the fillets. Add the rest of the fish to the stock and boil for another 20 minutes. Strain the stock through a sieve into a pan.

Wash the salt off the anchovy and remove the bones. Fry in olive oil in a casserole with 1 clove of garlic and the remaining parsley. Pour in the wine and allow to evaporate. Then add the chili pepper, the tomato, and a little salt, and simmer for 20 minutes.

Wash the broccoli florets, add to the casserole, and pour in the stock. Simmer for 5 minutes.

Break the spaghetti in pieces and cook in the stock *al dente* – until it is just tender.

Finally, cut the fish fillets into pieces, add to the stock, and serve the stew very hot.

SPAGHETTI ALLA CARBONARA
Spaghetti with bacon, egg, and Parmesan
(Illustrated in the background)

2 TBSP/30 G BUTTER
1/4 LB/100 G BACON
1 CLOVE OF GARLIC
14 OZ/400 G SPAGHETTI
SALT AND PEPPER
2 EGGS, BEATEN
SCANT 1/2 CUP/40 G PECORINO, GRATED
SCANT 1/2 CUP/40 G PARMESAN, GRATED

Heat the butter in a heavy pan, add the diced bacon and the garlic, and fry until they turn brown. Remove the garlic.

Cook the spaghetti *al dente* in plenty of salted water, pour off the water and drain well. Add the spaghetti to the fried bacon in the pan and mix thoroughly.

Remove from the stove and stir in a little pepper, the beaten eggs, and half of the grated cheese, until the eggs begin to set. Mix in the remaining cheese and serve immediately.

Spaghetti all'amatriciana
Spaghetti with bacon, tomatoes, and chili pepper
(Illustrated in the background)

1 TBSP OLIVE OIL
1/4 LB/100 G LEAN BACON
3/4 LB/350 G TOMATOES, SKINNED AND DICED
1 CHILI PEPPER
14 OZ/400 G SPAGHETTI
SALT
1/2 CUP/50 G PECORINO OR PARMESAN, GRATED

Heat the olive oil in a pan and fry the diced bacon
well for 5 minutes. Add the skinned, diced tomatoes
and the chili pepper, and sauté for a further 10
minutes, stirring occasionally with a wooden spoon.
Cook the spaghetti *al dente* in plenty of salted water,
pour away the water and drain well.
Remove the chili pepper from the sauce. Place the
spaghetti in a warmed dish, pour the sauce over the
top, and sprinkle with cheese.

Gnocchi di semolino alla romana
Semolina dumplings, Roman-style

4 CUPS/1 LITER MILK
SCANT 1 1/2 CUPS/200 G HARD WHEAT SEMOLINA
2 EGG YOLKS
6 1/2 TBSP/100 G BUTTER
SCANT CUP/80 G PARMESAN, GRATED

Bring the milk to the boil in a pan and gradually sprinkle in
the semolina, stirring constantly with a wooden spoon.
Cook the semolina for 15–20 minutes, then remove from
the stove. Beat the egg yolks in a basin with a few spoonfuls
of milk. Before the semolina cools, stir in half of the butter
and the beaten egg yolk, stirring constantly to prevent the
eggs curdling in the hot semolina. Pour the semolina on to
a wet plate and spread out to form a layer just under ½ inch
(1 centimeter) thick. Leave for several hours until
completely cold.
Turn the semolina on to a work surface and cut out small
circles using a thin-rimmed glass. Arrange the dumplings
alongside one another in a soufflé dish greased with butter.
Sprinkle with melted butter and bake in a preheated oven at
350 °F (180 °C) for 20–25 minutes, until golden brown.
Sprinkle with grated Parmesan and serve.

Bavette alla carrettiera
Bavette with pork, tuna, and mushrooms

2 OZ/50 G PORK CHEEK OR BACON
2 OZ/50 G TUNA FISH IN OIL
1/2 LB/200 G FRESH BOLETUS EDULIS MUSHROOMS
4 TBSP OLIVE OIL
1 CLOVE OF GARLIC, CHOPPED
SALT AND FRESHLY MILLED PEPPER
A LITTLE MEAT STOCK
14 OZ/400 G BAVETTE
1/2 CUP/50 G PARMESAN, GRATED

Cut the pork cheek or bacon into thin strips. Flake the tuna
fish. Clean the mushrooms thoroughly and cut into thin
slices. Fry the garlic and strips of pork cheek with the olive
oil in a pan until the pieces of meat become transparent.
Add the mushrooms, season with salt and pepper, and sauté
over a low heat for about 10 minutes. Pour in a few
spoonfuls of meat stock and stir in the pieces of tuna fish.
Cook the pasta *al dente* in plenty of salted water, pour off
the water, drain well, and mix with the sauce in a serving
dish. Sprinkle with grated Parmesan.

Spaghetti alla puttanesca
Spaghetti with anchovies and olives
(Illustrated right)

4 SALTED ANCHOVY FILLETS
2 CLOVES OF GARLIC
3–4 TBSP EXTRA VIRGIN OLIVE OIL
2 TBSP/30 G BUTTER
1 CUP/150 G PITTED BLACK OLIVES
1 TBSP SALTED CAPERS
5 RIPE TOMATOES
SALT
14 OZ/400 G SPAGHETTI
1 TBSP CHOPPED PARSLEY

Wash the salt off the anchovies, cut the fillets into small
pieces, and fry gently with the garlic in the olive oil and
butter over a low heat. Skin and dice the tomatoes and add
to the anchovies with the olives and capers. Season with salt
and simmer for approximately 20 minutes over a low heat.
Cook the spaghetti *al dente* in plenty of salted water, pour
off the water, drain and place in a warmed dish. Pour over
the hot sauce, mix thoroughly, and sprinkle with parsley.
Serve hot.

PAPAL CUISINE

In general, the supreme authorities in the Catholic Church have not been conspicuously hostile to sensual pleasure, or even ascetic in their culinary habits. Whereas, at the beginning of the 13th century, Pope Innocent III was still advocating spartan living, and insisting that only one main dish was served at his table, toward the end of that century Martin IV was showing a marked predilection for eel, particularly when it came from Bolsena. The pontiff is said to have procured live eels and stored them in special containers, so that he could eat them soaked in Vernaccia and broiled. About a hundred years later, Pietro Tomacelli was elected pope. Although his official name was Boniface IX, it was rumored that *tomaselle*, the liver dumplings enjoyed by His Holiness throughout his life, were named after him. Eugenius IV reintroduced a more economical culinary era, and even assembled independent observers around his meager table in order to demonstrate his moderation. As the 15th century drew to a close, Alexander VI had his daughter Lucrezia Borgia to cook for him, for nobody knew better than she which sweet delicacies her father loved best. In the years from 1513 to 1521, when Leo X was in office, dining in the Vatican accurately reflected Florentine cuisine. The festivities and exquisite banquets of the Medici popes were soon the talk of the entire city.

Any Roman who had aspirations began to take an interest in elevated gourmet cuisine. At papal banquets it now became the custom, not just to eat and drink a great deal, but to feast on noble, refined luxuries and to enjoy the tightrope walkers, musicians, and other artists who provided the program of entertainment. Neither was Leo X averse to a little joke from time to time. It is reported that once he arranged for a hemp rope to be served as eel, which a few unfortunate guests actually consumed, to the great delight of their table companions.

In the mid-16th century, Julius III reigned in the Vatican. He loved stuffed roast peacock and onions from Gaeta. After his successor, Marcellus II, had been on the apostolic throne for a short time, Paul IV became pontiff. It is known that he would sit at the table for up to three hours without interruption, and usually partook of up to 20 courses. Pius V, who was later canonized, engaged the most expensive chef of his times. This culinary genius was none other than Bartolomeo Scappi, author of *Opera dell'arte del cucinare*

THE CONCLAVE

The high life at the Vatican was punctuated by the repeated need to hold conclaves for the purpose of electing a new Holy Father. The procedure followed in the conclave was always subject to strict regulations. The members of the conclave were not allowed any contact with the outside world, and, in order to prevent secret information being passed to them, specially appointed inspectors had to examine all the food before the servants were allowed to place it before their ecclesiastical masters. Baked dishes that were browned on top, inside which a note might have been concealed, were forbidden, as was the use of silver cutlery on which messages might have been etched.

In the event of the election taking more than eight days, the dignitaries were to be served a meager diet consisting

Frontispiece from the *Opera dell'arte del cucinare* by Bartolomeo Scappi, printed in Venice in 1610. During a conclave, servants in procession are carrying baskets of cold appetizing morsels from the larder, hot dishes from the kitchen, and noble beverages from the cellar. Each basket bears the insignia of a cardinal.

of only bread and water – at least this is what is written in the canonical code – probably with the hidden motive of accelerating the procedure. In around 1700, officials nevertheless formed the opinion that such a regulation was unworthy, and subsequently installed an extremely well-appointed kitchen in the apostolic chambers, in which cooks, masters of ceremonies, cup bearers, and cellarers went about their business with alacrity.

and reformer of Western cuisine. In his standard culinary work of 1570, Scappi also recorded some favorite papal dishes, including fish from Lake Garda or Liguria, and caviar from Alexandria in Egypt. In the 19th century, too, high living was the order of the day in Rome. Gregory XVI was without doubt an accomplished gourmet, and we even know the favorite sequence of dishes of Pius IX: risotto, various items from the bakery, roast meat with vegetables and fruit, all accompanied by Bordeaux wines. The meal was always rounded off with a tart or pie and coffee. This, however, marked the end of the great era of kitchens

in the apostolic chambers. The plain meals of modern popes are prepared outside the hallowed walls of the Vatican. It is said that some degree of consideration is given only to certain regional preferences – depending on the geographical origins of the head of the Church.

Pope Martin IV
(pontificate: 1281–1285)

Pope Boniface IX
(pontificate: 1389–1404)

Pope Alexander VI
(pontificate: 1492–1503)

Pope Leo X (pontificate: 1513–1521)

Pope Julius III (pontificate: 1550–1555)

Pope Pius V (pontificate: 1566–1572)

BARTOLOMEO SCAPPI

Alongside Maestro Martino and the humanist Platina, Bartolomeo Scappi ranks as one of the most important innovators in Italian cuisine. Born in Veneto around 1500, by his mid-thirties he was in the service of Cardinal Campeggio, for whom he had to organize the festive banquet for the emperor Charles V. In 1549 – by which time Scappi was working for Cardinal Carpi – the conclave gathered to elect a new Holy Father following the death of Paul III. Scappi's catering for the committee of electors was so outstanding that it took over two months to reach the announcement *habemus Papam*. The new pope, Julius III, appointed Scappi as his *cuoco secreto*, his personal chef, a position held by this eminent cook throughout the reign of the next six heads of the Church.

In accordance with the spirit of the Renaissance, Scappi strove above all for harmony and balance in his creations. Expensive spices, which would disguise rather than emphasize the character of the food, receded into the background. Attention was directed toward conservative, "high-precision" cooking techniques, which admittedly presented a much greater challenge for the chef. In 1570 the book *Opera di Bartolomeo Scappi, maestro dell'arte del cucinare, cuoco secreto di Papa Pio Quinto divisa in sei libri* appeared in Venice. This work, published in six volumes with the blessing of the pope, became a culinary standard for both courtly and prosperous bourgeois cuisine. In it, Scappi not only divulges technical tips and tricks, but also lists numerous recipes for braised, roasted, poached, deep-fried, sour, robust, piquant, and sweet fare, many of which can be found in our modern cookery books today.

ANATRA ALLA SCAPPI
Duck à la Bartolomeo Scappi
(Illustrated below)

2 OVEN-READY WILD DUCKS WITH GIBLETS, EXCEPT FOR THE LIVER
1/2 LB/250 G COOKED HAM, CUT INTO SMALL PIECES
1 BOTTLE RED WINE
SCANT 1/2 CUP/100 ML RED WINE VINEGAR
2 1/2 TBSP/30 G SUGAR
SCANT 1/2 LB/150 G PITTED PLUMS
1/2 TSP FRESHLY MILLED WHITE PEPPER
4 CLOVES, GROUND
A LITTLE GROUND CINNAMON
GROUND NUTMEG
GROUND GINGER
GENEROUS CUP/120 G RAISINS, SOAKED IN LUKEWARM WATER
SALT

Clean the ducks and place in a casserole with all the ingredients except the salt. Cover with a lid and bring to a boil on top of the stove. Then transfer the casserole to a preheated oven and cook at 300 °F (150 °C) for about 1 hour. Depending on the size and age of the ducks, the cooking time can be extended. Then arrange the ducks on a plate with the plums and set aside in a warm place. Reduce the sauce on top of the stove and season with salt. Serve the sauce separately from the meat.

JEWISH CUISINE IN ROME

Before the birth of Christ a Jewish community was in existence in Rome, which even had a synagogue in Ostia. From the 10th century onward, the preferred place of residence of Jewish merchants and craftsmen was near the Ponte Fabricio, which was later renamed the Pons Judeorum. The quarter expanded rapidly during the Middle Ages, finally extending as far as the Regola and Sant'Angelo districts. In the mid-16th century, however, Pope Paul IV put an end to the flourishing Jewish way of life by creating a ghetto near the Teatro di Marcello. Roman Jews were forbidden by decree to move freely outside this area, and in addition the gates were locked at night. It was not until 1870 that the ghetto was dissolved.

Today, some hundred or so Jewish families live in the quarter, which has a somewhat dilapidated appearance. They cook, as they have always done, in accordance with the strict precepts of their faith: the flesh of animals that are not ruminants may not be eaten, nor may fish that have neither fins nor scales. Pigs, rabbits, hare, and marine mollusks are thus regarded as unclean. The animals that are permitted must be slaughtered using traditional methods, inflicting as little pain as possible, and must be bled completely dry before consumption.

Although Jewish cookery is simple, it always appears novel and interesting thanks to its oriental influences. The plain ingredients are frequently prepared with raisins, pine nuts, cinnamon, and cloves. Nowadays an increasing number of non-Jews are coming into the former ghetto to buy high-quality meats, stock up with delicious confectionery at the bakery, or to dine in one of the kosher restaurants.

PIZZA EBRAICA D'ERBE
Vegetable pizza

Serves 8

GENEROUS 3/4 LB/400 G SPINACH
3 ARTICHOKES
JUICE OF 1 LEMON
2 1/2 LBS/1.2 KG FRESH PEAS
1 ONION
1 BUNCH OF PARSLEY
3–4 TBSP EXTRA VIRGIN OLIVE OIL
2 EGGS
SALT AND PEPPER
1 LB/450 G SAVORY PLAIN CRUST PASTRY

Wash the spinach, drain well, and cut into strips. Remove the outer, hard leaves from the artichokes, and break off the stems. Cut the artichokes into thin slices and place in water containing lemon juice to prevent them discoloring. Shell the peas, and finely chop the onion and parsley. Heat the olive oil in a casserole and cook all the vegetables in it. Leave to cool, transfer to a dish, and mix with the eggs. Season to taste with salt and pepper.
Roll the pastry dough out to form two circles, one a little larger than the other. Use the larger circle to line the base and sides of a springform pan, fill with the vegetable mixture, and cover with the smaller pastry circle. Press the edges firmly together and prick the top several times with a fork.
Bake in a preheated oven at 350 °F (180 °C) for about 45 minutes.

THE CAMPO DE' FIORI

Tourists arriving in Rome who wish to see more than the doubtless interesting, but extremely crowded, St. Peter's Square or Sistine Chapel, should treat themselves to a rewarding walk through the most beautiful market in Rome, the market at the Campo de' fiori. However, the visitor will not understand much, even if his knowledge of Italian is good, for on many of the stalls the Roman dialect continues to be used for haggling, dealing, chatting with neighbors, and discussing the general political situation of the city and the country as a whole. This really is an unadulterated slice of Roman life, seen, as it were, in the flesh. The range of fresh fruit and vegetables on sale is also exceptionally good. Much of the produce is locally grown, which means it is not harvested until fully ripe. The best bargains are to be had toward the end of the day in the market, for it is then that the stallholders try to dispose of their remaining produce, sometimes at rock-bottom prices. It is not kept from one day to the next. On the next market day, a small farm truck will draw up again to deliver produce that has ripened to the peak of perfection. In addition to all the colorful varieties of fruit and vegetables, a huge range of herbs and spices is available, depending on the season. It is unlikely that any visitor will forget in a hurry the tremendously intense fragrance of these exotic wares.

Batavia is a variant of the iceberg lettuce that is common throughout northern Europe. It has wavy, curled leaves.

Lollo bianca, Lollo bionda or Lollo verde has very crinkly, wavy leaves with light green to yellow tips.

Lollo Rossa has the same shaped leaf as its paler relative, but has a nutty flavor and is sufficiently robust for a strong dressing.

Radicchio (red chicory, red endive) has a pleasantly bitter taste. There are many different varieties in Italy.

Lattuga (round lettuce, green salad) is grown in many different varieties all the year round throughout Italy.

Romana (romaine lettuce, summer endive, Romana) has fibrous, rather hard outer leaves, but its heart is tender.

Indivia belga (chicory, Belgian endive, blanched chicory) is forced in the dark so that the leaves stay pale in color.

Foglia di quercia (oakleaf lettuce) has reddish tips to the leaves, which resemble oak leaves, and a nutty flavor.

Dente di leone (dandelion) like *catalogna* or *puntarelle*, is a type of chicory, available in the spring.

Indivia (frisée chicory, curly endive) has curly leaves with pronounced indentations. It is aromatic and has a delicate flavor.

Scarola (escarole, smooth endive, winter endive) is equally suitable as a salad and as a cooked vegetable.

Rucola, Rughetta (arugula, rocket) has longish, often rather sharp and nutty-flavored leaves, which are used in salads.

Vegetables such as eggplants, tomatoes, zucchini, potatoes, leeks, onions, garlic, carrots, spinach, artichokes, and broccoli continue to play a significant role in Italian cookery, despite the influence of fast food, and are ultimately the reason why Italian food is so healthy and easily digested.

Alloro (bay) is added to fish and meat dishes, as well as to soups.

Aneto (Dill) is used to flavor fish and vegetable dishes.

As well as the Campo de' fiori market, which is a popular subject for the tourists' cameras, the Romans like to go to the large Mercato Trionfale and the Mercato Testaccio.

Anice (aniseed) is an ingredient in pastries, confectionery, and liqueurs.

Anice stellato (star anise) is used in confectionery and in the production of Sambuca.

Aromi (bouquet garni) can be used in almost all dishes.

Basilico genovese (Genovese basil) has small leaves and a delicate flavor. It is suitable for pesto.

Basilico napoletano (Neapolitan basil) has large leaves and an intense flavor. It is suitable for pizza and salads

Borragine (borage) is included in the Ligurian mixture of herbs known as *preboggion*.

Cacao (cocoa powder) is used in desserts, cakes, and confectionery.

Camomilla (chamomile) is used to make herbal and medicinal teas.

Cannella (cinnamon) can be used to flavor savory as well as sweet dishes.

Cappero (capers) add flavor to salads, pasta, sauces, and tuna fish.

Cardamomo (cardamom) adds spice to liqueurs, confectionery, and panforte.

Cerfoglio (chervil) is used in vegetable dishes, soups, and egg dishes.

Chiodi di garofano (cloves) go well with dark meat and pickles.

Coriandolo (coriander) is used to flavor sausage products (mortadella), as well as confectionery and liqueurs.

Cren, Rafano (horseradish) is found in northern Italian dishes, which are influenced by Austrian cuisine.

Crescione (cress) tastes particularly good in robust-flavored soups and salads.

Cumino (caraway) is used in northern Italian food such as bread and sauerkraut.

Estragone (tarragon) can be used in almost all dishes.

Erba cipollina (chives) goes well with egg dishes and soft varieties of cheese.

Maggiorana (marjoram) can be used in any savory dish.

Ginepro (juniper) is added in marinades for fish and game.

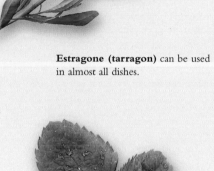

Noce moscata (nutmeg) is added to roast and braised dishes.

Pepe (pepper) is used for *panpepato*, pork dishes, and sauces.

Menta (mint) is used to flavor sweet dishes, but also roast meat and poultry.

Origano (Oregano) is used throughout Italian cuisine.

Salvia (sage) goes well with light meat, such as pork, and calf's liver.

Prezzemolo (parsley) is used for *salsa verde* and much else besides.

Peperoncino (chili pepper) is used to flavor anything that should be hot and spicy.

Rosmarino (rosemary) flavors marinades and broiled meat.

Vaniglia (vanilla) is an ingredient in *panna cotta* and is used in desserts and all types of confectionery.

Zenzero (ginger) is indispensable when preparing *panpepato* and panforte.

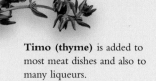

Timo (thyme) is added to most meat dishes and also to many liqueurs.

Zafferano (saffron) is used in *risotto alla milanese* and to color other dishes yellow.

THE LEGACY OF FALERNO

In ancient times, Lazio served not only as a larder for Rome, but also as its cellar. It was here that a grape variety called Aminea was used to produce the ultimate Roman house wine *par excellence*, Falerno. Apparently the Volsci people, the original inhabitants of the region in pre-Roman times, had pressed this wine and named it after the town of Falernum, situated in the center of the area where the vines were cultivated. According to Horace, Virgil, Propertius, and Martial, both red and white Falerno wine was available. Pliny the Elder nominated it as the best growth of his time, and recorded that it could be made sweet and light, but strong as well.

The modern DOC wine, Falerno del Massico, bears little resemblance to its historic forerunner. The grape variety disappeared from the range grown in Italy centuries ago, and, furthermore, the wine is no longer pressed in Lazio, but in neighboring Campagna. The full-bodied red Falerno in particular, which is made from Aglianico and Piedirosso grapes, can develop into a powerful wine that is full of character, but it is scarcely known beyond the borders of the region, and Romans nowadays do not drink it at all.

Modern Lazio, with its 150,000 acres (60,000 hectares) of vineyards, where at least 30 percent of the wine produced is DOC wine, is one of the most important winegrowing regions in Italy. Its reputation is mainly due to its white wines, the overwhelming majority of which are pressed using different varieties of the Malvasia and Trebbiano grape. At least as popular as Orvieto, the vineyards of which actually extend a little way into Lazio, and the northern Italian Soave, is Frascati, a white wine produced on the slopes south of Rome that stretch up to the Alban mountains, which should be drunk chilled when it is young. For centuries it was extremely popular with the Roman clergy, but in those days, unlike today, it was drunk mostly as a medium dry or even sweet wine – a fructose-laden variety known here as Cannellino.

DOC wines with characteristics similar to those of Frascati include Colli Albani, Colli Lanuvini, Marino, and Zagarola, as well as the white wines of Castelli Romani, Cerveteri, Cori and Velletri, of which there are also red versions. In the various vineyards of Lazio it is possible to find vintners experimenting here and there with imported grape varieties, including Chardonnay, Sauvignon blanc, Cabernet, Merlot, and, most recently, even Shiraz – and some of the wines pressed from these can be quite complex and suitable for aging. A few of these varieties of French origin had already been introduced at the beginning of the 20th century by Venetian settlers in the marshland of Lazio, which had at that time just been drained for the first time, making it suitable for winegrowing.

Unfortunately, the indigenous red variety, Cesanese, is seldom impressive, and could have even more of a struggle in future. Good vintners are already reducing the proportion of Cesanese grapes in their wines wherever the regulations for DOC wines permit this – usually in favor of the Sangiovese, which is also used in many red wines here, but also in favor of the imported grape varieties mentioned.

The winegrowing estates of Lazio cover about 150,000 acres (60,000 hectares) of vineyards in total, and account for the production of about 13,600,000 US gallons (515,000 hectoliters) of DOC wine.

Autumn in the Montefiascone vineyards. The winegrowing regions of Lazio are among the most traditional in the whole of Italy. Wine has been pressed here since ancient times.

Montefiascone lies in the province of Viterbo, near the Lago di Bolsena. Est! Est!! Est!!! di Montefiascone is produced here.

Halt! Good wine here!

Est! Est!! Est!!! di Montefiascone, one of Lazio's many wines, which is made mainly from Malvasia and Trebbiano grapes, comes from the province of Viterbo, and owes its unusual name to an anonymous German bishop. Legend has it that this bishop's prelate, while on his way to Rome, was under orders to look out for good wines. Whenever he found any, he was supposed to write the word "Est!" on the door of the cellar or bar in question. This would mark out the best places to drink for the benefit of dignitaries who made the journey later.

In Montefiascone the German taster was so enchanted with the local wines that he did not write the arranged code word on the wooden doors just once, but, in order to emphasize the outstanding quality of the wine, chose instead to repeat it twice. The legend goes on to say that the prelate liked Est! Est!! Est!!! di Montefiascone so much that he was indulging in this wine when he eventually breathed his last.

Today, Est! Est!! Est!!! di Montefiascone is a wine of a clear, pale appearance, which can taste dry and well-balanced. Unfortunately, its great success with later travelers to Rome of all nations has not been very beneficial, at least as far as quality is concerned. And so, for various reasons, one is obliged to conclude that neighboring Orvieto, the vineyards of which extend along the shores of the Lago di Bolsena into Lazio, is often the better choice.

Frascati

The most popular wine from the Eternal City originates from the slopes of the Colli Albani, situated to the south of Rome. For a long time the white wines produced here were the favorite wines of Romans and tourists visiting the Vatican, and were often drunk as medium dry rather than dry wines. Only with the advent of modern methods in the cellars has Frascati become a fruity, soft, harmonious white wine, which is a good accompaniment to fish.

Marino

Marino is one of the vine-growing areas that extends partly into Rome. The white wine is pressed mainly from the grape variety Malvasia bianca di Candia. There are just a small handful of very good producers, who sometimes mature their wine in large wooden barrels.

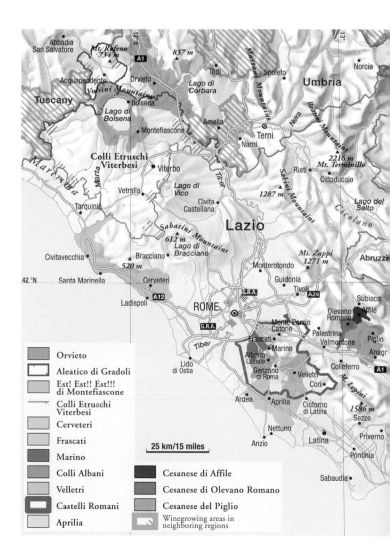

Orvieto	
Aleatico di Gradoli	
Est! Est!! Est!!! di Montefiascone	
Colli Etruschi Viterbesi	
Cerveteri	
Frascati	
Marino	
Colli Albani	Cesanese di Affile
Velletri	Cesanese di Olevano Romano
Castelli Romani	Cesanese del Piglio
Aprilia	Winegrowing areas in neighboring regions

25 km/15 miles

ABRUZZO
MOLISE

ABRUZZO · MOLISE

SHEEP AND GOATS

CHITARRA, CEPPA, AND
RONTROCILO

SAFFRON

MEAT AND MILK PRODUCTS

CANDY, SUGARCOATED
CANDY, AND
CONFECTIONERY

BRIGHTLY COLORED WORKS
OF ART

LINKING NORTH AND
SOUTH

Attractive to look at, stimulating to the senses, and decidedly fiery on the tongue – that's the red chili pepper or *peperoncino*, known affectionately by the people of Abruzzi and Molise as *diavolino*, little devil. Caution is advised when tasting the specialties of this region, because the cuisine here is hearty, cheering, and often devilishly spicy. With the exception of their desserts, everything seems to be flavored with chili powder. According to the hardened inhabitants of this harsh mountain region, you need fire to survive the frosty winter days. And by fire they mean three different sources of heat: the spicy preparations on their plates, the open fireplaces in their cozy kitchens, and the centerba: a strong, spicy herbal liqueur made from around a hundred herbs.

Livestock production and arable farming are the typical occupations of this region. Culinary traditions are thus also firmly rooted in the soil. Pasta, vegetables, and meat are the staples of Abruzzi cuisine. For many centuries, the ability of the chefs in this region to conjure up the tastiest dishes from these few ingredients has been unsurpassed. The Val di Sangro, a mountain valley in the Chieti province, has produced whole dynasties of chefs, and many large restaurants, hotels, and cruise lines continue to benefit from their ability to turn simple and sophisticated, nutritious and light, exotic and local ingredients into appetizing creations. These culinary conjurers have learned their trade not only from the shepherds but also from the farmers' wives. Many exquisite lamb dishes and aromatic cheeses owe their creation to pasture farming and the changeable everyday life of the shepherds, while in the kitchens of the resident farmers homemade pastas were prepared using a *chitarra*, a dough cutting frame stretched over with fine strings. A steaming plate of *Maccheroni alla chitarra con ragù d'agnello*, macaroni with lamb sauce, combines the two traditions in a simple but ingenious way.

But despite its earthy and modest roots, the cuisine of the Abruzzi and Molise regions is also perfectly capable of excesses. Weddings are traditionally celebrated in great style. Traditionally, guests bring magnificent baskets, which they then take home with them after the celebrations filled with anything they could not manage to eat up during the banquet. The more the guests take away with them after the celebrations, the greater the compliment to the chef.

Previous double page: People with a sweet tooth are in capable hands at the shop of Fratelli Nurzia in L'Aquila. One of the delicacies they can buy here is the famous *torrone* (nougat).

Left: L'Aquila lies at the foot of the Gran Sasso. Now the capital town of Abruzzi, it was founded in the middle of the 13th century by Emperor Frederick II.

SAFFRON

Considering the tiny portions in which saffron is sold and the few recipes that still require its use today, it is hard to imagine that the flower pistils of *Crocus sativus* were once one of the most sought-after items of merchandise in the West.

As long ago as in classical times, the Greeks and Romans loved saffron, even sprinkling it in the theaters to create a pleasant atmosphere for the performance. They also used the orange-red threads to dye precious silk fabrics or sewed it into pillows, as it was reputed to have a soporific effect. It was not until the Middle Ages that saffron became a status symbol. Throughout Europe, great importance was attached to making a meal look as good as possible, for the table decked with food was intended to display power and wealth. As a result, every meat dish, whether boiled or broiled on a spit, was "gilded," in other words covered with a brilliant yellow preparation made from saffron. However, the fragrant luxury spice was subject to high rates of tax, so even in those days gourmets had to dig deep into their pockets to pay for the quantities they required. A document written in English around 1400 states that a pound in weight (500 grams) of saffron was equal in value to one horse.

In the Abruzzi town of L'Aquila, which from the late 13th century had a flourishing trade with Venice, Milan, and Marseilles, tempted by the high profit margins, they began to grow crocuses themselves. The crocus growers' hopes were not disappointed, because L'Aquila came to be a major exporter. Particularly in Germany, there was such a high demand for the expensive commodity that the penalty for adulterating or falsifying Abruzzi saffron was death. It was not until 300 years later, when the nascent chemical industry made synthetic dyes and flavorings available, that the era of the yellow powder gradually came to an end.

There are, however, still some traditional dishes that from both a flavor and color point of view cannot do without genuine saffron. *Risotto alla Milanese* would be unthinkable without its beautiful, rich yellow, and the Spanish paella would also be a rather pale imitation without saffron.

Before use, saffron threads should be crushed with a pestle and mortar and left to infuse in a little warm water to release the flavor. The danger with the saffron powder frequently sold in shops is that it could contain undesirable additives.

Opposite and above: The saffron crocus *(Crocus sativus)* grows naturally only on the poorest of soils. Its pistils have long been valued for their dyeing and medicinal properties.

Opposite and below: At least 200,000 flower heads are required to obtain two and a quarter pounds (one kilogram) of saffron threads, making it correspondingly expensive.

Crocus blossoms are harvested in October. They have to be picked as quickly as possible, as the plants are in flower for only two weeks.

Saffron is usually sold in tiny jars or even as individual threads, because it takes a great deal of skilled handiwork to produce.

Mozzarelline allo zafferano
Mini-mozzarella cheeses with saffron
(Illustrated above)

A FEW THREADS OF SAFFRON
SALT
1 GENEROUS CUP/150 G WHEAT FLOUR
12 SMALL MOZZARELLA CHEESES
BREADCRUMBS
VEGETABLE OIL FOR FRYING

Infuse the saffron in 4 tablespoons salted water. Gradually stir in the flour and enough water to produce a thick batter. Coat the mozzarella cheeses in the batter and then roll them in the breadcrumbs. Heat the oil in a deep skillet, and fry the cheeses until golden yellow. Serve hot.

Frittatine di patate e zafferano
Saffron potato cakes

Serves 6

1 1/2 LBS/600 G POTATOES
A PINCH OF SAFFRON
EXTRA VIRGIN OLIVE OIL
3 EGGS
2 TBSP CHOPPED PARSLEY
ALL-PURPOSE FLOUR AS REQUIRED
SALT AND PEPPER

Boil and peel the potatoes, then pass them through a potato ricer. Soak the saffron in 3 tablespoons olive oil.
Put the potatoes, eggs, parsley, and saffron oil in a bowl and knead gently to form a dough. Add more olive oil or a little flour as necessary. Season with salt and pepper. The potato mixture should be soft and light. Spoon the mixture into a lightly greased skillet, press smooth, and fry over a low heat.

CANDY,
SUGAR-COATED
CANDY, AND
CONFECTIONERY

Even in ancient times, people enjoyed confectionery: The Chinese, the Egyptians, and later the Romans coated fruits, flower blossom, nuts, and seeds in honey. With the increasing popularity of sugar in the years after it was introduced from Persia, it was first added to the honey coating, but subsequently replaced the

Below: Since the Renaissance, confectionery has been made into flowers and other shapes in Sulmona. The tradition originated in the Santa Chiara monastery.

honey altogether, candy then being made solely with sugar coatings.

Italians differentiate between hard and soft confectionery by whether these sugarcoated candies have a hard or a liquid or creamy center. Soft confectionery is filled with liqueurs, almond paste, or flavored creams. Sometimes jellied or candied fruits are also added. Hard confectionery on the other hand has centers made from shelled or roasted almonds, pistachios, or hazelnuts. A *bassina* is used to coat the center. This hemispherical, slightly warmed copper vessel always hung from a chain and was moved by hand. In 1850, a clever inventor designed the first *bassina* with electric beaters. The nuts were first treated with syrup or gum Arabic so that they would retain the sugar layers. They were then coated in the *bassina*. At first, the syrup is fluid, but for the final few layers it needs to be stickier. When the coatings have dried, the confectionery is whitened and polished.

In the case of soft confectionery, the liquid filling has to be poured into the inside of the sweet morsel. Only

when this is done is it polished to a high gloss using a mixture of cocoa butter and a binding agent (gum arabic).

Since the Renaissance, Sulmona has been the confectionery-manufacturing center of Abruzzi. It is here that the greatest variety of dragées or Jordan almonds and other candies is created and then transformed using silk, plastic, colored paper, wire, and other accessories into flowers, blossom, ears of wheat, exotic fruits, and many other things. Even the color of the confectionery is important, as it has symbolic meaning. At the celebrations for weddings or 25th or 50th wedding anniversaries, there are white, silver, or golden dragées or Jordan almonds. When new arrivals are baptized, the candy is pale blue or pink in color depending on the sex of the child. Red is the color for academic success (the candies are put in a little fabric bag the color of the coat of arms of the faculty in question). Finally, confectionery is yellow for second marriages. However, the latter is not in widespread use in this part of Italy!

Sulmona is the confectionery capital. Six factories and numerous dealers are involved in producing the candy specialties and selling them to the customer in wonderfully attractive shops.

BRIGHTLY COLORED WORKS OF ART

The confectioners of Abruzzi are not only among the best in the world, but also certainly some of the most creative. For the celebration to mark the 500th anniversary of the discovery of America, the firm of Confetti D'Alessandro created a caravel, a 15th-century Spanish or Portuguese small, fast, light ship, entirely from candy. It can now be found in the New York Columbus Foundation museum. This workshop also produced a baseball bat, created to mark the visit of Joe di Maggio to Italy, and a table decoration for the G-7 summit in Naples. Among the particular specialties of Alessandro are the *panelle*, in which brightly colored confectionery is arranged like a mosaic.

U Dulcit

The 360-square-yard (300-square-meter) *Parco nazionale d'Abruzzo*, one of the four nature reserves in Abruzzi, has its own candy specialty. In addition to the chamois, wolves, golden eagles, otters, and lynx that roam Italy's oldest national park, there is also the rare Apennine brown bear, which inspired the baker Antonio from Civitella Alfedena to create his bear cake. This chocolate-coated cake is sold to its many fans under the name *U Dulcit – Il dolce del Parco* (Park candy).

This *panella* (mosaic made out of confectionery) by Confetti D'Alessandro shows an advertisement for the Post Office.

Confetti D'Alessandro also made this *panella* to help world food aid.

Decorated with sparkling stars and sporting festive red and green, this bouquet would make a wonderful Christmas gift.

It goes without saying that wedding confectionery like this pretty "bouquet of flowers" has got to be white.

Torrone by Nurzia

Sometime between the end of the 18th and the beginning of the 19th centuries, Gennaro Nurzia, a specialist in distilled liqueurs by trade, moved from the small mountain village of Arischia in Abruzzi to the capital, L'Aquila. Here he opened a store and soon broadened his range of commercial activities to include the production of confectionery, especially *torrone*. One of his descendents, Ulisse, created the *torrone Nurzia tenero al cioccolato*, an astonishing creation for the time, in that it neither melted in the heat nor became too hard in the cold. The secret lies in an old, closely-guarded recipe, and in the exact proportion of the ingredients.

Another *torrone* specialty, made with dried figs, comes from the province of Chieti. The people of Abruzzi particularly enjoy eating this full-flavored and calorific candy on cold winter days. Nowadays, there are even firms who import it from Italy.

CAMPANIA

aples immediately brings to mind the liveliness of
Italy – bustling, noisy, shimmering in the summer heat, and
full of unrestrained *joie de vivre*, even fearlessly defying the
volcanic threat. Neapolitans are said to have an exuberant
temperament and an inexhaustible supply of good humor that
enables them to overcome the vicissitudes of their far from
simple lives with stoic calm. Whether or not this gross gener-
alization is true, one thing is certain: there is nothing bland
about Neapolitan cuisine. Here people like to see tasty results
as quickly as possible. Life in Naples is hectic, so people do
not want to wait long for their food. It therefore comes as no
surprise that the cuisine of Campania has become famous for
its delightfully simple specialties. The farm produce – tomatoes, capsicums, spring onions, potatoes, artichokes, fennel,
lemons, or oranges – ripened on the fertile volcanic soils at
the foot of Vesuvius under the generous warmth of the southern sun, is all so good, that no expensive refinements are
necessary. Fish and seafood can be brought fresh each day
from the Gulf of Naples or other coastal waters. The durum
wheat needed to produce the world-famous Neapolitan pasta
is either grown in Campania itself or imported from neighboring Apulia. Livestock production provides meat for the
obligatory pasta meat sauce, and even buffalo milk, used to
make the extremely aromatic mozzarella cheese of Campania.
These are the only ingredients the Neapolitan kitchen
conjurers require to serve up the *pièces de résistance* of their
culinary tradition: vegetable dishes, omelets, spicy fish soups,
stir-fries, and, of course, the two staples of Campanian cuisine:
pasta and pizza.

Naples has experienced life under the ruling houses of the
Normans, Hohenstaufens, Bourbons, Aragon, Anjou, and
Savoy, but not one of these foreign powers was able to leave
any lasting mark on the region's cuisine. The only exception
is, perhaps, the influence of the French language dating from
1786, and the introduction of French etiquette at court,
broadening their vocabulary with culinary terms such as *ragù*
(meat sauce), *gattò* (cake), and *crocchè* (croquette). The excellent
dishes typical of the people of Campania, however, such as
*Maccheroni alla napoletana, Pizza margherita, Insalata caprese,
Mozzarella in carrozza* or *Costoletta alla pizzaiola*, do not need
any such embellishment.

Previous double page: Genuine mozzarella, as produced here at the Vannulo cheese-dairy, is
made from buffalo, not cow's milk.

Left: View over the Bay of Naples. The island of Capri can be seen in the distance. Each year
it attracts a small but sophisticated flock of visitors.

Southern Italy does not just provide tomatoes for its own people in the northern regions, but also exports them throughout the world. The tomato is an important commodity in the economy, and investments made by the major food companies go some way to helping to improve the chronically-strained economic situation in the south.

The regions of Emiglia-Romagna and Campania were the pioneers of the tomato processing industry. In northern Parma, some machine builders even specialize in manufacturing the large appliances the industry needs. Italy is now the world-leading supplier of high-quality tomato preserves. Each year, 25 million hundredweight of the red fruits from the Campania province of Salerno alone end up on the conveyor belt. Especially outside of Italy, canned San Marzano tomatoes are one of the cooking enthusiast's favorites, because the preserved fruits from the south often have a stronger flavor than fresh tomatoes from a greenhouse outside Italy.

Alongside *pomadori pelati*, the peeled tomatoes in a jar or can, *concentrato di pomodoro*, *passata di pomodoro*, and *polpa di pomodoro* are also sold. *Concentrato di pomodoro*, tomato paste, comes in various concentrations. *Estratto di pomodoro*, tomato extract, on the other hand, is a Sicilian specialty four to six times as concentrated as ordinary tomato paste.

Alternatively, there is *passata di pomodoro*. It is made from blanched, skinned, and sieved tomatoes, and is thicker than tomato juice, but runnier than tomato paste. A product that until recently has not always been easy to find outside Italy is *polpa di pomodoro*. It is similar in consistency to *passata*, but still contains whole pieces of tomato.

TOMATOES

The tomato has to be the Italians' favorite vegetable. They are served at mealtimes practically every day, no matter what the season, and in many guises: in pasta sauce, as a salad or accompaniment, or stuffed or stewed – Italian cooks are always coming up with something new. There are now around 5000 varieties of this typical Mediterranean fruit worldwide, and, particularly in the United States, breeders and biologists are in the process of developing new hybrids that are reported to be even more disease-resistant, quick-growing, and healthy.

Although the tomato had already reached Europe from the New World by the middle of the 16th century, it was not welcomed into the kitchen until 200 years later. Even in the kingdom of Naples, the red fruits were sometimes thought to be poisonous, and the plant was grown in ornamental gardens as an exotic novelty. The plants did not make it to the vegetable garden until about 1750 – well after people had discovered that the tasty *pomo d'oro*, the golden apple, fitted in extremely well with culinary traditions around Vesuvius. A carnival song from about this time even mentions the new delicacy.

Although the tomato was being cultivated in Campania by the middle of the 18th century, it had to wait a while longer to become the undisputed leader and hence the essential ingredient of southern Italian cuisine that it is today. However, vegetable growers gradually much improved the tomato through breeding, and cooks began to discover the versatility of this garden produce. From then on, there was no stopping

people's enthusiasm for the tomato. Even the nickname for the people of Naples changed to take into account their new eating habits: until then, they had been called *mangiafoglie*, leaf eaters, but this changed to *mangiamaccheroni*, because now, instead of salad and vegetables, people ate mainly pasta served with tomato sauce.

Tomatoes can be harvested from summer to late autumn. However, Neapolitans did not want to be without them during the rest of the year either, so processes to preserve them began to develop. During the 19th century, Italian scientists wrote learned tracts earnestly debating the question of how to ensure a supply of tomatoes throughout the year.

It was not until the 20th century that a whole sector of industry grew up around the city at the foot of Vesuvius, specializing in the cultivation and processing of this member of the nightshade family. The region's best varieties were developed by optimum selection and breeding to produce high yields of top-quality tomatoes. The best-known tomato from Campania has to be the San Marzano. This brilliant red variety produces small, plum-shaped, juicy, fleshy fruits with thin skins and not many seeds. They are suitable both for industrial processing and all domestic uses.

Tomato concentrate or tomato paste (*concentrato di pomodoro*) provides extra tomato flavor.

Canned chopped tomatoes, *polpa di pomodoro*, are a basic ingredient for quick and easy tomato sauces.

Peeled tomatoes (*pomodori pelati*) usually need to be seeded and chopped before use.

Sieved tomatoes (*passata di pomodori*) are a thick tomato juice ready for use in the kitchen.

San Marzano
The elongated or oval fruits of the San Marzano variety are used for canning and drying or to make freshly prepared pasta sauces. Its flesh is sweet and firm.

Sorrento
This variety of the well-known San Marzano tomato is softer and is therefore used only to produce tomato preserves for export.

Casalino
Casalino is a small, sweet-flavored tomato that grows in clusters. It used to be stored in cellars, hanging from the ceiling, and kept throughout the winter.

Pomodoro di Cerignola
The Pomodoro di Cerignola belongs to the large group of cherry or cocktail tomatoes. It has a sweetish flavor, and can be eaten raw in salads, or cooked quickly in sauces.

Marena
Like other tomatoes from the south, the Marena variety is also wonderfully ripe, red, and sweet. However, it is very demanding in terms of growing conditions, and, in addition to a lot of sunshine, it also requires potash-rich soil.

Roma
The Roma variety also needs potash-rich soil, so it is typical of the tomatoes grown in southern Italy. It is very good for preserving, whether canned or dried.

Pachino
The Italian cocktail tomatoes, also called *ciliegini*, are named for the Sicilian town of Pachino, where the best tomatoes of this type are grown. The Pachino tomato has an intense and slightly sour flavor.

Perino
With its firm skin and flesh, the elongated Perino tomato is used in the food industry, and usually ends up in a can as *pomodoro pelato*, peeled tomatoes.

Sardo
This variety can be used in any dish, pan, or salad bowl. It ripens in winter, and is particularly good eaten raw. At present, attempts are being made to breed yellow tomatoes.

Ramato
This tomato got its name because it grows on *rami*, strong branches, with several glowing red fruits hanging from each one. The tomatoes can weigh up to five ounces (130 g) each. They are easy to peel and very versatile in the kitchen.

Napoli
This variety needs potash-rich soils as found in the volcanic soil around Vesuvius. It is somewhat smaller and rounder than the San Marzano tomato.

Palla di Fuoco
The Palla di Fuoco, fireball, is also a popular variety in the north. It makes a particularly good tomato salad or *Insalata mista* or mixed salad.

Cuore di Bue
A Cuore di Bue (ox heart) tomato can weigh over eight ounces (250 g). This variety is very fleshy, but has very few seeds. Cuore di Bue is an excellent salad tomato, and is only eaten raw. In north-ern Italy, it is also eaten while still green, when it contains more acid than when ripe. "Ox heart" tomatoes are delicious served with a little oil, salt, and pepper.

PUGLIA

Types of bread

1 Pane di Altamura
This sourdough durum wheat bread, compact and full of holes, keeps well, and is now popular throughout Italy. In Apulia, the tasty, round, flat loaves can weigh up to 44 pounds (20 kilograms).

2 Pane casareccio
Not so very long ago, every family used to bake their own *pane casareccio*, Apulia's classic loaf made from durum wheat flour, salt, water, and yeast. Now the loaves you can buy from the baker as just as tasty and satisfying.

3 Puccia di pane
When baked, this small, soft, nutritious round loaf, enriched with olives, is tossed in white flour to remind people of the purity of the Virgin Mary. The province of Lecce is the main place for this bread, although it can also be found in Brindisi and Ostuni.

4 Puddica
The basic ingredients, ordinary bread dough and mashed potato, are kneaded to form a smooth dough, which is then rolled out into flat cakes. These are then covered with halved tomatoes, seasoned with salt, and pepper, drizzled with olive oil, and baked in the oven.

5 Focaccia ripiena
This parcel of bread dough is filled with mozzarella, tomatoes, ham, and onion or leek, baked in the oven, then cut into slices, and eaten.

6 Taralli
Wheat flour, lard, olive oil, brewer's yeast, fennel seeds, ground red pepper or freshly milled pepper, and a little salt are the main ingredients for these crispy bread rings. They are a popular aperitif in southern Italy.

7 Crostini
Slices of white bread roasted in the oven are drizzled with fresh olive oil and sprinkled with oregano. They can also be served with olive, anchovy, or tuna paste.

8 Friselle
These small, round, golden-brown loaves made of barley flour and durum wheat flour are baked twice, first in a hot oven, and then in a moderate oven. If an audible crack is produced when the loaf is broken open, it is a sure sign that it is really crusty and good. *Friselle* keep for a very long time, if kept in an airtight container.

If you want to discover Apulia's many different types of bread, you can do no better than to visit the Angelini bakery in Martina Franca, where they bake *taralli*, *friselle*, *focaccia*, and all the other tasty specialties in an authentic atmosphere full of Apulian cheer.

Taralli
Bread rings
(Illustrated below, no. 6)

4 CUPS/500 G FLOUR
SALT AND PEPPER
1/2 CUP/125 G LARD
2 OZ/55 G BREWER'S YEAST
FENNEL SEEDS (OPTIONAL)
WATER
OLIVE OIL

Combine the flour with a little salt and pepper, then knead together with the lard, brewer's yeast, and fennel seeds, if using. Add sufficient water to produce a smooth dough. Cut off small pieces of dough and shape into rings. Drizzle with a little oil, place on a greased baking sheet, and leave to rise for 1 hour. Then bake in a preheated oven at 300 °F (150 °C) for 1 hour.

WHEAT

There are more than 360 varieties of wheat throughout the world. Wheat can be roughly divided up into three groups: durum wheat provides heavy corn with lots of grits. It is not very strong. Soft wheat forms within white grains, from which white flour can be milled. The properties of semihard varieties are somewhere between these two groups. They are often used because they provide white flour, and it is easy to separate the bran. In Apulia, they cultivate mainly durum wheat (*triticum durum*), but sometimes also other varieties of wheat. The advantage of durum

wheat is that it thrives in the dry, hot climate of this region. Seed wheat is very demanding in terms of the mineral content of the soil and moisture, which is why it was preferable to grow durum wheat.

For centuries, life in Apulia has focused on arable farming and has been governed by the harvest calendar, so it is not surprising that they have taken equal care when processing field crops. Fresh, homemade pasta still features prominently on Apulian menus, but the various types of bread also have an established place. Throughout Italy, bread from Apulia is considered to be particularly good. They knead a great variety of pasta in their kitchens, and bake many different types of bread in their bakeries. Baked to varying degrees of crustiness, whether best enjoyed fresh, or suitable for the store cupboard, hearty, or delicate and sweet, the imagination knows no bounds. The quality of a loaf depends on various factors. Which flour or flour mixture does the baker use? Bread made from durum wheat may not be such a beautiful, radiant white, but it keeps very well, and does not go stale so quickly. How was the corn harvested, and how was it milled? Does the baker add yeast or other raising agents? What baking pans does he use? And finally, how does he bake them, and in what sort of oven? The bakers of Apulia are experts in all these questions. However, their various kinds of bread all have one thing in common: they taste fabulous.

Below: *Grano duro*, durum wheat (*triticum durum*), is primarily grown in southern Italy, because this variety tolerates the dry, hot climate. Milled durum wheat, known as semolina or *semolino* in Italian, is an essential ingredient in the cuisine of the Italian peninsula, because it is the basic ingredient for pasta.

BASILICATA

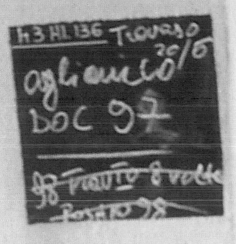

PEPERONCINO
LUCANICA SAUSAGES
HAPPY PIGS
BREAD
CONFECTIONERY
HOMEMADE PASTA
LAMB
HONEY
HELLENIC WINE

B asilicata is a tranquil, secluded region. Visitors rarely stray into this sun-drenched, inaccessible but nonetheless fascinating region between the heel and the sole of the Italian boot, and travelers who come only for the cuisine are even rarer, even though Basilicata definitely has a few specialties to offer. Even in ancient times, when this stretch of land was still called Lucania, Roman writers such as Cicero, Martial, and Horace praised the local sausages. And the Epicurean Apicius went so far as to provide the first description of the *lucanica*, a tasty, fresh pork sausage, served by Lucanian slaves to their Roman masters. Even today, pork continues to play an important role in the cuisine of Basilicata. Almost every family rears its own pig, and they throw a big party when the pig is slaughtered. If the meat is not being made into the excellent, traditional sausages, such as *lucanica*, *pezzenta*, and *cotechinata*, it is roasted on a spit. This is also their preferred way of cooking mutton and lamb.

Pasta is another mainstay of the regional cuisine. As in the neighboring southern regions, in Basilicata homemade pasta is made from durum wheat and water. Delicious vegetable or meat sauces transform this simple but nutritious dish into a distinctive culinary experience. On feast days, kitchens are filled with the aroma of *Ragù della mamma*, made to a recipe that has remained so secret that all we know is that it is made from large chunks of meat.

However, the most distinguishing feature of Basilicata's cuisine is the peperoncino. These bright red, devilishly hot chili peppers are used in almost every dish. Every market sells them, tied into pretty braids, and in this region, even the mild varieties have long been considered a healthy staple food. Pork, sausage, pasta, and peperoncini – that sounds like good, solid cooking, but hardly suitable ingredients for dessert. However, Basilicata is surprisingly good for desserts. Here, they finish a meal either with a spicy cheese, preferably a *provolone*, which should be ripened over your own fireplace, or a delicious dessert, either baked or that has been mixed with lots of honey.

After a sumptuous Lucanian feast, people like to take a time-tested digestive, the bitter Amaro Lucano, which is now enjoyed throughout Italy.

Previous double page: Wine is prepared for transport at the vineyards of Armando Martino in Rionero Vulture (province of Potenza).

Left: Rivello, situated beneath Monte Sirino, is one of Basilicata's most beautiful small towns.

HOMEMADE PASTA

The cuisine of Basilicata may be simple, but it is by no means unimaginative. Quite the opposite, in fact, for even the simplest ingredients are treated here with patience and love. The basic pasta dough, which is still often made at home, consists almost solely of durum wheat and water. The addition of eggs is practically unheard of. The fact that, despite this, the simple, but very nutritious food has become a culinary highlight is due to the wealth of imaginative ideas of the Lucanian cooks. They have invented not only spicy sauces and stews, but also an infinite variety of pasta shapes, sometimes made using very simple devices.

Take the *cavarola*, for example. It is a small, grooved wooden chopping board usually handcrafted by shepherds. The pasta dough is rolled over the board to make *strascinati*, literally meaning dragged pasta shapes. The *maccarunara* is another special pasta board used to make *tagliolini*, which are similar to *maccheroni alla chitarra*. To make *triid*, on the other hand, all you need

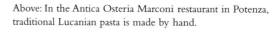

Strascinati, literally meaning dragged pasta shapes, are made by rolling small portions of dough over the *cavarola.* This gives the pasta its characteristic pattern.

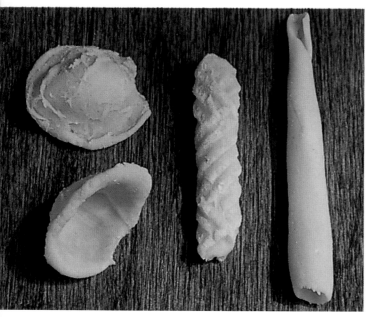

From left to right: *Orecchiette, strascinati* and *ferrettini.*

Above: In the Antica Osteria Marconi restaurant in Potenza, traditional Lucanian pasta is made by hand.

is nimble fingers. This very traditional pasta is said to be derived from the Sicilian *trie* and was brought to the southern Italian mainland in the early 12th century by the Norman prince Roger II. To make these long pasta strips, which in other regions are called *vermicelli* or *spaghettini*, a hole is pressed into the center of a ball of dough weighing approximately three-quarters of a pound (300 grams). The ring of dough is then rolled using jerky hand movements to form an increasingly long strip, which is then wound up like wool. The soft strips should not tear, nor should they stick together.

You need a lot of pasta-making experience in order to make *triid.* A single "cord of dough" has to be produced from a ring of dough.

The "cord of dough" is then drawn out further until it is a "string of dough." The great skill is to avoid breaking the dough.

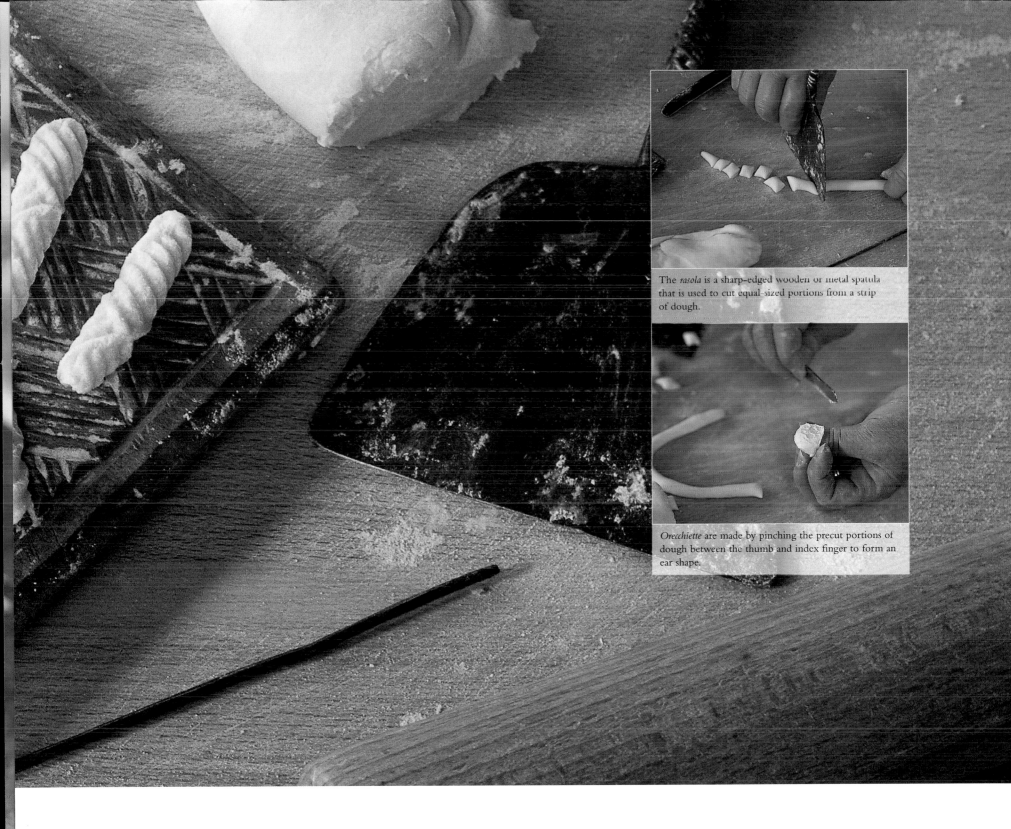

The *rasola* is a sharp-edged wooden or metal spatula that is used to cut equal-sized portions from a strip of dough.

Orecchiette are made by pinching the precut portions of dough between the thumb and index finger to form an ear shape.

A *ferretta*, a special metal rod, is used to make *ferretti* or *ferrettini*.

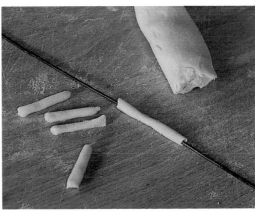

The thinly-rolled dough is first wrapped around the *ferretta*. The dough is then cut and the pasta shapes carefully twisted off the rod.

STRASCINATI ALLA MENTA
Strascinati with mint

14 OZ/400 G STRASCINATI (OR ANY OTHER HOMEMADE PASTA)
1 SLICE/30 G BACON, FINELY DICED
1 CLOVE OF GARLIC, CHOPPED
1 PEPERONCINO, CHOPPED
3–4 TBSP EXTRA VIRGIN OLIVE OIL
A FEW LEAVES OF MINT

Boil the pasta in copious salted water until *al dente*.
Meanwhile fry the diced bacon, garlic, and peperoncino in the olive oil. When the pasta is almost cooked, add the mint leaves to the bacon.
Drain the pasta, arrange on plates, and pour over the sauce.

HELLENIC WINE

Basilicata may have more vineyards than the famous north Italian combined region of Trentino-South Tyrol, but its quality wine accounts for barely ten percent of its DOC production. The decidedly mountainous region, which goes down to sea level only in the southeast, is one of the poorest in Italy. It

has only one mark of origin, which in terms of quality has no need to hide its light under a bushel, that of the red Aglianico del Vulture. Most of the wine produced, however, is sold as anonymous bulk wine and is used to no small extent to enrich many a reputable table wine from the more northern regions of the Italian peninsula.

On the slopes of Monte Vulture, an extinct volcano in the north of Basilicata, at a height of between 1500 and 2000 feet (450–600 meters), grow the famous Aglianico grapes. These are said to have originated from the Ancient Greeks – Aglianico is only a derivation of *ellenico*, the Italian word for Greek – and form the basis of probably the most well-known and most important DOC wine of

The winegrowers have dug their cellars in the high loessial cliffs of the valleys around Monte Vulture.

southern Italy. With their dark color, powerful bouquet and full body, and provided they receive the correct viticultural attention and careful cellar management, the best wines from Aglianico have nothing to fear even from the Sangiovese and Nebbiolo wines. They can even be stored in oak casks, and a few concerns have been using this method of production with great success for more than ten years now.

An unusual feature of the rugged landscape around the towns of Barile (Italian for barrel or cask) and Rionero are the earth cellars that have been dug into the loessial cliffs of the small river valleys. Another typical feature of winegrowing in this region is the way the vines are

grown on old, almost pyramidal poles. These can still be seen in most of the vineyards today and many wine-

growers believe this method is considerably better for high quality Aglianico grapes than the modern, productive, and easy-to-work wire frames.

Beyond Basilicata, the Aglianico grape plays a significant role only in Campania and Apulia, where the famous Taurasi and the Castel del Monte wines are pressed from its grapes, whether as single varietals or as a blend with other varieties. Italy's other DOC wines that contain Aglianico grapes, such as Taburno, Cilento, Sant'Agata de' Goti, or Lacryma Christi, play a very subordinate role in the world's wine markets.

Above: Basilicata's annual production may be an impressive 12,400,000 U.S. gallons (470,000 hectoliters), but almost 90 percent are sold as blended wines in other regions.

Opposite and below: The popular bitters from Basilicata is called Amaro Lucano. Its fans attribute remarkable properties to the tincture.

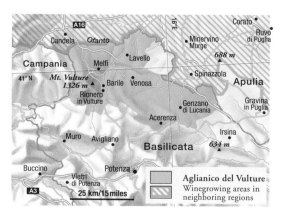

Liqueur

Many families in Basilicata still make liqueurs themselves (background), the most popular being Nocino, Amarello, and Rosolio. Nocino is actually a specialty from Emilia-Romagna, but is also very popular in the south. It is made from green walnuts steeped until soft in high-proof alcohol. After about 40 days, the mixture has transformed into a brownish and very effective digestive.

Rosolio gets its name from the rose petals that are steeped together with wild berries or other flavorings in sweetened alcohol. Citrus fruits are a favorite in Basilicata. Amaro Lucano is manufactured in the small Lucanian town of Pisticci. You will find this famous bitters in any well-stocked bar in the cities of Milan, Venice, Rome, or Naples.

CALABRIA

Corigliano
Calabro
Acri
Rende Cosenza
Calabria
Crotone
Lamezia Terme
Catanzaro
Vibo Valentia
Tropea
Bagnara Calabra
Reggio
di Calabria

Calabria's strategically favorable position providing direct access both to the Tyrrhenian and Ionian Seas has attracted the attentions of foreign rulers since time immemorial. During the 8th century B.C., this region was ruled by the Greeks after they had absorbed the area comprising the sole, instep, and toe of the Italian boot into their large colony to the West. The Calabrians not only profited from the culinary know-how of these occupying nations but also took over their traditions and customs, some of which continue to this day. Whenever a pig is slaughtered – an occasion for celebration in itself – it is a not-to-be-missed opportunity for a family to have its future read or have the sex of an expected baby predicted from the entrails.

Around 500 years after the Greeks, Calabria was occupied by the Romans who derived great pleasure from the viniculture which their predecessors had introduced into the region. After the collapse of the Roman Empire, there followed a continuous stream of Teutons, Goths, Lombards, Franks, Sicilians, Saracens, French, and Spaniards one after the other. Naturally enough, all of them left their imprint on Calabrian cuisine. The Arabs brought oranges, lemons, raisins, artichokes, and aubergines – all of which remain to this day important ingredients in the traditional dishes of the region. The Cistercian monks, who held large estates in the Sibari region, introduced new agricultural methods and the art of dairying, which at that time constituted a major advance in farming. During the rule of the House of Anjou and, later, Napoleon, French influences were assimilated and the Spaniards likewise left their mark. The word for cake, *gatò*, derives from the French *gateau* and the delicious meat paté *murseddu* or *mursiellu* has its origins in the Spanish word *almuerzo* (breakfast, meal).

Despite all these foreign influences, Calabrian cuisine has an identity very much its own. All too often, the inhabitants of the toe of Italy were forced to flee from invaders into the mountains where they continued to cook their traditional dishes based on simple produce coaxed from the poor soil and some livestock farming. Although they may sometimes have been slow to absorb foreign tastes, once Calabrians finally do take to something, then they do so in a big way. Just as a visitor will eventually be welcomed with great hospitality after some initial wariness, the eggplant likewise has been embraced wholeheartedly by the people of the region.

Previous double page: The fishwives of Bagnara Calabra, the so-called *bagnarote*, displaying their wares in the morning.

Left: A swordfish boat – known as *luntru* in Calabrian dialect – entering Bagnara harbor.

CULINARY FESTIVALS

The whole of southern Italy is home to a wealth of culinary celebrations. Although the Church tolerates these festivals, all of which openly flaunt their pagan origins to a greater or lesser degree, they are not always liked. This does not deter the gourmets, however, who gather at specific times of the year to indulge in some particular delicacy or other. In July, for example, Bagnara in Calabria celebrates its swordfish festival, at which the landed catch is not only duly admired but also enjoyed in a variety of dishes. These festivals, which even ancient Roman writers such as Ovid and Makrobius mentioned in their writings, date from a time – almost inconceivable to us nowadays – when the rhythm of life was determined by people's work on the land or the needs of their livestock. In the spring, people celebrated the seed sowing and looked forward to the newborn lambs, while summer was the season to enjoy the blessing of the ripe fruits. Autumn was the time to give thanks for a good harvest and in the depths of winter, all kinds of magic ceremonies were performed to banish the cold weather and keep people's spirits up.

Today, more and more communities are remembering their old customs, consulting the chronicles and lovingly trying to revive these traditional festivals. Not only does this delight the tourists, who feel they are experiencing a real authentic piece of Italy, but, above all, it helps the villages, towns, or communities to revive a part of their culture and preserve their country's diversity from the uniformity that is the legacy of supermarkets.

Anyone who is keen to experience a typical *fiera* or *sagra* on a trip to Italy should note down some dates. The following have, of course, merely been selected as samples. It is not true, by the way, that it is only southern Italy that celebrates such "food festivals." It is just that they are somewhat jollier, more colorful, and certainly more boisterous down here than they are in the more reserved north. In July, Casalfiumanese holds its apricot festival and in April the orange has pride of place in Ribera near Agrigento. A visit to San Damiano d'Asti in September is a must for anyone with a passion for *bollito misto*. In autumn, the sweet chestnut is center-stage in Marradi near Florence while gnocchi can be sampled in Castel del Rio near Bologna in June. Figure-conscious visitors can have a field day at the salad festival in Treviso in December while August is the month for celebrating the famous Castelluccio lentils in Norcia and mozzarella cheese in Eboli. Anyone with any room left can visit the pizza festival in Albanella, in the Campanian province of Salerno, also in August. Torrone (nougat) can be sampled in Cremona or Faenza in October and November and if you find yourself in Sardinia in August, you can enjoy the tomato festival (Zeddiani, Oristano province) or the Vernaccia grape festival (Nurachi, also in the Oristano province) at which Sardinian traditional costumes are worn.

Background: Strings of colored lights light up Bagnara which plays host to the swordfish festival. This spectacular event attracts crowds of visitors to this small village from all over the region as well as from neighboring Sicily.

INVOLTINI DI PESCE SPADA
Swordfish rolls

Serves 6

About 1 1/2 lbs/600 g fresh swordfish, cut into
thin rectangular slices about 2 1/2 inches by
4 inches (6.5 x 10 cm)
4 oz/100 g steamed swordfish meat
1/2 cup/50 g caciovallo, freshly grated
1 cup/60 g fresh breadcrumbs
12 stoned black olives, chopped
Onion rings
Bay leaves

Salsa salmoriglio:
1/3 cup/100 ml olive oil
1 handful of chopped parsley
2 garlic cloves, minced
Chopped capers, as required
1 tsp oregano
Salt and pepper

Lay the swordfish steaks on a marble board and
tenderize with a rolling-pin, taking care not to split
them. Dice the steamed swordfish meat and mix with
the *caciovallo*, the breadcrumbs, and the olives. Spread
this mixture over the slices of fish, then roll them up.
Put the rolls on a skewer, alternating them with the
onion rings and bay leaves, then cook over a charcoal
grill, brushing them with the *Salsa salmoriglio* marinade.
To make the *Salsa salmoriglio*, mix the olive oil with 4
tablespoons of hot water, adding parsley, garlic, capers,
oregano, and salt and pepper to taste.

PESCE SPADA ALLA GHIOTTA
Swordfish rolls in tomato sauce
(Illustration below, foreground)

1/2 lb/200 g tomatoes, passed through a sieve
4 basil leaves
Salt
4–5 cups/250 g fresh breadcrumbs
4 oz/100 g stoned black olives, chopped
3 tbsp capers
1 small bunch of parsley, chopped
1 peperoncino, chopped
Generous 2 lbs/1 kg swordfish, cut into thin slices
3–4 tbsp olive oil

Cook the tomatoes in a saucepan with the basil until the
mixture forms a sauce. Season with salt and set aside. In a
bowl, mix together the breadcrumbs, olives, capers, parsley,
and peperoncino, adding a little water and salt. Spread the
paste onto the slices of swordfish and then roll up, securing
each one with a cocktail stick. Fry these in olive oil. Pour
the tomato sauce over the fish rolls and let them simmer for
a few more minutes over a low heat. Serve hot.

PESCE SPADA IN SALMORIGLIO
Grilled marinated swordfish
(Illustrated below, background)

For the mariade:
Extra virgin olive oil
Juice of 1 lemon
Oregano
1 small bunch of parsley, chopped
1 clove of garlic, chopped
Salt and pepper
1 tbsp chopped capers
Grated lemon zest

1 3/4 lbs/800 g swordfish, cut into 4 steaks

Mix the olive oil, lemon juice, a generous amount of
oregano, chopped parsley, and the chopped garlic together
in a bowl to form a marinade and season with salt and
pepper. Add the chopped capers and a little lemon zest.
Sprinkle the swordfish steaks with olive oil and cook over a
very hot grill. Sprinkle with the marinade and serve hot.

SICILIA

SICILY

Tuna fish

Fish from three seas

Salt

Primi piatti from nine
provinces

Opulent cuisine

Pumpkins and zucchini

Sicilian vegetable dishes

Citrus fruits

Prickly pears

You'll be for it
tonight…

Sweet occasions during
the church year

Marzipan from
Martorana

Ice cream

Winegrowing

Marsala

Lipari Islands
(Aeolian Islands)

S.Vito
lo Capo

Messina

Trapani
Palermo

Straits of Messina

Favi-
gnana
Marsala

Etna
3350 m

S i c i l y

Mazara
del Vallo

Enna
Caltanisetta

Catania

Agrigento

Francofonte

Siracusa

Ragusa

As far as Sicilians are concerned, the best things in life include good company, family life, sunny days by the sea, and, above all, an appreciation of the culinary arts. Just how important good food and fine wines are here is obvious from the region's culture which exhibits a fair amount of preoccupation with matters of a gastronomic nature. In his novel entitled *The Leopard* – which is actually about something else entirely, namely the political turmoil within Italy prior to Unification – Giuseppe Tomasi di Lampedusa profiles the eating habits of Sicilian aristocracy in loving and minute detail. Similarly, Domenico Modugno, the singer – who despite his claims to the contrary, is not a native of Sicily himself – has immortalized in song the tradition of fishing for swordfish which goes on in the Straits of Messina. Sicilians have a long tradition of enjoying their culinary pleasures. Long ago in prehistoric times, when people still worshiped Dea Madre, ritual little cakes were baked in honor of the goddess who was, essentially, motherhood. Then came the Greeks, colonizing the eastern Mediterranean. They dispensed with these female goddesses and devoted themselves to the cult of the grape as personified by the god Dionysus. The Romans introduced elaborate goose dishes to the island, the Byzantines brought with them their fondness for sweet and sour and the Arab invasion between the 9th and 11th centuries brought about a minor culinary revolution: To this day, apricots, sugar, citrus fruits, sweet melons, rice, saffron, raisins, nutmeg, cloves, pepper, and cinnamon are cornerstones of Sicilian cuisine. The Normans and Hohenstaufen invaders, in turn, were fond of meat dishes and the Spaniards magnanimously shared their latest discoveries from the New World: cocoa, maize, turkey, tomatoes, and other produce of the Solanaceae family. They were followed by the Bourbons, the "continental" Italians, and many other races who helped fashion the Sicilian menu.

Eating and drinking in the heart of the Mediterranean, therefore, is always synonymous with a journey back in time to cultures of a bygone age. The ingenuity of Sicilian cooks ensures that the result will be a highly individual interpretation of a multicultural cuisine: colorful, sweet, hearty, aromatic, exotic, typical of the region, and sometimes very mysterious. Just like the island itself.

Previous double page: Sicily is not the only province where street stalls provide instant refreshment in the form of ice cream and *granita*.

Left: The Sicilian landscape, as pictured here near San Vito lo Capo, can appear harsh and romantic at the same time.

SALT

Man could not survive without salt. Sodium chloride keeps the body's muscles and nerves in working order, enables it to digest food and helps maintain a proper water balance. Without salt in his diet, he would suffer from tooth loss, heart disease, and general disability. Prehistoric man got what salt he needed from eating plenty of meat, but the quantities he required forced him to live the life of a hunter and nomad. Life depended on the salt and protein derived from animals. It was not until people discovered that the gray or white crystals obtainable from seawater or from natural deposits were equally capable of supplying the body's vital salt requirements that they could contemplate a change in their diet and life style. People began to settle, to live off the fruits of their land and they supplemented their daily food with salt. This reduction in meat consumption and a switch to a diet based on virtually salt-free grain and vegetables led inevitably to a dependence on the "white gold." Salt became the most important trading commodity in the early civilized world and the demand for it increased dramatically after resourceful cooks discovered that this crystalline substance with its characteristic taste could also keep meat, fish, and vegetables from spoiling – thus was born the art of preserving, an important new cultural advance as this also meant that salted food rations now made intensive military operations and invasion campaigns feasible. Towns along the salt routes flourished, a salt embargo could mean the ruin of an entire region, and the local princes were at pains to safeguard their access to salt resources. Salt was also used as currency – as the word "salary" reminds us.

Sicily is particularly blessed with salt. Sea salt is extracted around Trapani, Marsala, and Augusta while Cattolica Eraclea has extensive deposits of rock salt in its vicinity. In earlier days, large trading ships used to call at the western tip of the island to carry Sicilian salt all over the world.

The traditional methods of salt extraction have not changed all that much over the past 140 years and so it is well worthwhile recalling how Sicilian scholar Giuseppe Pitré described the Trapani salt pans in his book published at the end of the 19th century entitled *La famiglia, la casa, la vita del popolo siciliano* (Family, home and life of the Sicilian people). He wrote: "A large area to the east of Trapani is divided into numerous squares. These are linked by a system of small canals which gradually allow sea water to penetrate right the way inland to the salt pan farthest from the shore. Its color changes as it progresses, starting off a reddish color, then turning bluish, and finally ending up white after the water has been evaporated by the baking African sun, leaving a layer of salt crystals which gleam like glistening white snow."

Around a century earlier, an English traveler described the process of salt extraction at the salt-works in some detail: "The salt-works is divided into numerous pans. The cold seawater is pumped into the largest one, the so-called 'cold' basin or 'mother'. This is where the evaporation process begins. Once the

Background: The extensive salt extraction plants and windmills for crushing salt near Trapani lie on the Via del Sale, the salt route, which runs along the coast between Trapani and Marsala.

WHITE GOLD

Salt is mankind's oldest preservative. No other substance has had such a strong influence on cooking or life style. Transportable, salted provisions mean mobility, freedom from concerns about food shortages, and insurance against diseases caused by nutritional deficiencies. This was particularly crucial to seafarers, soldiers, and settlers in undeveloped areas. But those who remained close to home also benefited from the new kinds of preserved food. Salted cod and herring, vegetables salted down in barrels, and salted meat specialities like ham and sausage transformed the culinary landscape. Trapani assumed an important role in supplying this valuable commodity. The situation has changed somewhat since then. Nowadays, cheap industrial salt is produced all over the world. Gone are the days when the Phoenicians used to load up their maneuverable ships on Sicilian shores. The Greeks and Romans came next, followed by Arab feluccas and later the ocean-going vessels of the Normans. Valuable Sicilian salt was eventually introduced to Brittany, England, and later the towns of the Hanseatic League. It would have been impossible to process the large herring catches without salt and on Norway's Lofoten islands, it was used in the preparation of klipfish and stockfish. Cod, salted and dried in the cold northern air, soon became popular in the Mediterranean region and Sicilian salt, after this excursion to northern climes, returned home again. Norman ships brought consign-

ments of this hard but tasty fish to southern Italy and returned home again with cargoes of citrus fruits, Marsala, wine, and, of course, "white gold."

The advent of modern refrigeration methods and industrial preserving techniques, including sterilization and pasteurization, has meant that Trapani sea salt has lost its key role. It is, however, currently experiencing a small renaissance as more and more cooks are using these large crystals of coarse grain salt on focaccia or other types of flat bread.

water has had time to warm up a little, it is channelled into the next basin, known as the *frittedda* or 'no longer quite so cold'. It remains here for two weeks before being channelled along a canal into a third chamber known as *ricauda* or *idicauda*, or 'lukewarm', which is further subdivided into three sections. Buckets and ladles are now used to transfer the water into a tub before being poured yet again into the *casa calda* or 'warm house', again divided into three sections. From here, it goes to the penultimate chamber, the *caldissima*, the 'hot basin'. The seawater's journey finally ends in the last pan where the water, five inches deep to start with, crystallizes into a roughly two-inch layer of salt. The water…is channelled along the canals into the respective basins by means of a system of sluice-gates. The resulting salt crystals are piled into pyramids away from the salt works and left to air-dry for a year. During this time, a crust forms which protects the salt underneath. The salt is crushed into coarse grains by means of a vertically-turning mill-wheel."

When the summer season is over, the pyramids of salt are protected by terracotta tiles.

Luchino Visconti's film version of *The Leopard*, based on the novel by Giuseppe Tomasi di Lampedusa, used spectacular sets and starred top names like Claudia Cardinale and Burt Lancaster.

Above: In the 19th century, the San Nicola monastery in Catania was the second largest monastery in the world.

OPULENT CUISINE

Until Italy became a liberal centralized state in the 1870s, Sicily's inheritance laws were based on primogeniture, the right of the firstborn to inherit. This meant that younger siblings were, to some extent, destined from the outset to have no financial means of their own, even if they came from rich, aristocratic backgrounds. The notion of earning money from gainful employment was, by and large, an unknown concept to them and often the only course left open to these lower-ranking nobles was to embark on a career in the church. In order to cushion their harsh fate a little, these sons and daughters of Sicilian princes, barons, and counts naturally made every effort to

provide themselves with a fitting life style within the monastery walls. It was for this reason that feudal cuisine in 19th-century Sicily branched off in two main directions which still retained many surprising similarities. On the one hand, there was the culinary magnificence seen in the great palaces, and on the other, the sumptuous cuisine of the monasteries which often employed their own French *monzu*, a type of latter-day gourmet chef.

One of the most powerful and richest monasteries was San Nicola, in Catania. This was the second largest monastery in the world after Cisnerros in Portugal. In 1894, Federico de Roberto, in his epic novel *The Viceroys*, painted a revealing portrait of monastic life: "The monks lived according to the motto 'Good food and drink, not forgetting a little gentle exercise.' On rising, every monk went to celebrate mass in church, usually behind closed doors so as not to be disturbed. After returning to his cell, he would partake of a small

bite to eat in anticipation of the midday meal, for which preparations would be underway in the vast kitchens, often staffed by no fewer than eight cooks and their helpers. To keep the fires in the kitchen ranges burning, four loads of oakwood charcoal were delivered each day. The cellarer also supplied four bladders of lard and two kafis of oil each day just for the fried dishes alone. Such quantities would have lasted a prince's household six months. Grills and fireplaces could accommodate half a calf or a whole swordfish at a time. Two kitchen boys would spend an hour grating two whole cheeses. Even the oak chopping board was so gigantic that two men could not reach around it with their arms. So heavily used was it that a carpenter had to be summoned once a week – in return for a fee of four taris and half a cask of wine – to plane off about an inch of wood from the surface to make it smooth again. The opulence of Benedictine cuisine was the talk of the whole town. It included *Timballo di maccheroni*, a baked pasta dish, topped with short pastry, *arancini*, so-called rice balls as big as melons, served with stuffed olives and honeysweet *crespelle*…And, believe it or not, for ice cream dishes like *spumone* and *cassata*, the monks would actually send to Naples for Don Tino, the young man from the Caffè Benvenuto." According to literary history, were it not for *The Viceroys*, there would have been no *Leopard*, in other words, no book by the Prince of Lampedusa about the life of the fictitious Prince Salina. Giuseppe Tomasi di Lampedusa obviously knew his subject well. Having been brought up by his maternal grandparents at the Palazzo Cutò-Filangieri in Santa Marìa Belice and at the castle of Palma di Montechiaro, Lampedusa was very well acquainted with the cuisine of his day. His novel consequently reads like a treatise on the gastronomic traditions of Sicilian aristocracy, which, after years of Bourbon rule, found itself on the threshold of a new, unified Italy. The Prince of Salina, the Leopard, is summoned to Naples by King Ferdinand because his nephew is propagating new-fangled, liberal ideas. Having aired his – entirely justified – displeasure, the king then amiably shows his Sicilian guest that there are no hard feelings by inviting him to a small, private repast – consisting, naturally, of macaroni and pleasant female company – thereby indicating that he wishes to let the matter rest.

When Garibaldi lands near Marsala with his famous "Thousand", the Salinas simply withdraw to their summer residence at Donnafugata, as if nothing has happened. A gala dinner is held on the evening of their arrival, given by the Leopard in honor of the mayor and local nobility. Lampedusa's description of the banquet reads like an excerpt from the culinary history of an Italy whose upper classes, though all for the sort of refined, aristocratic life style cultivated elsewhere in Europe, are more concerned with eating their fill and are not interested, therefore, in any kind of experimentation. The Prince of Salina takes account of this by unceremoniously ignoring existing rules of haute cuisine and instead, having nourishing, home-cooked Sicilian dishes served at his table. Lampedusa makes fun of the fact that the guests' sole concern as the banquet gets underway is that the first course might turn out to be the clear, pale soup that has gained popularity as the latest culinary fashion. Soup as a starter is an intolerable notion for the local dignitaries of Donnafugata and its environs and they mutter about such a "dreadful, foreign custom." However, all their fears prove unfounded as the liveried servants carry in a huge mountain of pasta which turns out to be *Timballo di maccheroni*. Unfortunately, Lampedusa did not provide a recipe for this work of art, but it is obvious from the story that it must have been quite a spectacular affair.

IL TIMBALLO DEL GATTOPARDO
Sicilian pie
(Illustrated below)

1/2 LB/250 G FROZEN PLAIN (SHORTCRUST) PASTRY
2 LB/1 KG DRIED BEANS

2 pints/1 liter Salsa spagnola:
1 LB/500 G VEAL ON THE BONE
4 PINTS/2 LITERS BOUILLON

For the sauce:
SCANT HALF CUP/100 ML MARSALA VERGINE SOLERAS
OLIVE OIL
1/4 CUP/25 G ONIONS, DICED
1/4 CUP/25 G CARROTS, DICED
2 SLICES/50 G RAW HAM, DICED
1 SMALL/50 G CHICKEN BREAST, SKINNED AND CUT UP INTO SMALL PIECES
1/8 CUP/25 G DICED LIVER
1/3 CUP/80 G DICED HARD-BOILED EGG
A GOOD PINCH OF CINNAMON
A FEW CLOVES
1 1/2 TBSP/30 G TOMATO PASTE
ALL-PURPOSE FLOUR
BUTTER
SALT AND PEPPER
TRUFFLES OR WILD MUSHROOMS

1/2 LB/250 G FROZEN PUFF PASTRY
2 LB/1 KG PENNE RIGATE
GRATED PARMESAN OR CACIOCAVALLO
1 EGG WHITE, WHISKED TO A FROTH
1 EGG YOLK
MILK
FRESH FLOWERS FOR DECORATION

Roll out the thawed out plain pastry to a thickness of just less than ¼ inch/1 cm and line the base and sides of a 13-inch/33-cm springform cake pan with the pastry. Cover the pastry with aluminum foil which has been pierced several times with a fork. To keep the pastry flat while baking, place about 2 lb/1 kg of dried beans on top of the base and bake blind in a preheated oven for 15 minutes at 350 °F (180 °C). Remove the beans and foil and bake for a further ten minutes. Leave to cool, then carefully undo the springform. Refrigerate the pastry base until required.
To make the *salsa spagnola*, first brown the veal in the oven, then add the bouillon and cook until the liquid is reduced to about 2 pints/1 liter.
To make the sauce, slowly reduce the 2 pints of *salsa spagnola* over a low heat. Remove from heat and leave to cool, then add the Marsala Vergine Soleras or any other good, dry marsala. Meanwhile heat the oil in a skillet and saute the onions, carrots, ham, chicken, liver, and eggs. Season with cinnamon and cloves and add the tomato paste thinned down with a little water. Brown some flour in butter, add a little water and pour over the vegetable and meat mixture. Season with salt and pepper and add the reduced *salsa spagnola*. Simmer a while longer and allow the mixture to thicken further. Finally, fish out the cloves, then add the butter, truffles, or sliced wild mushrooms.
Roll out the layers of puff pastry to a thickness of about ⅛ inch/3 mm. Cook the pasta until *al dente* in plenty of salted water, drain, quickly sprinkle the cheese over and toss. Stir the sauce into the pasta.
Remove the baked pastry case from the refrigerator and fill with the hot pasta. When it is still just warm, brush the edges of the pastry with egg white. Cover the pasta with layers of puff pastry, pressing it down around the edges to hold it in place. The pie can be decorated with shapes, for example, Sicilian motifs, cut from the remaining plain pastry. Brush the lightly beaten yolk of an egg, mixed with a little milk, over the pastry lid and bake in a preheated oven for 45–50 minutes at 340–350 °F (170–180 °C). Decorate with a few small, fresh flowers.

Il timballo del Gattopardo – Sicilian pie

Farsumagru

Stuffed veal roulade
(Illustrated below left)

1/4 LB/100 G HAM OR BACON
3/4 CUP/175 G SALSICCIA, DICED
1/4 LB/100 G CACIOCAVALLO
2 CLOVES OF GARLIC
1 TBSP CHOPPED PARSLEY
1 EGG
SALT AND FRESHLY MILLED PEPPER
1 1/4 LBS/600 G PIECE OF VEAL FOR A LARGE ROULADE
2 HARD-BOILED EGGS
A PINCH OF DRIED MARJORAM
4 TBSP EXTRA VIRGIN OLIVE OIL
1 ONION
1/2 CARROT, DICED
1 BAY LEAF
1/2 CUP/125 ML BOUILLON
1 GLASS RED WINE

Dice the ham and cheese, and combine with the diced salsiccia, one crushed clove of garlic, the chopped parsley and the lightly beaten egg to make the filling. Season with salt and pepper.

Carefully flatten the veal with a meat mallet and spread the mixture over it. Slice the hard-boiled eggs and arrange on top of the mixture. Roll up the meat and secure tightly with kitchen string. Sprinkle with marjoram. Heat the olive oil in an ovenproof dish and sauté the veal roulade on all sides. Add the onion, sliced into rings, the diced carrot, bay leaf, and remaining garlic. Pour in half the bouillon and cover. Cook the meat for about an hour in a preheated moderate oven (about 340–350 °F/ 170–180 °C) until tender, basting occasionally with the meat juices. Top up the liquid with more bouillon if necessary.

Place the meat on a warmed platter and keep warm. Put the ovenproof dish back on the burner, pour in the wine, and simmer until the liquid is reduced by half. Remove the bay leaf. Cut the veal roulade into slices, arrange on a warmed platter, cover with the sauce, and serve.

Farsumagru – Stuffed veal roulade

Arancini alla siciliana

Rice balls with ground beef
(Illustrated below center)

2 RIPE TOMATOES
1/2 ONION, DICED
EXTRA VIRGIN OLIVE OIL
1/2 CUP/100 G GROUND BEEF
1 1/2 CUPS/250 G FRESH PEAS
SALT AND PEPPER
1 CUP/250 G RICE
3 1/2 TBSP/50 G BUTTER
1/2 CUP/50 G PECORINO, GRATED
2 EGGS
1/2 CUP/50 G DRIED BREADCRUMBS
OIL FOR FRYING

Blanche and peel the tomatoes, then press them through a sieve. Lightly sauté the onions in olive oil, add the ground beef and peas and cook for a few more minutes. Add the tomatoes, season with salt and pepper, and cook slowly over a low heat.

Boil the rice in salted water, drain and mix with the butter, the grated pecorino, and 1 egg. Allow the mixture to cool, then, taking small amounts at a time, mold into small pockets and fill with the meat mixture. Firmly press the open edges together to seal and shape into balls. Dip the rice balls first in the beaten egg, then in breadcrumbs and fry in hot oil. Drain off any excess fat on a paper towel and serve warm or cold.

CANNELLONI RIPIENI
Stuffed cannelloni
(Illustrated below right)

Serves 4–6

For the dough:
1 GENEROUS CUP/150 G PLAIN FLOUR
1 CUP/150 G DURUM WHEAT SEMOLINA
2 EGGS
1/2 TSP SALT
FLOUR (FOR ROLLING OUT THE DOUGH)

For the filling:
1 LB/500 G BRAISED BEEF WITH A GOOD THICK SAUCE
SALT AND FRESHLY MILLED PEPPER
FRESH NUTMEG
1 CUP/100 G CACIOCAVALLO OR PECORINO, GRATED

5 TBSP OLIVE OIL
2 EGGS

To make the dough for the pasta, mix together the flour and durum wheat semolina and pile in a mound on a work surface. Make a well in the center. Break in the eggs and add salt, then add ⅓ cup plus 1 tablespoon of lukewarm water and knead by hand until the dough is smooth. Cover the dough with a cloth and set aside for 20 minutes. Sprinkle the work surface with flour and roll out the dough to form a flat sheet about ⅟₁₆ inch/2 mm thick. Using a pastry wheel, cut out 10 x 4-inch/10 cm squares. In a large saucepan, bring 6 ½ pints/3 liters of salted water to a boil with 2–3 tablespoons of oil and cook the squares of pasta, a few at a time, for 5 minutes. Remove with a spatula and hold under cold running water for a moment, then leave to drain.

Dice the braised beef into very small pieces or grind briefly in a food processor. Place in a saucepan with half the cooking juices and cook until a thick meat sauce is formed. Season with salt, pepper, and freshly grated nutmeg. Grease a large, ovenproof dish with 3 tablespoons of olive oil. Pile 2 tablespoons of the meat sauce along one edge of a pasta square, sprinkle with grated cheese and roll up the pasta. Do the same with the other pasta squares. Lay the cannelloni side by side in the greased dish. If there is any meat sauce left over, pour this over the top and sprinkle with the remaining cheese. Finally, drizzle 2 tablespoons olive oil over the whole and cook in a preheated oven for 15 minutes at 390 °F (200 °C). Lightly beat the eggs, pour over the cannelloni, and bake for a further 5 minutes until a crisp golden crust has formed.

Canneloni ripieni –
Stuffed cannelloni

Arancini alla siciliana –
Rice balls stuffed with meat

435

PUMPKINS AND ZUCCHINI

The pumpkin family, which incorporates the various varieties of garden pumpkin as well as cucumbers, melons, and zucchini, plays a key role in Italian cooking. Whether it is braised, sautéd, tossed in flour and fried, broiled, stuffed, used as a salad or dessert ingredient, the possibilities are endless. And yet, the fruit got off to something of a shaky start when it was first introduced to Europe by the Spanish Conquistadores. Discovered in South America, it was initially regarded as no more than an ornamental feature for the flower garden – a fate which the pumpkin shared with the tomato and the eggplant. The latter was even given the name *mela insane*, unhealthy apple, from which the Italian word for eggplant *melanzana* is obviously derived.

The word *zucca* was not exactly flattering in meaning either. This word in local dialect meant "dimwit," "quarrelsome person" or "idiot". As is often the case, however, the palate eventually won the day and now that the pumpkin and its relatives have gained acceptance in the kitchen, people have forgotten that they were once viewed so derisively.

Zucchini flowers and other flowers of the pumpkin family can be bought all over Italy. They can be stuffed before frying or else simply sautéd just as they are.

The long, green zucchini, in particular, have had spectacular success – not just in Italy but all over the world where they are regarded by many people as a symbol of Mediterranean cuisine. They can be used in a wide variety of dishes.

ZUCCHINI AL POMODORO E BASILICO
Zucchini with tomatoes and basil

2 LB/1 KG RIPE TOMATOES
2 LB/1 KG ZUCCHINI
4 CLOVES OF GARLIC
1 BUNCH OF FRESH BASIL
OLIVE OIL
SALT

Blanch, peel, deseed, and dice the tomatoes. Wash and dice the zucchini. Peel and mince the garlic and chop the basil. Lightly sauté the garlic in hot olive oil. Add the tomatoes, basil, and cubes of zucchini. Cook over a low heat until the zucchini is cooked but still firm to the bite. Season with salt to taste.

FIORI DI ZUCCA RIPIENI
Stuffed pumpkin or zucchini flowers
(Illustrated left)

2 EGGS
1/2 CUP/50 G FLOUR
12 ZUCCHINI FLOWERS
10 OZ/275 G RICOTTA
A PINCH OF FRESHLY GRATED NUTMEG
1 BUNCH OF CHIVES, SNIPPED
1 EGG, LIGHTLY BEATEN
4 TBSP FRESHLY GRATED PARMESAN
SALT AND FRESHLY MILLED PEPPER
OLIVE OIL

To make the batter, lightly beat the two eggs in a bowl. Add the flour a bit at a time and mix in. Stir in 4 tablespoons cold water to make an even batter. Set aside.
Carefully clean the zucchini flowers, rinsing the outside under running water and removing any insects from the inside of the flower. Carefully pat dry.
To make the filling, combine the ricotta, nutmeg, chives, egg, parmesan, salt, and freshly milled pepper and spoon this mixture into the flowers. Carefully twist the tips of the flowers closed to prevent the mixture falling out.
Heat a generous amount of oil in a large pan. Dip the flowers in the batter and fry one at a time in the hot oil until golden brown in colour, turning occasionally. Drain off excess oil on paper towel and serve.

Assemble the ingredients for stuffing the zucchini flowers.

Lightly beat the cheese, chives, and egg together and season.

Dip the stuffed flowers in the batter and fry.

Use paper towels to absorb any excess oil before serving.

SICILIAN VEGETABLE DISHES

One of the oldest Sicilian recipes is the *Maccu di San Giuseppe*. Despite its Christian-sounding name, this dish was actually brought to Sicily by the Ancient Romans. The *Maccu* is made from dried, hulled lima beans which are mashed during cooking with a wooden spoon. It is said that the word *maccari*, Sicilian dialect meaning "to mash," was derived from this procedure and this led, in turn, to the term "macaroni." If this is true, then *Maccu* is, if nothing else, the etymological forefather of our pasta. It was only later that "San Giuseppe" was added to its name in recognition of the St. Joseph's Day tradition in Siracusa of treating all the poor young women of the town to a plate of *Maccu*.

Another dish with a long, colorful past to its name is *Caponata* - another typically Sicilian dish. Nowadays, the *Caponata* is made exclusively from vegetables, but it originally started life as a fish dish, served in the *caupone*, the taverns around Sicily's ports, and consisted of squid, celery, and eggplants, served with a sweet-and-sour sauce. The most unusual variation of this is *Caponata San Bernardo*: The eggplants are combined with a sauce made from plain dark chocolate, almonds, sugar, vinegar, and toasted breadcrumbs.

CAPONATA
Eggplants with tomatoes and olives
(Illustration top right)

1 LB/500 G EGGPLANTS
SALT
1 LB/500 G ONIONS
4 STALKS/100 G CELERY STALKS
1 CUP/150 G GREEN OLIVES
1 LB/500 G TOMATOES
4 TBSP VEGETABLE OIL
6 TBSP EXTRA VIRGIN OLIVE OIL
FRESHLY MILLED BLACK PEPPER
2 TBSP/25 G SUGAR
7 TBSP WINE VINEGAR
2 TBSP CAPERS

Wash and slice the eggplants, sprinkle with salt and place in a sieve to allow the bitter juices to drain off. Finely dice the onions, blanch the celery and cut into small pieces. Cut the olives in half and remove the stones. Blanch the tomatoes and pass them through a sieve. Rinse the eggplants in cold running water, drain, and pat dry.
Heat the vegetable oil in a skillet and sauté the eggplants on both sides until golden brown. Place on paper towels to remove any excess oil.
Put the olive oil in a saucepan and gently sauté the onions. Add the celery, olives, and sieved tomatoes and season with salt and pepper. Simmer for 5 minutes. Add the sugar, vinegar, capers and eggplant and simmer for a further 10 minutes until the vinegar fumes have evaporated. Leave the vegetables to cool before serving.

MACCU DI SAN GIUSEPPE
Bean paste with fennel

1 LB/500 G DRIED LIMA BEANS
3/4 CUP/100 G DRIED LENTILS
3/4 CUP/100 G DRIED PEAS
5 OZ/150 G DRIED CHESTNUTS
1/2 LB/250 G FENNEL
1 CELERIAC
3 DRIED TOMATOES
1 ONION
SALT AND PEPPER
EXTRA VIRGIN OLIVE OIL

Soak the dried pulses and chestnuts overnight in water. Pour away the water and put the beans, lentils, peas, and chestnuts in a large pan of fresh water. Coarsely chop the fennel and celeriac, dice the tomatoes and onion, and add all these ingredients to the pulses. Season with salt and pepper and cook over a low heat for about 3 hours until it forms a paste
Serve on deep plates, drizzling a few drops of olive oil on each portion, with white bread as an accompaniment.

CAPERS

The hardy and undemanding caper bush can be found all along the Italian coast and grows well on dry, stony soil, or even crumbling old brickwork. Capers are not actually the fruit of the caper bush but its as yet unopened buds.
After being picked in spring – the tiniest buds are best – the capers first have to be made edible. To eliminate their bitter taste, they are placed in vinegar water or brine for several days. Both solutions are also ideal for preserving the buds on a long-term basis. Before being eaten, the capers must be rinsed in order to remove most of the vinegar or salt which would otherwise overpower the other flavors of the dish. The little buds with their distinctive taste go well in salads, tomato sauces, pasta dishes, and vegetable specialties. They are a crucial ingredient of the tuna fish sauce in the famous *Vitello tonnato*. Capers should not be cooked along with the food, however, but should be added at the very last minute, or else they will lose their flavor. The best capers grow on the Aeolian islands and on Pantelleria which lies off Sicily's southern coast.

GOETHE IN ITALY

Towards the end of the 18th century, Johann Wolfgang von Goethe, who loved traveling in Italy, kept a diary recording some of his impressions from his travels in southern Europe. In his *Italian Journey*, the entry for April 13, 1787, tells us about some of the thoughts that occurred to him during his visit to Palermo, about the weather, the culinary specialties and about Sicily's importance in general: "One cannot think of Italy without having a picture of Sicily in your heart: this is the key to everything. One cannot praise the climate enough: it is the rainy season at the moment, but even so, there are breaks in the rain; it is thundering and lightning today and everything is turning very green. Some of the flax is already in bud, the rest is in bloom. The flax in the fields below is such a beautiful shade of bluish-green that it looks as if there are little pools of water in the valleys. There are countless charming sights! … I

tion. Fish are of the best and tenderest. We have also enjoyed very good beef this time even if it is normally not much praised."

Eleven days later, on April 24, during a visit to Girgenti, Goethe observes the local method of pasta making: "Since there are no inns here, a hospitable family made room for us and accommodated us in a raised alcove in a large room. A green curtain separated us and our luggage from the other members of the household, who were preparing pasta in the main room. This was pasta of the finest, whitest and smallest kind, the most expensive kind, which, after first being shaped into long ribbons the length of an arm, were then twisted by nimble young girls' fingers into a spiral shape. We seated ourselves with the pretty children and had the process explained to us. We learned that they were made out of only the best and strongest wheat, *grano forte*. The process is

Johann Heinrich Wilhelm Tischbein, *Goethe in der Campagne,* Oil on canvas, 164x206 cm. Städelsches Kunstinstitut, Frankfurt am Mein.

have as yet said nothing of the food and drink hereabouts despite the fact that this is a matter of some significance. The garden produce is wonderful – the lettuce, especially, is extremely tender and tastes like milk; you can see why the ancients called it Lactuca. The oil and wine are all very good and could be even better if more care were taken in their prepara-

done mainly by hand rather than by machine or mold. They then cooked us the most delicious pasta dish, whilst at the same time regretting that their stores did not include a dish comprising the most perfect of all pastas, a pasta that could not be made by anyone outside Girgenti, indeed anyone outside their own home. This was said to be unparalleled in whiteness and delicacy."

CITRUS FRUITS

If anyone who has been to Sicily is asked Goethe's question "Do you know the land where lemons bloom and grow, where amidst the dark foliage the golden oranges glow," he will answer with a very heartfelt "Yes, of course." No other Italian region has achieved such fame as a result of one single fruit. Even in the Middle Ages, if the citrus fruit was of Sicilian origin, then its quality was guaranteed to be of the best. This provided the island with a reliable source of income.

The Arab poet, Ibn Zaffir, who resided at the court of the Hohenstaufen King Friedrich II, was very fond of extolling the citrus trees in the groves of Palermo: "The trees in Sicily have their heads in the fire and their feet in water." The Arabs were indeed proud of their irrigation methods, which they then bequeathed to the Sicilians when their rule came to an end. Cultivated with the aid of Arab know-how, lemon and orange trees caused a sensation on this Mediterranean island. The original home of citrus fruit is apparently China and Japan in the Far East, although the bitter tasting variety of orange probably stems from India and, along with the citron, was already familiar to the Greeks and Romans. The lemon may also come originally from northern India where it seems to have been known prior to the 8th century B.C.

Thanks to the Arabs, lemon and orange trees with their bitter-tasting fruit became firmly established in Sicily between the 11th and 12th centuries. Five hundred years later, monks planted sweet varieties for the first time. The plains of Palermo proved ideal for growing this fruit and became known from that time on as the *Conca d'Oro*, the golden basin. Cultivation of the mandarin orange, which originated on the island of Samoa, did not begin until the early 19th century. The grapefruit likewise was cultivated for the first time in East India during the same century and, along with the clementine, is still one of the comparatively new fruits to be found in Sicilian citrus groves.

Today, the island supplies 70 percent of Italy's oranges and 90 percent of its lemons. Despite the excellent reputation of its citrus fruit, however, Italy's lemon and orange growers are having to struggle harder and harder to survive. This is because imports from North Africa and other states with lower production costs, not to mention fruit from other European Community countries, keep forcing down the prices.

439

Biondo commune

The "common blond" is one of Sicily's most traditional orange varieties. Because of its numerous pips, however, it is being replaced more and more by the "Ovale" and "Washington navel" varieties.

Ovale

The "oval" with its compact, juicy flesh is good for storing. It ripens late, between April and May.

Sanguigno comune

This type of orange, found all over the island, is harvested from January to April.

Washington navel

This attractive, aromatic and almost seedless variety was introduced from Brazil during the 40s and 50s. It is grown largely around Ribera and Sciacca and can be harvested from November to January.

Tarocco

Blood oranges constitute more than three-quarters of Sicily's entire orange production. Tarocco is a popular, fast-growing variety, which can be cropped from November to January in Catania, Siracusa and Francofonte.

Tarocco dal muso

The Tarocco dal muso is recognizable from its distinctive bell shape. It is a fast-growing variety found mainly in the groves of Francofonte.

Although Sicily produces 90 percent of Italy's lemon crop, the best lemons are said to come from Amalfi in Campania.

Insalata di finocchio ed arance

Fennel and orange salad

2 LARGE RIPE ORANGES
3 FENNEL BULBS
2 SMALL RED ONIONS
JUICE OF 1/2 LEMON
6–8 TBSP OLIVE OIL
1 PINCH OF ENGLISH MUSTARD POWDER
SEA SALT, WHITE PEPPER
3 TBSP COARSELY CHOPPED WALNUTS

Peel the oranges with a sharp knife, removing all the white pith from the flesh and saving the juice. Cut the oranges into segments.
Thinly slice the fennel and onions, setting aside some of the feathery green fennel leaves. Arrange the sliced fennel and orange segments in a fan shape on a large platter which you have already covered with the onion rings.
Mix together the orange and lemon juice, olive oil, mustard powder, salt and pepper, and pour over the salad. Allow to stand for at least 30 minutes before sprinkling finely chopped fennel leaves and chopped walnuts over the salad.

Sanguinello
The Sanguinello is an oval–shaped variety with a pleasantly bitter taste. It is harvested from January to April in Paternò Santa Maria di Licodia, Palagonia, Scordia, and Francofonte.

Valencia
The Valencia orange, which is also used for confectionery, is similar to the Ovale variety.

Moro
This variety has crimson-colored flesh and is grown around Lentini, Scordia, and Francofonte. It is harvested from mid-January to the end of April.

SORBETTO D'AGRUMI DEL SULTANO
Sultan's tropical sorbet

2 CUPS/500 ML MANDARIN JUICE
2 CUPS/500 ML ORANGE JUICE
2 CUPS/500 ML JUICE SQUEEZED FROM RIPE LEMONS
1 CUP/500 ML JUICE FROM GREEN LEMONS
2 CUPS/400 G SUGAR
3/4 CUP RUM

Strain the juices and mix together. Add 2 cups of water and stir in the sugar. Lastly, add the rum. Pour it all into an ice-making machine and leave to freeze.
If you do not have an ice-making machine, pour the liquid into a flat metal tray and place in the freezer for several hours. When the sorbet is half frozen, put it into a well cooled bowl and beat thoroughly. Put it back into the metal tray and return it to the freezer. Repeat this process once or twice more.

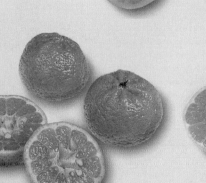

Femminello
This variety of lemon, which is mainly grown in Catania, Siracusa, Messina, and Palermo, constitutes 80 percent of Sicily's lemon crop.

Verdello
Thanks to intensive cultivation, this variety is ready to pick between May and September.

Monachello
The "little monk" is better able to withstand periods of drought than the Femminello variety and is harvested from October to March.

Comune
Comune is a common variety of mandarin orange.

Tardivo Ciaculli
Tardivo Ciaculli is the other type of mandarin in Sicily

MARZIPAN FROM MARTORANA

Sicilians learned the art of confectionery from the Arabs. After the departure of the Muslims, their recipes for sweetmeats were adopted and improved upon in mediaeval monastery kitchens. Luckily, the former occupiers left behind their distillation equipment. This useful apparatus made possible the manufacture of an essence, called "orange flower water," an essential ingredient in the making of marzipan. The pious confectioners pounded almonds in mortars, mixed the result with sugar, cooked the two together in orange flower water, flavored the result with some vanilla and the resulting product was Sicilian marzipan.

Its name comes from the Arabic word *manthaban*, which was originally just the container in which the sweet almond paste was stored. Later, this term was used for measuring the correct ratio of sugar and almonds used in the manufacture of marzipan. So quickly did marzipan become a regular fixture on the tables of kings that Sicilians gave it a fitting nickname: *pasta reale* or royal paste.

The Martorana cloister became particularly famous for producing this specialty. In 1143, George of Antioch, a trusted admiral of Roger II, the first Norman king, had a church built which he handed over to an order of Greek nuns. The nuns lived in a nearby convent where they devoted themselves primarily to producing sugar figurines for All Saints' Day and All Souls' Day. These already famous delicacies were colored with dyes made from roses, saffron, and pistachio. About 50 years later,

Eloisa Martorana built another cloister which was joined to the building belonging to the Greek sisters. The entire complex became known from that time on as "Martorana," the same name that was also given to the sweetmeats. Even after 1435, when the buildings were taken over by Benedictine monks, the name remained the same.

Although the secrets of marzipan making and confectionery made their way into ordinary households during the course of time, the sweetmeats produced in the cloisters retained their special reputation. So high was the demand that the nuns were kept busy round the clock, producing marzipan and other confectionery for special festivals. So much so that in 1575, the religious authorities of Mazara del Vallo were forced to prohibit the local nuns from making it so that they would not be distracted from their religious duties during Holy Week. These gentlemen had not reckoned with such resistance on the part of the holy sisters, however. Passionate confectioners all, they refused to obey the order from the synod, continued to manufacture their *frutti di Martorana,* and created new delicacies. Unfortunately, we have no record of what the Bishop said on the subject of the *minni di Virgine,* maiden's breasts, decorated with tiny glacé cherry halves!

The independent confectioners of Palermo meanwhile put their trust in lucky charms of a more pagan nature and competed with each other to see who would create the best marzipan pig for January 20, St. Sebastian's Day. These appetizing little pigs quickly found their way north across the Alps – today you can buy them in every confectioner's shop, especially at New Year and during carnival time.

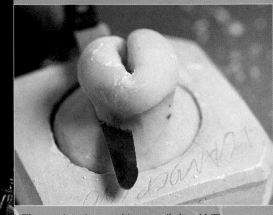

The marzipan is shaped into a fat roll and cut into sections, the size of which depends on the figure to be modeled.

The marzipan is pressed into an oiled mold. The excess marzipan is squeezed together and trimmed off with a knife.

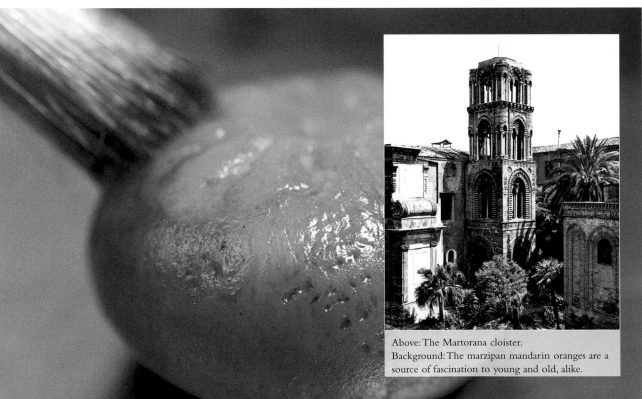

Above: The Martorana cloister.
Background: The marzipan mandarin oranges are a source of fascination to young and old, alike.

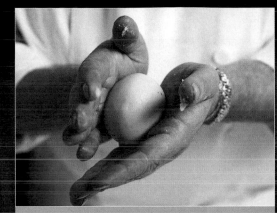

Small amounts of marzipan are rolled by hand into smooth, round balls.

The marzipan fruit has to be left to dry for several days. Once a thin crust has formed, colors can be applied. Fresh marzipan would absorb the color.

Background: Giuseppe Caruso, the pastry chef of the Palermo bar, Italico, holds up a basket full of fresh fruit or are they really marzipan fruits?

WINEGROWING AND MYTHOLOGY

Even in classical times, Sicily was well-known for its agricultural produce. Even before the Greeks, Phoenicians had introduced grape vines from the Middle East to this island where previously only wild grapes had grown. The Phoenicians were followed by Greek settlers who brought with them the latest grape-crushing technology as well as new varieties of grape, such as the Greganico. Greek mythology and its wines also came onto the scene. The cult surrounding Dionysus and his maenads, later called bacchantes by the Romans, began to spread and the poetess, Sappho, expelled from her native island of Lesbos, is also said to have cultivated wine here. Her famous nuptial songs celebrate the bridal pair who, at their marriage ceremony, drink wine out of the same goblet by way of asking for the blessings of Eros and Aphrodite. The

town of Erice, near to present-day Trapani, had a sacred place, a shrine to temple prostitution. As evidenced by large numbers of amphora shards, the priests and priestesses drank wine before the sacrifice. In the days of the Roman Empire, Sicilian wine was regarded as a welcome change from the Falerner wine and it is even claimed, though on no reliable evidence, that Caesar's favorite tipple was Mamertino wine from Capo Peloro.

Even Arab rule had no adverse effect on Sicilian viniculture. Despite the Koran's ban on alcohol, the new rulers not only tolerated the cultivation of the grape but even introduced the technique of distilling wine into alcohol with the aid of a still.

Hidden away in monastery cellars, Sicilians continued to brew secret elixirs which were sold to numerous customers. And yet there was no real need for the abbots to switch to distilling. The church's immeasurable wealth came not least from the vast vineyards in its possession and the monopoly that these gave it in producing and selling wine.

The wines' outstanding reputation soon extended far beyond the island's shores and Sante Lancerio, the cup bearer of Pope Paul III, praised them very highly

indeed in a letter sent to Cardinal Guido Ascanio Sforza in 1559. The star of Sicilian wine cultivation did not begin to set until the Spanish Viceroys took control. Instead of cultivating wine, they grew wheat. It was not until 1773 that Sicily managed to resume its accustomed place in the world of wine. Quite by chance, an Englishman, John Woodhouse, discovered Marsala and helped to make it popular. A further market for the island's wines opened up in 1870 when France's vineyards were so devastated by phylloxera that French vintners had to import wine by the barrel. All too soon, however, the pest crossed the Alps and continued its destruction in far off Sicily. Within a few years all hope of large and continuing profits was destroyed and once again wine cultivation had a hard struggle beginning all over again.

For a long time, Sicilian wine had a difficult time of it on today's world market with cheap mass-produced wines adversely affecting its reputation. Nevertheless, over the past few decades, some wine producers and wineries have managed to develop good quality wines of their own and gradually been able to establish themselves on the Italian market as well as some important foreign markets.

Initiation ceremonies into the mysteries of Dionysus, as depicted on a wall painting in the Villa dei Misteri in Pompeii, around 50 B.C.

THE ROAD TO MODERN WINE-GROWING TECHNIQUES

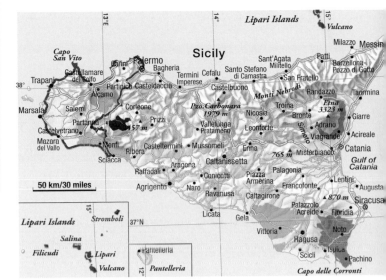

As far as winegrowing is concerned, Sicily is surely one of the most amazing regions in Italy. Not only does it share the lead with Apulia for the extent of its vineyards and the size of its grape harvest – each year 2.4 to 2.6 million U.S. gallons (9 to 10 million hectoliters) of wine are produced from an area extending over 370,000 acres (150,000 hectares) – but for more than a decade, it has been developing its potential as a producer of top-class wines. This is despite the fact that for decades, Sicily produced only the simplest mediocre wines and vast quantities of the popular sweet, sickly Marsala.

The region, whose most distant outposts of Pantelleria and Lampedusa are nearer to Tunisia than Italy, boasts perfect conditions for wine-growing: Barren soil, lots of sunshine, warmth, and low rainfall all conspire to create perfect growing conditions. At the same time, the winegrowing slopes of the central mountain region, which rise up to 3000 feet (900 m), experience sharp swings between

daytime and nighttime temperatures, a factor which helps the grapes develop their fruity flavor. The main area of vineyards is situated in the westernmost province of Trapani, where Marsala, Sicily's most most famous wine, is produced. The countryside on the north and south of the island are also major winegrowing areas, whereas the eastern part is mainly given over to the production of dessert grapes.

Thanks to an enormous improvement in quality, the Sicilian wine industry now boasts a number of outstanding vintners and wineries – and this, despite the fact that only about 120 of the altogether 100,000 or more wine producers bottle and market their product themselves. The main varieties used are not only native grapes such as the white Catarratto, Inzolia, and Grillo or the red Nero d'Avolo and Nerello Mascalese but also so-called "international" varieties such as Cabernet Sauvignon and Chardonnay, which a small number of winegrowers are now turning into some of Italy's most coveted "modern" wines.

Catarratto and Grillo, which are mainly cultivated in the Trapani area and used for Marsala, can also be used for dry, fairly robust white wines. The white Inzolia grape has an even greater potential for quality wine and also does well in higher locations. Malvasia is an ancient Greek variety, or rather a whole family of vine stock with an endless number of different varieties, which can be found in nearly every region of Italy. It

The area between Selinunte and Castelvetrano, to the southwest of Marsala, produces more than 2.4 million U.S. gallons (9 million hectolitres) of wine.

forms the basis for a rare, top-quality dessert wine native to the Lipari islands. Of the native red grapes, it is the Nero d'Avolo, also known as Calabrese, which has the greatest quality potential. This produces a red wine that is both elegant and powerful.

Modern technology is the key word in winegrowing and wine-making. Consequently, extensive winegrowing areas can be seen to have departed from the traditional methods of growing vines where they were kept pruned into bush-type growths and have switched to modern techniques of training vines on wire trellis supports. Similarly, wine-making procedures have witnessed the advent of steel tanks, computers, and cooling systems, by means of which fermentation can be controlled with precision. Many of the top wines nowadays are produced in small, new wooden casks, so-called *barriques*, and these can easily hold their own against the best vintages of Tuscany or the Piedmont.

With regard to the groups of islands surrounding the Sicilian mainland, they have successfully continued

the region's old traditions of sweet wine. Heavy, full wines with powerful bouquets and a rich, sweet flavor are produced here from Malvasia and Zibibbo (Moscato) grapes. As part of the general upturn in the wine industry, the producers of Marsala have also bethought themselves

	Marsala
	Alcamo
	Contessa Entellina
	Menfi
	Etna
	Cerasuolo di Vittoria
	Moscato di Noto
	Malvasia delle Lipari
	Moscato di Pantelleria, Moscato Passito di Pantelleria

of their past glory and now boast a variety of fortified products. The fact that winegrowing in Sicily is becoming a booming industry again has come to the notice of winegrowers and wineries in northern Italy who, for some years now, have been investing heavily on the island. The region's future has only just begun!

SICILIAN WINES

Alcamo
Alcamo or Bianco d'Alcamo is the name given to wines produced from Sicily's largest DOC region covering more than 50,000 acres (20,000 hectares) in the Trapani province. Although this area for a long time produced only fairly run-of-the-mill wine in barrels, a few wine producers have, over the past few years, gained a reputation for some pleasant, fresh new wines. The Catarratto variety of grape, which is fairly neutral in character and is one of the main ingredients of Marsala, is grown in most of the region's vineyards. If its yield is correspondingly limited, it can produce robust, full, dry white wines which are excellent served with fish and antipasto.

Cerasuolo di Vittoria
These red wines from Sicily's southeast corner are produced largely from the native varieties of Frappato – which can also be used on its own – and Calabrese. They are sometimes quite high in alcohol content and the best of them have a pleasant, fruity aroma that some drinkers find reminiscent of sour cherries.

Malvasia delle Lipari
The grapes with this DOC label of origin, which have experienced a dramatic comeback over the past decades, grow on the volcanic slopes of the Lipari islands situated off Messina. A variety of Malvasia and the native Corinto nero form the basis for this delicious dessert wine, the balsamic overtones of which are unmistakable. In its ordinary form, Malvasia delle Lipari has an alcohol content of just 8 percent but it also exists as a 20 percent proof fortified Liquoroso and Passito made from dried grapes. It is good either as an aperitif or dessert wine, depending on which type it is.

Moscato di Pantelleria
The Moscato di Pantelleria, which comes from the island of the same name situated half way between Sicily and Tunisia, is produced from the Moscato di Alessandria grape, known here as Zibibbo. This golden dessert wine, which is only produced in small quantities, has become so popular that the island's winegrowing industry is thriving once more. Like the Malvasia delle Lipari, it is also available as a fortified liqueur version, which can be powerful with an almost oily sweetness.

MARSALA

Marsala wine is often stored for many years in wooden barrels before it is finally bottled. It is then called Fine, Oro or Stravecchio.

In 1770, a storm forced the young Englishman, John Woodhouse, to seek refuge in the port of Marsh-allà. This anchorage with its Arabic name, which roughly means the "port of God", belonged to the western Sicilian town of Marsala. Woodhouse was to make a discovery here that would fundamentally change the world wine market. This ambitious son of a Liverpool merchant had actually been on his way to Mazara del Vallo to purchase soda ash. After almost being ship-wrecked, he now found himself stuck in Marsh-allà while the storms raged. What better way to pass the time than to go and explore the local inns? Sampling the native wine, he soon realized that this was a drink which could easily compare with expensive Spanish and Portuguese sherry or Madeira. Hoping to have his own impressions endorsed, he sent for his betrothed who worked for a wine producer on Madeira. After some intensive sampling, they both agreed about the potential of Marsala wine: It could easily rival Madeira and sherry and thus finally break the Portuguese and Spanish monopoly on fortified wines. Woodhouse faced a fairly difficult task, however. Although Sicilian grapes were easy to obtain and local labor fairly cheap, a three-year trial period followed before the production of Marsala could get fully underway and Woodhouse could send the first shipment back to England where it quickly became popular. It was not longer before Woodhouse had to institute regular shipping runs between Marsala and Liverpool to cope with the growing demand.

After seven hard years, a break-through occurred in the form of a state order. In 1800, Admiral Nelson sent a written commission for 500 barrels of Marsala to be supplied annually to the English Mediterranean fleet based in Malta. Just five years later, His Majesty's navy, under Nelson, won the decisive victory of Trafalgar by destroying the united fleets of Spain and France. From then on, the Sicilian wine became known in England – as well as the rest of the world – as Marsala victory wine.

When the high demand began to lead to a shortage of grapes, Woodhouse had another ingenious idea. In order to encourage more wine production, he began to advance interested farmers the necessary capital. At the same time, he reserved the right to set the prices for any grapes or basic wines supplied. During his long sojourn on the island, he had obviously taken to heart the Sicilian saying *nenti ppi nenti nuddu fa nenti*, nothing comes from nothing. The farmers saw things in a similar light and were only too happy to cooperate with the Englishman.

Other English entrepreneurs tried to cash in on the success of Marsala victory wine. In 1806, Benjamin Ingham, a 22-year-old with an eye for business, arrived in Marsala. In 1812, he opened a new, bigger, and technically better equipped establishment at Lungomare Mediterraneo, situated a decent distance from the Woodhouse stronghold. Ingham knew that he was dependent on the farmers' cooperation so he began his own PR campaign: At harvest time, town-criers traveled all over the winegrowing areas around Marsala giving small-time farmers tips on harvesting intended to improve the quality of the wine. Ingham listed ten points for ensuring quality and some of these are still followed by the region's wine producers to this day.

In 1833, a Sicilian entrepreneur finally took the fate of marsala into his own hands. Using the name of a friend, Vincenzo Florio acquired a vast estate on Lungomare, which bordered Woodhouse's property on one side and Ingham's land on the other. Thus began the unstoppable rise of Marsala Florio S.O.M., with its familiar trademark of a drinking lion. The deeds founding the firm belonging to Vincenzo Florio and

his friend, Raffaele Barbaro, which were signed on October 20, 1834, curiously enough still refer to a Madeira-type wine. Even though it is John Wood-house who is credited with discovering and marketing the wine, it was Ingham and Florio who first trans-formed Marsala into a really marketable product, the demand for which grew year by year. Despite initial difficulties, Florio was gradually able to win over the local grape producers and Marsala's worldwide success was thus guaranteed.

FINE, ORO, AND VERGINE STRAVECCHIO

There are various types of Marsala, some of which – such as the notorious and often inferior quality Marsala all'Uovo – have fortunately gone out of fashion. The varieties which have the lowest alcohol content are the Oro made from white grapes and the Rubino made from red. Cremovo is a variety aroma-tized by various means but the most interesting ones are called Fine, Superiore, Vergine, or Vergine Stravecchio. These wines are up to 18 percent proof and have matured for four, six, or even ten years in the cask before being bottled and sold. Marsala, in its various forms, is ideal to drink either as an aperitif or dessert wine.

Melone cantalupo al Marsala
Cantaloupe melon with Marsala
(Illustrated below)

Serves 2

1 CANTALOUPE MELON
DRY MARSALA, ACCORDING TO TASTE

Cut the melon horizontally through the middle, remove the seeds and excess juice. Place the two halves of melon in suitable dishes into which they fit snugly. Using a melon baller, scoop out balls of melon and return them to the melon halves. Pour over a measure of good-quality, dry Marsala and refrigerate before serving.
Serve as a starter or a dessert.

Scaloppine al Marsala
Veal escalope in Marsala

1 LB/500 G VEAL, CUT INTO SLICES 1/4 INCH/5 MM THICK
FLOUR FOR DUSTING
6 TBSP EXTRA VIRGIN OLIVE OIL OR 4 TBSP/50 G BUTTER
2/3 CUP/150 ML GOOD QUALITY, DRY MARSALA
SALT AND FRESHLY MILLED, BLACK PEPPER

Toss the escalopes in flour, tap off any excess flour. Heat the oil or butter in a large, heavy skillet. Sauté the escalopes one at a time for several minutes on each side. Remove from the pan and set aside.
When all the escalopes are cooked, put them back in the skillet. Pour over the Marsala and season with salt and pepper. Stir for a few seconds. The mixture of wine and flour should coat the meat in a thin sauce.

SARDINIA

S ardinia, the island that lies farthest from the Italian mainland, is an isolated place. Surrounded by emerald green sea, blessed with majestic mountains and fertile plains, criss-crossed by cool mountain streams and clear rivers, this region, which is still relatively unblighted by tourism, must seem like paradise to the visitor – and Sardinians do indeed maintain that God was especially generous when creating their island, providing fishermen and farmers, shepherds and seafarers, all with a place where they could live happily and in harmony with each other.

Sardinia is far from being an "Elysian island," however. Its strategically favorable position has throughout history attracted invaders not just from the Mediterranean region but from even farther afield. Attacked by the Phoenicians and Carthaginians, occupied by the Romans, overrun by the Arabs, a bone of contention between Pisa, Genoa, the popes, Aragon, Austria, and Savoy, the Sardinians had good reason for coining the saying that "all evil comes from across the sea." Even if the comment is nowadays accompanied by a wink, external influences are still regarded with some suspicion. The same attitude applies to unfamiliar faces, but once these islanders are satisfied that the visitor has come, not out of some sinister ulterior motive, but simply to visit and enjoy their captivating island, their legendary hospitality knows no bounds.

However, as stated earlier, there was every reason in times gone by to avoid the proximity of the sea and to withdraw to the safe, mountainous regions of the hinterland which were almost impassable to strangers to the island. As a result, fish and seafood do not traditionally figure in Sardinian cuisine and came into the picture much later. The true original culinary specialties of the island are unmistakably biased toward traditional country dishes. Sucking pig and wild boar roasted on the spit, rustic stews with wild vegetables and hearty beans, *carta da musica*, the dry bread which keeps fresh for long periods, a distinct fondness for fresh herbs such as myrtle and mint – these are all traditional elements of a cuisine which dates back a thousand years and has remained unchanged throughout history in country villages.

Previous double page: A rich catch – typical of the splendid specimens which Luigi Ledda, a Bosa fisherman, takes from Sardinian waters.

Left: Daniele Licheri not only runs the Azienda Mandra Edera holiday farm near Abassanta with his wife Rita, but is also a shepherd and horse-breeder.

SARDINIAN BREAD

Traditional Sardinian dishes were – and in some remote areas still are – based on practical considerations. In the same way that meat was mainly roasted on the spit because the herdsmen were unable to carry heavy cooking equipment around with them, many types of bread were likewise made with the needs of men in mind who often spent weeks on end in lonely mountain regions far away from the possibility of fresh supplies. The bread had to be light in weight with a low moisture content so that it would be less likely to go moldy and, at the same time, be versatile enough to form the basis for a variety of quick, complete meals. *Carta da musica* or *pane carasau*, as it is called in Sardinia, fitted the bill perfectly: The once-baked flat bread could be rolled up and carried in a shepherd's bag and the twice-baked version was practically immune to mold.

Pane fratau is the "filled" version of the *carta da musica*, whereby the crisp rounds of bread are turned into a nourishing meal with diced tomatoes, eggs, pecorino or other cheese, and herbs. Bread was also an important part of the menu of farmers and townsfolk except that they preferred heavier and doughier bread: *moddizzosu-* or *mazzosu-*loaves could weigh up to 22 pounds (10 kilograms).

Whether it is bread for wandering herdsmen or for townspeople, nothing much has changed with regard to the Sardinians' preference for country-style breads made from bread flour, wheat, or barley flour. One look inside local bakeries will dispel any idea that southern Europeans only eat white bread, as is commonly supposed.

Another very popular bread is *ciabatta*, which is now also fairly common north of the Alps. Although *ciabatta* is not really a typical Sardinian bread, there is hardly a bakery – either in Sardinia or the rest of Italy – which does not sell this aromatic wheat bread with its lightly floured, somewhat leathery crust. *Ciabatta* is made from "Grade 0" flour, in other words, not as fine or white as the bread made from "Grade 00" flour, but it does have more bite and flavor. This soft and fairly moist bread has large holes in it which are formed during the six hours in which the dough is left to rise. They give the bread its characteristic appearance.

CARTA DA MUSICA

This distinctive Sicilian bread is actually called *pane carasau*. Its old Sardinian name is becoming increasingly uncommon as visitors from the mainland call it *carta da musica*. These thin almost transparent rounds of bread resemble sheets of parchment-like music manuscript paper and the distinctive sound of these crisp sheets when they are broken also provides the *musica*.

Making *pane carasau* the traditional way is fairly expensive. First of all, a dough is made from durum wheat semolina, wheat flour, yeast, water, and a little salt. This is left to rise for half a day. Then it is kneaded again and left to rise a second time. The dough is then divided into balls and rolled out into wafer-thin rounds. After being left to stand for several more hours, the bread finally goes into the oven. As soon as the rounds of bread balloon up, they are removed from the oven and cut horizontally through the middle. The halved bread circles are then baked a second time until they are a delicious golden brown color.

Because the preparation is so time-consuming, most Sardinians leave it to the baker to make this musical bread. He sells it in stacks of ten or twenty, wrapping his delicate product in paper to protect it.

Carta da musica is a tasty snack just as it is, but it can also be brushed with oil and briefly reheated to make it even crispier. It can also be soaked in water to restore its original elasticity and then made into a type of lasagna by layering it with different fillings in an ovenproof dish. The most popular dish of all must be *pane fratau*. For this, the bread rounds are spread with tomato paste, layered with poached or fried eggs and then sprinkled liberally with grated cheese.

Pane carasau has even made a name for itself in the expensive restaurants of the famous tourist resorts. The bread is broken into pieces, brushed lightly with oil and sprinkled with coarse sea salt – this is as addictive as crackers or crisps. Once you start nibbling – as with *pane carasau* – you can't stop.

Civraxiu
This bread speciality from Cagliari is baked from bread flour. In order to get a smooth, homogenous dough, it must be well kneaded. As soon as it has risen, it is shaped into loaves, each weighing about two pounds (1 kilogram) and baked in a wood oven. Since the method of making it varies from place to place, *civraxiu* comes in strong and soft, thin, and thick versions.

Coccoi pintatus or pintau
The dough for this exceptionally attractive bread is made by mixing bread flour, lukewarm water, and yeast together. It is often decorated with a cross to ensure that it turns out well! It is then shaped by nimble fingers, using scissors, knives, and pastry cutters, into a vast number of figures ranging from plants to animals. You can see fish, birds, little pigs, turtles, roses, and many other things. These small works of art are mainly made for festival days.

Pistoccu
Pistoccu, which, like the *carta da musica*, is a snack for wandering herdsmen, is made from bread flour. The dough, which is mixed only with water, is shaped into small, rectangular loaves which are pierced several times with a fork to prevent air bubbles forming. They are then baked twice in succession. This bread is commonly found in and around Cagliari and the shepherds take it with them on their wanderings as it keeps fresh for long periods. It is often served with tomatoes, basil, oregano, garlic, and a strong local cheese.

Carta da musica
Flat rounds of bread
(Background illustration and below left)

1/2 LB/250 G ALL-PURPOSE FLOUR
1/2 LB/250 G DURUM WHEAT SEMOLINA
WATER
SALT
1 1/2 CAKES/20 G YEAST (IF USING ACTIVE
DRY YEAST, FOLLOW THE MAKER'S
INSTRUCTIONS)

Mix the flour and semolina into a dough
with lukewarm salted water, adding the
water a little at a time. Knead the dough
carefully with your hands and fists until
it is smooth. Add the yeast and continue
to knead until it has been completely
worked into the dough. Finally, cover the
dough with a cloth and leave to rise in a
warm place. Knead thoroughly one more
time and roll out the dough into a thin
round. Bake in a preheated oven at 465°F
(240°C) until the dough balloons.
Quickly remove it from the oven and
cut horizontally through the middle so
that you end up with two large rounds
of bread. Bake these briefly in the oven
for a second time.

CHEESE AND SAUSAGE

CASUMARZU

Casumarzu, the maggot cheese, is a Sardinian specialty which will definitely not appeal to vegetarians. This is basically a harmless, slightly mature pecorino. What causes this cheese to be viewed with suspicion, however, are the residents which are introduced into it. A small channel is bored through the rind on top of the cheese, into which small white maggots are inserted. To keep the new arrivals in tiptop condition, they are initially given a few drops of milk every now and again. After a few days, however, the maggots become accustomed to their new, not unappetizing, surroundings and begin to consume the pecorino from within. Once the maggots have worked their way through the whole cheese, the *casumarzu* aficionado breaks it open and scrapes out the mixture of cheese and maggots onto a chunk of bread.

The **Pecorino sardo**, with its own DOC label, is Sardinia's own version of the same sheep's cheese that is produced in central and southern Italy.

Some Sardinian cheese shops occasionally stock *pecorino romano*. If it has not actually been produced in Rome itself, it is called **Pecorino tipo romano**.

Calcagno is a strong, full-flavored cheese used for slicing, which is made from unpasteurized milk. It can be served as it is or be used in the kitchen for grating.

The milk for **Semicotto** is curdled with calf rennet. As a young cheese, it is quite mild, but it becomes stronger in flavor as it matures.

Pepato is a mild cheese, ideal for slicing, which develops a sharp taste as it matures. Goat rennet is used in its preparation and it gets its name from the peppercorns in its rind.

The **Dolce di Macomer** is a traditional cheese made from cow's milk which comes from Macomer, Sardinia's cheese-making center. This relatively low-fat specialty with its soft, light rind has a pleasantly mild flavor.

Sausage and air-dried salami from Macomer are among Sardinia's main meat products.

MACOMER

Every Sardinian is familiar with the little town of Macomer, which lies halfway between Oristano and Sassari. It is the island's equivalent of Tilsit – the only difference being that Macomer offers the visitor not one, but numerous different cheese specialties. The first cheese-producing cooperative is said to have been founded here back in 1907. This cheese-making industry, therefore, goes back a relatively long way – relatively, insofar as the actual town of Macomer boasts a much longer history. The parish church of San Pantaleo, for example, dates from the 16th century. Although there is no concrete evidence that the congregations of that time were already enjoying locally produced cheese, there seems every likelihood that they were.

Even several hundred years earlier, when Bernhard von Clairvaux dispatched Cistercian monks to Sardinia in the middle of the 12th century to found the Santa Maria di Corte monastery about six miles (ten kilometers) to the west of Macomer, it is likely that cheese products appeared on the monks' menu. In view of such an august past, the hundred or so years of history clocked up by the cheese-producing cooperative seems comparatively short. If measured in human terms, however, around four generations have enjoyed Macomer cheese since 1907. Its continuing popularity is the best proof of the quality which Macomer represents. Cheese is not the only specialty of this small town, however. If you like strongly flavored, air-dried salami or would like to sample other genuine Sardinian sausage varieties, Macomer is well worth a visit.

Left: The Buon Gustaio store in Macomer offers a large selection of cheese and sausage specialties.

PECORINO SARDO

About half the area of Sardinia is used for grazing. The island supports one third of all Italy's sheep, and livestock farming is the main source of income for the 1.6 million or so inhabitants. An offshoot of this is a very productive and renowned milk-processing industry: *Pecorino sardo* is one of the most sought-after cheeses "on the continent," as the Sardinians call the Italian mainland.

Background (left): After the whey has been skimmed off, the curdled milk is removed from the vat and pressed into a cylindrical sieve.

Only sheep's milk is used for *pecorino sardo*.

Calf rennet is added slowly and gradually mixed in.

The whey which has formed is skimmed off.

The curdled milk is pressed into a sieve.

Any remaining whey is drained off and the young cheese takes shape.

The pecorino is carefully rinsed in brine.

465

Gray mullet bottarga

Fishing for gray mullet is especially worthwhile in August and September when the female fish are full of eggs. The precious *bottarga di muggine* is somewhat more expensive than tuna *bottarga*, which is not exactly cheap itself. It is no wonder, therefore, that the female fish is opened with the greatest of care to avoid damage to the coveted eggs. The fish roe is salted to preserve it, and then pressed into characteristic oblong shapes using wooden paddles. After being stored for three to four months in cool, well-aired rooms, the blocks of pressed roe will have matured to a nutbrown or amber color. They are firm but not too dry and have an incomparable aroma of the sea. *Bottarga di muggine* is popular as an antipasto, served in thin slices with fresh white bread. Crumbled into small pieces and mixed with high-quality olive oil, this fine delicacy also makes a wonderful sauce for spaghetti or other long pasta.

There are over a hundred species of gray mullet worldwide. They live in coastal waters and can even be found in brackish water or rivers near the coast.

There are over a hundred species of gray mullet worldwide. They live in coastal waters and can even be found in brackish water or rivers near the coast.

Nowadays, genuine *bottarga di muggine* is only found in selected delicatessens. The fish roe is removed immediately after the fish has been caught and placed in salt.

Muggini in teglia
Gray mullet in oil and vinegar

4 GRAY MULLETS, WEIGHING 3/4 LB/350 G
EACH, READY TO COOK
3–4 TBSP OLIVE OIL, SALT
4 TBSP RED WINE VINEGAR
1 GLASS OF DRY WHITE WINE
FRESHLY MILLED PEPPER

Rinse the mullet under running water, allow to drain and place in a lightly oiled, ovenproof dish. Salt the fish and brush with olive oil, sprinkle with 2 tablespoons red wine vinegar and bake in a preheated oven for about 15 minutes at 320 °F (160 °C). Pour over the remaining vinegar and white wine and cook the fish for a further 15 minutes. Remove the fish, fillet them with the aid of a spoon and arrange on a platter. Pour the cooking juice over the fish and season with freshly milled pepper. Serve with rice or a green salad.

FRESHLY CAUGHT FISH

Sardinian specialties are strongly biased toward the food popular with shepherds and farmers. Sardinians have never felt much affinity with the sea as they are not a seafaring people, although, being an island, it has always been and will always be home to fishermen. Sardinian fish dishes are simple and uncomplicated. They rely on the freshness and delicate flavor of the fish itself, as well they may, since the sea surrounding Sardinia, with the exception of the stretches of coast either side of the major ports, has very high water quality. Wherever you find the tourists recuperating from hectic everyday life on the fine sandy beaches and in the blue-green shimmering, crystal-clear waters of the bays around Sardinia, the fish, too, are similarly happy in their environment. Sardines, gray mullet, and tuna are the most commonly caught fish.

The Sardinian way of preparing the small, flavorsome sardines is just to wash them well without scaling or filleting them. Plenty of salt is rubbed in before they are barbecued. They are so tender that they can be eaten "top and tail." Local cooks have another clever tip for frying fish: semolina produces a much crispier coating than flour. Fresh gray mullet, the best specimens of which come from the waters around Cabras in the west of the island, are also prepared whole. Not only do they have tender, delicately flavored flesh, they are also the source of the valuable *bottarga*, which is rather like caviar and only found in the best delicatessens.

The southern side of the island used to depend on tuna fishing. The large shoals of tuna which existed in the past went to the local factories to be processed into canned fish. Nowadays, however, the conveyor belts have more or less come to a standstill. Tuna from the oceans, especially from Japan, has pushed Sardinian products into the background. A few family concerns, which concentrate on the small-scale manufacture of specialties for the gourmet market, have regained some of their importance over the past few years. *Ventresca*, the belly fat of this big fish, and *tarantello*, a type of salami made from belly fat, popular in Campania, Calabria, and Apulia, are now being rediscovered by chefs and gourmets alike.

SARDINE AL POMODORO
Sardines with tomatoes

I ONION
EXTRA VIRGIN OLIVE OIL
3/4 LB/400 G TOMATOES
GENEROUS 3/4 LB/500 G SMALL SARDINES
SALT
FLOUR

Finely chop the onions and lightly sauté in a little olive oil. Peel and dice the tomatoes, add them to the onions, and continue to cook gently for about 20 minutes.
Wash and drain the sardines, season with a little salt and toss in flour. Heat plenty of olive oil in another skillet, fry the sardines in this and drain on paper towels. Arrange the sardines on a serving dish, cover with the tomato sauce, and leave to stand for 24 hours in the refrigerator. Serve cold.

TONNO ALLA CATALANA
Catalan style tuna fish

4 TUNA FISH STEAKS, EACH WEIGHING ABOUT 5 OZ/150 G
7–8 TBSP EXTRA VIRGIN OLIVE OIL
I CUP/250 ML DRY WHITE WINE
3 RIPE TOMATOES, PEELED AND PURÉED
SALT
I RED ONION, SLICED INTO RINGS
2 POTATOES
1/2 YELLOW BELL PEPPER
1/2 RED BELL PEPPER
1/2 PEPERONCINO

Rinse the tuna fish steaks under running water, then pat dry. Heat 2 tablespoons olive oil in a skillet and sauté the tuna on both sides. Pour in the wine and, after a few minutes, add the prepared tomatoes. Simmer for a further 10 minutes, season with a little salt and then stand in a warm place.

At the Oristano fish market you will find imported fish as well as local Sardinian varieties, including gray mullet from the marshy areas of nearby Cabras — and *bottarga*.

Heat the remaining olive oil in a skillet and lightly sauté the onion rings. Peel the potatoes and dice into small cubes, then add to the onions. Cut the peppers into strips and add these as well. Season with salt and add the half of the peperoncino. Simmer for a short while over a low heat. Arrange the tuna on plates with the vegetables, pour over some of the cooking juices and sprinkle with freshly milled pepper just before serving.

CASSOLA
Fish casserole

Serves 6

4 TBSP OLIVE OIL
I ONION
I CLOVE OF GARLIC
I PEPERONCINO
GENEROUS I LB/500 G TOMATOES
I GLASS DRY WHITE WINE
SALT AND FRESHLY MILLED BLACK PEPPER
1/2 LB/250 G BABY OCTOPUS
2 1/2 LBS/1.3 KG MIXED SEA FISH
6 SLICES OF WHITE BREAD

Heat two tablespoons of olive oil in a large saucepan. Finely dice the onion, garlic clove, and peperoncino and sauté for 5 minutes in the olive oil. Peel the tomatoes, dice, and add to the saucepan. Pour in the wine, season with salt and pepper, and slowly bring to the boil.
Cut the octopus into pieces and sauté in the remaining olive oil for 4 to 5 minutes, then add to the tomatoes in the saucepan and simmer with the lid on for about 30 minutes. Remove the bones from the sea fish, cut into pieces, add to the saucepan and allow to simmer for about 15 minutes. Toast the bread or bake it in the oven, arrange each slice on a deep plate, and pour over the fish casserole.

FISH PREPARATION

Round fish

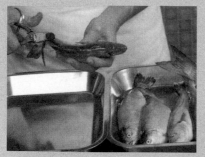

Starting from the tail, remove all fins and any barbels with a kitchen knife.

Carefully trim the tail fin to make a perfect "fish-tail" shape.

Holding the fish by its tail, remove any scales with a fish scaler or a sharp knife.

Lift the gill flap and, using a small kitchen knife, loosen and carefully remove the gills.

Partially clean the fish through the gill opening, taking care not to damage the head or body.

Make a deep 1-inch/2–3-cm opening in the stomach cavity from the tail toward the head to clean out the rest of the fish.

Thoroughly rinse the cleaned fish inside and out under running cold water.

Drain the cleaned fish and carefully pat dry with paper towels.

Filleting salmon

Cut through the middle of the salmon just above the backbone.

Using a sharp knife, remove the skeleton together with the head.

Cut away any bones or fatty meat on the upper side.

Remove any small bones with tweezers.

Carefully remove the skin with a flat knife.

Finally, remove any remnants of skin or fatty meat.

UTENSILS USED IN FISH PREPARATION

Oyster tongs with curved grips (tenaglia Inox per ostriche)
These tongs are also useful for opening up crabs and lobsters.

Heavy cast-iron skillet (padella in ferro)
Fish can be cooked without oil in this non-stick skillet.

Heavy oval cast-iron skillet (padella in ferro nero ovale)
This is designed for cooking plaice and other flat fish.

Tweezers for removing bones (molla levalische)
These are useful for removing any bones left in the filleted fish.

Scaling knife with compartment to collect the scales (squamapesce)
The scales can be scraped off without getting sprayed all over the kitchen.

Scaling knife (squamapesce)
Only large fish like gray mullet or carp are scaled. Others have scales which are too small to be removed.

Sea urchin tongs (tenaglia per ricci di mare)
These tongs can be used to cut a sea urchin in half without injuring yourself on the sharp spines.

Lobster crackers with tweezers (pinza per astice)
Once the claws have been broken open, the meat can be removed with the tweezers.

Lobster crackers (pinza per astice)
Lobster crackers are used to break open the strong shell of the claws to expose the delicious meat inside.

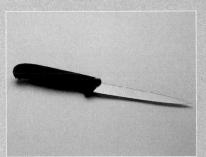

Deep-frying thermometer (termometro per frittura)
The temperature of the oil is important in deep frying.

Flexible spatula (spatola flessibile)
This is a useful kitchen utensil for turning the fish without it disintegrating.

Filleting knife with wooden handle and flexible blade (coltello per filettare)
This utensil is essential for filleting the fish cleanly.

Filleting knife (coltello per filettare)
This knife can be used to open up shellfish.

ROCK LOBSTERS

There is only a small part of Sardinia that is renowned for its rock lobsters: namely, a strip of west coast, stretching from Capocaccia in the north, through Alghero, down to Bosa in the south. Here are found a wealth of delicious fish and a wealth, too, of rock lobsters which cling to the picturesque cliffs.

Capocaccia itself, surely one of the most beautiful spots of the Mediterranean, is a paradise for anyone looking for rock lobsters or sea urchins. Alghero, the main town of this bay, is likewise a real jewel where the blue of the sea meets the gold of the chalk cliffs; Bosa, in turn, with its colorful little houses, is a picturesque fishing village. This corner of the island seems more like Catalan than Sardinia in atmosphere. This is because a thousand years ago this area around Alghero was conquered by Catalonia invaders. Whereas the Sardinians are traditionally a pastoral folk and the Sardinian diet does not lean toward the sea and its inhabitants, the Catalans from Alghero – known as Barcelloneta – Bosa, and Capocaccia have been fishermen since time immemorial and had always lived in close contact with the sea. Nowadays, fish is an important part of Sardinian cuisine.

Rock lobsters are traditionally caught with special nets, known as *nasse*. These are long nets drawn over a structure – formerly made from rushes, but nowadays constructed from wire – to make a tunnel. The rock lobsters swim into the wide opening, which eventually narrows into a funnel shape, lured in by small calamari bait. In days gone by, the fishermen used to tie the *nasse* containing the trapped shellfish to the boat, thus ensuring that the catch would remain alive and fresh until it was sold. Nowadays, however, modern ships have refrigeration equipment and the traditional methods of keeping the catch fresh have long since been replaced.

In Alghero, rock lobsters are prepared in many different ways. What to us is a rather expensive delicacy, was to the fisherfolk of Alghero a staple food, so much so that they sometimes wearied of it. It became imperative in Alghero kitchens to introduce some variety into the monotonous diet of rock lobsters – and anyone who could afford it, dished them up in a stew, enhanced by precious potatoes and vegetables, considered great delicacies.

Rock lobsters can be caught in fish-traps or nets. Here, Marco Sotgiu, is carefully hauling in the net, hoping for a catch.

To avoid damaging the catch, the net, up to 1 mile/1.5 km in length, is wound in over a spool (see also background illustration).

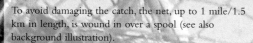

Skilled, experienced hands untangle the lobsters, which can weigh up to 1–1¼ lbs/400–600 g, from the net without damaging it.

Freshly caught rock lobsters are a delicacy. They are kept in water tanks at the market or fish counter until sold.

HOW DO YOU TELL WHETHER SEAFOOD IS REALLY FRESH?

The same rule that applies to fresh fish also applies to the sometimes very delicate and easily spoiled seafood, namely always buy it from a reliable source. Even then, it does no harm to check the merchandise.

Bivalves must always be firmly closed. Even a tiny gap between the two halves of the shell indicates that the creatures have dried out and spoiled after being caught. Any open shells should be thrown in the garbage, not in the cooking pot, as should any specimens that float to the surface in a bowl of water or do not open up during cooking.

Crabs, lobsters, or shrimps should have their shells intact, feel heavy, and smell fresh. Your nose is a reliable guide in this respect. The slightest hint of an unpleasant smell should make you wary. Never ever buy "fishy" smelling seafood. It is a sign that the fish is not fresh.

May is the best season for catching lobsters off the Sardinian coast. This prized catch does not need sophisticated preparation as its delicious meat already has a wonderful flavor of the sea of its own. Rock lobsters are delicious barbecued or baked in the oven with olives, salt, pepper, and rosemary, and need only a short cooking time.

Scampi a zuppetta
Scampi with tomato sauce

2 LBS/1 KG SCAMPI
1 ONION, DICED
1 GARLIC CLOVE, MINCED
4–5 TBSP EXTRA VIRGIN OLIVE OIL
2 BAY LEAVES
1 SMALL PIECE OF PEPERONCINO
1/2 CUP/100 G TOMATO SAUCE
SALT
1 GLASS OF DRY WHITE WINE
1 TBSP CHOPPED PARSLEY

Halve the scampi lengthwise and wash thoroughly under running water. Lightly sauté the onion and garlic in olive oil and add the bay leaves and finely chopped peperoncino. Pour in the tomato sauce and simmer for a few minutes over a low heat before adding the scampi and a little salt to taste. Pour in the wine and simmer for a few minutes, then add a little water and simmer with the lid on for about 10 minutes. Arrange the scampi on a plate, pour over some of the cooking juices, and garnish with the parsley.

Aragosta al forno
Baked rock lobster
(Illustrated below)

1 ROCK LOBSTER, ABOUT 2LBS/1 KG IN WEIGHT
1/2 CUP/50 G FLOUR
4 TBSP/100 G BUTTER
1 TBSP VEGETABLE OIL
SALT AND PEPPER
1 SPRIG OF ROSEMARY
1 GLASS OF DRY WHITE WINE

Halve the lobster lengthwise and remove the intestine, which runs from the tail end to the rump. Wash under running water, dry on paper towels and dust with flour.

Heat the butter and oil in a ovenproof dish. Add the lobster, season with salt and pepper and sauté on both sides. Add the rosemary, pour in the wine, and cook in a preheated oven for ten minutes at 350 °F (180 °C).
Serve immediately with the cooking juices.

Spaghetti all'aragosta
Spaghetti with rock lobster
(Illustrated right)

1 SMALL ROCK LOBSTER, ABOUT 1 LB/500 G IN WEIGHT
3–4 TBSP EXTRA VIRGIN OLIVE OIL
4 GARLIC CLOVES, MINCED
1 ONION, DICED
4 BAY LEAVES
1 GLASS OF DRY WHITE WINE
1/2 PEPERONCINO, GRATED
1 TBSP CHOPPED PARSLEY
1 CUP/200 G TOMATO SAUCE
14 OZ/400 G SPAGHETTI
SALT

Halve the lobster lengthwise and remove the intestine, which runs from the tail toward the rump. Cut the meat into small pieces, removing the shell where possible.
Heat the olive oil in a saucepan and sauté the onion and garlic together. Add the lobster meat and the bay leaves and sauté. Pour in the white wine, the grated peperoncino, chopped parsley and tomato sauce and simmer for 30 minutes over a low heat.
Cook the spaghetti in plenty of salted boiling water until *al dente*, drain into a bowl, and combine with the lobster mixture. Serve hot.

Calamari ripieni –
Stuffed squid

SEAFOOD

A wide variety of seafood can be found along the Sardinian coast which boasts a total length of 830 miles (1340 kilometers) in all. You will find crabs and shrimp everywhere and even a novice fisherman can catch the delicate octopus – he virtually only needs to dip his hand in the water to do so. The trattorias invite visitors to the island to sample delicious mussels from Marceddi and the squid season is a must for seafood lovers. Artificial breeding grounds for common mussels and, to a lesser extent, oysters produce top quality seafood which is a crucial feature of a typical Sardinian *Antipasto misto di mare.*

CALAMARI RIPIENI
Stuffed squid

1 3/4 LBS/800 G FRESH EQUAL-SIZED SQUID
JUICE OF 1 LEMON
SALT
2 EGGS
1 CUP/50 G BREADCUMBS
2 ANCHOVIES, CUT INTO SMALL PIECES
1 GARLIC CLOVE, MINCED
1 TBSP CHOPPED PARSLEY
1/2 CUP/30 G PECORINO, GRATED
PEPPER
2 TBSP/30 ML OLIVE OIL

Remove the ink sac, innards, and head from the squid. Wash and pat dry. Cut the tentacles into small pieces and cook in salted water, to which the lemon juice has been added, for about 15 minutes, then drain. Place the tentacles in a bowl with the eggs, breadcrumbs, anchovies, garlic, parlsey, and cheese. Season with salt and pepper and mix thoroughly. Stuff the squid with this mixture and secure the openings with a skewer or kitchen string. Place them on a greased baking sheet and bake in a preheated oven for about 20 minutes at 320 °F (160 °C). Leave to cool, then cut into ¾-inch/2-cm slices and serve.

FRUIT AND VEGETABLES

The fertile plains of Sardinia are ideal for growing fruit and vegetables. Every ingredient used in Mediterranean cooking is grown in small plots and fields, be they large or small, commercial or private. Even in the heart of towns, you can stumble upon hidden plots, surrounded by high walls. If you do succeed in getting a peep through the securely bolted wooden or iron door, you will glimpse a shady, cool, well-watered garden which supplies its proud owner with figs, oranges, lemons, cherries, plums, pomegranates, melons, chestnuts, hazelnuts, and also almonds.

No one actually needs to cultivate prickly pears, a fruit popular all over Sardinia, since these fleshy-leaved cacti grow wild by the wayside almost everywhere. If you want to pick any, however, you need to go armed with gloves. It is inadvisable to stand on a wobbly ladder when picking the fruit at the top for a tumble into this prickly plant is not one of the more enjoyable experiences in a gourmet's life.

Pomodori ripieni –
Stuffed tomatoes

SARDINIAN – A LATIN LANGUAGE

Est tundu e non est mundu,
est rubiu e non est fogu,
est birde e non est erba,
est abba e non est funtana.
(su forastigu)

Even if you paid only scant attention during Latin lessons at school, you can see from this old Sardinian riddle that this is a Latin-based language *par excellence*. You might almost think you were hearing a Roman from Ancient Rome. According to linguistic researchers, Sardinian is not just a dialect of Italian, but a language in its own right which, to this day, is still closely related to Latin. Words have been retained in Sardinian, for example, which have long since become obsolete in Italian in favor of other expressions.

"House" is *domus* in Latin, *domu* in Sardinian and *casa* in Italian. The word for "door" is *janua* in Latin, *janna* in Sardinian, but *porta* in Italian. Similarly, the word for "large" likewise demonstrates the greater Latin bias of Sardinian compared with Italian: *magnus* in Latin, *mannu* in Sardinian, and *grande* in Italian.

For all non-Latin students, here is the translation of the riddle – with the answer, of course:

It is round, but it is not the earth,
It is red, but it is not fire,
It is green, but it is not grass,
It is water, but it is not a spring.
(Answer Watermelon)

Minestra di piselli con ricotta –
Pea soup with ricotta

Sardinian vegetable gardens are fully on a par with fruit as far as diversity is concerned. Artichokes are grown here; varieties such as the thornless Violetto di Provenzo and Violetto di Toscana or the thorny Spinoso sardo. The latter is particularly tender with a delicately pleasant flavor and is even shipped in large quantities to the mainland. Along with the artichoke, its relative the cardoon is also cultivated successfully on Sardinia. Over the past few decades, tomatoes have likewise become one of Sardinia's national products and have found their way to the markets of Turin and Milan. The fleshy, juicy, almost seedless fruit tastes exceptionally good and has a fine, smooth skin. Generally speaking, Sardinian vegetables do seem to develop a bit more flavor than their counterparts elsewhere. Many traditional salad recipes require only the addition of salt, since an oil and vinegar dressing is usually not necessary. Celery has so much flavor that it has to be used sparingly so as not to overpower the main dish. Radishes (particularly the long Arreiga variety) go well with a joint of meat – and only require a sprinkling of salt. Peas are particularly tender and juicy. The eggplants are just as good as those from Calabria and beans easily stand comparison with those from Apulia. Many herbs, such as the saffron crocus, mint, rosemary, basil, garlic, sage, bay, and marjoram also grow well here.

Pomodori ripieni
Stuffed tomatoes
(Illustrated above left)

4 LARGE, FIRM TOMATOES
2 EGGS
1/2 CUP/60 G PECORINO, GRATED
2 CUPS/100 G FRESH BREADCRUMBS
1 TSP SUGAR
SALT AND PEPPER
A PINCH OF NUTMEG
EXTRA VIRGIN OLIVE OIL

Wash the tomatoes, remove the tops, core, and deseed. Lightly beat the eggs in a bowl and add the grated pecorino, breadcrumbs, and sugar. Season with salt, pepper, and a pinch of nutmeg and mix together well. Fill the tomatoes with the mixture and replace the tops.
Put the tomatoes in an oiled pan and bake in a preheated oven for about 30 minutes at 320 °F (160 °C).

Tortino di carciofi
Artichoke gratin

6 ARTICHOKES
JUICE OF 1 LEMON
4 EGGS
3–4 TBSP EXTRA VIRGIN OLIVE OIL
3 TBSP CHOPPED PARSLEY
1/2 CUP/50 G GRATED PECORINO OR GRANA
SALT AND PEPPER
BUTTER
BREADCRUMBS

Remove the tough outer leaves of the artichoke. Cut the tips off the remaining leaves and cut the artichokes into thin slices and place in a bowl containing the lemon juice and some water. In a second bowl, lightly beat the eggs and olive oil together. Add the parsley and cheese and season with salt and pepper. Grease an ovenproof dish and sprinkle in the breadcrumbs. Drain the artichokes, pat dry, and spread

Flavor-filled vegetables and garden fresh fruit continue to play a major role in Sardinian cooking. Since every housewife needs fresh supplies of these every day, the business of shopping is organized very simply – as it is all over the Mediterranean world. People shop either at the market or a nearby store. If you suddenly remember that you are short of an ingredient, you can always get it from a traveling tradesman by the roadside.

out in the dish along with the egg mixture. Sprinkle with more breadcrumbs and bake in a preheated oven for about 30 minutes at about 320 °F (160 °C). Cut the gratin into slices and serve warm or cold.

Minestra di piselli con ricotta
Pea soup with ricotta
(Illustrated below left)

1 LARGE ONION, FINELY DICED
3–4 TBSP EXTRA VIRGIN OLIVE OIL
4 LBS/2 KG FRESH PEAS
2 TBSP TOMATO PASTE
SALT
1/2 LB/200 G SMALL PASTA
8 OZ TUB/200 G RICOTTA

Lightly sauté the onions in olive oil. Shell the peas, add them to the onions, and sauté for about 15 minutes, stirring occasionally with a wooden spoon. Add the tomato paste and a little water. Season with salt and simmer for a further 20 minutes. Add the pasta and cook with the lid on until they are firm to the bite.
Crumble the ricotta onto deep plates. Pour the soup over the ricotta and stir together.

Favata
Bean stew

1/2 LB/250 G DRIED BEANS
1 ONION
1/2 STICK OF CELERY
1 CARROT
1/2 LB/250 G SAVOY CABBAGE
1–2/250 G PIG TROTTERS AND RIND
1/2 LB/200 G FAIRLY OLD SALSICCIA
1 VERY LOOSELY FILLED CUP/40 G DRIED TOMATOES
1 GARLIC CLOVE, CRUSHED
1 BUNCH OF DILL
SALT
TOASTED SLICES OF BREAD
GRATED PECORINO

Soak the beans overnight in water. Next day, put these into a large saucepan with about 12 cups/3 liters of water. Dice the vegetables and add to the beans along with the meat, tomatoes, and garlic. Cook for about 40 minutes over a low heat. Then, add the dill, season with salt and continue to cook until the beans are done. This bean stew improves in flavor if it is allowed to stand overnight. It should then be reheated and poured over pieces of toasted bread arranged on deep plates. Sprinkle with grated pecorino and serve.

CAKES, CANDIES, AND COOKIES

Sweetmeats are very appropriately named in Sardinia for they really are extremely sweet. Different types of sponge and pastry, themselves already sweetened with honey or sugar and including a variety of ingredients, such as almonds, mixed spices, yeast, or marzipan, are used for the bases of little delicacies. This decorative confectionery, in the shape of cubes, balls, diamonds, or even animal and human figures, is similar to French *petits fours* and is covered with thick glacé icing or marzipan and decorated with candied fruit or sugar pearls in all colors of the rainbow – including real gold and silver.

Sardinian birthday cakes from the local bakery can also be wonderful works of art. Layers of sponge are liberally soaked in schnapps or other spirits before being alternately layered with sweet crème patisserie or cream. The color of the icing depends on who is celebrating the birthday: Adults get a white or pale lemon cake, while girls will find a pink and boys a blue creation to marvel at among their gifts. Cakes with an alcoholic content, however, are reserved exclusively for the adults. It will almost certainly have "Happy Birthday" written in icing on top. It is not only birthday cakes that are reserved for special occasions, however. The other *dolci* are likewise kept mainly for special events, but since even a neighbor dropping in can constitute such an occasion, some excuse can always be found for bringing out these sometimes costly sweet delights.

Sardinian confectioners are not only famous for their candies but also produce various kinds of small pastries which are sold in every bar, especially around breakfast time. These snacks of puff or yeast pastry are freshly baked every day and are available with a custard filling. Another very popular type of cookie is the so-called *ciambelle*, a cookie the size of a saucer, which is decorated in the middle with a dollop of bright red jelly. Anyone who does not trust the products from their local bakery can take their custom to a nearby convent: Even today it is quite common for people to buy their confectionery from convent bakeries. Many compulsive candy eaters would go so far as to say that the nuns, who depend on the income to keep their convents going, still bake the best *ciambelle*. Unfortunately, there is rarely an opportunity to compliment these pious confectioners on their art, since many Sardinian nuns belong to enclosed orders and maintain a strict vow of silence. Even the sale of the goodies is conducted in silence. Anyone wanting to buy cookies must knock at a certain door or window, which is opaque, naturally. The money is then placed in a sort of two-sided hatch. Once the outer door is closed, the nuns open up the inner door, collect the money and replace it with fragrant *ciambelle*, attractively wrapped in snow white paper and usually still warm from the oven. Only when the inner door is heard to close again may the outer door be opened and the delicious cookies removed. The very first bite will be enough to convince you that this silent purchase was definitely worth it.

AMARETTUS
Almond macaroons

1 LB/500 G SWEET ALMONDS
3 OZ/80 G BITTER ALMONDS
3–4 EGG WHITES
2 CUPS/500 G SUGAR
ALL-PURPOSE FLOUR

Soak the almonds for a while in boiling water, then peel and chop very finely. Whisk the egg whites until stiff, add the sugar and almonds and mix in well. If necessary, add 1 to 2 tablespoons of flour to make the mixture a little firmer. Shape small, light balls from the mixture and place on a baking sheet lined with waxed paper. Bake the macaroons until golden in a preheated oven for about 10 minutes at 300 °F (150 °C).

TORTA DI MANDORLE
Almond cake

4 EGGS
3/4 CUP/150 G SUGAR
1/2 CUP/50 G FLOUR
1/4 LB/100 G ALMONDS
2 1/2 LEVEL TSP BAKING POWDER
1 TSP VANILLA ESSENCE
GRATED ZEST OF 1 LEMON
1 TBSP BUTTER
FLOUR FOR DUSTING
CONFECTIONERS' SUGAR

Separate the egg yolks from the whites. Whisk the yolks with the sugar until frothy, then add the flour, the peeled and finely chopped almonds, baking powder, vanilla essence, and lemon zest. Whisk the egg whites until stiff and carefully fold in to the mixture. Grease a cake pan with butter and dust with a little flour. Pour the mixture into the pan and bake for about 40 minutes in a preheated oven at 350 °F (180 °C). Tip the cake out of the pan and leave to cool. Serve on a cake platter, liberally sprinkled with confectioners' sugar.

SEBADAS
Cheese ravioli with honey

1 1/3 CUPS/200 G DURUM WHEAT SEMOLINA
4 TSP/20 G SHORTENING (OR MARGARINE)
SALT
4–5 TBSP EXTRA VIRGIN OLIVE OIL
2 OZ/60 G FRESH CHEESE (CACIOTTA SARDA)
1 TBSP ALL-PURPOSE FLOUR
2 LEVEL TBSP HONEY

Mix the semolina with the shortening, a little water, salt, and one tablespoon of olive oil to make a soft, smooth dough. Roll out the pastry very thinly and cut out circles measuring about 2½–3 inches (6–7 cm).
Cut the fresh cheese into pieces and add to a saucepan with some water and one tablespoon of flour. Melt over a low heat until the mixture is thick and creamy. Drop a small amount of melted cheese onto half of the dough circles, using the remaining half as lids. Press the edges together firmly and fry in hot olive oil. Drizzle honey over the *sebadas* and serve hot.

GATTÒ AND OTHER WORKS OF ART

The festival calendar inspires Sardinian confectioners to greater and greater heights of achievement. Every year, a *gattò* is produced for the festival in honor of the local saint. This is more than just a confection of almonds and sugar – it is almost an architectural work of art. Great efforts are made to reproduce in cake form the town's main church or the leading convent and this scale-size replica is given pride of place at the celebrations. Nor would carnival time be complete without the saffron yellow, deep fried *zipulas*. Sumptuous cakes, as well as modest quark or ricotta tartlets called *pardulas*, are traditional features of the Easter table. All Saints' Day is an occasion to serve colorful confectionery and at Christmas and New Year, every region creates its own individual candy specialties.

Bianchini

Pardulas

Amarettus

Pabassini

Aranzadas

Pistoccheddus

Gueffos

Pastissus

WINEGROWIN ON THE SUN- SHINE ISLAND

Situated just 125 miles (200 kilometers) from the Italian mainland and on the same latitude as Campania and Basilicata, Sardinia, boasts one of the oldest wine industries in the country. In the course of history, it has been occupied by Byzantines, Arabs, and Catalans and the Spanish influence on wine cultivation is still evident to this day. The most important grape varieties in Sardinia, such as Cannonau and Carignano, originate from the Iberian peninsula. Winegrowing in Sardinia, far more so than in the rest of Italy, is dominated by large cooperatives of growers.

Apart from these, there are just a few wineries and a handful of talented vintners who have achieved a degree of success, both nationally and internationally. A large proportion of the island's wine production is still for domestic consumption or sent for blending with other wines on the mainland.

Only a few of Sardinia's DOC wines, therefore, can really be classed as quality wines, including, as mentioned above, Cannonau di Sardegna, the Vermentino di Gallura, Vernaccia di Oristano as well as Carignano del Sulcis.

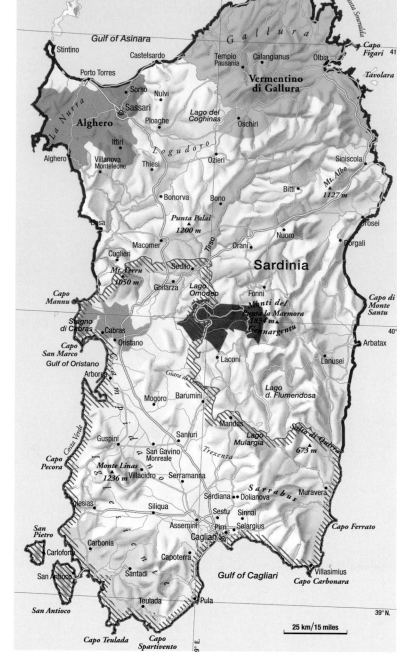

- ▣ Cannonau di Sardegna, Malvasia di Cagliari, Monica di Cagliari, Moscato di Cagliari, Vermentino di Gallura (DOCG)
- ▨ Moscato di Sorso-Sennori Alghero
- ▢ Nuragus di Cagliari
- ▨ Giro di Cagliari
- ▨ Vernaccia di Oristano
- ▨ Mandrolisai
- ▨ Carignano del Sulcis

Cannonau di Sardegna

In its Spanish homeland, the Cannnonau, sometimes written Cannonao, is known as Garnacha. This is the second most common variety of grape in the world and covers 20 percent of Sardinia's grape-growing area. It forms the basis of many a famous Spanish wine, such as the Rioja. It has also become one of the main grapes grown in southern France – under the name of Grenache – where it is also used in the production of many excellent Châteauneuf-du-Pape wines. It can also be found here and there around Maremma on the Tuscan coast, where it is called Alicante. It produces deeply-colored, strong, full-bodied red wines which are also popular for mixing with other varieties, like the Cabernet Sauvignon, for example. The best Cannonau wines go well with roast meat and game dishes and are produced in the province of Nuoro in eastern Sardinia.

Vermentino di Gallura

The island's best Vermentino, a lively fresh white wine, which is an excellent accompaniment to simple fish dishes, comes from the Gallura province in the northern tip of Sardinia. This grape is also widely cultivated on the neighboring island of Corsica and in the Liguria region as well as in southern France, where it is known as Rolle. The best results are really only obtained if the winegrower is meticulous about restricting the yield – a crucial factor in producing flavor-intensive wine.

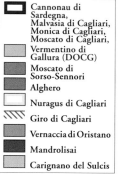

Carignano del Sulcis

The Carignano, known as Carinena or Marzuelo in Spain and Carignan in southern France, is primarily a simple mass-produced wine without much character or distinguishing features. In Sardinia, however, it can, in the right hands, produce some interesting wines, which can be seductive with their lingering bouquet and round, full flavor.

Monica, Vernaccia, and Malvasia

In addition to several native grape varieties, Sardinia also grows many unusual types of some of the more widely cultivated Italian vines. These include the Monica (M. di Cagliari or M. di Sardegna), a dry red with an intense bouquet, the Vernaccia (V. di Oristano), which produces strong, dry, white wines and can also be used in a kind of liqueur, similar to sherry, as well as the Malvasia.

IL VINO DELLO ZIO

Even up to 20 years ago, *il vino dello zio*, in other words, wine made by your winegrowing uncle – and nearly every family had one among its relatives – was still what Italians drank as an everyday wine. You brought it home with you in a wicker bottle from a visit to your relatives and if you lacked the necessary *zio*, uncle, or *nonno*, grandfather, in the family, then you simply took your empty bottle to the wineshop round the corner or went to the nearest *cantina sociale*, one of the numerous cooperatives, armed with a plastic canister or wicker basket, and filled this up for a few lire from large storage tanks.

In those days, cheap wines did not afford much enjoyment, however. Badly made from inferior grapes, they frequently did not withstand the long journey back from holiday and by the time they reached home, had a distinct vinegary taste and a similarly unappealing bouquet. By and large, only a sumptuous family meal in the countryside or a sunny day on the beach in holiday mood could make them reasonably palatable to most people.

The picture began to change somewhat in the eighties. As the production of top quality wines began to increase throughout Italy, Italian wine drinkers became correspondingly more demanding. Holidays were no longer spent exclusively on the Adriatic or Riviera, but people began instead to explore the fascinating world of foreign travel. Young Italians, in particular, returned home from increasingly exotic destinations with newly discovered tastes and higher expectations in wine drinking.

It is true that even today, a large proportion of everyday wine, especially in the less renowned winegrowing areas of Italy, is still collected in canisters from the filling point at the nearest *cantina sociale*, as is also the practice in France, Germany, and elsewhere in the world. During the past two decades, however, Italy has developed a really distinguished viniculture. Fine, perfectly made wines from best-quality grapes, which are bottled in modern designer bottles and sold in elegant stores and restaurants at uniformly steep prices, have taken the place of the *vino dello zio*, once the Italians' everyday tipple.

The Cantina Sociale della Vernaccia in Oristano was founded in 1953. It has always been the winery's aim to combine the traditional hand methods of Vernaccia production with up-to-the-minute winemaking techniques – the result is a high-quality DOC wine.

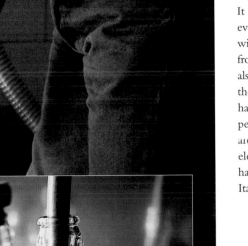

The large, bulbous Vernaccia bottles used in Oristano resemble the wicker bottles once used to collect wine from the *cantina sociale*.

Left: The Vernaccia di Oristano is one of the best Sardinian DOC wines. Here we see Giuseppe Atroni of the Cantina Sociale della Vernaccia tapping the wine straight from the stainless steel tank.

479

WATER

The interior of Sardinia has a wealth of high mountains and unspoilt landscapes. The many mountain streams are sources of clean, clear drinking water for which there is widespread demand.

Even though nowadays a large amount of spring water is bottled and sold in supermarkets with a laboratory analysis on the label, some Sardinians still like to go, or rather drive, to "fetch water," in other words, they take their own containers to fill from accessible streams or springs. Since some spring water is said to have special curative properties, people are skeptical as to whether the supermarket water possesses the same powers.

If you have the time and suitable transport, you can collect your own drinking water fresh from the famous mountain springs. Many people mistrust the plastic bottles that are widely sold in the supermarket.

San Leonardo has long been one of the most popular and frequented Sardinian springs. The local authorities have even had to improve the access road to the spring.

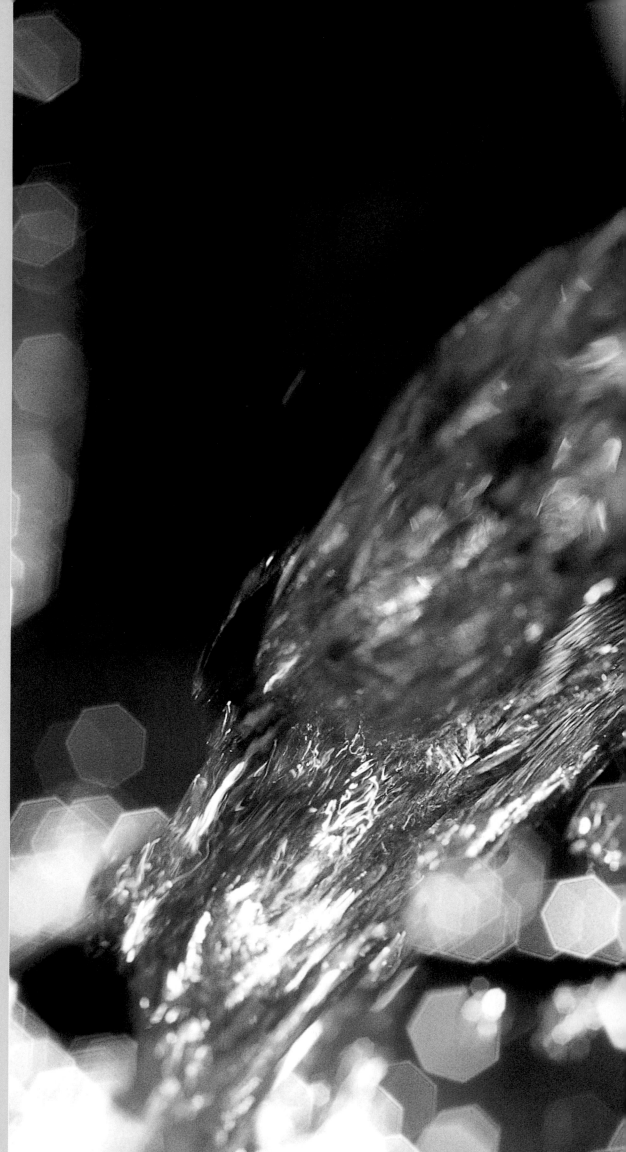

WELL-KNOWN ITALIAN MINERAL WATERS

The **Rochetta** spring in Umbria produces water with a low mineral and carbonic acid content.

Levissima comes from Italy's highest spring in the Bormio mountains of Lombardy.

Water rich in potassium bubbles up from the **Sangemini** spring in Umbria.

Ferrarelle still water comes from the Riardo source in Emilia Romagna.

Vera comes from the Veneto and is said to stimulate the metabolism.

The **San Pellegrino** from Val Brembana has been famed for its healing powers since around 1200.

Uliveto a still water from Vico Pisano in Tuscany, is low in natural carbonic acid.

Monteforte comes from the Coveraie spring, situated high in the Apennines.

Boario originates from four springs in a Lombardy nature reserve.

The province of Orvieto in Umbria is home to **Panna**, a completely uncarbonated water.

Cerelia water from Emilia Romagna is said to be good for bladder infections.

Fiuggi water from Lazio is recommended for disorders of the urinary tract.

The **Limpia** source in Lombardy produces water with a low mineral content.

Lora Recoaro comes from the Veneto. The spring lies at an altitude of 2625 ft/800 m.

San Francesco from Caslino al Piano (Como province) rises from a spring deep underground.

Tavina mineral water comes from a spring in Salò on Lake Garda.

GLOSSARY

abboccato	medium sweet
acciuga/alice	anchovy
aceto balsamico	balsamic vinegar
aceto di vino	wine vinegar
acqua di rose	rose water
acquavite	schnapps
affettato	cold cuts
affogare	poach
affumicare	smoke
affumicato	smoked
agarico delizioso	saffron milk cap
aglio	garlic
agnello da latte	sucking lamb
agro	sour
agrodolce	sweet-and-sour
aguglia	needlefish
al dente	firm to the bite
al forno	baked in the oven
alalunga	mackerel
albicocca	apricot
alborella	whitefish
alcolici	alcoholic drinks
alice	anchovy
alimentari	foodstuffs
all'arrabbiata	spicy, with peperoncino
alla casalinga	homemade
alla griglia	broiled
alloro	bay leaf
amabile	sweet
amanita cesarea	imperial mushroom
amaretto	almond macaroon
amaro	bitter
aneto	dill
anguilla	eel
anice	aniseed
anice stellato	star anise
antipasto	antipasto
aperitivo	aperitif
aragosta	rock/spiny lobster
arancia	orange
aromatizzato/aromi	seasoned/herbs
arrosto	roasted
artemisia, assenzio	artemisia
arzilla	flat fish
asparago selvatico	wild asparagus
astice	lobster
attaccarsi	burn
baccalà	dried salt cod
baccello	pod
bacca	berry
bagnare	soak
bagnomaria	bain-marie
bevanda	drink
bietola	Swiss chard
bisso	beard (of a mussel)
bistecca	steak
bocconcino	nibbles
bollito	boiled (especially meats)
borragine	borage
branchie	gill breather
branzino	sea bass
brasato	braised
brodo	bouillon/broth

bruschetta	toasted bread
buccia	peel, skin
budino	pudding
bulbo, tubero	bulb
burro	butter
caffè	espresso
caffè corretto	espresso with almond liqueur, grappa, or Sambuca
caffè latte	coffee with milk
caffè macchiato	espresso with a dash of milk
caffè ristretto	doubly concentrated espresso
calamaro	squid
camomilla	chamomile
canederlo	dumpling
cannella	cinnamon
cannocchia	Mantis shrimp
cantarello	chanterelle
cappero	caper
cappone	capon
carciofo	artichoke hearts
cardo	cardoon
carne d'asino	donkey meat
carne di camoscio	chamois meat
carne di cavallo	horse meat
carne di montone, di castrato	mutton
carota	carrot
carpa	carp
caviale	caviar
cavolfiore	cauliflower
cavolino di Bruxelles	brussels sprout
cavolo	cabbage
ceci	garbanzo bean/chickpea
cedro	citron
cereali	cereals
cerfoglio	chervil
cernia di fondale	sea bass
cervella	brain
cetriolo	cucumber
chiodi di garofano	cloves
chiodino	honey agaric mushroom
cibo kascer	kosher food
ciccioli	crackling
cicoria	chicory
cieca	glass eel
ciliegia	cherry
cime di rapa	turnip tops
cinghiale	wild boar
cipolla	onion
cipollotto	scallions
cirenga	sea bass
coccio	clay pot
colazione	breakfast
concentrato di pomodoro	tomato paste
conciglia di San Giacomo	pilgrim scallops
condire	season
confetto	dragée
congelato	frozen, iced
coniglio	rabbit

conservabile	keeps well
contorno	vegetables
coriandolo	coriander
corteccia	bark
coscia	leg, haunch
costola	rib
co(s)toletta	cutlet
cotechino	pork sausage
cotenna	rind
cotto	well done
cozza	common mussel
crauti	herbs
crema	cream
cren	horseradish
crespella	pancake
croccante	crisp
crocchetta	croquette
crosta	crust
crosta di sale	salt crust
crostacei	crustaceans
crostino	toasted bread
crudità	crudités
crudo	raw
crusca	bran
cucinare	cook
cucinato al forna	baked in the oven
cumino	caraway
cuocere e far addensare	thicken
dattero di mare	date mussels
dentice	dentix (sea bream)
di giornata	fresh each day
digestivo	digestive
disossare	bone
disporre a strati	layer
dolce	candy, dessert
dorare	sauté until transparent
dragoncella	tarragon
eleta	morel mushroom
erba cipollina	chive
erbette aromatiche	herbs
estragone	tarragon
estratto	extract
evaporare	evaporate
fagiano	pheasant
fagioli	beans
famigliola buona	honey agaric mushroom
far legare	bind
faraona	guinea fowl
farina di riso	rice flour
farina di segale	rye flour
faro	spelt
fatto in casa	homemade
fegato	liver
fegato d'oca	goose liver
fermentare	ferment
fetta biscottata	crispy, toast-like bread
fico d'India	prickly pear
filettare	fillet
filetto	fillet
finferlo	chanterelle
finocchio	fennel
fiore di sambuco	elderberry blossom

focaccia	focaccia
fonduta	cheese fondue
formaggio di pecora	sheep's cheese
formaggio duro	hard cheese
formaggio fresco	soft cheese
formaggio fresco tipo ricotta	curd cheese
fragola	strawberry
frattaglie	innards
fresco	fresh
friggere	fry
frigorifero	refrigerator
fritto	fried
frizzante	sparkling (wine)
frutta secca	dried fruit
frutta di bosca	fruits of the forest
frutti di mare	seafood
fungo imperiale	imperial mushroom
fungo ostrica	oyster mushroom
fuoco, piastra	hot plate
gamberetto	shrimp
gambero	(king) prawn
gelato	ice cream
ginepro	juniper
girare, voltare	turn
gnocchi	little semolina or potato dumplings
gocciolare	sprinkle
grancevola	spider crab
granchio	crab
grano duro	strong wheat
grano integrale	wholegrain
grano saraceno	buckwheat
grano tenero	wheat
grano turco	maize
grassetti	crackling
grasso del pesce	fish fat
gratinato	gratin
grattugiato	grated
grissino	bread stick
impanato	breaded
impastare	knead
in agro	marinated in vinegar
in agro-dolce	marinated in sweet and sour
in brodo	in a broth
in marinata	marinated
in padella	in a skillet
in umido	braised in sauce
indivia	endive
insalata brasiliana	iceberg lettuce
integrale	wholemeal
involtino	roulade
lampone	raspberry
larderellare	grease
lardo	lard
lasca	roach
lasciar andare	leave to rise
lasciare in concia	allow to stand
latte di bufala	buffalo milk
latte intero	full-cream milk
lattuga	lettuce
lavarello	whitefish
legumi	pulses
lenticchie	lentils
lepre	hare

lessato	boiled	pasta frolla	plain pastry	ripieno	stuffed	spinaci	spinach
lievito	yeast	pasta leggera tipo biscotto	sponge mixture	riscaldare	heat up	spolverare	sprinkle
lime	lime	pasta lievitata	yeast dough	riso commune	rice	spugnola	morel mushroom
limone	lemon	pasta sfoglia	puff pastry	riso fino	medium-grain rice	spumante	sparkling wine
lingua	tongue	pasticcio	paté	riso semifino	round-grain rice	squama	(fish) scales
liquirizia	liquorice	patata	potato	riso superfine	arborio rice	stagionato	mature
liquore	liqueur	patata dolce	sweet potato	rombo	turbot	storione	sturgeon
lisca	fish bone	pelato	peeled	rosmarino	rosemary	stufare	stew
lombo	loin	pepe	pepper	rospo/rana pescatrice	monkfish	succo d'arancia	orange juice
lumaca di mare	sea snail	peperoncino	chili pepper			succo di limone	lemon juice
macerare	steep, soak	peperone	bell pepper	rucola	garden rocket (hedge mustard)	sventrare	clean
macinato	ground meat	pera	pear			svuotare, scavare	hollow out
maggiorana	marjoram	pernice	partridge	salame di fegato	liver sausage	tacchino	turkey
magro	lean	pesare/pesato	weigh/weighed	salamoia	brine	tagliare, tagliato	cut/sliced
maiale	pork	pesca	peach	salato	salted, seasoned	tagliare a dadini	diced
maionese	mayonnaise	pesce	fish	sale	salt	tagliare a tranci	sliced
mandorla	almond	pesce persico	perch	salmone	salmon	affettare	
manzo	beef	pesce San Pietro	John Dory	salsa	sauce	tagliuzzato	cut into small pieces
marinare/marinata	marinate, marinated	pesce spada	swordfish	salsiccia	pork sausage	tarassaco	dandelion
marmora	mormyr (bream)	pestello di legno	wooden pestle	salsiera	sauceboat	tartaruga	turtle
marrone	chestnut	petto di pollo	chicken breast	salsina	dip	tartufo bianco	white or Alba truffles
marzapane	marzipan	piatto da magro	Lenten fare	salvia	sage	tartufo nero	black, winter or Norcia truffles
mazzetto	bouquet	piccante	spicy, hot	sanguinella	blood orange		
mazzetto di aromi	bunch of herbs and vegetables for soup-making	piccione selvatico	wood pigeon	sarago	white bream	temolo	mullet
		pietanza	dish	sardina	sardine	temperatura di cottura	cooking temperature
mela	apple	pimento	pimento	savoiardo	sponge finger		
melanzana	eggplant	pinna	fin	sbollentare	blanche	timballo	timbale
melograno	pomegranate	pinolo	pine nut	scalogno	shallot	timo	thyme
menta	mint	piselli	peas	scaloppina	escalope	tinca	tench
meringa	meringue	pizzoccheri	buckwheat pasta	scampi	langoustines	tonno	tuna
merluzzo	cod	pleuroto	oyster mushroom	scavare	scoop	tordo	thrush
mescolare	stir	polenta	polenta	schiacciare	mash, pound	tortelli	ravioli
mettere ammollo	soak	pollame	poultry	sciogliere	dissolve, melt	tortino	tartlet
mettere in concia	pickle	pollo	chicken	sciroppo	syrup	tramezzino	sandwich
miele	honey	polpa	pulp	scorzonera	black salsify	triglia	red mullet
miglio	millet	polpa di pomodoro	canned chopped tomatoes	scottare	overheat	trippa	tripe
minestra	minestrone			scremato	semi-skimmed	tritare	ground
mirtillo rosso	cranberry	polpo	octopus	secco	dry	trota	trout
misto	mixed	pomodoro	tomato	secondo piatto	second course	tuorlo	egg yolk
molluschi	mollusks	pompelmo	grapefruit	sedano	celeriac	uovo all'occhio di bue	fried egg
mora di rovo	blackberry	porcellino da latte	sucking pig	selvaggina	game		
mostocotto	fruit syrup	porcino	boletus mushroom	seme, nocciolo	seed, kernel	uovo	egg
muggine	gray mullet	porro	leek	semi di finocchio	fennel seed	uva	grape
nasello	hake	pralina	praline	semi-secco	semi-dry	uvetta	raisin
nocciola	hazelnut/filbert	prataiolo	field mushroom	semolina	semolina	vaniglia	vanilla
noce	nut	preparazione	preparation	seppia	squid	verdura	vegetables
noce moscata	nutmeg	presa	pinch	servire	serve	versare	pour in
orata	gilthead	prezzemolo	parsley	sesamo	sesame	vinacce	marc
origano	oregano	primo piatto	first course	sformato	flan	vino da tavola	table wine
orzo	barley	prodotti caseari	dairy produce	sgocciolare	drain	vino liquoroso	liqueur
orzo perlato	pearl barley	prosciutto	dry-cured ham	sgombro	mackerel	visciola	wild cherry
osse con il midollo	marrow bone	prugna	plum	sobbollire	sieve	vitello	veal
pagello	bream	pulire	clean	soffriggere	sauté	vongola	clam
palombo	shark	quaglia	quail	sogliola	sole	zafferano	saffron
pan grattato	fresh breadcrumbs	rafano	horseradish	soppressata	pressed meat	zampone	pig trotter
pancetta	belly fat	raffreddare	cool	sorbetto	sorbet	zenzero	ginger
pane	bread	raffreddare in acqua	cool in water	sott'aceto	marinated in vinegar	zucca	pumpkin
panino	bread roll	ragù	ragout	sott'olio	preserved in oil	zuccherare	sugar
panna	cream	rapa	turnip	spalla	shoulder	zucchero a velo	confectioners' sugar
passato	sieved, puréed	ravanello	radishes	spalmare	smooth	zucchero di canna	cane sugar
passera di mare	flounder	reni	kidneys	spazzolare	brush off	zucchero vanigliato	vanilla sugar
pasta	pasta	residuo, fondo	residue	spennellare	brush	zuppa densa	thick soup
pasta asciutta	lit.: dried pasta = pasta with tomato sauce	resistente alla fiamma	heat resistant	spezzettare	dice		
		riccio di mare	sea urchin	spianare	roll out		
				spiedo	kebab		
				spigola	sea bass		

COOKING TECHNIQUES

Artichokes

Cut off the stem of the artichoke. Only stalks from very tender artichokes are edible, but even they must be peeled. Remove the tough outer leaves and, using kitchen scissors, cut a generous amount off the tips of the remaining leaves. Place the prepared artichokes in a water and lemon juice mixture to prevent discoloration. Use according to the recipe instructions. Before eating, remove the choke from the base of the artichoke, taking care not to damage the delicate heart, the choicest part of the vegetable.

Blanching

This entails cooking the ingredients for a few moments in plenty of boiling water, then plunging them into cold water. This not only partly precooks the food, but also helps it retain its color and, in the case of soup bones, removes protein, fat, and foreign particles.

Braising

Cooking food in its own juices or in a small amount of fat and/or liquid over a constant, moderate heat. Some vegetables, such as onions, are lightly sautéed until they are translucent.

Calf's sweetbreads

Soak the sweetbreads for 2 hours in cold water to remove any traces of blood, frequently changing the water. Blanch in boiling water for about 5 minutes and then plunge in cold water. Use a knife to peel off the skin, removing any blood vessels, then prepare according to the recipe.

Cannelloni

Roll the fresh pasta dough into a thin sheet and cut into small squares. Pipe a small amount of filling in the center of each square and moisten the edges with water and roll up into tubes. Place the cannelloni in a dish with the join facing downward.

Carpaccio

To slice carpaccio, wrap the loin of beef in foil and place in the freezer compartment for about 1 hour, after which the meat can be cut into paper-thin slices using a large, sharp kitchen knife or an electric carving knife.

Chestnuts

To roast chestnuts, first make a small incision in the shell of the chestnut to prevent it bursting during roasting. Chestnuts should be roasted for 30 minutes at most in a hot oven. Any longer than this and they become hard.

Coating with breadcrumbs

Season meat, fish, or other ingredient, toss in flour, then dip in egg yolk and coat with breadcrumbs before frying.

Coloring pasta

Add the following ingredients to egg-based pasta dough (See: Pasta dough):
For green pasta, substitute about ¼ lb/100 g well drained spinach purée for one egg. For red pasta, add 2–3 tablespoons tomato paste or 1 small puréed beetroot; for golden yellow pasta, 1 small packet of saffron strands, ground in a mortar, and for black pasta, use the ink from about 1 lb/500 g squid.

Crabs

These must be boiled for about 20 minutes and then left in the cooking water for a further 15 minutes. The best way to open them is to press firmly between their eyes which will cause the shell to lift like a lid. Remove the gills and extract the meat from the body and claws.

Dried beans and pulses

Dried beans and pulses are generally soaked for 8–12 hours before use. In this way, they cook faster and are easier to digest. Any beans that float to the surface during soaking should be discarded as these could contain insects. Drain off the water they have soaked in, as this contains indigestible substances. Rinse the beans or pulses well in fresh water and cook for up to 3 hours, depending on variety. Beans are cooked when they have doubled or trebled in size. Do not add salt until the beans are nearly cooked (as adding it early on will make the beans tough).

Eggplants

Slice the eggplant, sprinkle with salt and leave to stand until the salt has drawn out the bitter juices and excess moisture. After 15–30 minutes, rinse the salt off under cold running water and pat the eggplants dry. Before frying, blanch the eggplants briefly to prevent them absorbing too much oil.

Excess fat removal

Remove excess fat from broths, soups, and sauces by pouring or skimming it off, soaking it up into paper towels or lifting off the solidified layer of cold fat.

Farfalle

Roll the pasta dough out thinly and cut into small squares using a pasta wheel. Squeeze these together in the middle between thumb and forefinger to make little "bows."

Gnocchi

Boil about 2 lbs/1 kg of potatoes, peel them while they are still hot and mash them straight onto the work surface. Gradually knead in 1 teaspoon salt and about ½–1 lb (250–500 g) flour. The amount of flour required depends on how floury the potatoes are. The resulting dough should be smooth without being sticky. Leave to stand covered for about 15 minutes. Mold the dough into rolls each about the thickness of a finger. Cut these into pieces about ¼ inch/2–3 cm in length. Using a fork, press in both sides to give the gnocchi their characteristic shape. Leave for a further 15 minutes. Cook in gently (not fast) boiling water for about 5 minutes.

Gratin

This means cooking a dish under a high top heat in the oven or broiling under a high temperature so that a brown crust forms. To form the crust, sprinkle small amounts of butter, grated cheese, breadcrumbs, or a creamy sauce over the surface.

Kidneys

Peel off the thin outer skin of the kidneys. Halve them and cut out the white core, taking care not to damage the kidneys.

Marinating

This means placing food in any seasoned liquid to give it flavor, or, in the case of meat, to tenderize it. Game can be treated similarly.

Marinating and preserving vegetables in vinegar

Vegetables and mushrooms need to be precooked but must remain al dente at all costs. To ensure that the vegetables remain crisp and retain their color, they should be plunged into ice-cold water. To marinate about 2 lbs/1 kg vegetables (e.g. zucchini, eggplants, bell peppers, green beans, carrots, fennel, or mushrooms), peel and quarter 4 cloves of garlic and crumble 2 dried bay leaves. Finely chop a bunch of parsley and half a bunch each of marjoram and thyme. Pour a little olive oil into a large glass jar, add a layer of prepared vegetables, season with salt and pepper and some of the herbs. Sprinkle over some white wine vinegar and cover the whole lot with plenty of oil. Repeat this process until the jar is full, ending with a thick layer of oil. Leave the vegetables to stand for a week in a cool place (ideally in a cellar or cool pantry). Mushrooms should be left to stand for two days in the refrigerator. Following this, vegetables can be kept for a further week, mushrooms for about another two days. The ingredients must always remain well covered with the marinade

Mushrooms

Avoid washing mushrooms if at all possible as they soak up water. To clean them, wipe with a damp cloth or paper towels, scratching off any particles of dirt left with a small knife and cutting away any unwanted parts. Morel and chanterelle mushrooms, however, do need rinsing to remove any sand or grit from the lamella.

Mussels

Wash and brush mussels thoroughly under running water and scrape off any calcium deposits with a knife. Remove the beards by giving them a sharp twist. Discard any open mussels as they will have gone off. Cook the mussels over a high heat for about 5 minutes until they open up. Discard any unopened shells.

Omelets

To make an omelet for 2 people, lightly beat 4 eggs with 1 tablespoon milk, water, or cream and season the mixture with salt and pepper. Melt some butter in a large skillet and cook the egg mixture gently over a moderate heat. Keep stirring with a fork without disturbing the bottom layer. When the omelet is almost set, but still runny on the surface, remove the skillet from the heat and fork along the edge, while simultaneously shaking the skillet, so that the front edge of the omelet folds over slightly. Important: remove the skillet from the heat while the surface of the omelet is still runny as it will carry on cooking in the hot pan. This ensures the omelet retains its perfect consistency and is not too dry.

Pasta

Pasta must be cooked in a large saucepan in plenty of water. Use 4 cups/1 liter of water and one generous teaspoon of salt for every ¼ lb/100 g of pasta. Do not add the salt until the water is boiling. A dash of oil in the water will prevent fresh pasta and lasagna sheets from sticking together. Oil is not necessary with other types of pasta. Once the pasta has been added to the boiling water, cover with a lid for a moment until the water returns to a boil. Stir briefly with a wooden spoon to prevent the pasta from sticking to the base of the saucepan, then continue to cook in rapidly boiling water without the lid. Check the pasta a couple of minutes before the end of the recommended cooking time to see if it is al dente, firm to the bite. It should be soft on the outside but still firm inside. Drain in a sieve. Pasta should not be rinsed in cold water as this would wash out the flavour and nutrients. Mix immediately with a prepared sauce.

Pasta dough
To make egg pasta, mix 2½ cups/300 g all-purpose flour with 3 eggs, 1 tablespoon oil, and a little salt and knead for at least 5 minutes until the mixture forms a smooth elastic dough. Wrap the dough in foil or plastic wrap and leave to stand for 30–60 minutes. Either using a pasta making machine or a rolling pin, roll out the dough into a thin sheet, dusting with more flour as necessary. This amount makes about 1 lb/500 g (enough for 4 portions).
To make pasta without eggs, mix 3⅓ cups/400 g flour with 3 eggs, ⅞ cup/200 fl. oz lukewarm water and a little salt and knead for at least 5 minutes until the mixture has formed a smooth, elastic dough. Wrap in foil and leave for 30–60 minutes. Using a pasta machine or a rolling-pin, roll out into a thin sheet, dusting as required with a little flour. The pasta dough will make about 1¼ lbs/600 g (enough for four portions).

Pizza
To make pizza dough, dissolve 30 g/1¾ cakes compressed yeast in some hand-hot water, add 2–3 tablespoons flour and mix to a smooth paste. Leave to rise for 30 minutes. (If using active dry yeast follow maker's instructions.) Mix a generous 4 cups/500 g of flour with the paste and add ½ teaspoon of salt. Knead well for at least 10 minutes, adding a scant ½ cup/100 ml hand-hot water a little at a time. Divide the dough into four, sprinkle with flour. Cover and leave to rise in a warm place for two hours. Roll out the four pizza bases and cover with the desired ingredients. The best pizzas are baked in Italian stone ovens over a wood fire. These reach a temperature of 340 °C (620 °F) and the pizza is cooked within minutes. If using an electric or gas oven, bake for about 20 minutes on the second shelf from the bottom at 220–250 °C (430–480 °F) until the base of the pizza is crisp and the cheese has melted.

Pizza dough preparation
Whether you use fresh or dried yeast: pizza dough must be thoroughly kneaded for a good 10 minutes until it is smooth and elastic. Then, it has to be covered and left to rise in a warm place for about two hours until it has doubled in volume. Knock back the dough once more and knead again. Sprinkle a little flour on the work surface and roll out the dough. Cover and leave to rise for a further 12 to 15 minutes.

Polenta
Slowly sprinkle 1 cup/250 g polenta flour into boiling salted water (3 cups/750 ml) or boiling broth, stirring all the while to prevent any lumps forming. Cook over a low heat, stirring constantly, for about 45 minutes. When air bubbles begin to form, remove the saucepan from the heat, otherwise the mixture will start to splash. Press any clumps that form against the side of the saucepan to dissolve them.

Ravioli
Roll out some fresh pasta dough (See: Pasta dough) into a thin sheet. Pipe equal amounts of filling onto one half of the sheet of dough. The distance between the mounds of filling depends on the size of ravioli required. Brush the spaces in between with water and carefully place the other half of the sheet on top of the first, firmly pressing the sheets together around the filling. Cut out the ravioli with a pastry wheel, or with metal ravioli shapes or a wooden ravioli press, which is even easier. Cooking time: about four minutes.

Risotto
Always add risotto rice to the saucepan without washing it so that none of the starch is washed out. About 7 cups/1.75 liters of liquid (broth) is required for 2½ cups/500 g of rice. Lightly sauté the rice in butter and oil with finely diced onion and herbs and spices until the onion is soft and translucent. Gradually add the hot liquid a bit at a time, stirring constantly. More or less liquid may be used but test from time to time to see if it is cooked. The rice must be soft on the outside but still be firm inside.

Salt (dried) cod
Leave the fish in water for 24 hours, changing the water three to four times. Very thick specimens should be soaked for 36 hours. For the last two hours of this procedure, use warm water in order to ensure that all the salt has been dissolved out of the fish. Pat the fish dry and it is ready to use.

Shrimp
Twist the heads off and remove the tail flesh from the shell. Using a sharp knife, lift and remove the threadlike black intestine which is visible along the back.

Sieving
Strain soups, sauces, or puréed food through a sieve or muslin cloth to get a fine, even consistency.

Skinning bell peppers
Cut the peppers in half and lay on a baking sheet lined with waxed paper. Bake in the oven until the skin turns dark brown and begins to blister. Remove from the oven, cover with a damp dish cloth, and leave to cool. Carefully scrape off the skin with a sharp knife.

Squid (calamari)
Remove the innards along with the tentacles from the body. Separate the tentacles from the head, leaving them still joined together at the top end. Remove the cartilage from the tentacles. Peel off the outer skin from the body sac and slide out the translucent bone. If you wish to use the ink, carefully remove the ink sac from the innards and set aside.

Steaming
To steam food, it is placed in a colander, covered, and cooked over boiling water. This method of cooking is ideal for retaining vitamins and other nutrients, as well as preserving the natural taste.

Tagliatelle
Even without a pasta machine, tagliatelle is simple to make from fresh pasta dough: Roll the dough out thinly into a roughly rectangular shape. Starting from both sides, roll the dough up towards the middle and then cut into strips with a sharp knife. Cooking time: about 2 minutes for narrow, and 6 minutes for wide ribbon pasta.

Thickening
Sauces, soups, and creamy mixtures can be thickened by stirring flour, cornstarch, cream, eggs, butter, roux, grated potatoes, or puréed vegetables into the liquid.

Tomatoes
To preserve tomatoes, pour boiling water over about 2 lbs/1 kg of tomatoes, peel off the skins, cut them in half, and remove the core. Lightly sauté one shallot and one stick of celery in one tablespoon olive oil. Add the tomatoes, a pinch of sugar, salt and freshly milled pepper, and cook for about 20 minutes uncovered in a saucepan. Pour the hot tomatoes into a clean glass jar, screw the lid closed, and stand upside down for 5 minutes. If the tomatoes are to be stored for any length of time, the jars should first be sterilized by standing them in boiling water for one hour. Makes about 2½ cups/600 ml.

Tortellini
Roll out fresh pasta dough (See: Pasta dough) into a thin sheet and cut out circles. Place the filling in the center of each circle and fold in half. Wrap these semicircular shapes around your forefinger and press the ends firmly together. Cooking time: about 6 minutes.

Trimming and dicing
Cut off the fat, sinews, and skin from pieces of meat or fish and cut into equal sized pieces. These discarded bits can be used for stock or go into the cooking juices.

Vegetables in sweet and sour marinade (in agrodolce)
Prepare about 1 lb/500 g of eggplants (See: Eggplants) and dice into cubes. Sauté in 2 tablespoons olive oil and dry on paper towels. Sauté several tender stalks of celery in the oil, then remove them from the skillet. Cut an onion into rings and fry in the oil for a few minutes along with 4 cored and seeded tomatoes. Add one tablespoon of pine nuts and soaked raisins, respectively, and one teaspoon of sugar, a little red wine vinegar, the eggplants, and celery. Cook over a moderate heat for about 30 minutes. Sweet and sour zucchini can be prepared in the same way. To preserve it, see Marinating.

Zucchini flowers
To stuff the flowers, cut off the stem and dip the flowers briefly into cold water, drain, and pat dry with paper towels. Carefully open up the center of the flower and cut out the pistil with a sharp knife. Pipe the filling into each flower cup and twist the ends closed to seal in the filling.

RECIPE INDEX

Recipes with illustrations have page number in **bold** type.

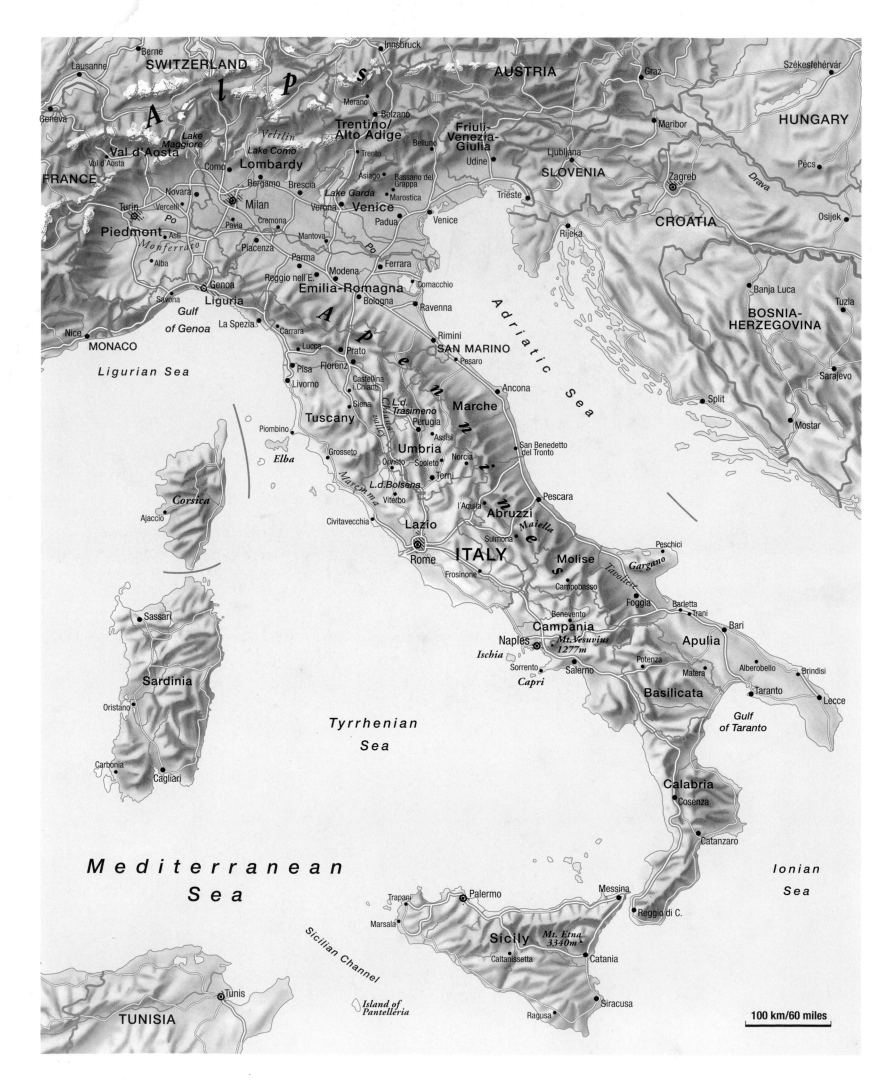